Jerry Baker's

Terrific Tomatoes,
Sensational Spuds, and
Mouth-Watering Melons

Jerry Baker's

Terrific Tomatoes, Sensational Spuds, and Mouth-Watering Melons

1,274 *Super* Secrets for Growing
Prize-Winning Vegetables

by Jerry Baker,
America's Master Gardener®

Published by American Master Products, Inc.

Executive Editor: Kim Adam Gasior
Published by American Master Products, Inc.,
by arrangement with
Storey Communications, Inc., Pownal, Vermont 05261

Contributing Writer and Project Editor: Vicki Webster
Editors: Gwen W. Steege and Eileen M. Clawson
Horticulture Editor: Charles W.G. Smith
Illustration Editor: Ilona Sherratt
Cover and Text Design: Betty Kodela
Text Layout: Susan Bernier, Deborah Daly,
Erin Lincourt, Beth Peters, and Jennifer Jepson Smith
Indexer: Susan Olason, Indexes and Knowledge Maps

Jerry Baker
P.O. Box 1001, Wixom, MI 48393
www.jerrybaker.com

Printed in the United States of America
2 4 6 8 10 9 7 5 3 1 hardcover

Contents

The Homegrown Advantage   **1**

CHAPTER 1   Strategies for Success   **5**
- Veggie Necessities: Giving Plants What They Need   6
- Picking the Perfect Plot   17

CHAPTER 2   Planning Your Plot   **20**
- Drawing the Plan   21
- Memories Are Made of This   23
- What Goes Where?   24
- Good Things Come from Small Plots   29
- A Seed and Plant Shopping Spree   30

CHAPTER 3   Ready, Set, Grow!   **37**
- A Head Start Pays Off   38
- Those Unmistakable Signs of the Vernal Equinox   45

CHAPTER 4   Weedin', Feedin', and Waterin'   **51**
- Be Good to Your Garden . . .   52
- From Rocks to Riches   54
- Rise Up and Be Planted   57
- A Little Help from Your Friends   59
- Black Gold: Compost   63
- Gimme Some of That Old-Time Nutrition   68
- Make Mine Sour, Please (but Just a Tad)   72
- Water Wisely and Water Well   73
- Great Garden Cover-Ups: Mulches   76
- Take the Work Out of Weeding   78
- Get Your Garden to Grow Up, Up, Up   80
- Keeping Things Under Control   82
- All Tooled Up   83
- Baby, It's Cold Out There   86

CHAPTER 5 Keeping Plague and Pest(ilence) at Bay 89
- The Defensive Line 90
- Botanical Warfare 93
- Garden Cure-Alls 99
- Telling Good Guys from Bad 103
- Giving the Good Guys a Chance 112
- The Vilest Villains 120
- Not-So-Fine Feathered Friends 124
- When the Big Guys Come Around 126

CHAPTER 6 Reaping — and Keeping — the Rewards 131
- Bringing In the Bounty 132
- How to Capture Summer in Jars 142

CHAPTER 7 Jerry's Favorites:
A Vegetable Family Album 151
- Bean and Pea Family 152
- Beets and Greens Family 169
- Cabbage Family 192
- Carrot Family 232
- Onion Family 244
- Squash and Cucumber Family 257
- Tomato Family 282
- Extended Family 315
- Perennial Vegetables 333

CHAPTER 8 Jerry's Terrific Tonics 346

Zone Maps 362

Index 364

The Homegrown Advantage

Not long ago, I was poking around in a big old trunk in my attic, and I came across the very first garden scrapbook that Grandma Putt and I ever made together. It was a record of the garden she helped me grow just after I'd gone to live with her that spring. Talk about bringing back memories! That book was crammed full of notes, drawings, lists, pages torn from seed catalogs — even recipe cards — and lots of old, faded photographs.

It's Magic!

Back then, gardening was a whole new, magical world, and it seemed to me that Grandma Putt knew more about it than any person could possibly know about anything! Every day, as we were tending our gardens, she showed me how to take care of every plant just the way it liked, and what it needed in the way of soil, water, and food.

The Old Neighborhood

Grandma Putt knew what plants made good neighbors and which ones liked to be as far away from one another as they could get. She knew which crops to plant when the moon was full and which did better if you waited until the new moon. Plus, she knew how to build fences that would keep the most determined deer in the county away from the corn patch, and how to get toads to set up housekeeping and solve bad-guy bug problems lickety-split.

Veggies in Wonderland

Best of all — at least from the standpoint of a 10-year-old boy — she knew how to make gardening fun! She gave me old-time seeds that grew into vegetables I'd never even imagined, like white tomatoes and red corn, and beans that were splotched just like the neighbors' Appaloosa horse.

And she taught me how to save my own seeds so I could grow those same crops again and again.

She showed me how to build beanpole teepees where I could hide out on warm summer afternoons and daydream about Wild West adventures. She also helped me grow cucumbers in bottles and make lanterns out of turnips.

The Thrill of Victory

And every time I turned around, it seemed that she was organizing another neighborhood contest. We were always setting out to harvest the earliest crop of peas, grow the biggest pumpkin, or build the scariest scarecrow. Thanks to Grandma Putt's old-fashioned grow-how, we usually won, too!

Mmm-mmm . . . Good!

All summer long, friends and neighbors would come by to visit — and more likely than not, Grandma Putt would insist that they stay for supper." She'd cook up one of her special recipes and serve up platters full of corn and tomatoes fresh from the garden. For dessert, we'd have chocolate-mint cake made with our own homegrown mint, or if we were really lucky, her strawberry-rhubarb pie that took a blue ribbon at the county fair.

Tricks of the Trade

Naturally, the conversation always turned to gardening, and Grandma Putt made sure I didn't get left out just because I was still a little guy. She knew that the best way to learn about gardening — next to gardening itself — is visiting with other gardeners. We'd swap stories about our favorite plants and promise to save seeds for one another come fall, or we'd talk about problems we were having with pests, the weather, or some temperamental kind of plant.

And you know, I don't think I can remember a single time that Grandma Putt didn't help at least one guest solve some problem or another. Sometimes, the solution was one of her old-time remedies; at other times, it was a clever tip, trick, or tonic she thought up on the spot.

What's in a Name?
Grandma Putt had her own special names for just about everything, and I was no exception. My parents named me Gerald F. Baker, Jr., in honor of my father. But to Grandma (as you'll soon see), I was affectionately referred to as "Junie" — short for Junior.

Come One, Come All!

At the end of the season, those same folks would come on over for harvest bees and help us get in the crops — and we'd do the same for them. Grandma Putt knew all kinds of games to turn the work into fun, of course, like stomping our popcorn off of the cobs and whacking away at sacks of dried beans the way kids swing bats at piñatas at parties nowadays. And there always was a pumpkin-carving contest and corn-shucking races.

Taking Home the Blue

Harvesttime was also county fair time, and we didn't miss one for as long as I can remember. We'd take our best vegetables and Grandma Putt's tastiest pies and cakes, and we always came away with a fine crop of blue ribbons.

Wild, Wild Eatin'

You'd think that canning and drying and socking away veggies would be the worst kind of torture for a young boy. But Grandma Putt had a way of making it almost as much fun as tending the garden. For one thing, she always made sure that, besides regular canned tomatoes and pickled onions, we made up special treats like "leather britches" beans and fruit and vegetable "leathers" just like the ones cowboys carried on those long trail drives. While we worked, she'd tell me tales about the Wild West, and we'd sing cowboy songs.

The Family Heirlooms

Grandma also told me about how all the vegetables came to be in our gardens. She said that Native Americans, including some of her own ancestors, had grown lots of crops, like corn and squash, for thousands of years before folks from Europe had even arrived on the scene. And the Europeans, she said, brought plenty of others with them, like peas and beets. She told me about a lot of old-time varieties that had gone away, like the dinosaurs, because folks hadn't kept growing them.

Use 'em or Lose 'em

Grandma Putt taught me that antique vegetables aren't like that big clock my Grandpa left me. She always said, "The only way to pass vegetables on to your kids is to grow them." Then we'd talk about the ones that were still around, like 'Big John' pole beans that she said folks in Kentucky have been growing since Revolutionary War times, and 'Carolina' lima beans that Thomas Jefferson grew for years at Monticello.

Sometimes, just the names were enough to make me want to grow them and pass on the seeds to other folks — after all, what kid could resist 'Yellow Tommy Toe' or 'White Rabbit' tomatoes, or 'Pink Banana' squash? Not me, that's for sure!

Eat Up!

Come winter, we chowed down on all that good food we had put by, and we'd make up baskets of the fancy things (like Grandma Putt's special watermelon pickles and her honeyed carrot-ginger marmalade) to give to family and friends during the holidays.

Sittin' by the Fire

On long cold evenings, we'd pop ourselves a big bowl of homegrown popcorn, light a fire in the fireplace, and set about having some of the best fun we could have: planning next year's garden, which we just knew would be the best garden anyone in the whole world ever saw!

Good Old-Fashioned Grow-How . . .

All of those good times with Grandma Putt and all of her solid country wisdom found their way, in one form or another, into that first garden scrapbook and the ones that followed. A lot of them have found their way into this book, too, along with more than a few tips, tricks, tonics, and recipes that I've come up with myself over the years.

In these pages, we'll look at everything it takes to grow the best darned vegetables you ever tasted — from surefire strategies for getting your seedlings growing on the right foot to harvesting your bumper crops and putting your plot to bed for the winter. We'll learn tried-and-true secrets for choosing plants and seeds that will perform like champs no matter where you live, fighting — and winning — the war against pesky pests and dastardly diseases, and protecting your garden from all those curve balls Mother Nature sends its way.

. . . and Where It All Leads

Finally, we'll get up close and personal with 38 of America's favorite vegetables. Most important, we'll have fun at every step of the way, because, for Grandma Putt, that's what gardening was all about — and for me, it still is!

The Good Old New Days

Grandma Putt would be pleased as punch if she could see what's going on in the gardening world today. Every year, more and more folks are discovering how satisfying — and how much fun — it is to grow their own vegetables. At the same time, more and more seed companies and even nonprofit groups are offering seeds of those old-time varieties Grandma Putt set so much store by. Why, folks are even turning away from all of those pesticides and chemical fertilizers that were all the rage for so many years, and going back to the simpler (and less expensive) methods that worked like magic for Grandma and her friends.

CHAPTER 1

Strategies
for Success

Grandma Putt taught me that a garden chock-full
of great-tasting, great-looking vegetables doesn't just
happen all by itself. Like most of the good things in
life, it takes work — but first it takes preparation.
Here's the basic groundwork she used — and I still
use — to get growing in the right direction.

Veggie Necessities: Giving Plants What They Need

Just like you and me, plants have certain basic needs, and they haven't changed since Grandma Putt's day. Before I ever set foot to shovel in a new garden, I study the terrain to see how well it measures up as a home, sweet home for my vegetables.

Your Climate and Whether the Weather

Ever notice how some folks don't even bother to put on an overcoat until the first snowfall, and just seem to shrivel up when the temperature inches above 75°F? Other folks reach for a down jacket at the first nip in the air and don't get going in high gear again until it's hot enough to fry an egg on the sidewalk. Well, vegetables are the very same way. Some, like lettuce and potatoes, for instance, prefer the temperature to be on the cool side. Others, like peppers and okra, want all the heat they can get for as long as they can get it.

So how do you know what veggies will thrive in your garden? Grandma Putt always said that two things determine your climate from a veggie's point of view: how long the growing season lasts and how much of it is cool or hot weather.

'Tis the season. Because most vegetables are annuals — that is, they begin and complete their life cycles in a single year — the most important bit of knowledge you need is the length of your growing season. Simply stated, the growing season starts with the last frost in the spring and ends with the first frost in the fall. When you know when those two events usually happen in your area, you know when to start seeds, indoors or out, when to set out transplants, and — most important — whether that crop you're hankering to grow will have time to ripen.

You could look it up. In the U.S., the average number of frost-free days in a year ranges all the way from just 67 around Laramie, Wyoming, to a whopping 322 in Brownsville, Texas, and thereabouts. To find out where your garden fits into that range, check out the chart on pages 8 and 9.

Taking the heat. Even if your growing season lasts for months on end, how high the temperatures get will determine how well heat lovers like tomatoes or cool-weather fiends like peas will perform in your garden. To learn that important bit of information, look at the American Horticultural Society Plant Heat Zone Map on page 363.

Take a number. In almost every garden book and seed catalog, you'll find another map: the USDA Plant Hardiness Zone Map on page 362. It's put together by the U.S. Department of Agriculture and divides the country into zones numbered from 1 through 11. That number indicates the average low temperature each year for the region. In the coldest section, Zone 1, the wintertime low averages a staggering -50°F. Brrrrrr. Makes my teeth chatter just thinking about it! Way down in Zones 10 and 11, on the other hand, frost rarely rears its veggie-killing head.

Jerry Baker Says

"Even when the garden you're planning will be a home for annual veggies, it's still useful to know your USDA Zone number, because it's the number that gardeners — and garden writers — toss about more than any other. I refer to it most often when I'm growing perennial vegetables like asparagus or rhubarb, or herbs like thyme or rosemary, or when I'm planting a windbreak of trees or shrubs around my vegetable garden."

All Maps Are Not Created Equal

The zone map we use in this book has been put together by the U.S. Department of Agriculture. It's the one you see most often in books and catalogs, but it's not the only one. A few seed companies use their own maps with different numbering systems. So whenever I pick up a new seed catalog, I always glance at the map and the temperature chart next to it. That way, I don't accidentally order seeds that would be happier growing up two states to the south of mine.

How Long Does Your Garden Grow?

Unless you live in territory that Jack Frost rarely visits — parts of Florida and California, for instance — your garden lives and dies by two dates: the last frost in spring and the first frost in autumn. Here's a sampling of some of those dates and the number of growing days in between. (For the dates in your area, contact the closest Cooperative Extension Service Office.)

CITY	LAST SPRING FROST	FIRST FALL FROST	DAYS IN GROWING SEASON
Mobile, Alabama	Feb. 27	Nov. 26	272
Juneau, Alaska	May 16	Sept. 26	133
Phoenix, Arizona	Feb. 5	Dec. 15	308
Pine Bluff, Arkansas	March 19	Nov. 8	234
Eureka, California	Jan. 30	Dec. 15	324
Denver, Colorado	May 3	Oct. 8	157
Hartford, Connecticut	April 25	Oct. 10	167
Wilmington, Delaware	April 13	Oct. 29	198
Tampa, Florida	Jan. 28	Jan. 3	338
Savannah, Georgia	March 10	Nov. 15	250
Boise, Idaho	May 8	Oct. 9	153
Chicago, Illinois	April 22	Oct. 26	187
South Bend, Indiana	May 1	Oct. 18	169
Cedar Rapids, Iowa	April 29	Oct. 7	161
Topeka, Kansas	April 21	Oct. 14	175
Lexington, Kentucky	April 17	Oct. 25	190
New Orleans, Louisiana	Feb. 20	Dec. 5	288
Portland, Maine	May 10	Sept. 30	143
Baltimore, Maryland	March 26	Nov. 13	231
Boston, Massachusetts	April 6	Nov. 10	217
Detroit, Michigan	April 24	Oct. 22	181
Duluth, Minnesota	May 21	Sept. 21	122

CITY	LAST SPRING FROST	FIRST FALL FROST	DAYS IN GROWING SEASON
Vicksburg, Mississippi	March 13	Nov. 18	250
Jefferson City, Missouri	April 26	Oct. 16	173
Helena, Montana	May 18	Sept. 18	122
North Platte, Nebraska	May 11	Sept. 24	136
Las Vegas, Nevada	March 7	Nov. 21	259
Concord, New Hampshire	May 23	Sept. 22	121
Newark, New Jersey	April 4	Nov. 10	219
Carlsbad, New Mexico	March 29	Nov. 7	223
New York, New York	April 1	Nov. 11	233
Fayetteville, North Carolina	April 2	Oct. 31	212
Bismarck, North Dakota	May 14	Sept. 20	129
Akron, Ohio	May 3	Oct. 18	168
Tulsa, Oklahoma	March 30	Nov. 4	218
Portland, Oregon	April 3	Nov. 7	217
Pittsburgh, Pennsylvania	April 16	Nov. 3	201
Kingston, Rhode Island	May 8	Sept. 30	144
Charleston, South Carolina	March 11	Nov. 20	253
Rapid City, South Dakota	May 7	Sept. 29	145
Nashville, Tennessee	April 5	Oct. 29	207
San Antonio, Texas	March 3	Nov. 24	265
Spanish Fork, Utah	May 8	Oct. 12	156
Burlington, Vermont	May 11	Oct. 1	142
Norfolk, Virginia	March 23	Nov. 17	239
Spokane, Washington	May 4	Oct. 5	153
Parkersburg, West Virginia	April 25	Oct. 18	175
Janesville, Wisconsin	April 28	Oct. 10	164
Casper, Wyoming	May 22	Sept. 22	123

Wind-Sock Wisdom

Average temperatures, winds, humidity, and frost dates are just that: averages. They all vary from year to year, day to day — even hour to hour. So I always keep a wind sock flying in my garden and a wind gauge fastened to the garden fence, and I always have two thermometers handy — one for soil and one for air. That way, I know for sure when it's time to put my seeds in the ground, pull the covers over my most tender plants, or scurry like mad to get the crops in before an early freeze bowls them over.

Two to grow on. Here's a duo of other climatic factors you need to keep in mind when you plan your garden:

• **Humidity.** Some plants can take the heat just fine, but the combination of heat and muggy air — and the damp soil that often goes with it — will do them in.

• **Day length.** A few vegetables, including onions and spinach, are sensitive to the number of daylight hours they get. If it's not just right, they won't produce the bountiful harvest you want them to.

A Breath of Fresh Air

Plants need room to breathe. When you're looking for a place for your garden, just say no to dips and hollows where cool air hangs around. And steer clear of tight spaces, especially the kind between building walls and solid fences. Grandma Putt used to say that planting a garden where air can't circulate freely is like throwing an open house for diseases.

The New Kid on the Block

If you've just moved to a new part of the country, or you're starting your very first garden, call the closest Cooperative Extension Service or a local nursery. Either of them can clue you in on what to expect from the local weather, tell you what vegetables do especially well (or poorly) in your new neighborhood, and even warn you about diseases and veggie-gulping critters to watch out for.

Let There Be Light

And plenty of it! Most vegetables perform their best when they can bask in sunshine all day long. If your site doesn't command that much of ol' Sol's time, don't worry: Your garden can still produce bountiful crops if it gets 6 to 8 hours of sun a day.

Make mine morning. If no place in your yard gets full sun, but you can choose between morning and afternoon sun, go with the morning. It's less intense, which encourages a higher rate of photosynthesis, the greening-up process. (This is especially true if you live in the steamy South.)

Please pass the sun screen. Not all veggies are die-hard sun worshipers. This crew can tolerate some shade — especially during the hottest part of the day:

Chard
Chicory
Collards
Kale

Lettuce
Parsley
Peas
Spinach

Be wary of walnut. Whatever you do, keep your vegetable garden far away from walnut trees — both black and English kinds. They produce a chemical called juglone that's toxic to many plants, including potatoes and tomatoes. Make that far, far away — the roots of a walnut tree sometimes extend more than 3 or 4 times the width of the tree's leafy canopy.

Jerry Baker Says

"When I'm looking for a new planting site, I always venture out early in the morning and look for the spot that feels the toastiest: A place that warms up early in the day will also warm up early in springtime, giving you a jump on the growing season."

SUPER Growing Secrets

PLAN AHEAD

Don't wait until it's almost planting time to find your garden's place in the sun. Instead, explore your yard the year before you choose the spot. Do it in summer or early fall, when trees and shrubs are full, leafy, and casting their longest shadows. That way, you'll know the shady spots to avoid come spring.

Beware of Wind

An easy breeze mixes different pockets of air and helps keep temperature and humidity on the moderate side. But a strong wind will dry out leaves, rob moisture from the soil, even break stems and send trellises flying. On a calm day, it's hard to know whether wind will be a problem, but look for these clues:

• If you can stand there and see across the hills to the back of beyond, it's almost guaranteed to be too windy.

• A spot along the shore of an ocean or a big lake will get heavy gusts, at least from time to time.

• A site with western or northern exposure will leave your garden wide open to storm fronts moving through.

Slope Sense

The best place for a garden is on a gentle, easy slope, with no buildings, trees, or big shrubs nearby to block light or airflow. In the North, a south-facing incline is best. It will warm up quickly in the spring and take its time welcoming Jack Frost in the fall. In the South, look for a slope that faces north; it won't get quite so hot during the dog days of summer.

Water

All living things need water. Most vegetables need about an inch of water every week, especially when they're just starting to grow, and later, when they're blooming and setting fruit. That comes to a whopping 62 gallons for every 100 square feet of planting area! Most years, in most parts of the country, rain won't provide nearly enough water to keep your plants thriving, so you'll have to give Mother Nature a hand. Make sure you put your garden as close as you can to a hose hookup, so you don't have to tote a heavy watering can back and forth.

Drinking habits. Some vegetables need more water than others. On an inch-per-week basis, celery and asparagus are two of the heaviest drinkers.

Beets and peppers rank among the modest imbibers. Many herbs, including marjoram, oregano, thyme, and garlic, need very little liquid. In fact, they'll taste best if you grow them in soil that's on the dry side.

Jerry Baker Says

"Don't be too quick on the hose trigger: Too much water can be worse than too little. It will drown plant roots and wash away the nutrients that plants need to grow up strong and healthy."

Putting Down Roots:
The Soil in Your Garden

Anybody who thinks of soil as just a lot of boring old dirt should have spent some time with Grandma Putt. To her, a spade full of healthy garden soil was like a magical miniature world, full of millions of tiny critters just going about their business — and, in the process, making everything around us blossom and grow.

Oh, soil-o-mio. As important as soil is, when Grandma Putt was looking for an area for a new garden plot, she always considered soil *after* she thought about sunlight, fresh air, protection from harsh winds, and closeness to a water supply. When I asked her why, she said that those things are hard, and sometimes impossible, to change, but you can always improve your soil — and it's fun to do, besides. Before you can make it better, though, you have to know what you're starting with.

Loam, loam on the range. When you're standing on plain old garden-variety dirt, you're actually standing on a combination of air, water, organic matter, and billions of mineral particles. The biggest ones — rocks — we gardeners chuck by the wayside. The smallest ones we rank by size as either sand (the biggest of the tinies), silt (medium-sized), or clay (microscopic).

Sandy soil — "light" soil in gardeners' lingo — tends to drain quickly and not hold nutrients very well. Clay, or "heavy," soil holds nutrients, but it also holds water too well. When it gets wet, it sticks together like two sides of a peanut butter sandwich — not a good condition to encourage plants to grow in.

A vegetable's dream soil is a nicely balanced mix of sand, silt, clay, and organic matter — what we call loam. It holds a good supply of nutrients, doesn't dry out too fast, but doesn't stay soggy.

Bring On the Chow!

For a vegetable plant, dinnertime means chowing down on many nutrients in the soil. We'll talk a lot more about plant diets and nutritious soil in Chapter 4, but here's a quick rundown on "The Big Three," as Grandma Putt used to call them.

NUTRIENT	WHAT IT DOES	WHO NEEDS IT MOST
Nitrogen (N)	Keeps plants green Promotes good leaf and stem growth	Leafy crops like lettuce, cabbage, and spinach
Phosphorus (P)	Makes for good, strong root development Helps plants produce fruit and resist disease	Root crops like potatoes, beets, and carrots
Potassium (K)	Makes plants grow Fends off diseases	All plants

Sweet and sour: your soil's pH. You can pour all of the nutrients in the world into your soil, but if those nutrients can't dissolve in water, they can't get to the plants' roots. That means you might as well pour all that good plant chow down the drain. One of the factors that determine if the nutrients in the soil actually get into the plants is pH. If your soil is either too acid (sour) or too alkaline (sweet), the nutrients in it have no way of getting into the plant. That's when knowing your soil's pH comes in handy.

Test time. When I'm in a hurry to get growing, I buy a nifty little kit at the garden center, follow the directions, and presto! I know my soil's pH and how much nitrogen, phosphorus, and potassium are in it.

When I have a bit more time, I mail off a soil sample to my County Extension Service or a private testing lab, and they test it for me. It sometimes takes 6 to 8 weeks to get the results, but it's worth the wait, because I get a much more thorough analysis, including levels of all those other important nutrients besides "The Big Three."

The pH Scale

The letters pH stand for "potential of hydrogen," and the pH scale runs from 1.0 to 14.0, with 7.0 being neutral. A measurement below 7.0 means that you've got acid soil; above 7.0 indicates alkaline soil. Most vegetables do best with a pH between 6.0 and 7.0, though there are some significant exceptions. (For more about those, see the individual plant portraits in Chapter 7.)

Five Simple Steps for Taking a Soil Sample

Step 1. Remove any sod, mulch, or surface litter in the area.

Step 2. Dig a hole about 5 inches in diameter and as deep as the topsoil layer. This could be anywhere from 6 to 18 inches deep.

Step 3. With a trowel, slice about a ½-inch strip of soil from the side of the hole, and lay the slice on a piece of clean newspaper.

Step 4. Take samples from at least nine more areas of your future garden, then mix all of these samples together. (Be sure to break up soil clumps and remove any sticks, stones, or other debris.)

Step 5. Follow the instructions that come with your kit or that you get from the testing lab.

How to pass with flying colors. As we all learned in high school chemistry, the accuracy of any scientific test depends on the quality of the sample. These tips will put you on the honor roll:

• Test your soil in fall, if possible.

• Take your samples *before* you work or add anything to the soil.

• If you use a do-it-yourself test, mix your samples with distilled water; tap water contains minerals that can sometimes alter results.

• Be extra careful not to include sticks and stones — or anything other than soil — in your sample.

• Do your sampling when the soil is warm and neither bone-dry nor sopping wet.

• Don't take a sample from an atypical spot, like the place the former owners had a compost pile or a low area where puddles form after a rain.

• If you added fertilizer to the soil, wait at least 2 weeks before you sample.

• Keep records of the date you took your samples, where you took them from, and the weather conditions that day, as well as the results of the test, for future reference.

The Worms and I

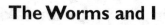

In Grandma Putt's time, there weren't any of those fancy soil test kits. But she sure as shootin' knew how to find out whether her soil was healthy. How? She'd take a worm count (see box below). She knew that for worms to call a chunk of earth home, it has to be well drained and well aerated, with a pH between 6.0 and 7.0, and it has to be chock-full of organic matter. In other words, it's just the kind of soil vegetables need in order to grow big and juicy.

The numbers. If your worm census counts more than 10 slithering pink guys, congratulations! It means your garden has laid out a welcome mat for worms and other tiny critters that'll keep the soil healthy and productive. The higher the head count (so to speak), the better. When it comes to these underground structural workers, there's no such thing as overpopulation.

On the other hand, a count of fewer than 10 means that there's work to do. You'll need fancier tests than this one to figure out exactly what the problem is. One thing is almost certain, though: You can make any soil healthier by adding a big helping of organic matter.

Soup's On!

Want to really lure the neighborhood worms to your garden? Dish up frequent servings of my veggie scrap soup. To make it, simply whirl up your dinner peelings and leftovers in the blender (minus sauces and dressings). Then dig a hole anyplace in your garden, pour in the soup, and cover it up with soil. Worms will charge in and eat hearty!

Anybody Home?

Grandma Putt and I always took our worm census in the spring or fall, when the soil temperature was about 60°F. (When it's any warmer than that, worms have to head for deeper territory or they die.) She'd hand me a spade and I'd dig out a block of soil about 1 foot square and 7 inches deep. I'd ease the soil onto a board and — very gently — Grandma Putt and I would break up the clumps with our fingers and lift out the worms. Then we'd count them as quickly as we could and send them home again before they dried out.

Picking the Perfect Plot

So much for what it takes to make plants happy in the garden. What about you? You wouldn't expect vegetables to grow in conditions that don't meet their needs. It's no different for you: If conditions don't meet *your* needs, you can't give your plants the time and attention it takes to keep them thriving (or you won't want to, which amounts to the same thing when you're gardening for fun and relaxation).

Don't Bite Off More . . .

When I first went to live with Grandma Putt, World War II was raging, and here on the home front, we were giving our all to support the troops. I knew that the more vegetables we could grow in our home gardens, the more farmers could send to our boys overseas, including my Uncle Art. Why, I saw my first garden spreading across acres, feeding our whole town and Uncle Art's regiment to boot.

When Grandma Putt pointed out a plot that looked to me about as big as her kitchen table and said, "That'll be all yours, Junie," I couldn't believe my ears! Did she think I couldn't handle anything bigger than that? As always, though, she was right. There was so much to learn, and it all took so much more time than I thought it would.

Since then, I've developed my own rule of thumb for how big to make a garden: Decide how much you can take care of with no trouble at all, then reduce it by a third. (After all, you probably don't have to feed the Seventh Armored Division.) You can always enlarge your garden next year, after you know how much you *really* enjoy digging and watering and mulching and weeding. By then, you'll also know how much food your garden produces — which will be a lot more than you probably think.

Location, Location, Location

Always put your garden as close to the house as you can. That way, you'll spot those little weedlings before they become big bullies. You'll notice insect pests while there's still time to pick them off with your fingers or send them packing with a blast from the garden hose. Best of all, you'll know just when those new baby carrots, peas, and greens are ready for picking, and you won't waste a minute of their sweet, fresh flavor.

Pretty as a Picture

It seems that every time I walk into a supermarket or a drug-store these days, I see another glossy magazine or a fancy picture book about "ornamental kitchen gardens." Why, the way those writer folks carry on, you'd think they invented the whole idea of a good-looking vegetable patch!

They should have seen my Grandma Putt's place. She knew that lots of plants that are good to eat are as beautiful to look at as any just-for-show flowers. She also knew that the way you divide up your space makes all the difference in the world between a ho-hum garden and a veggie plot you're proud to show off! Her garden was full of little squares, rectangles, triangles, even circles — and I learned firsthand that they were easier to take care of than those long rows that, to my 10-year-old eyes, at least, looked like they stretched into the next county.

What will the neighbors think? In some neighborhoods, folks still seem to think that a house needs to be surrounded by nothing but clipped lawn with maybe a few trees and shrubs here and there. If you're not sure your neighbors will take kindly to a vegetable garden in your backyard, keep these ideas in mind:

• Situate your garden where it can't be seen easily from the street.

• Instead of making a compost pile, use a special plastic bin. They speed up the composting process, and they look like the garbage cans everyone else has, only nicer.

• Put up a nice-looking fence around your garden and grow flowering vines on it. Just make sure the fence is low enough, or has enough openings in it, so that air can circulate freely.

• Instead of planting everything in straight rows, divide up the space into planting beds of different shapes and sizes.

• Cover pathways between beds with brick, stone, or an attractive mulch like small wood chips, gravel, or cocoa hulls. Besides looking great, the mulch will help keep down weeds.

• Make a brick or stone terrace right in the middle of your garden, and put a table and chairs on it. Then, when your tomatoes are practically bursting with juicy flavor and you're pulling up new potatoes that are cute as buttons, invite everyone over for a good old-fashioned neighborhood social. And don't be surprised if, come January or so, they start asking for advice on their seed orders.

Making the Most of What You've Got

Not many folks these days have that perfect garden site: a big plot of rich, loamy soil on a gentle, sunny, south-facing slope that's protected from harsh winds. There are plenty of other challenges for a gardener to cope with, too: short growing seasons, harsh climates, not to mention the droughts that seem to hit more of the country every year. When I complained about any of those kinds of things to Grandma Putt, she'd just look at me and say, "Junie, there's nothing more boring than perfection."

Divide and conquer. No law says that your whole garden has to grow in the same place. If you don't have the right spot for a single garden, do what I do. Find all the sunny, sheltered spots in your yard, and plant whatever will fit comfortably there and grow well together. (That's an old-time technique called companion planting, and we'll talk more about it in the next chapter.) Here are a few of my very favorite mini gardens:

• Cherry tomatoes surrounded by a border of basil

• A bed of mixed salad greens with a border of parsley

• Peas planted on a trellis with turnips growing underneath

• Beets intermingled with bush beans

Mix and match. Some vegetable plants are so pretty, they'd be worth planting even if you didn't want to eat them. Grandma Putt always kept rhubarb and asparagus growing in her perennial flower beds, and she always put eggplant right in with the cosmos and zinnias in her cutting garden.

Hostile territory. Most veggies have a general preference for a certain kind of climate: dry, wet, cool, hot. Chances are, though, you can grow whatever you're hankering for. Just adjust your planting and harvesting times to suit your climate, and plant varieties that are bred to thrive in your particular growing conditions. (See Chapter 7 for more specific suggestions.)

Well, now that you know what your veggies need in the way of "creature" comforts, let's move on to planning their home, sweet home.

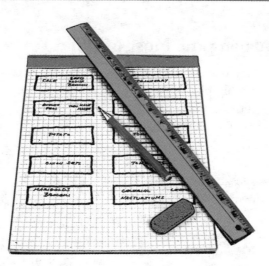

CHAPTER 2

Planning
Your Plot

For Grandma Putt and me, a big part of wintertime
fun was planning next year's garden. On cold, blustery
evenings, we'd pop ourselves a big bowl of popcorn.
Then we'd pull up a table in front of the fireplace,
get out pencils, paper, seed catalogs, last year's garden
scrapbook, and set to it. Even today, after all these years,
careful planning in my garden pays off just as much as it
did back then — and it's just as much fun!

Drawing the Plan

Back when Grandma Putt helped me lay out my first little garden, I was amazed at how careful she was about what went where and how much space to give everything. Later, as all those plants grew up and I started picking basket after basket full of beans and tomatoes and carrots, I was more than amazed: I was just about bowled over at how much food I had grown in that tiny plot!

Give Yourself the Test

The first step to planning a garden — especially if it's your first — is to take my "Why I Want to Grow My Own" test. Treat this test as an exercise in amateur self-analysis: Your answers will help you decide how big to make your garden, how to lay it out, and what to grow in it.

Just check off all of the statements that apply to you, and keep them in mind when you start the real planning. And remember: There are no wrong answers to this test — this is *your* garden!

From my garden, I want:

❏ Vegetables with old-time, fresh-picked flavor

❏ Vegetables and herbs that I keep reading about in magazines, but can't find at my local supermarket

❏ Produce that's been grown without pesticides or synthetic fertilizers

❏ Food that I know hasn't been genetically engineered

❏ A lower food bill

❏ A big harvest for preserving and sharing

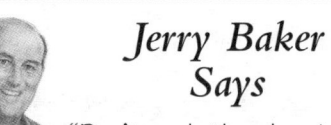

❏ Just enough for my family and me to eat fresh, with a little extra for company

❏ Relaxation and exercise

❏ An attractive addition to my yard

Jerry Baker Says

"Don't rush the planning process. It always takes me several long winter evenings (and lots of popcorn) to figure out everything I want to grow this year and exactly where I want to grow it."

Get It in Writing

Once you know what you want from your garden, and where you want to put it, you need to measure the site and draw its outline on a paper. It's best to draw your plot to scale, or as close to it as you can. (Don't worry: It's a lot easier than it sounds.) I use graph paper that has 10 squares to an inch, and I let 1 inch on the paper equal 1 foot in my garden.

Ready, Set, Plan

Here's what I always have handy when I sit down to make my garden plan:

- Graph paper
- Ruler
- Compass
- Stencils for fancy shapes
- Sharp pencils with erasers
- Seed and plant catalogs
- Garden encyclopedia for reference
- My old garden scrapbooks

East is east. On your plan, be sure to mark north, south, east, and west, and label any trees, buildings, or fences that block the sun during the day. (If you know where significant shadows fall in the garden, mark them too.) If you're like me, it's easy to lose track of those things when you're inside.

Plain and Fancy

To draw round beds on my garden plan, I use the kind of old-fashioned compass that we used to carry to school in our pencil boxes. You can still get these at any store that sells craft or school supplies.

If you want to make fancier beds, buy plastic stencils in shapes like triangles, crescents, and teardrops. You can even use cookie cutters if they're the right size! (In chapter 5, we'll talk about some simple tricks for transferring those shapes onto the ground.)

Plotting the Feast

Here's my rule of thumb for figuring out a family-size plot that will keep you in fresh veggies all summer long, with a plentiful supply to put by for the winter.

IF YOU'RE FEEDING	MAKE YOUR GARDEN
3 or 4	10' X 10'
4 to 6	15' X 15'
6 or more	30' X 30'

SUPER Growing Secrets

THINK THIN

Whatever shape you make your beds, keep them narrow enough that you can reach into the center comfortably without stepping on the planting area. Stepping on cultivated soil compacts it. That can even damage the roots of big trees, so imagine what it will do to your tender young seedlings!

Memories Are Made of This

I've been keeping a garden scrapbook every year since I first started to garden — and that's a lot of scrapbooks! It's a real kick to look through them from time to time, but they're more than just sentimental souvenirs — they're also an important part of my garden reference library. I like to use great big artists' sketchbooks, because they're sturdier and look great, but a big three-ring notebook also works just fine.

The Makings of a Scrapbook

Like my seedlings, my scrapbook starts out small, but during the spring and summer, it just grows and grows. Here are some of the things that wind up in it by the time I call it quits at harvesttime:

• Soil-test results, both the scientific type and the old-time kind (like my yearly worm count)

• Snapshots of the "before," with notes I've made about things that affect the results, like wind and sunlight

• All my plans for this year's garden — even the ones I wind up not using, because they might turn out to be just the ticket for some other year

• Lists of whatever I add to beef up the soil, complete with quantities and dates

• My original "wish list," along with the real, shorter version I wound up with, as well as the clipped-out catalog descriptions of everything I ordered

• All of the seed packets and those plastic tags that come tucked in with plants from the garden center

• Notes about my garden in progress from the time I start seeds indoors to the time I bed down my asparagus and rhubarb for the winter

As you can see, there's everything from soup to nuts in there. And you'll be amazed at how useful it can be.

Jerry Baker Says

"A garden scrapbook is a lot like a ship's log. I like to keep track of dates, like when I sow seeds, indoors and out, and harden off and transplant seedlings. It's the only way I can remember how every kind of plant performs, when it blooms and sets fruit, when I get my first and last harvest, and — most important — how it tastes."

What Goes Where?

When it's time to go on summer vacation, a friend of mine just throws a dart at a map and treks off to wherever it lands. That might be a great way to have yourself an adventure, but it's no way to plan a vegetable garden. Grandma Putt used to say that vegetables have strong opinions about the place they bed down in, even if it's for just a few months out of the year. So here's what you need to know.

The Long, Green Row

If you decide to stick with old-fashioned rows for your veggies, make sure you break them up with pathways every now and then. If that line stretches on too far, you'll be tempted to take a shortcut through the plants to the other side — stepping on the soil and the plants in the process.

Tall in the Saddle

Where you plant tall crops, like corn and sunflowers, and ones that ride high on trellises, like tomatoes and some beans, depends on the climate. In most parts of the country, it's usually best to put them on the far west side of your garden, so they can shield the more tender plants like lettuce from the west wind and the hot afternoon sun. But if you live way up North, where heat can be hard to come by even in summer, you'll probably want to keep those high, vertical shapes on the north side. That way, they won't cast cold shadows on their shorter neighbors.

And with Whom?

Most of the plants in a particular family have pretty much the same nutritional needs. They also tend to have the same enemies when it comes to pests and diseases. And both of those factors figure into a part of garden planning called crop rotation.

When Grandma Putt started teaching me about gardening, I didn't have a clue about what to plant with what, so she explained her basic rule of thumb: When in doubt, plant vegetables near other members of the same family. Even if they don't help one another in some special way, at least they'll mind their manners and get along in the row.

Vegetable Families: What's in a Name?

In any two garden books or catalogs, you're likely to see two different names for the same plant family. That's why, besides knowing the common family names of the veggies you want to grow, it's useful to know their scientific monikers, which are the same all over the world. (Don't worry: You just want to recognize them when you see them — you don't have to spell them or pronounce them!)

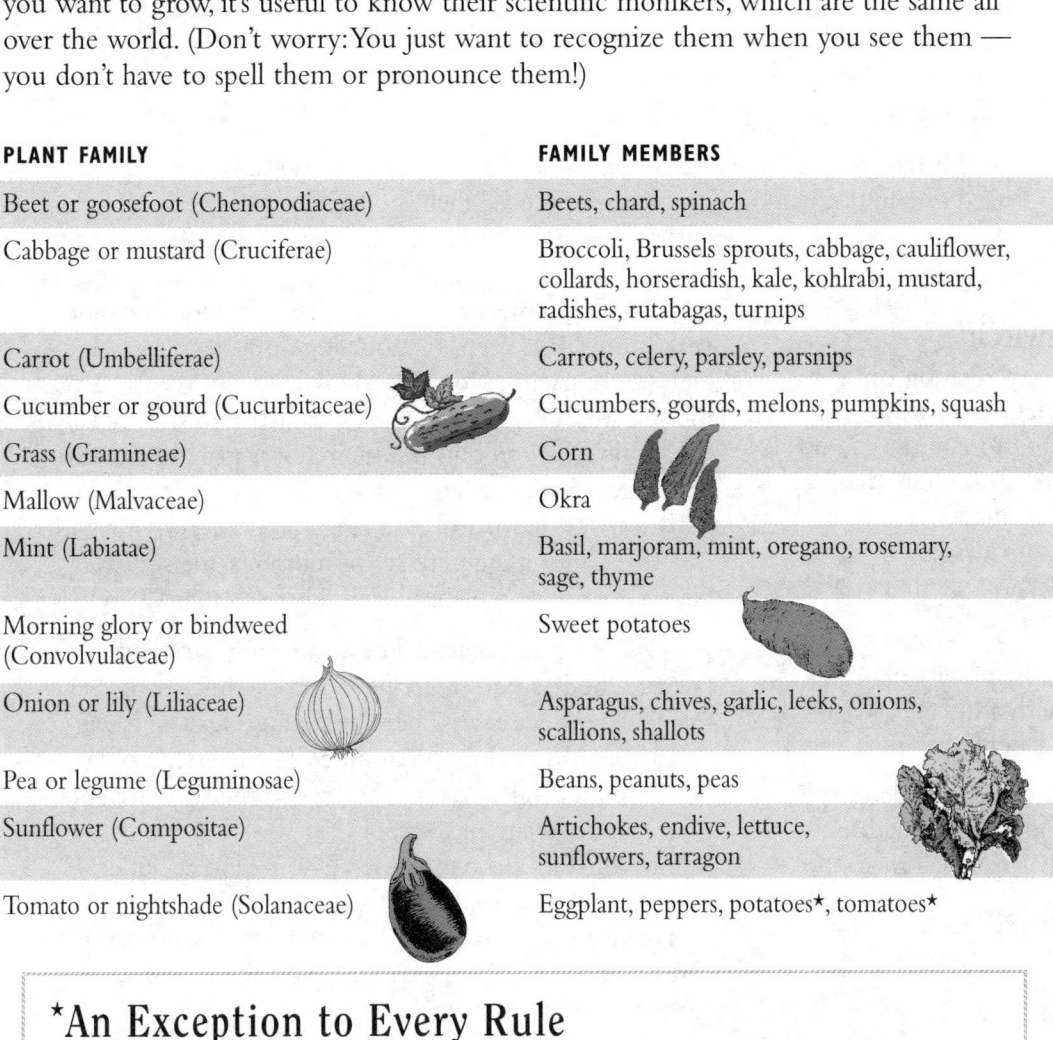

PLANT FAMILY	FAMILY MEMBERS
Beet or goosefoot (Chenopodiaceae)	Beets, chard, spinach
Cabbage or mustard (Cruciferae)	Broccoli, Brussels sprouts, cabbage, cauliflower, collards, horseradish, kale, kohlrabi, mustard, radishes, rutabagas, turnips
Carrot (Umbelliferae)	Carrots, celery, parsley, parsnips
Cucumber or gourd (Cucurbitaceae)	Cucumbers, gourds, melons, pumpkins, squash
Grass (Gramineae)	Corn
Mallow (Malvaceae)	Okra
Mint (Labiatae)	Basil, marjoram, mint, oregano, rosemary, sage, thyme
Morning glory or bindweed (Convolvulaceae)	Sweet potatoes
Onion or lily (Liliaceae)	Asparagus, chives, garlic, leeks, onions, scallions, shallots
Pea or legume (Leguminosae)	Beans, peanuts, peas
Sunflower (Compositae)	Artichokes, endive, lettuce, sunflowers, tarragon
Tomato or nightshade (Solanaceae)	Eggplant, peppers, potatoes*, tomatoes*

*An Exception to Every Rule

While cozy family life is just fine for most veggies, there is an exception: the tomato clan (a.k.a. nightshades). Tomatoes will be happy as clams living next door to their pepper and eggplant cousins. But, like feuding siblings, tomatoes and potatoes just don't care for each other's company. And, because potatoes need a lower pH than the rest of the Solanaceae family, they're usually not grown with their relatives.

Keep 'em Movin'

Crop rotation is a fancy-sounding name for a pretty basic concept. It simply means growing plants in different parts of your garden every year — very much like the game of musical chairs we used to play as kids. Keeping your crops marching around your garden pays off in two ways:

• **Nutrition.** Just as people do, plants have different eating habits. Though they all need certain basic kinds of nutrients, they need them in different quantities and different combinations, and they take them from different levels of the soil.

When the same kind of plant grows in the same spot year after year, it keeps on gobbling up its own special blend of nutrients. No matter how hard you try to keep the soil stocked with that plant's favorite chow, eventually the supply will run out, and the result is malnutrition for your green, rooted friend.

But if you let that plant change places every year with one that favors a different set of nutrients, the soil will have a chance to replenish itself. That's all there is to it.

• **Pests and diseases.** Just as various plants have favorite foods, so do insect pests and the microscopic critters that cause diseases. These pesky guys feast on their veggie victims during the summer. Then, instead of taking off on a tropical cruise, they spend the winter right there, sound asleep in the soil. That way, they'll be Johnny-on-the-spot when the all-you-can-eat buffet opens up in the spring.

Fortunately for both plants and gardeners, most vegetable villains won't go galloping after the chuck wagon. If they wake up from their long winter's nap and find that their favorite meal has been replaced by something they don't care to eat, they simply lie back down and starve to death.

One, Two, Three: Switch!

Crop rotation can get tricky. The whole thing used to confuse me no end. But Grandma Putt told me not to worry: You can't go wrong if you remember these rules:

1. Replace a big eater with a lighter eater or a caterer (see next page).

2. Replace a deep-rooted plant with one that has shallow roots.

3. Never put a plant where a member of its own family grew the year before.

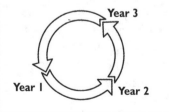

Some Giveth and Some Taketh Away

One thing to keep in mind as you rotate crops is plant appetite levels. Like folks, plants fall into three categories: big eaters, lighter eaters, and caterers. This last batch of plants actually returns nutrients to the soil.

When I use this method, I plant a big eater like eggplant in an area one year. The next year, I put the eggplant someplace else, and replace it with a moderate eater like onions. The year after that, bush beans might go in that plot, so that when they're plowed under, they can replenish or "fix" the nitrogen the onions and eggplant have used up.

Home, Sweet Home

A Word to the Wise from Grandma Putt

Grandma Putt used to say, "There's an exception to every rule." In the case of crop rotation, there's one group of plants that you have to just let stay put: perennials. The three most common perennial vegetables are asparagus, rhubarb, and some varieties of artichoke. Once you've made a happy home for them, they like to stay right where they are.

Planting Buddies

Nowadays, you hear a lot about "companion planting." But it's nothing new. Way back in ancient times, people noticed that certain plants seemed to do better — or worse — when they were growing next to each other. Today, scientists know that all plants send out chemicals from their roots and leaves. These substances can repel pests, attract beneficial insects, inhibit a plant's ability to grow, or make it generally healthier. The study of such things is called allelochemistry.

Eat Hearty, Me Lads!

Big Eaters	Light to Moderate Eaters
Broccoli	
Brussels sprouts	Beets
Cabbage	Carrots
Cauliflower	Chard
Celery	Kale
Chinese cabbage	Kohlrabi
Corn	Leeks
Cucumber	Parsnips
Eggplant	Radishes
Lettuce	Rutabaga
Melons	Spinach
Okra	Sweet potatoes
Onions	Turnips
Peppers	
Potatoes	**Caterers**
Squash	Beans
Tomatoes	Peanuts
	Peas

Boon Companions

I'm not a scientist, but from everything I've seen over the years, I know that companion planting really does work. As we go along, we'll talk more about the ways plants give each other a hand (or club each other over the head), but for starters, here are some good and not-so-good neighbors to keep in mind as you plan your garden.

VEGETABLE	GOOD NEIGHBORS	BAD NEIGHBORS
Asparagus	Basil, parsley, tomatoes	Garlic, onions
Bush beans	Beets, cabbage, carrots, cauliflower, celery, corn, cucumbers, potatoes	Basil, kohlrabi, onions
Pole beans	Carrots, cauliflower, chard, corn, cucumbers, eggplant, peas, potatoes	Basil, beets, cabbage, onions
Beets	Bush beans, cabbage, lettuce, onions	Pole beans
Broccoli	Dill, mint, potatoes, rosemary, sage	Tomatoes, pole beans
Cabbage	Dill, mint, potatoes, rosemary, sage	Pole beans
Carrots	Chives, lettuce, onions	Celery, parsnips
Cauliflower	Dill, mint, potatoes, rosemary, sage	Pole beans
Celery	Bush beans, cabbage, cauliflower, leeks, tomatoes	Carrots, parsnips
Corn	Beans, cucumbers, melons, peas, pumpkins, squash	Tomatoes
Cucumbers	Cabbage, chives, corn, potatoes, radishes	Potatoes
Lettuce	Carrots, radishes	None
Onions	Beets, carrots, lettuce, tomatoes	Asparagus, beans, peas
Peas	Beans, carrots, corn, cucumbers, potatoes, turnips	Late potatoes, onions
Potatoes	Beans, cabbage, corn, horseradish, peas	Cucumbers, pumpkins, rutabagas, spinach, squash, tomatoes, turnips
Pumpkins	Beans, cabbage, corn, horseradish, peas	Potatoes
Radishes	Cucumbers, lettuce, peas	Hyssop
Rutabagas	Peas, onions	Potatoes
Spinach	Cabbage, celery, lettuce, onions, radishes	Potatoes
Squash	Corn	Potatoes
Tomatoes	Bush beans, cabbage, carrots, celery, cucumbers,	Pole beans, potatoes

Good Things Come from Small Plots

You don't have to have a big yard to have a great vegetable garden. For that matter, you don't need a yard at all! I've seen some mighty fine harvests come from small patios, tiny balconies, and even rooftops and houseboats.

Save That Space!

When space is tight, it pays to have a few tricks up your sleeve. Here are a few of my favorites:

• **Go compact.** No matter what kinds of veggies you decide to grow, look for compact varieties. (See Chapter 7 for some good suggestions.)

• **Get wide.** Instead of planting in long, narrow rows, grow your crops in wide, raised beds. That way, you can set plants closer together, and make the paths between beds narrower — so you'll save space two ways.

• **Stay full.** Don't let any bed sit empty. Instead, replace every crop you harvest with another one. The fancy term for this is succession planting.

• **Grow up.** Grow vine crops like cucumbers, vining tomatoes, and squash on trellises, walls, or fences. They'll take up less space, and you can use the ground at their "feet" for lower-growing, less-sprawling veggies.

• **Grow in pairs.** Put fast-growing plants close to ones that take longer to mature. This is another old-time gardening trick, called intercropping or interplanting.

• **Spread around.** You don't have to grow your garden all in one place. Take advantage of all those little nooks and crannies around your yard. Grow pole beans up the lamppost, or cherry tomato plants by the back door.

• **Use containers.** You can grow a fine crop of lettuce or radishes in a window box. And if you pick the right variety, almost any veggie will feel right at home in a big pot or a wooden barrel sawed in half.

A Seed and Plant Shopping Spree

Grandma Putt used to say that shopping for plants is the same as going to the grocery store: If you don't have a list, you're likely to wind up with some interesting things, but they might not be what you really want. That's why, long before the planting season ever rolls around, I spend some time pondering what I really want to grow in my garden this year.

Exercising Restraint

All of those colorful pictures in the seed catalogs can be mighty enticing, especially in the depths of winter when the days are gray, the nights are long, and it feels like spring will never come. When you look at all of those plump, ripe veggies, you can almost feel the warm sun beating down on your back. It makes you want to crank up your pencil and order one of just about everything. I know, because I've done it — more than once! That's why I came up with a few rules for deciding what to grow.

Rule no. 1 — Grow only what you and your family love to eat. So what if 90 percent of the gardeners in the country grow tomatoes? If nobody in your family cares about them one way or another — homegrown or not — forget about them. Devote your time, energy, and space to the things that disappear the minute you put them on the table.

Rule no. 2 — When it comes to quantity, play it by year. Maybe your kids used to love Brussels sprouts (mine did), but now they're going through an "I-won't-touch-that-yucky-stuff" stage (mine did that, too). So cut back on the sprouts section this year, and plant more of their current favorites.

Rule no. 3 — Vote for flavor. The tastiest varieties of most vegetables never appear in supermarkets and rarely even on farm stands. That's because the most flavorful kinds don't hold up well in shipment, or they ripen a few at a time instead of in one fell swoop, as most commercial growers need them to do. And regardless of variety, some vegetables, like corn and peas, start losing their sweetness the minute you pick them. To get the biggest bang for your gardening buck, grow veggies that have the kind of flavor money can't buy. How do you know what they are? Ask other gardeners, check out seed catalogs, and above all else — experiment!

The Containment Policy

When you're planning your plot, don't over-look some of my favorite places to grow veggies: containers. A lot of folks think container gardening is just for people who don't have yards to sink their shovels into. That's one way to look at it, but even if your territory stretches as far as the eye can see, you've got a lot to gain by growing some of your food crops in pots. Here are some of the reasons I like to use them:

• **Rein 'em in.** They let me corral spreading plants like horseradish and mint that would take over my whole garden if I planted them in the ground and turned my back for 10 minutes.

• **Cater to needs.** A container holds any kind of soil and any kind of nutrients I put into it. That means, for instance, that I can grow potatoes in big barrels full of the sour soil they like, and use my garden space for crops that hanker for sweeter surroundings.

• **Outfox the weather.** In containers, I can grow cooking herbs like bay and rosemary that can't last the winter in my climate. They have a grand old time outdoors until the first frost approaches. Then I bring them inside, give them a sunny window to bask in, and they're happy campers all winter long.

• **Perk up your place.** There are some mighty pretty pots in the garden centers; filled with good-looking veggies, they make fine additions to any landscape. I grow peppers and eggplant in big clay pots right out beside the front porch.

Trace Elements

When you're planning your plot, here's a simple way to figure out where to put your container veggies: Just draw the outline of each container on tracing paper. (Make sure it's drawn to scale.) Then lay that sheet on top of the scale drawing you've made of your yard, and move the tracing paper around until you've found exactly the right spot for each pot!

CONTAINER GARDEN BOOSTER MIX

When it's time to plant your container veggies, add this miracle mix to a peck of a half-and-half mixture of commercial potting soil and compost.

½ cup of Epsom salts
¼ cup of coffee grounds (rinsed clean)
1 tbsp. of instant tea granules
4 eggshells (dried and crushed to powder)

Mix the ingredients together well, and then plant away!

Jerry Baker Says

"Every year, whatever I decide to grow in my garden, I always plant a little more than I need, and give my extra harvest to the local food bank."

Treasure on the Vine

Grandma Putt told me that when she married my Grandpa Putt, her grandfather gave them seeds for a wedding present. But they were no ordinary seeds. They came from plants *his* grandfather — and his grandfather's grandfather — had grown.

There weren't many seed companies back then, so every year people would save seeds from the healthiest, hardiest plants with the tastiest vegetables, and they'd plant those seeds the following year. When children left home to start their own families and their own gardens, their parents would give them a little treasure chest of seeds to take with them.

Later, when big seed companies and garden centers came along, more folks started buying seeds every year instead of saving their own, and a lot of those special old-time vegetables went the way of the dinosaurs.

Everything Old Is New Again

Or, as Grandma Putt would say, "What goes around comes around." Fortunately, Grandma Putt and a lot of other gardeners kept right on growing their favorite plants, saving the seeds, and passing them around to one another. Nowadays, folks call those old-time varieties "heirlooms," and they're popping up in more and more catalogs and garden centers every year. I've always given heirlooms prime real estate in my garden, for plenty of good reasons.

• **Flavor.** Heirloom varieties often taste better than newer hybrids, because most often our forefathers saved seeds only from the plants that produced the best-tasting crops.

• **Hardiness.** Besides demanding good taste from their crops, old-time gardeners passed on seeds from the toughest hombres in the row — the ones that could stand up best to whatever the territory delivered in the way of pests, diseases, and ornery weather. And those had to perform without all those fancy fertilizers and pesticides we have today.

• **A long harvest.** Many modern varieties ripen all at once. That's fine for people who want bushels of produce to sell at market. But I'd rather have what most of the older kinds offer up: veggies that keep ripening in dinner-sized batches for a long time.

• **Good looks.** A lot of heirlooms are so gosh-darn pretty, I'd grow them even if I didn't want to eat them. I plant 'Pruden's Purple' tomatoes, 'Rainbow' Swiss chard, and 'Baby White Tiger' eggplant right out in the open, where I can look at them all summer long.

An Education in the Mailbox

A good seed catalog is a lot more than attractive pictures and lists of plants. Why, Grandma Putt used to say that studying a first-rate catalog is just like taking a course in gardening. Every year, when my favorites arrive in the mail, I read them from cover to cover — and I always learn something new!

Plant Breeding 101 — It's Easy!

In any good catalog, right up beside a plant's name, you'll see either OP, which stands for "open-pollinated," or F_1, which is short for F_1 hybrid. (Don't panic: This is a lot simpler than it sounds.) Open-pollinated plants are what scientists term "genetically stable." That means that if I save seeds from my plants and use them the following year, I'll get a plant that is nearly identical to the one I started with.

On the other hand, an F_1 hybrid is a plant that scientists have bred to be a superplant with an extra dose of desirable qualities, like compact size, high yield, or disease resistance. Unfortunately, F_1 hybrids are genetically unstable and produce offspring that are much inferior to their parents. To get a plant with those same good traits next year, I have to buy new seeds.

Extra! Extra! Read All About It!

When a catalog offers up these extras, I'm in gardener's heaven:

- Recipes and tips on how to store the harvest
- Just-for-fun nuggets about a plant's history and where it came from
- Tips on fending off bugs, thugs, and diseases
- Drawings of garden plans to give me ideas for my own
- Good descriptions of gardening books and cookbooks — because there's always more to learn!

Jerry Baker Says

"Look for seed companies that have test gardens in your part of the country. That way, you can be pretty sure the varieties they're selling will find a happy home in your garden."

SUPER Growing Secrets

COLD STORAGE

When the seeds you've ordered show up in your mailbox, stash them in the fridge. That way, they'll be rarin' to go when it's time to put them into the ground.

Green Thumb Tip

Whether you order your plants from a catalog or buy them from the local garden center, be sure to find out when the seedlings were started. You want plants that have been started at the recommended time for your area.

The Best of the Best

The best catalogs are well written, easy to understand, and give me the complete scoop on each variety they offer, and there's a lot more besides.

Here's the basic information I look for:

- **Days to maturity.** This tells me how long it will take a crop to grow to harvest — the best-tasting veggies in the world won't do me much good if my growing season isn't long enough for them.

- **Complete growing information.** A glance at the description should tell me the variety's pH preference, the best air temperature for seed germination, how long it takes seeds to sprout, how warm the soil needs to be, how well the plant resists pests and diseases, and how well it stands up to heat, cold, or drought.

- **Mature size for both plant and vegetables.** This is especially important if I'm looking for crops to grow in containers or in a small garden — or if I want to grow things like giant pumpkins or yard-long beans.

- **Taste, and the best ways to eat the harvest.** A good catalog entry won't say just that a veggie tastes good. It will tell me that it's sweeter than another popular variety, for example, that it has a "nutlike" flavor, or that it's great to eat fresh, but not so good for canning or freezing. In short, it doesn't always tell me what I want to hear, but it sure does tell me what I need to know!

A-Shopping We Will Go!

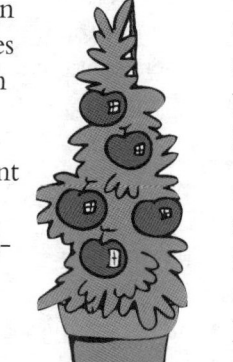

Nowadays, if you walk into any big garden center, you'll see table after table just covered with vegetable seedlings. Except for root crops and a few others that are almost never sold as started plants, you can find a wide variety of veggies. So doesn't it make sense just to buy plants, take them home, and tuck them into your garden? Well, sometimes yes, and sometimes no.

Buy started plants when:

🌱 The vegetables you want to grow need an early start indoors, and you don't have the time, the space, or the inclination to do the job.

🌱 You want to be certain that you will get varieties that will perform well in your climate.

🌱 You want almost instant results for a container garden or an ornamental-edible planting.

🌱 You're happy with whatever varieties the garden center has for sale.

Start from seed when:

🌱 You want varieties you can't find at the garden center. Many vegetables come in hundreds of varieties, and even the biggest garden center in the world can't carry all of them. If you want something extra special in the way of flavor, giant size, or color worth bragging about, you'll have more options with seeds.

🌱 The vegetables you want to grow don't like to be transplanted. Root crops aren't the only vegetables that resent having their underground parts disturbed. Cucumbers, squash, and melons don't like it any better. As for corn and beans, their seeds all but carry signs saying *Just plant me and let me settle down!*

Before You Leave Home

Before the busy spring shopping season starts, let your fingers do the walking. Call a few garden centers and ask:

• What kinds of vegetable plants are they planning to carry and will they have the varieties you want?

• When will their shipments start arriving, how often do they resupply, on what days of the week do shipments arrive, and for how long will they continue to arrive?

• What are the best days and times to find the freshest plants and the best selection?

Buying Day

- Try to be at the garden center when it opens the day a new shipment has been put out, or the first day they put their own home-grown seedlings out for sale. That way, you'll have the best selection of plants, and the staff will have time to answer your questions before the crowds descend upon them.

- Look for young, sturdy, stocky plants without blossoms. A plant that's leggy, lanky, or already in bloom is too old and stressed to perform well in your garden.

- Gently remove a plant from its container and make sure no roots are growing around the sides of the soil clump. That means that it was started too early.

- If you find any plants with a whitish powder or a chemical odor on their leaves, take your shopping list elsewhere. Those plants have probably been sprayed with a pesticide, and that's a sure sign that either the grower or the store has problems that you don't want in your garden.

- Find a staff member who has time to help you, and ask questions about what you're buying. The people who work in the best garden centers are usually gardeners themselves. I've found that, time permitting, most of them enjoy sharing their know-how and their enthusiasm.

It's All in the Game

Grandma Putt loved gardening contests. She said she caught the competition bug from one of her favorite garden writers, Thomas Jefferson. Every year, he and his neighbors in Virginia would have a contest to see who could grow the earliest peas. The winner would invite the also-rans for dinner and serve up the evidence. Talk about humble pie!

In the neighborhood where Grandma Putt and I lived, we went beyond peas. We'd all try to outdo one another with the biggest pumpkins and the earliest corn and tomatoes. That's when I learned to pay extra-special attention to big sizes and early maturity dates in catalog descriptions. When it comes to growing winners, technique is important, but first you need to find seeds with the right stuff. There's no substitute for good genes!

Okay, you've found that perfect spot for your garden to call home, and you've chosen your seeds or plants. Now it's time to get growing!

CHAPTER 3

Ready, Set, Grow!

When I lived with Grandma Putt, I never needed a calendar to tell me when spring was on its way. All I had to do was hear her say, "Well, Junie, it's getting on near planting time," and I knew Old Man Winter was a goner.

I also knew there were some good times ahead as we put all our careful wintertime planning into action. I get as big a kick out of planting time today as I did all those years ago. And I'm just as careful to follow all the important steps Grandma Putt taught me, so my plants get off and growing on the right root.

A Head Start Pays Off

Grandma Putt used to say that starting seeds indoors was a lot like sending a team of baseball players to spring training. Most of the guys could manage to get through the season all right without that head start, but you could bet your last pepper seed they wouldn't break many records on the field!

The Great Indoors

If you live in a nice warm, balmy climate, you can start just about any kind of vegetable seed right in the garden, and it'll take off like a superstar. But in many places, most crops — like most baseball players — do perform better with a preseason warm-up.

The bare essentials. Some seeds are picky about what they want in the way of light and temperature. (We'll talk about that in Chapter 7.) But most plants are pretty easygoing. Their basic needs are few:

- A well-drained container
- A well-drained, disease-free starting mix with lots of organic matter
- Steady, even moisture
- The right kind of food, in the right amounts, at the right time
- The right amount of light
- The right temperature

The Maternity Ward

Nowadays, you can find all kinds of seed-starting containers, and even complete kits, at your local garden center or in gardening catalogs. They all work just fine. But, as Grandma Putt used to say, seedlings don't need a room at the Ritz. They're happy starting life in anything that holds soil and has holes to let the extra water run out. Here are some containers I like to use (after I've poked holes in the bottoms, of course):

- Milk cartons
- Pie and cake tins
- Plastic shoeboxes
- Paper and plastic foam drinking cups
- Margarine, cottage cheese, and yogurt containers
- Plastic and plastic foam take-home boxes from restaurants and delis

Mellow Yellow JELL-O®

To get your seeds off to a disease-free start, lightly sprinkle JELL-O powder on them with a salt shaker. Any flavor will work, but lemon is the best choice because it repels some bugs. As your young plants grow, feed them more JELL-O — the gelatin helps the plants hold water, and the sugar feeds the micro-organisms in the soil.

Starting Seeds: A 12-Step Program

Here's how to get those baby plants off to a good, healthy start.

1. Give your seeds a day to chill out before you plant them. Wrap them in cheesecloth (one kind to a bundle!), and put the bundles into containers that have my Seed Starter Tonic in them.

SEED STARTER TONIC

1 tsp. of baby shampoo
1 tsp. of Epsom salts

Mix these ingredients in 1 quart of weak tea. Then wrap your seeds in cheesecloth (one kind to a bundle), tuck them into the liquid, and put the container into the fridge to soak for 24 hours.

2. Meanwhile, head off any bad-guy germs that may be waiting to attack: Wash all of your containers and a pair of tweezers in a solution of 1 part bleach to 8 parts hot water.

3. Beef up your seed-starting mix by adding 2 tablespoons of Epsom salts to each quart of mix. Then fill all of your containers. Dampen the mix, but don't soak it. Gently tamp it down to level it.

4. Use a large nail to make holes in the planting mix. For most seeds, they should be about ¼ inch deep and 2 inches apart. (See Chapter 7 for the preferences of particular plants.) Then sprinkle a little milled sphagnum moss into each hole. (Sphagnum moss has an antibiotic quality that will kill the damping-off fungus, which is seedlings' Public Enemy Number One.)

5. Take your seeds out of the refrigerator and spread them on paper towels to dry. Then pick up each seed with the tweezers, and set it into a hole. (Don't worry: This isn't as tedious as it seems.)

6. To prevent damping-off disease, sprinkle more sphagnum moss on top of the seed mix and press down lightly.

7. Mist the surface of the newly planted containers with my Seed and Soil Energizer Tonic.

SEED AND SOIL ENERGIZER TONIC

1 tsp. of liquid dish soap
1 tsp. of ammonia
1 tsp. of whiskey

Mix these ingredients in 1 quart of weak tea, pour it into your mist-sprayer bottle, shake gently, then mist the surface of newly planted seed containers.

8. Set the containers on a tray. Dampen a towel with the Seed and Soil Energizer Tonic, and cover the containers with the towel. (Drape it over the sides of the container to keep it from touching the surface of the soil.) Put the tray in a warm spot — the top of your refrigerator is perfect! Each day, lift the towel to check on the seeds. Mist the soil and dampen the towel with the Energizer Tonic, then cover the tray again.

9. When you see little bits of green poking out of the starter mix, take off the towel and mist-spray the little tykes with my Damping-Off Prevention Tonic (see page 42). Then move the tray to a spot where it will get at least 12 hours of light a day, whether from the sun, grow lights, or a combination of both.

10. As soon as the first two real leaves appear, your seedlings are ready for bigger quarters.  Gently lift each one with a small spoon, and set it into an individual pot filled with pasteurized commercial potting soil. For most seedlings, 2¼-inch pots are fine, but tomatoes, peppers, and eggplant need more legroom: Give them 4-inch pots.

11. Initially, feed the youngsters with my Seedling Starter Tonic.

12. Make these new seedlings feel at home, just as you would any other houseplants, until it's time to move them to the great outdoors. Once they get 3 to 4 inches tall, mist-spray them every few days with my Seedling Strengthener Tonic.

SEEDLING STARTER TONIC

2 tsp. of fish fertilizer
2 tsp. of liquid dish soap
1 tsp. of whiskey

Mix these ingredients in 1 quart of water. Feed the Tonic to your baby seedlings while they're young, and they'll grow up to produce tasty, bountiful harvests.

SEEDLING STRENGTHENER TONIC

To get your older seedlings off to a healthy start, mist-spray your plants every few days with this Tonic:

2 cups of manure
½ cup of instant tea granules
warm water

Put the manure and tea into an old nylon stocking, and let it steep in 5 gallons of water for several days. Dilute the "tea" with 4 parts of warm water before feeding your plants.

No Lunch for Me, I Brought My Own

Remember, fertilizer is for plants, not seeds. Sow your seeds in good soil and just let them sprout: Even the tiniest seed has all the food energy it needs to send out roots and push its little head through the soil.

Help Your Seedlings See the Light

If you don't have a sunny window — or any window at all — for your seedlings to bask in, don't worry. I've started healthy, happy vegetable plants in a dry basement. I just put my trays of containers on a table, hang fluorescent lights over the trays, and keep them on for 12 to 16 hours a day. (I buy inexpensive, adjustable light fixtures from the hardware store.)

As the seedlings grow, I keep raising the lights so that they're always about 3 inches from the tops of the plants. Otherwise, the little tykes will stretch for the light and get leggy. And you don't want leggy seedlings!

Sink or Swim

If you've saved seeds from last year and you're not sure they're rarin' to grow this season, try this trick: Pour the seeds into a glass of water. The ones that sink have a good chance of growing up big and strong. The seeds that float to the top are losers, so throw them onto the compost pile.

A word of warning, however: Once you've done this trick, you'll have to sow the seeds you're saving, because they'll have soaked up some water and are well on their way to sprouting.

Stamping Out Damping-Off

Grandma Putt was a great believer in that old adage "Experience is the best teacher." So when it came time for me to start my very first seedlings, she gave me the seeds and equipment I needed, showed me the basics, and then turned me loose. It's a good thing those seeds weren't her valuable heirlooms; when those poor little plants were only a few inches tall, they keeled right over and died. The morning I discovered them, I went running to Grandma Putt and told her what I'd found. She took one look at my dead seedlings, shook her head, and said, "Damping-off." Then she told me how to make sure it wouldn't happen again.

Damping-Off 101

The Causes of Damping-Off

- Dirty pots
- Nonsterilized soil
- Stagnant air
- Dirty hands or tools

To Prevent Damping-Off

- Always use a commercial sterile potting mix that has no soil in it, which is made especially for starting seeds. (You can find it at any garden center.)

- If your containers have been used for planting before, soak them for 15 minutes or so in a solution that's 1 part bleach to 8 parts hot water.

- When the first bits of green appear above the soil, spray the little tykes with my Damping-Off Prevention Tonic.

- Keep your seedlings in a place with good air circulation. Air that just hangs around is exactly what fungi like best.

- As your seedlings grow, keep the soil moist by spraying with my Seed and Soil Energizer Tonic (see page 355).

- Water your seedlings early in the day. Baby plants that head into the night with wet leaves are prime candidates for damping-off.

- When you transplant the seedlings, keep your *hands off* their stems. Use a small spoon to move them, and take as much of their starter planting mix with you as you can.

DAMPING-OFF PREVENTION TONIC

4 tsp. of chamomile tea
1 tsp. of liquid dish soap

Mix these ingredients in 1 quart of boiling water. Let steep for at least an hour (the stronger the better), strain, then cool. Mist-spray your seedlings with this Tonic as soon as their little green heads poke out of the soil.

A Leaf or Not a Leaf?

After you tuck your seeds into their flats, the first sign of life you'll see from most veggies is a thin, arched stem, followed by a pair of small, plump leaves. These are preliminary leaves, or seed leaves. (Scientists and garden writers call them cotyledons.) These leaves are standard equipment on seeds and provide much of the energy the seedlings need to get above ground. The second set of leaves you see will be the true leaves.

Homebodies at Heart

Most vegetable plants like the travelin' life just fine. They'll sail through their early days in a group flat, move right along to bigger pots of their own, then settle into the garden without a care in the world.

But a few veggies want to sink their first little roots into a good home and settle in for the long haul. If your growing season is too short for these stay-at-homes to start life in your garden, give them their own pots right from the get-go. That way, you won't disturb their roots when you move them outdoors to the wide-open spaces. Use pots that are 2 to 2½ inches wide, and sow several seeds in each pot. When the youngsters have two sets of true leaves, snip out all but the strongest seedling.

These are the not-so-rugged individualists, who can't stand to be moved:

Beans	Dill	Peas
Carrots	Melons	Radishes
Corn	Okra	Rutabagas
Cucumbers	Parsley	Squash
	Parsnips	

A Single Room to Go, Please

A Word to the Wise from Grandma Putt

Besides starting some of her seeds in eggshells (see page 44), Grandma Putt used to make what she called "travelin' pots" for seeds that don't like to have their roots tampered with. She had two favorite kinds.

NEWSPAPER POTS

Nowadays, catalogs and garden centers sell special molds to make newspaper pots. They're mighty handy things to have, but they're not absolutely necessary. All you really need is some newspaper and a tin can (a soft drink can is just the right size).

Cut a strip of newspaper about 12 inches long and 6 inches wide. Wrap the paper around the can lengthwise, with about 4 inches covering the side of the can and 2 inches hanging over the bottom. Fold that extra piece onto the bottom of the can, press it tight with your fingers, and bingo! Take away the can, and you've got yourself a pot. Make as many as you need, fill them with seed-starting mix, and put them into flats with holes in the bottom for drainage. Be sure to pack 'em in tight so they don't unravel.

SOD-BUSTER POTS

I use this kind for big seeds like melons and cucumbers. First dig up a piece of turf that's about 3 inches deep, and cut it into 2-inch-square chunks. (Just make sure the grass hasn't been treated with an herbicide — that'll do your seeds in almost before they're in the soil.) Turn the sod pieces upside down, set them into a flat that has drainage holes in the bottom, and poke two or three seeds into each piece.

Seeds in the Half Shell

Grandma Putt used to start her seeds in eggshells, and I still do. In fact, I save my shells and cartons all year long, so that I have plenty come spring. Here's how to do it:

• When you break an egg, carefully remove only the top third or so. I use a special egg-cutting tool that's like a pair of scissors, with a circular opening where the pointy blades should be. Put the opening over the top of the egg, squeeze the handles, and presto! A sharp blade slices right through the shell.

• Rinse the shell carefully and set it into an empty egg carton. Set the carton aside until next time.

• Come planting time, poke a hole in the bottom of each shell.

• Set the shells back into the carton, fill them with seed starting mix, and plant your seeds.

• When it's time to transplant the seedlings, plant the whole shebang. Crack each shell gently as you set it into its hole, so that the roots won't have to struggle to get out.

Don't Rush the Season

I hear a lot of folks say that no matter how well they nurse along their seedlings, those little guys just never grow up right in the garden. More often than not, the problem is that these folks were just a little too quick with the seed packet.

I get as eager as anybody else to see spring come charging round the bend, but I'm careful not to start my indoor seeds too soon. I know that if I do, my seedlings will get tall, weak, and spindly before transplanting time rolls around. And that means they'll never perform their best when they get to the great outdoors — and they might not even survive.

To make sure your seedlings are just the right age at transplant time, sow your seeds according to this schedule:

Jerry Baker Says

"Picking up a seedling by its stem can cause permanent damage. Always handle a young plant by its leaves or rootball."

VEGETABLE	WEEKS BEFORE TRANSPLANTING	VEGETABLE	WEEKS BEFORE TRANSPLANTING
Broccoli	4–5	Lettuce	3–4
Brussels sprouts	4–5	Melons	3–4
Cauliflower	4	Peppers	7–8
Celery	10	Pumpkins	3
Cucumbers	3–4	Squash	3
Eggplant	6–7	Tomatoes	4–5

Those Unmistakable Signs of the Vernal Equinox

Or, as Grandma Putt would say, "Let's head for the garden, Junie. Spring has sprung." As much fun as it was to start seeds indoors, Grandma Putt and I both knew we were just getting ready for the real thing: the day we'd get our rakes and trowels off of the tool rack and set to it. There's still nothing I look forward to more than tucking all my seeds and seedlings into good, healthy spring soil.

Sowing Time — or Not?

Nowadays, most folks decide when to sow seeds by looking at the calendar and watching the weather forecasts on TV. Grandma Putt had other methods for figuring out when to put her vegetable seeds into the ground.

Plant prognostication. One way Grandma Putt knew when to plant was by looking at what the flowers and trees in our yard were doing. Here's how she figured it:

PLANT	WHEN
Corn	Dogwood trees are in full bloom
Cole crops (like cabbage, broccoli, and cauliflower)	Dogwoods have dropped their petals
Swiss chard, spinach, beets, and onions	Daffodils bloom
Peas	Maple trees flower
Potatoes	The leaves of white oaks are the size of a cat's ear
Bush beans, pole beans, and cucumbers	The petals are dropping from apple blossoms

Moon Sense

Grandma Putt was a great believer in planting according to what phase the moon was in. When I asked her about it one night, she gazed up at the sky and said, "Stands to reason, Junie. Just look what the moon does to the water in the ocean. Why, land sakes, most of what's in vegetables is water. Why shouldn't it make a difference in how they grow?"

It made sense to me. After all, 95 percent of a tomato is water, and a common spud is 80 percent good old H_2O. (Of course, Grandma Putt also made sure that her soil was in tip-top shape and weather conditions were right.)

Here's how to do the moontime two-step:

• Plant all vegetables that produce their fruits above ground during the waxing moon (that's the period from new moon to full moon).

• Plant all bulb and root vegetables by the waning moon (from full moon to new moon).

String Along with Me

Tiny seeds, like those of lettuce and carrots, can be real corkers to sow. Either they bunch together and end up on the ground in a big glob, or a gust of wind comes up and — poof! — they're gone.

But Grandma Putt had a nifty trick for putting them in their place. She'd take her seed packets out to the garden along with a shallow dish, a bucket of water, and some string. First she'd pour the seeds into the dish (only one kind at a time, of course). Then she'd dip a piece of string in water and press it into the seeds. Finally, she'd lay the string on the ground and cover it with soil. The seeds stayed where she wanted them, and she used up all those pieces of string that she could never bring herself to throw away.

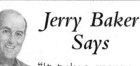
Tape It Up, Kids

If you have kids or grandkids who like to help you garden, but the seeds they plant seem to wind up everywhere but in the holes where they belong, here's a great solution: seed tapes. These are seeds on long strips of laminated paper coated with water-soluble material, and they're already spaced the right distance apart. All you — or the youngsters — need to do is prepare the soil, place the seed tape on top, cover it lightly with soil, firm it down with your hand, and water. The seeds sprout, and the paper dissolves from the moisture in the soil. Your future gardeners get a kick out of "planting," and you'll know that the seeds have been sown right where you want them, not scattered across the lawn!

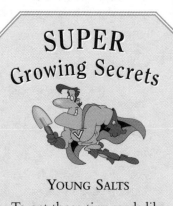

SUPER Growing Secrets

YOUNG SALTS

To get those tiny seeds like carrots and lettuce evenly spaced in their beds, put them into an old salt shaker. Then just sprinkle them over the soil.

Coffee, Comin' Right Up

Tiny seeds can be the dickens to plant evenly. To keep them from clumping up, mix them with dried coffee grounds before you sow them. They'll be as easy to handle as the biggest of the big guys!

Four Steps to Vegetable Power

Here's all you need to know about feeding your vegetable garden all season long. If you follow this routine, your garden will perform like a champ and bless you with a tremendous harvest in the fall.

Step 1. Two weeks before you start planting, get your garden ready for the big season. First, apply some of my Vegetable Power Powder to your garden, and work it into the soil.

Step 2. Then overspray the area with my Spring Soil Energizer Tonic.

Step 3. Before you plant your seeds, soak them overnight in my Seed Starter Tonic (see page 355). It'll help those little guys burst out of their shells like racehorses at the starting gate.

Step 4. Ten days after planting, it's time to put your garden on its regular training diet. That morning, and every 3 weeks for the rest of the growing season, feed your vegetable plants with my All-Season Green-Up Tonic.

VEGETABLE POWER POWDER

25 lbs. of organic garden food
 5 lbs. of gypsum
 2 lbs. of diatomaceous earth
 1 lb. of sugar

Mix all of these ingredients together, and put them into a handheld broadcast spreader. Set the spreader on medium and apply the mixture over the top of your garden. Follow up by immediately overspraying the area with my Spring Soil Energizer Tonic.

SPRING SOIL ENERGIZER TONIC

1 can of beer
1 cup of liquid dish soap
1 cup of antiseptic mouthwash
1 cup of regular cola (not diet)
1 tsp. of instant tea granules

Mix these ingredients in a bucket or other container, fill a 20 gallon hose-end sprayer, and apply to the soil to the point of run-off. Then let the area sit for 2 weeks before you start planting.

ALL-SEASON GREEN-UP TONIC

1 can of beer
1 cup of ammonia
½ cup of liquid dish soap
½ cup of liquid lawn food
½ cup of molasses or clear corn syrup

Mix all of these ingredients in a bucket or other container, fill your 20 gallon hose-end sprayer and overspray your garden with this Tonic 10 days after planting and every 3 weeks for the rest of the growing season.

It's Not Magic

Folks ask me how the contents of their medicine chest and kitchen cabinets can help vegetables grow big and strong. Well, it's not magic, and it's not snake oil. It's the chemical components of the products that do the trick. Here's a brief rundown on how they work. (For the full scoop, see page 347.)

• **Ammonia** is a great source of nitrogen that helps encourage leafy plant growth.

• **Antiseptic mouthwash** does for your garden just what it does in your mouth — kills germs.

• **Beer** releases nutrients that are locked in the soil and sends them to your plants' roots.

• **Regular (not diet) cola** feeds the good bacteria that condition your soil and keep your veggie plants healthy and thriving.

• **Epsom salts** stimulate your plants' root structure.

• **Sugar/molasses/corn syrup** do what cola does: feed the good soil bacteria.

• **Liquid dish soap** helps soften soil, removes dirt and pollution from plants, and helps them green up more easily.

• **Tea** contains tannic acid, which helps plants digest their food faster.

• **Tobacco Tea** (see page 358) poisons bugs and treats some plant diseases.

SUPER Growing Secrets

TAKE UP A COLLECTION

After you've set your transplants into the ground, use a finger to draw a ring in the soil around each one. When you water, or it rains, the water that collects in this mini basin will go straight to the plants' roots.

Egging Them On

Here's a handful of my favorite, not-so-common uses for eggshells in your garden:

♂ **Growing great peppers and tomatoes.** Soak all of your crushed eggshells in water for 24 hours, and then give your plants a drink.

♂ **Sweetening sour or acidic soil.** Don't add lime to raise the pH level. Add crushed, dried eggshells instead.

♂ **Making nutritious compost.** Add the dried shells to your compost pile for a good dose of calcium.

♂ **Supercharging soil for container veggies.** Dry eggshells in the microwave or oven, crush them, and add the powder to your potting soil.

Graduation Day

Along about the time that Grandma Putt and I started putting our seeds into the ground, we'd start moving our indoor seedlings out to the garden. We didn't plant them all at once, of course. Different kinds of vegetables are ready to graduate from the seedling nursery to the garden at different times. (You can find all of those special timetables in Chapter 7.)

And we didn't just take those little plants from their nice, sheltered spots and sink them into the cold soil, either. Instead, we spent a week or so getting them used to the idea of living in the great outdoors. Grandma Putt called this process hardening off. She said it always reminded her of rehearsing for high school graduation.

Toughen up, kids. When a seedling has spent its whole life basking in grow light, enjoying gentle breezes from a window, and bathing in soft sprays from a mist sprayer, it can be a real shock to crash head-on into honest-to-gosh weather. If you're not careful, steady rain, strong sunlight, cold soil, and heavy winds can wipe out your whole graduating class in no time flat.

The good news is that it's a cinch to get those little guys toughened up and ready to take anything Mother Nature cares to dish out (well, almost anything). Here's what you should do:

A week before transplanting time, stop feeding and cut back on watering.

Set your seedlings outside in a sheltered, partially shady spot for part of each day. I like to put my young plants under a big old maple tree in my yard, but a covered porch works fine, too.

Begin with a couple of hours in the afternoon and gradually increase the time. But if a strong wind comes up, or a heavy rain starts falling, rush those little guys back inside.

It's All in the Timing!

Grandma Putt knew *exactly* when to transplant the warm-weather crops like tomatoes, peppers, and eggplant that we'd started indoors. We always did it when the peonies and black locust trees flowered.

It's a Frame-Up

Hardening off seedlings is even easier when you have a cold frame. This handy gadget is nothing more than a box with a glass or plastic lid that opens up. You just set the flats inside, keep the lid open a little longer each day, and close it at night. If the weather is really sunny, rig up a little shade over the box for the first couple of days. I like to use an old piece of lattice propped on top of two sawhorses. (Garden centers and catalogs sell inexpensive cold frames, but Grandma Putt and I made our own. I'll tell you how in Chapter 4, page 87.)

Jerry Baker Says

"If you have a lot of seedlings, toting all those flats back and forth twice a day can be mighty time-consuming. I make the daily commute less of a grind by setting my flats on a couple of old coaster wagons at the start of hardening-off week. Then I just roll out the wagons, park them under a tree, and roll them back in again when it's time for the plants to call it a day."

SEEDLING TRANSPLANT RECOVERY TONIC

Give your transplanted seedlings a break on moving day by serving them a sip of this Tonic. It will help them recover more quickly from the shock of transplanting and make them feel right at home.

1 tbsp. of fish fertilizer
1 tbsp. of ammonia
1 tbsp. of Murphy's Oil Soap
1 tsp. of instant tea granules

Mix all of the ingredients in 1 quart of warm water. Pour into a handheld mist-sprayer bottle, and mist the seedlings several times a day until they're back on their feet.

Your veggie plants are in the garden and rarin' to grow. So let's move on and find out how to give them a big helping of TLC in the great outdoors!

CHAPTER 4

Weedin', Feedin', and Waterin'

To Grandma Putt, a garden wasn't just a bunch of plants. She said she thought of a garden as "a living, breathing critter." She always told me, "Junie, if you treat your garden kindly, give it the right kind of nourishment, and protect it from harm, it'll grow up big and strong. Then it'll repay you the best way it knows how."

Be Good to Your Garden . . .

And it'll be good to you. Grandma Putt taught me that the time to start being good to your garden is long before you ever sink a single seed into the ground. In fact, to give your plants the very best home possible — and to get the biggest harvest they can offer up — your TLC should start the year before you plant your garden.

Out with the Riffraff

Some folks are born lucky: They move into a house with a nice, tidy plot out back, all cleared and rarin' to grow. But more often than not, before you can even start beefing up the soil in your new garden, you've got to get rid of some unwelcome settlers: the grass or weeds that think that your place is their own private territory.

Jerry Baker Says

"The very first thing I learned about gardening was that a lawn has magical powers: All you have to do is start digging it up, and it gets bigger, right before your eyes. Back when I set out to dig my first garden, it looked to me like the whole thing could fit in the back of a pickup truck. But by the time I'd spaded up just a few pieces of turf, I'd have sworn that ol' plot stretched clear into the next county!"

It's Newsworthy

Here's the easiest way to get rid of a lawn that's standing in the way of a vegetable garden. It takes about 6 months, but it's worth the wait!

1. In late summer, the year before you plant your garden, stake out beds.

2. Lay a 1-inch layer of newspaper on top of each bed and weight down the papers with rocks. Give the papers a good soaking and keep them moist through the summer.

3. In the fall, remove the rocks and spread 6 to 8 inches of leaves on top of the papers.

4. On top of the leaves, put a foot or so of good soil. I like to use a nice, sandy loam that I buy at the garden center. (And I have them deliver it.) If you've got access to a good supply of compost, that works well, too.

5. Sit back and relax while worms and other little organisms spend the winter hard at work, breaking down all those layers of stuff. Come spring, that grass will be history, and you'll have a raised bed full of good, rich soil.

Weed It and Reap

Weeds can be a whole lot harder to get rid of than plain old lawn grass. If a nice, healthy crop of dock and dandelions has settled in where you want your corn and tomatoes to grow up, it often pays to serve the eviction notice in early spring, a whole calendar year ahead of planting time.

Here are three methods I use to get rid of really stubborn weeds and make my soil richer in the process. It means giving up a whole growing season, but I figure that's a small price to pay for a weed-free place for my veggies to put down their roots.

The big straw hat. Cover the weeds with cardboard or at least two layers of newspapers. On top of that, pile about a foot of straw. Wet it down once in a while to keep it from blowing away. But otherwise, give it the cold shoulder until next spring rolls around.

The black plastic sheet. Spread a piece of black plastic over the weedlot and weight it down with rocks. The sun will cook those weeds to a crisp. In the fall, remove the plastic and replace it with an 8- to 12-inch layer of leaves or straw.

The pre-crop (a.k.a. cover) crop. Plant a thick-growing plant such as rye or clover right in among the weeds. (Buckwheat is my favorite weed-killer crop.) As soon as it flowers, dig it into the soil, or mow it down and throw the clippings onto the compost pile. Then repeat the whole process, from planting to digging or mowing. If there's time left in your growing season, do it a third time. By the time the first killing frost knocks down everything, those weeds will be long gone, and your soil will be richer to boot!

A Word to the Wise from Grandma Putt

The Eyeball Test

Grandma Putt knew that not all weeds are villains. In fact, many wild plants — including some pesky weeds — offer dandy clues to what kind of soil you've got. These useful wonders are called "indicator plants." When you see a lot of them thriving in one place, it's a good indication of soil conditions beneath the surface. Here are some of Grandma Putt's favorites:

SOIL TYPE	PLANTS THAT LIKE IT
High-acid	Mosses, sorrel
Alkaline	Goosefoot, poison ivy
Good drainage	Chicory, dandelion
Poor drainage	Joe-pye weed, mosses

From Rocks to Riches

There's almost nothing more frustrating than getting all fired up to grow your own fresh veggies, and then finding out that your soil is worthless. But with a little patience and a few tricks up your sleeve, you can start with a plot that's practically nothing but rocks and rubble, and turn it into the best danged garden you've ever seen!

SUPER Growing Secrets

IT'S COARSE, OF COURSE

If you're trying to bring *clay* soil up to snuff, feed it organic matter that's on the chunky side, like straw, pine needles, wood chips, or mature plant stalks. These materials take longer to break down than fine-textured stuff like grass clippings or leaves, and during that waiting time, they'll open up the soil so that water, nutrients, and worms all can navigate better.

No Drain, No Gain!

I know it seems almost too good to be true, but there is an honest-to-gosh wonder drug that's guaranteed to make soil drain well, retain just the right amount of water, and serve up wholesome, well-balanced meals to your vegetable plants. What is it? *Organic matter.* All you need to do to improve drainage, soil structure, and fertility is dig in plenty of Mother Nature's bounty, like leaves, grass clippings, straw, or wood chips.

Where, Oh Where Has the Nitrogen Gone?

Fresh organic matter uses lots of nitrogen during the breakdown process. When you add large amounts of fresh leaves, straw, or clippings to your garden all at once, it takes a month or so for the imbalance to right itself. But you can correct the temporary nitrogen shortage quickly by adding any one of this trio to each bushel of material you add to the soil.

  1 pound of nitrate of soda
  ½ pound of ammonium nitrate
  ¾ pound of ammonium sulfate

Soil: I Really Dig It

The very best time to dig up a new garden site is in the fall, so that all of the added organic matter has time to break down before next spring. And, unfortunately, the best way to do it is still the good old-fashioned way: by hand. The job will go a whole lot easier, though, if you do a little at a time. I like to spread the work over a week or two. Here's my method:

1. Outline the edge of your garden with a spade. Shove it all the way down each time, so that the top of the spade is even with the ground; this will give you a clear mark to go by.

2. Make parallel cuts, 6 or 8 inches apart, across the bed. When you're done, your plot will look like a piece of lined notebook paper.

3. Now just move across a cut, turning over small chunks of soil, one at a time. Keep going until you're tired, then stop for the day.

4. When you've dug up the whole plot, chop the soil chunks and spread organic matter over the whole area.

5. Rest for a day or two. Then mix the soil and amendments together, top it off with my Spring Soil Energizer Tonic (see page 357), and curl up with a good book until spring rolls around.

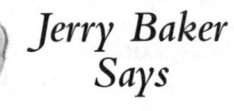

Jerry Baker Says

"It's easy to mark off straight-edged beds with stakes and string, but when I'm laying out fancy-shaped beds like circles and crescents, I 'draw' the outlines on the ground with lime or all-purpose flour. If I don't get it right the first time, I just brush the powdery stuff away and try again."

Fork It Over

In the main part of a garden, it's a cinch to keep the soil good and loose. I just go all over the plot with a garden fork. I stick it as deep into the soil as it will go, put my foot on top, and rock back and forth until I feel the soil loosen. Then I pull back the fork, and let the tines lever and loosen the soil. After I pull the fork from the soil, I move back 8 inches or so, and shove it in again. This is a good time to add lots of organic matter. Before I know it, I've got a whole garden full of soil that's as fluffy as a jarful of cotton balls.

Deep Thoughts

I prepare the spots where perennial crops like rhubarb and asparagus bed down using a method called double-digging. Frankly, it's a lot of work; but remember: You only have to do it once. Here's the method I use:

1. Dig a trench one shovel length deep (about 8 or 9 inches) across the bed, and pile the soil along the outside edge.

2. Loosen the soil at the bottom of the trench for another 8 or 9 inches.

3. Add organic matter, like leaves, straw, or compost.

4. Make a second trench that is parallel to the first.

5. Use the topsoil from that trench to fill the first one. Then work more organic matter into the soil with a garden fork.

6. Repeat the whole process until you've double-dug the whole bed. Then fill in the last trench with the topsoil you took from the first one.

7. Plant your rhubarb or asparagus, and watch it take off.

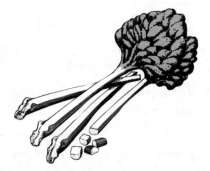

When Does Spring Spring?

Grandma Putt used to say, "All kids love to play in the dirt. The ones who never stop loving it grow up to be gardeners." That's me, all right. When I was a boy, I couldn't wait to get out there in the garden and start turning over all that good, rich soil, and then planting my seeds. Why, if she'd have let me, I'd have gone out there and dug right through the snow.

But Grandma Putt knew that working the soil too early can damage it by making it cake — and destroy all of that hard work we did in the fall. Her way to make sure the time was right for springtime tilling was to dig up a spadeful of soil and check its texture. If it crumbled easily and wasn't soggy, it was time to grab our shovels and forks and go to it.

Loosen Up

There are three reasons I like to mix deep-down soil with topsoil:

1. Micronutrients. Subsoil (the soil below the top 8 inches or so) is chock-full of minerals that plants need in small quantities but can't always get from the topsoil. And they can't get it from the subsoil, either, unless you loosen it, then mix it up.

2. Moisture. If you keep the subsoil fluffed up, it can hold more moisture, which means you don't have to water as much. That'll be really important if a drought hits your territory!

3. Worms. When you loosen the subsoil, you make it easy for roots and worms to get around in. Then they can open it up even more.

Rise Up and Be Planted

The best way I know to guarantee good drainage is to plant your garden in raised beds. There are two kinds: one with walls to contain the soil, and one without. Whichever type you use, there are lots of reasons besides drainage to elevate your plants. Here are some of the best.

What Raising 'em Up Means

Earlier planting. Soil in raised beds warms up earlier in the spring, because more of it is exposed to sunlight. That means you can get those heat lovers off and running sooner.

No washout. A heavy rain can flood a normal garden row and send newly planted seeds floating off. In a raised bed, because the soil is so light and well drained, seeds stay where you put them.

Longer, straighter roots. In a raised bed, root crops like carrots, beets, and turnips have a lot more nice, fluffy soil to sink down into, so they grow straighter and longer.

Less stooping and bending. Because raised beds sit above the ground, you won't have to reach so far to pull weeds and harvest crops.

Traffic control. Even the gardener in charge steps on a planted row now and then. As for the kids and the dog . . . hmmm . . . well, you can't blame them for their springtime exuberance, but they can compact the soil, and that's bad for a plant's roots. With raised beds on the scene, everybody — even the dog — sticks to the pathways.

Freestanding Beds

I use this kind when I'm tilling a big plot and want to lift up the soil just in the planting area. Get out your ruler, because here we go:

1. Mark the edges of each bed with stakes and string. The size and shape are up to you. Just make sure they're narrow enough so you can reach into the center without stepping on the soil.

2. Work your soil down to a depth of 6 to 8 inches. Get it good and loose, then work in plenty of organic matter.

3. Pull up the soil from the walkways and pile it onto the beds. I like to get a good 4 to 6 inches on each one.

4. Spread compost across the bed, and till it into the top few inches.

5. Smooth out the surface with the back of a rake, and bingo! You're good as gold and ready to plant.

Keep Your Cool

The soil in raised beds warms up faster and stays warm longer than it does in traditional garden rows. That's great if you live in the cool-as-a-cucumber North. But in places with sweltering summers, a veggie's roots will fry if you leave too much soil exposed to the sun. So, if you live in hot climates, don't build freestanding beds more than 4 inches above the ground.

Enclosed Beds Are Best

I use this kind of bed as individual gardens in my lawn. You can also build them on a hard surface like a patio or parking area. They have some big advantages over freestanding beds:

• They retain moisture better.

• Your soil is guaranteed not to slide away.

• The walls hold pesky weeds at bay.

• It's easy to give each plant exactly the kind of soil it likes.

• You can use all of your cultivated space, because there are no sloping sides as there are on in-ground beds.

• You can make them as high as you want them, which means you can garden comfortably even if you use a wheelchair or have trouble bending. (If you live in a hot climate, use light-colored material that reflects the sun's rays, like stone or white-painted wood.)

• Because the walls can be made of just about any material that will hold soil, these beds can make a good-looking addition to your landscape.

The Building Process

An enclosed raised bed is just a big, bottomless box filled with soil. I've made them out of wooden beams, salvaged lumber, rocks, bricks, cement blocks, even recycled metal from the junkyard. Here's how I do it:

Step 1. Mark off the site.

Step 2. If there's soil under your bed site, loosen it down to a depth of 8 inches or so, and add about an inch of compost or aged manure.

Step 3. Dig a trench around the edges, several inches deep and as wide as your boards, bricks, or blocks. The walls will be more stable if they're sunk into the ground.

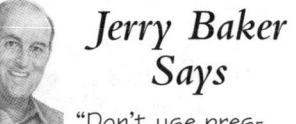

Jerry Baker Says

"Don't use pressure-treated lumber for your raised beds. It contains toxic chemicals that can leach into the soil."

Step 4. Build your box to whatever height you want.

Step 5. Fill the box with a half-and-half mix of soil and compost. Leave 2 or 3 inches between the soil and the top of the frame.

Step 6. Let the soil mix sit for 2 weeks, then plant to your heart's content.

A Little Help from Your Friends

The four-legged kind, that is. For just about as long as folks have been growing food crops, they've been using animal manure to aid in the process. It still makes mighty fine plant chow, and forking a load of it into your soil is a great way to add organic matter to it.

Manure Pointers

Consider the source. Use only manure that comes from vegetarian critters. Other kinds are so hot, they'll burn plants' roots.

Let it age. Before you add any kind of manure, cure it (see page 60), or add it to the compost pile. The heat generated will kill any lurking seeds.

Be careful what you serve it to. Manure is great for nitrogen lovers like corn, tomatoes, and leaf crops, but not for root veggies like potatoes and carrots.

Come and Get It

You don't have to keep a barnful of livestock to get your hands on good manure. I've found that plenty of places have mountains of it (all mixed in with good, nutritious bedding straw), free for the taking.

Whenever I need a supply, I let my fingers do the walking, contacting the usual suspects and asking if I can come and get some. Here are some of my favorite sources:

- **Riding stables**
- **Dairy farms**
- **Livestock auction lots**
- **Racetracks**
- **Rodeos**
- **Circuses**
- **Fairgrounds**

Taking the Cure

Once you get your manure home — or once that young fella you've hired has delivered it in his pickup truck — you need to cure it. Here's how I make mine cool, weed-free, and — believe it or not — all but odor-free! I like to start a new batch every 2 or 3 months, so my plants always have a full pantry.

1. Spread a big tarpaulin on the ground and dump the manure on top.

2. Fold up the edges of the tarp around the pile of manure.

3. Lay another tarp across the top, and add a few rocks, so it stays put.

4. Cut three or four small slits in the tarp, so the heat can get out.

5. Let it sit for 6 months or so and — presto! — you've got the best lunch a garden could ask for.

Manure of Another Color

Green, that is. *Green manure* is another name for a "cover crop," one of the greatest inventions known to plantkind. I have at least one cover crop going in my garden all of the time. And I plant my whole garden with green manure for the winter. Here's why I've become such a fan:

- **A little goes a long way.** You can start off with 5 or 10 pounds of seed and about 6 weeks later, you've got 2 or 3 tons of organic matter to plow into your garden. You can't beat that for cheap fertilizer!

- **Cover crops liven up sandy soils.** Water and nutrients wash right through all of those sand particles. I've found that after I till in a couple of green-manure crops, though, all that good stuff stays put, and right up close to the surface, where my plants can get at it.

• **Cover crops open up clay soils.** All those chunky leaves and stems wedge in among the tiny clay particles and shove them apart. That means air, water, and roots have space to move around.

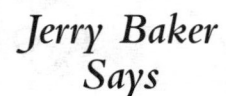

• **Planting a cover crop** is like taking your soil to an all-you-can-eat buffet. Worms and other tiny critters break down all that tasty organic stuff into chow for your next crop of veggies. What's more, some acids in green manure react with minerals in the soil to release extra nutrients. Talk about health food!

• **A cover crop** keeps your topsoil in the garden, not blowing away in the wind or floating off in a heavy rain. Whenever I've harvested a vegetable crop and don't have time to tend another, I plant green manure in that space. It takes no time at all to spread some seed and later on to till it into the soil. And I plant a cover crop on my whole vegetable garden after the harvest, so the soil stays covered through the winter.

• **Some green manure crops,** like peas and beans, give you free fertilizer and good eatin' for the price of one pack of seeds. Being legumes, they snatch nitrogen from the air and stash it in their leaves, stems, and roots. When you till the plants into the soil after you harvest their goodies, you put back all of that nitrogen and other important nutrients where other plants can use them.

• **Fast-growing cover crops** like buckwheat smother weeds like nobody's business. Buckwheat grows like Topsy, and its leaves are so close together that sunlight can't get through to nurture any weeds down below. Just plant two or three crops of it, and you can kiss your weed problems goodbye!

• **A green manure crop** acts like an insulating blanket. It keeps the ground cooler in summer, and in winter it keeps the soil warm near the surface, where worms put in their duty time. Without that cozy cover, they'd have to head down deep or they'd freeze.

Jerry Baker Says

"Some folks call cover crops 'catch crops,' because their roots dive down deep in the soil and snatch up moisture and nutrients that other plants can't reach. Then, when you plow the catch crops under, you put all that good stuff high up in the soil, where all your veggies can use it."

Top Coverage

There are dozens of great cover crops, but these four perform like real troopers in my garden. I keep sacks full of these seeds on hand, so that anytime there's a bare spot in my garden, I can fill it up in a snap.

CROP	AMOUNT NEEDED PER 1,000 SQ. FT.	BEST TIME TO PLANT	WHY I LIKE IT
Peas	10 lbs.	Early spring or early fall	I can plant them very early in the season and get a great cover crop, and great-tasting early peas, besides. They grow fast and keep weeds from sprouting. Plant in either spring or fall.
Beans	10 lbs.	Anytime after the last spring frost and up to 8 weeks before the first fall frost is due	They sprout fast in warm weather, so I can plant them after the early peas and get another "two-for-one" crop: one for eatin' and one for plowin' under. Beans make a dandy spot cover crop. I'm partial to green and yellow bush beans, but any kind will do the trick.
Buckwheat	2–3 lbs.	1–2 weeks before the last spring frost until 4–6 weeks before the first fall frost is due	It's inexpensive to buy, and you don't need much. It grows well anywhere, in all kinds of soil. It's fast-acting: In warm weather, it's ready to turn under about 6 weeks after planting. It has nice white flowers that attract pollinating insects to my garden. (Let 'em do their work for a few days before you till in the crop.) The stems are tender and hollow, so the plants are a snap to dig under, even with hand tools.
Annual ryegrass	2–3 lbs.	Midsummer through early fall	Like buckwheat, it grows well anywhere, in any kind of soil. Because it's an annual, it dies down when frost hits it. Then it just lies there like a woolly blanket. It keeps the topsoil cozy all winter long, so earthworms can stay on the job instead of diving down to deeper, warmer territory.

Black Gold: Compost

"Black gold" is what Grandma Putt used to call compost, and the longer I garden, the better I know just how on the mark she was. Compost does for plants what a nutritious, well-balanced diet does for kids: It makes them grow up strong, healthy, and ready to take on the world. Here is Grandma Putt's 12-step program for making gourmet compost.

Step 1. Find a spot that's not in prime viewing territory but is convenient to the kitchen. (That's so it'll be easy to step outside and toss your coffee grounds and fruit and veggie scraps.)

Step 2. Dig up the sod and turn it over. Then thoroughly soak the spot.

Step 3. Build a simple frame out of wood strips, and staple on hardware cloth or chicken wire. For the fastest results, make your pile 3 to 4 feet high, wide, and deep. Put hinges on one side so you can open the bin to get the compost out.

Step 4. Put a 10-inch layer of grass clippings on the bottom. Then start piling in your material at a ratio of 3 parts high-carbon to 1 part high-nitrogen. (See page 65 for a rundown of carbon browns and nitrogen greens.)

Step 5. On top of the grass clippings, stack about an inch of old newspapers and wet them down thoroughly.

Step 6. Add a 2-inch layer of manure (fresh or cured).

Step 7. Follow that layer with 4 inches or so of grass clippings, veggie scraps, or other plant waste.

Step 8. Add more newspaper, and wet it down again.

Step 9. Sprinkle on a good, thick layer of topsoil.

Step 10. Keep building your pile, alternating the layers of newspaper/manure/grass clippings/newspaper/topsoil until your pile is 3 to 4 feet high.

Step 11. Keep the pile moist but not soggy; cover it loosely with black plastic, so the rain won't wash it away.

Step 12. Turn the pile every 10 days to 2 weeks, so air can get at it, and spritz it every month or so with my Compost Feeder Tonic (see page 64).

When your black gold is dark, rich, and crumbly, scoop it out and work it into your garden soil.

COMPOST FEEDER TONIC

To boost your compost pile every now and again, spray it with Thatch Buster or sprinkle my Compost Activator/ Accelerator on top of it. Then, once a month, saturate it with this Tonic:

1 can of beer
1 cup of liquid dish soap
1 can of regular cola (not diet)

Mix these ingredients in your 20 gallon hose-end sprayer, and let 'er rip. It'll keep your compost cookin' right along.

SUPER
Growing Secrets

LEAVE THEM BE

There's nothing I know of that makes better garden food than leaf mold — and nothing could be easier to make. I cook up a big batch every winter. Here's how: Simply shred leaves with a lawn mower (smaller pieces will decompose faster), scoop the shreds into garbage bags, add water, close the bags, and go about your business. Come spring, you'll have a big supply of superchow!

Keep Your Cool

Or, as Grandma Putt used to say, "Different strokes for different folks." If balancing ingredients to keep your compost pile cooking at the right temperature is not your idea of fun, try cold composting instead. In this method, anaerobic bacteria break down the organic material, without the help of oxygen.

All you need are some plastic garbage bags, yard waste, and vegetable scraps from the kitchen. Be forewarned, though: When you open the bags, you'll be hit with an odor that will make you want to run for the next county. Fortunately, the . . . um . . . "rich" aroma soon disappears as the compost is exposed to oxygen. Here's my cold composting method:

• **Fill a large plastic garbage bag** with a mix of chopped leaves, grass clippings, and vegetable scraps. Add some Compost Activator/ Accelerator for every couple of shovelfuls of bulky, carbon-rich material (see The All-They-Can-Eat Buffet). When the bag is nearly full, sprinkle a couple of quarts of water over the contents, and mix thoroughly until all ingredients are moistened. Shake small or light bags; roll large or heavy ones.

• **Tie the bag shut, and leave it** in an out-of-the-way place where the temperature will stay above 45°F for a few months. For faster results, roll it every few days. That's all there is to it!

No More Tossing and Turning

If turning a binful of compost every week or so sounds like a lot of work, there's a good reason: It is. But I've found an easier way to get air into the center of my compost pile: I just stick a few ventilating stacks inside.

Before I start a new pile, I buy some perforated plastic pipe about 4 inches in diameter, and cut it into 5-foot lengths. (I use six pieces for every 16 square feet of surface area.) I lay one or two lengthwise on the pile. Then I just pile the material over them. When they're covered, I put down the next set, cover them, and so on. Air goes right through all those openings and into the center of the pile, and I don't have to lift a finger!

Mix and Match

Building a compost pile in layers is the standard, old-time way to do it, but it's not the only way. What really matters is that you get the right balance of high-carbon and high-nitrogen ingredients to make the pile heat up to about 160°F. That's the temperature all those microscopic critters need to quickly break the stuff down into good plant chow.

If you have too much carbon, you could wait years for your compost to cook. Too much nitrogen, and the odor will be so bad that your neighbors will show up on your doorstep, mad as hatters and wearing clothespins on their noses. Fortunately, it's easy to stay in everyone's good graces. When you add ingredients to your pile, just make sure you toss in 3 parts dry brown material (that's the carbon) for every 1 part green, succulent ingredients (that's the nitrogen).

The All-They-Can-Eat Buffet

To make a tasty compost buffet, you want three high-carbon ingredients (what I call "browns") for every one that's high in nitrogen (the "greens").

THE BROWNS

Hay	Paper
Horse manure	Sawdust
with bedding	Straw
Oak leaves	

THE GREENS

Coffee grounds	Horse and cow
Cover crops	manure (fresh)
Eggshells	Legume plants
Feathers	Pig and poultry
Fruit and vegetable	manure
scraps	Seaweed
Grass clippings	Tea bags
Hair (pet or human)	Young weeds

Undercover Compost

There's no getting around it, a compost pile isn't the best-looking part of anybody's landscape. If you don't care to look at your black gold in the making — or if you're concerned about what the neighbors will think — get yourself a compost bin, or make your own from a plastic trash can. Just cut off the bottom and drill holes in the sides and lid, so air can get in and circulate.

No, Thanks, That's Not on My Diet

Anything that comes from plants or animals will break down over time, but that doesn't necessarily mean you want it on your compost pile. Turn thumbs down on these menu items:

• **Kitchen scraps with fats, oils, bones, or meat in them.** They'll attract rats and other vermin, and will smell up your pile in the process.

• **Colored paper, including the colored parts of newspapers and magazines.** If you know that they've been printed with soy-based inks, it's okay. Otherwise, you could be adding harmful chemicals to your compost.

• **Diseased plants.** They'll pass germs to your compost — and to your garden.

• **Poisonous plants.** Castor beans and oleander are two of them.

• **Plants that have been sprayed with pesticides or herbicides.** Some chemicals will kill the worms and microscopic critters that make your compost.

• **Anything with plastic in it.** It will never break down.

• **Weeds that have gone to seed or that spread by creeping roots and stems.** You'll just have to dig them out of your garden all over again!

• **Charcoal from the barbecue grill.** It's treated with toxic chemicals. (Don't confuse this kind with horticultural charcoal, which is perfectly safe.)

• **Anything that comes from black walnut, red cedar, or eucalyptus trees.** They all produce chemicals that will harm, or even kill, your vegetable plants.

• **Manure from cats, dogs, humans, and other meat eaters.** It can transmit disease to your plants, or even to you.

Jerry Baker Says

"Before you put anything on your compost pile, chop it up as fine as you can. The smaller the pieces, the faster it will break down."

Troubleshooting Your Compost

If your compost isn't cookin' along the way it should, don't give up hope. There's a very good chance you'll find the problem — and its solution — in my handy-dandy troubleshooting chart.

PROBLEM	WHAT TO DO
Critters like raccoons are paying nightly visits.	Grind up fruits and veggies in a blender before you add them to the pile, and steer clear of meats, fats, and oils. You can also place fruits and veggies in the center of the pile — this makes them less attractive to critters.
Seedlings are coming up on top.	Pull them up. If they're volunteer veggies or flowers, replant them in the garden. If they're weeds, toss 'em into the trash can. Add more greens so the temperature gets high enough to kill seeds. And don't add any more plants that have already set seed.
Some things in the pile are not breaking down properly.	Take them out, chop them up, and add them to the next pile.
The whole pile is cold.	Add more greens, like grass clippings or fresh manure. Then turn the pile.
It smells bad, and it's wet.	Add lots of browns, like straw, sawdust, and leaves, and stir the pile more often.
It's dry in the center, and nothing seems to be happening.	Give the pile a good turning, wet it down, douse it with my Compost Feeder Tonic (see page 64) and cover it with black plastic, so the moisture stays in, where it belongs.
It's warming up but doesn't get hot, and it's damp in the middle.	Start over again, and make the pile bigger this time. Remember: To get good and hot, it needs to be at least 3 feet high, 3 feet wide, and 3 feet long.

Rescue Mission

My favorite time to go for a walk around the neighborhood is just after it's stopped raining on a warm summer evening. That's when earthworms like to wander around, too, and they often wind up squashed on the sidewalk. I always take along a small plastic bag with a handful of soil in it. Then, when I come upon a wayward worm, I stick him into the bag, take him home, and put him to work in my compost pile.

Gimme Some of That
Old-Time Nutrition

Back in Grandma Putt's day, folks didn't have all of the fancy chemical fertilizers we have now. They had to use whatever was on hand that suited the purpose. I still reach for this old-fashioned, stick-to-your-roots food.

 Eggshells. Crush 'em, let 'em soak in water for 24 hours, then use the water for your plants. All that calcium is especially good for peppers and tomatoes.

Fish. Any fish parts will make your plants take off like a buffalo stampede. Just make sure you bury the stuff deep in the garden. Tossed onto the compost pile or dug in too close to the soil surface, it'll create quite an odor and attract unwanted wildlife.

Hair. Whether it comes from a human or any other kind of animal, hair is good, healthy plant chow, full of iron, manganese, and sulfur. Work it into the soil or toss it onto the compost pile, and watch your plants eat it up.

Sawdust. Mixed into a compost pile, it's a great source of carbon. But don't use sawdust that came from pressure-treated lumber. Its toxic chemicals will leach into your garden.

Jerry Baker Says

"Vegetable plants really work up an appetite churning out all that good food for us, and even the most well-balanced diet needs a little kick now and then. So every 3 weeks during the growing season, feed your garden with my All-Season Green-Up Tonic (see page 349)."

Snack Time

Even vegetable plants appreciate a little variety in their diet. My All-Season Green-Up Tonic is great stuff (see page 349), but every so often, use one of these two tonics as a change of pace.

VEGGIE TONIC #1

1 can of beer
1 cup of ammonia
4 tbsp. of instant tea granules
2 tbsp. of baby shampoo

Mix these ingredients in your 20 gallon hose-end sprayer. Then spray everything in the garden to the point of run-off.

VEGGIE TONIC #2

½ cup of fish fertilizer
2 tbsp. of whiskey
2 tbsp. of Epsom salts
2 tbsp. of instant tea granules
1 tbsp. of baby shampoo

Mix these ingredients in your 20 gallon hose-end sprayer. Then spray everything to the point of run-off.

Food Group Fancies

To grow up strong and healthy, all plants need a diet that has each of the seven basic food groups in it. Usually, a well-balanced blend of organic matter will give them everything they need. But once in a while, a particular kind of plant or a particular spot in the garden gets a hankering for a specific kind of snack. When that happens, I choose from this smorgasbord:

FOOD GROUP	SOURCES	FOOD GROUP	SOURCES
Nitrogen	Alfalfa meal	Calcium	Aragonite
	Bird guano		Bonemeal
	Blood meal		Clam and oyster shells
	Coffee grounds		Eggshells
	Cottonseed meal		Gypsum
	Feathers		Limestone
	Fish emulsion		Rock phosphate
	Fish meal		
	Legume crops	Magnesium	Dolomitic limestone
	Manure (all kinds)		Epsom salts
	Soybean meal		
		Sulfur	Epsom salts
Phosphorus	Bonemeal		Ground sulfur
	Colloidal phosphate		Gypsum
	Fish emulsion		Manures (all)
	Poultry manure		
	Rock phosphate	Micronutrients	Alfalfa hay
	Seaweed		Compost
			Eggshells
Potassium	Bananas (both peels		Granite meal
	and fruit)		Grass clippings
	Cow manure		Kelp meal
	Granite meal		Leaves
	Greensand		Rock phosphate
	Kelp meal		Soybean meal
	Wood ashes		Wood ashes
			Worm castings

Jerry Baker Says

"Don't use any nitrogen-rich fertilizer (organic or otherwise) late in the growing season: It will stimulate leafy growth and make your plants more likely frost victims."

Don't Go for the Burn

Professional growers know that you should never put chemical fertilizers into the soil just before setting out seedlings. Why? Because if the fertilizer comes into contact with small plant roots, it will burn them — causing serious injury, or even death. But that doesn't mean you can't feed your seedlings. Just remember to first dilute and then dissolve the fertilizer in water so that the plant roots can absorb it safely.

Help! My Diet's out of Whack!

It's not always easy to know when your plants are getting enough, or too much, of the different nutrients they need. After all, they can't say "Please pass the potassium" or "No more nitrogen, thanks." Fortunately, though, there are clues. If your veggies are getting too little or too much of the Big Three nutrients, you'll usually see the telltale signs on old foliage near the base of the plant. Here's what to look for:

NUTRIENT	TOO LITTLE	TOO MUCH
Nitrogen	Stunted growth Small leaves or vegetables Pale green or yellow foliage	Too much leafy growth Foliage too dark Plant slow to mature Lush foliage with reduced flowering
Phosphorus	Red, purplish, or bronzed leaves Few blossoms or vegetables	Other essential nutrients get tied up, so plants exhibit signs of other deficiencies
Potassium	Reduced vigor Thin stems Small, misshapen vegetables with thin skins Curling, scorched-looking leaves with brown edges Plants become diseased easily	Poorly colored, coarse-looking vegetables

SUPER Growing Secrets

PLANTS' BEST FRIEND

Dry dog food contains many of the same nutrients found in organic fertilizers such as blood meal and bonemeal. For an added boost, work it into the soil at planting time or sprinkle it around growing plants.

Ask the Experts

A diet that's too low or too high in other nutrients, like iron, calcium, and magnesium, can cause problems, too, but they're trickier to diagnose. If your plants start showing signs that don't match anything in the chart on page 70, like yellow leaves with green veins, just give them a good dose of an all-purpose organic fertilizer that also contains trace minerals. If that doesn't perk them up, call your local Cooperative Extension Service and ask for help.

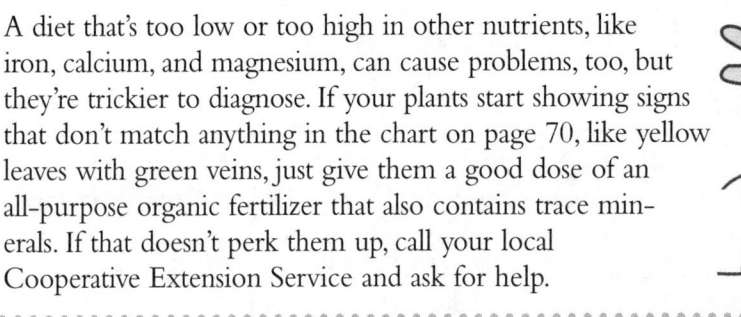

Help from the Hearth

When you're through roasting chestnuts this year, don't throw those fireplace ashes out! Here are some tips for using them in your vegetable garden for better results next year:

Tip #1. Control cucumber beetles by mixing ½ cup of wood ashes with ½ cup of hydrated lime in 2 gallons of warm water; spray this mix onto both upper and lower sides of the leaves.

Tip #2. Protect your plants from snail and slug damage by sprinkling a 2-inch-wide band of ashes around them. Replenish the supply whenever it rains.

Tip #3. Lower the pH of acidic soil by working in wood ashes at a rate of 1 pound per 25 square feet.

Tip #4. Energize your garden soil in spring by mixing 5 pounds *each* of gypsum, bonemeal, and ashes per 100 square feet of soil area.

Tip #5. Protect and feed rhubarb through the winter by mixing a shovelful of wood ashes with ground-up leaves and heaping them around the plants.

Tip #6. Keep your walkways slide-proof in winter by covering them with a mixture of 1 pound of ashes and 1 pound of gypsum. (Don't worry if you get some on the lawn — unlike salt or snow-melting chemicals, this mix is *good* for grass!)

Tip #7. Say "so long" to maggots, club root, and all sorts of nasties by sprinkling ashes around the base of trouble-prone plants. (See the individual plant entries in Chapter 7 for more about aid from ashes.)

Tip #8. Keep rascally rabbits at bay by lightly sifting wood ashes onto all of your plants.

Just Right!

If your soil can produce a great-looking crop of spinach, you know for sure that it has just the right balance of nutrients.

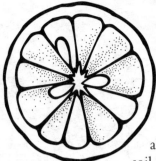

Make Mine Sour, Please (but Just a Tad)

Most vegetable plants grow best when the soil's pH measures between 6.0 and 6.8, which is just a hair on the acid side. (A measurement of 7.0 is neutral; above that is alkaline.) That's because in this range, organic matter in the soil breaks down most easily and the plants can get at the nutrients they need. Getting the right pH for your plants is a lot like taking them to a fast-food restaurant with healthy chow on the menu.

The Quick-Change Artists

The easiest way to change pH is to add either sulfur (to make alkaline soils more acid) or ground limestone (to make acid soils more alkaline). This chart shows how much of either one you'll need, depending on the type of soil you've got. One word of caution, though: Don't apply more than 1 pound of sulfur or 5 pounds of limestone per 100 square feet at any one time. If you need to add more than that, do it over two or more seasons, so the pH change is gradual.

Adjusting Soil pH

PH CHANGE			SANDY SOIL	LOAM	CLAY SOIL
FROM	TO	MATERIAL USED	(LBS. TO APPLY PER 100 SQUARE FEET)		
7.5	6.5	Sulfur★	1½	2	2½
7.0	6.5	Sulfur★	¼	½	¾
6.5	6.5	—	—	—	—
6.0	6.5	Limestone	3	4	6
5.5	6.5	Limestone	5	8	11
5.0	6.5	Limestone	7	11	15
4.5	6.5	Limestone	10	13	20
4.0	6.5	Limestone	12	16	23

★You can use iron sulfate or aluminum sulfate in place of sulfur, but you'll need about 2½ times more material to make an equivalent pH change.

Sweet or Sour?

When you need to change your soil's pH, sulfur and limestone are good fixes, but they don't last forever. Eventually, you'll have to crank up the old spreader all over again. You'll get longer-lasting results — and improve the content and structure of your soil besides — if you add the right kind of organic matter. Here are some of my favorite sweet and sour condiments.

To lower your soil's pH, add:
Aged sawdust
Coffee grounds
Cottonseed meal
Fresh manure
Oak leaves
Pine needles

To raise your soil's pH, add:
Bonemeal
Ground clamshells
Ground eggshells
Ground oyster shells
Wood ashes

Water Wisely and Water Well

It used to be that we thought dry weather was something only folks way out West had to worry about. Nowadays, though, it seems you hear about droughts and water shortages all over the country, almost every summer. That's why I try to get the most out of every drop of water I give my plants.

It's Thirsty Work Being a Plant!

Some vegetable plants get thirstier than others, but most of them need about an inch of water every week. That's about 62 gallons for every 100 square feet of garden — and that's a lot of H_2O! These days, most of us can't just sit back and wait for Mother Nature to open up the clouds and let the rain pour down. But you can make your chores easier, and your water bill lower, if you follow some basic guidelines.

H₂0 Guidelines

Water your plants only when they're thirsty. After a while, you'll learn to tell just by looking whether they're hankering to belly up to the bar. But I like to be on the safe side: I keep a rain gauge handy so I always know just how much H_2O is coming from the sky — then I supply the rest.

Cultivate before you water. Soil that's nice and loose lets the water filter right down to the plants' roots. If you don't at least scratch up the surface, a crust will form, and the water will just sit right there on top or run off to who knows where.

Water slowly and evenly. Get the moisture down at least 6 inches below the surface, to encourage deep roots that can snag water from different levels in the soil.

Water in the morning. That's when temperatures are lowest and humidity is usually at its highest. Evaporation is slow, letting the water seep into the soil, not disappear into the air. The morning is when your plants make the most efficient use of the water you give them.

Don't water in the late afternoon or evening. Moisture that stays on stems or leaves overnight encourages pests and diseases to pounce.

SUPER Growing Secrets

WHAT A CAN CAN DO!

Here's a trick for making sure water gets down to the roots of your plants: Cut both ends off big coffee and juice cans. Then dig a hole every few feet in the garden, put a can in each hole, and fill it up with gravel. When you water, fill those cans to the brim. That way, your veggies' roots can drink their fill.

Go Soak

A soaker hose does most of the things a permanent irrigation system does, for a lot less money. It's perfect if you plan to move in a couple of years, or if you're new to gardening and not sure how involved you want to get.

A soaker hose is a snap to use: Just snake it through the beds, so that it reaches the base of each plant, and leave it there. Then, when it's time to water, turn on the faucet and everybody drinks up. There's no more dragging a heavy hose back and forth. What's even more important from the plants' standpoint is that the water goes right into the soil. It doesn't get on the leaves and stems, thus inviting disease to set up housekeeping.

How Dry Am I?

When you want to find out whether it's watering time and you don't have a rain gauge handy, do this simple test: Pull back any mulch that's on the soil, and dig down 4 or 5 inches. Then scoop up a handful of soil and squeeze it. If the soil holds together, it's moist enough. If it crumbles in your hand, go for the hose: You need to water. (Very sandy soil never forms a ball. If it's gritty and sticks to your skin, it's moist enough. But if the grains run through your fingers, your plants need water.)

Jerry Baker Says

"Don't get carried away at watering time: Too much water will cause as much damage as too little water will. It will drown your plants' roots and wash away important nutrients."

Give It Some Guidance

Nothing can knock a plant to its knees faster than a battle with a garden hose. Avoid accidents by putting in hose guides at the corners and outward curves of your beds. I make these out of 2-foot lengths of either rebar or galvanized pipe that's about ½ inch in diameter. I sink the pipe into the ground, leaving about 8 inches sticking up. Then I slip a piece of bamboo or PVC pipe over each guide, so that the hose glides easier and doesn't get snagged on the pipe's sharp edges.

Three Ways to Cut Back

Here's a trio of ways to ease up on the water flow without cheating your plants out of a single drop of their drinking supply:

1. **Keep your soil well stocked with organic matter.** It's the best way to improve the soil's structure and increase its ability to hold water. One study found that increasing organic matter by just 5 percent will enable your soil to hold 4 times more water! Good soil structure also encourages large, healthy root systems, and that's a plant's best defense against drought.

2. **Mulch heavily.** You'll conserve water, keep down weeds, and discourage pests all at the same time. Talk about triple-threat maneuvers!

3. **Plant drought-tolerant varieties.** Garden centers and catalogs have more every year. In particular, many heirloom types tend to need much less water than do newer hybrids.

Water on Wheels

An old tire rim makes a great holder for your garden hose. Just mount the rim on the wall or a post right by the water spigot, paint it so it won't rust, and hang up your hose. You'll never have to fight with a snarled-up hose again.

The Efficiency Experts

When it came to figuring out what vegetables were pulling their weight waterwise, Grandma Putt had a rule of thumb: The more you eat of a plant, the more water thrifty it is. At the top of her list were beets, onions, turnips, lettuce, and other greens, because we ate the whole plant. Corn came at the very bottom of her efficiency list, because a single cornstalk will use 54 gallons of water during the growing season to produce just one or two ears of corn.

Great Garden Cover-Ups: Mulches

Laying down a good mulch is one of the best things you can do for your garden — and yourself. Why, the right mulch warms up your soil or keeps it cool, saves on your water bill, and fends off weeds and all kinds of pesky critters. It can even turn your garden into the neighborhood showplace!

Organic vs. Plastic

Plastic mulches can come in mighty handy. (You can't beat them for smothering weeds and warming up soil in the springtime.) But organic mulches have three things going for them that plastic will never have.

1. They break down over time, add nutrients and structure to your soil.

2. They're a darn sight nicer to look at than plastic.

3. No matter where you live, there's a terrific organic mulch that's free for the taking, either because it's just lying around somewhere or because somebody needs to get rid of it.

Free Mulch

Here are some organic, nutritious, and good-looking mulches that might be only a phone call away:

Chopped tobacco stalks
Cocoa hulls
Cottonseed hulls
Ground corncobs
Ground oyster or
    clamshells
Manure
Mushroom compost
Peanut hulls
Pine needles
Salt hay
Seaweed
Shredded bark
Shredded oak leaves

Which Mulch for Me?

There are so many kinds of mulches that deciding on which one to use can cause a real muddle. The thing to remember is that, just like everything else in life, no mulch is perfect for every job or every garden. The trick is to balance the pros and cons, and come up with the one that's right for you.

MATERIAL	PROS	CONS
Straw	Easy to get and simple to apply Good for cooling the soil Good source of organic matter	Can be expensive
Grass clippings	Inexpensive Generally easy to find Add organic matter	Can mat down
Manure	Easy to find, sometimes for free Rich in nutrients	Must be cured to kill weed seeds, prevent burning plants, and stop the awful stink Unattractive
Leaves	Great source of nutrients and organic matter	Break down very quickly and must be replaced often
Newspaper	Easy to get and apply Worms love it!	Must be weighted down
Plastic	Eliminates weeds if it's opaque Warms the soil Can be reused if it's heavy	Unattractive Expensive Adds no nutrients or organic matter to the soil Must be weighted down Must be cleaned up and stored in the fall
Wood shavings	Easy to find Easy to apply Free of weeds and disease germs	Can be acid Tend to tie up nitrogen in the soil

Take the Work Out of Weeding

Even if some weeds do have pretty flowers, in the vegetable garden, they're nothing but a pain in the grass! They crowd out other plants, attract pests, use up important nutrients — and make one heck of a lot of work if you don't keep on top of them. That's why the war against weeds takes top priority around my place.

My Weed Management Policy

To get the best of your weeds before they get the best of you, follow my 10-point prevention plan.

No. 1. Keep it small. The more space your garden covers, the more weeds you'll have. Stick to the size you can manage comfortably.

No. 2. Smother 'em in the pathways. Plant clover in the pathways between rows and beds. Weeds won't have room to grow, and the clover flowers will attract beneficial insects. Mow it now and then, and use the clippings as mulch.

No. 3. Mark your territory. Plant borders of fast-growing radishes around each bed or row. That way, you'll know exactly where your seedlings should come up. Anything that raises its head outside the border will be a candidate for elimination by the Weed Patrol.

No. 4. Cool your heels. When you've tilled your garden plot, instead of scooting indoors to grab your seed packets, just sit back and wait for the first rain. The next thing you know, your seedbeds will be chock-full of baby weeds, and you can hoe 'em right up. If there are so many weedlings that you can hardly see the soil, repeat the whole process before you plant your seeds. You'll save a lot of time in the long run.

WEED WIPEOUT TONIC

For those hard-to-kill weeds, zap 'em with this wild Tonic.

1 tbsp. of gin
1 tbsp. of vinegar
1 tbsp. of liquid dish soap
1 qt. of very warm water

Mix all of the ingredients together in a bucket, then pour into a handheld sprayer. Drench the weeds to the point of run-off, taking care not to get any on the surrounding plants.

No. 5. Use transplants. Young plants take off the minute you plant them. That means they can start shading out weeds right from the get-go. Plus, when something green does pop up, you'll know it's a weed and you can oust it without worrying that you might be giving the heave-ho to a future salad fixture.

No. 6. Procrastinate. Don't rush to plant warm-weather veggies like tomatoes, peppers, and melons. Wait until the soil gets good and warm. When heat lovers have to struggle to grow in cold soil, weeds will do them in pronto.

No. 7. Seed heavily. Weeds pop up in any bare soil they find. But you can beat them to it by covering the space with the plants you want in the garden. Later you can thin your crops to the right distance — and have plenty of tender young greens for the salad bowl.

No. 8. Weed early. Even if you keep on top of your weeds for only a month in late spring, you'll still be way ahead of the game. The people who study these things have found that the most critical period of weed control is the 4 weeks after the seeds germinate.

No. 9. Weed often. Every 2 weeks, to be precise. Those same studious folks pondered bell peppers for a while and discovered that if you weed all summer long, you'll get twice as many peppers as you will if you weed just twice, at 2 and 4 weeks after planting.

No. 10. Kick 'em when they're down. Perennial weeds often depend on the food that's tucked away in their roots. This stash is at its lowest just before the plants flower. If you've got a crop of strong-rooted villains, lay down the law when they're about to burst into bloom.

Off with Their Heads!

If the weeds in your veggie patch have gotten the upper hand and you can't hope to get them all out if you pull from now till Christmas, do the next best thing: Keep the rascals from propagating. Cut them down with a scythe before they bloom, and toss them onto the compost pile (minus the roots, if they're the creeping kind).

If You Can't Beat 'em . . .

To most folks, dandelions may be nothing but nasty old weeds, but to Grandma Putt, having a patch of them growing in the yard was like having a drugstore right on her doorstep. She said the whole plant was good for whatever ailed you, especially indigestion, or kidney and liver problems. She served up the young leaves in salads, steamed the older ones just like she did spinach, and roasted the roots to make coffee. And 3 times a day — morning, noon, and night — she brewed herself a cup of her All-Purpose Dandelion Cure. It must have worked: Grandma Putt was the healthiest woman in town.

Wild, Wild Salad

Dandelions aren't the only weeds that make good eatin'. There's nothing better than young purslane and lamb's quarters. I pick off individual purslane leaves when the plants are small, and clip off the top 2 or 3 inches of lamb's quarters when the plants get to be 3 to 4 inches tall, toss them all in a big salad with an oil-and-vinegar dressing, and eat my fill before the roots get dug up and sent off to never-never land.

ALL-PURPOSE DANDELION CURE

Brew up this tea to cure whatever ails you — or to keep away anything that might.

2 tsp. of fresh dandelion roots and leaves
½ cup of springwater

Put the roots and leaves into the water. Bring the water to a boil, then remove the pan from the heat and let the mix steep for 15 minutes. Make a cup 3 times a day, and drink to your good health!

Get Your Garden to Grow Up, Up, Up

The first time I heard Grandma Putt talk about "vertical gardening," I got a picture in my head of a lot of people swinging from a mountainside on those climbers' ropes, tucking seeds into straight up-and-down walls, and trying like crazy to make them stay put. It didn't take me long to learn that Grandma was really talking about growing vegetables on trellises and other kinds of supports. I also learned that there are plenty of good reasons to grow upstanding crops — and there are plenty of ways to do it, too!

Onward and Upward

Most everyone knows about propping up peas and pole beans, and staking tomatoes. But I like to get other crops on the up-and-up, too, like cucumbers, squash, and even small pumpkins and melons. Vertical growing pays off in several ways:

Space. Sprawling vines take up a whole lot of room. When I grow them on trellises, I can make my garden smaller or use the extra space to grow more crops.

Pesky pests. Slugs and other pests can slither right into vegetables that are lying on the ground. But most of those critters can't climb up strings and trellises.

Appearance. When crops like squash and cucumbers grow on trellises, Mother Earth's good old gravity field tugs down on them and makes them grow longer and straighter.

Versatility. A trellis with a nice, thick coat of leaves and veggies on it is a good garden worker. It can protect tender crops from wind and strong sunlight. Or it can block out things you'd just as soon not look at, like your compost pile and your neighbor's porch.

It's Electrifying

Some trellises and supports can actually supercharge your garden. It has to do with an old-time kind of gardening called electroculture. Have you ever noticed how your lawn suddenly greens up after a thunderstorm? That's electroculture at work: Electricity flying around in the air joins oxygen and nitrogen to form nitric oxide, and that's great for plants!

To create this same condition in your garden, use metal supports and trellises — especially copper ones — to draw static electricity. Don't just take my word for it. You'll see the difference in the health of your plants and the size of your harvest. Here's all you have to do:

• Grow melons and other vine crops on metal fences.

• Use only metal poles for staking.

• Tie up plants with strips of old panty hose. (If you don't know how that could attract electricity, just ask any woman about "static cling"!)

• Make sure you get out of the garden the next time you hear thunder!

Tennis, Anyone?
If you've got an old badminton net moldering in the garage, you've got a dandy instant trellis for up-and-coming crops like peas, cucumbers, and melons. Just sink a couple of posts into the ground, attach the net, and bingo! Your garden just got sporty.

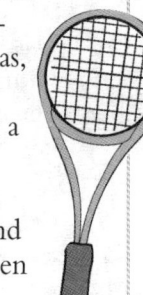

Keeping Things Under Control

Come summertime, the livin' gets easier — even for us vegetable gardeners. It's not like springtime, when you're rushing to get everything into the ground, or later in the fall, when you're scrambling to harvest all your crops before frost bowls 'em over. Oh, there are still plenty of chores to do in summer, but everything moves at a slower pace. It's more like tending a flock of quiet sheep than trying to keep up with a litter of 5-week-old puppies.

The Agenda

I always keep this chore list taped to the fridge, just so I don't overlook anything when I get an attack of the midsummer lazies.

❑ Make sure the garden is getting enough water.

❑ Check for sagging stems and tie 'em up before they break.

❑ Pick veggies as soon as they're ripe.

❑ Wash down the whole garden every 2 weeks with my All-Season Clean-Up Tonic to keep bugs, slugs, and garden thugs away.

❑ Inspect the mulch now and then, and add more if needed along about midsummer; overspray it with my Mulch Moisturizer Tonic.

ALL-SEASON CLEAN-UP TONIC

1 cup of liquid dish soap
1 cup of antiseptic mouthwash
1 cup of Tobacco Tea

Combine all these ingredients in a 20 gallon hose-end sprayer, filling the balance of the sprayer jar with warm water. Soak your entire yard (garden beds, trees, shrubs, and everything in between) to the point of run-off. Do this every 2 weeks in the early evening during the growing season.

MULCH MOISTURIZER TONIC

1 can of regular cola (not diet)
½ cup of ammonia
½ cup of antiseptic mouthwash
½ cup of baby shampoo

Mix these ingredients in your 20 gallon hose-end sprayer, and soak the mulch in your vegetable garden.

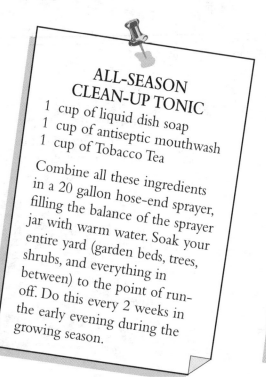

Tobacco Tea

I used to call this "chewing tobacco juice," but one of my loyal readers suggested that I rename it to more accurately reflect what it is and how it is made. That was a darn good idea, so here's how to make my Tobacco Tea: Place a thumb-and-three-fingers' worth of chewing tobacco in an old nylon (panty hose) stocking. Boil a gallon of water, then soak the tobacco-filled stocking in the hot water until the mixture turns a dark brown. Put it into a container, label it, then use 1 cup when a tonic calls for it.

Just Let Me Alone!

Like people, plants tend to stress out when the weather turns sticky and sweltering or when a drought hits. At those times, give your plants their own space. Don't spray or prune them, and don't pick any veggies unless they're ripe. Just give your garden a good drink of water and let it rest awhile.

All Tooled Up

When it comes to tools, I like to stick to the basics. Why, if I got all fired up and bought even half of those fancy contraptions I see at the garden center, I'd have to build another garage to put them in. These are the tools I can't get along without.

Tools You Can't Live Without

TOOL	WHAT I USE IT FOR
Garden fork	Loosening large areas of soil; breaking up clods and heavy soil
Digging or spading fork	Loosening soil; digging up clumps of weeds (and leaving the soil behind); breaking up chunks of soil
Hand trowel	Digging small holes for transplanting seedlings; mixing small amounts of soil and plant food; scooping out rocks; working among plants that are close together
Shovel	General digging and lifting of soil
Spade	Edging beds; cutting through sod, weeds, and tree roots
Weeding hoe	Slicing and dicing weeds

The Un–Tool Chest

The right tool makes any job easier and more fun. Some of the "tools" I use most often don't come from the garden center. Here are my favorites:

• **Old shower curtains and bedspreads.** Whenever I'm working in the garden, I spread one out nearby. I toss all of my weeds, plant clippings, and other debris on top; then, when it's full, I fold it up and carry it off to the compost pile.

• **Kitchen forks.** They're the best tools I know for cultivating small spaces, like between young seedlings and in the herb garden.

• **A retired golf bag.** When my kids gave me a new bag for Father's Day, I turned my old one into a wheeled garden carryall. Hoes, rakes, and shovels slide right into the plastic tubes, and the zippered pockets hold hand tools, seed packets, and all kinds of odds and ends. Best of all, the big wheels make it a cinch to pull my garden necessities!

Right from the Drawer

One of the handiest garden helpers I know of is right in your (or your wife's) dresser drawer: panty hose. Here are a footful of the ways I use them:

• **Clean it up!** Tuck a bar of soap into the toe, and hang it up near your handiest outdoor faucet. Then scrub up outside without taking the mess inside.

• **Tie it up!** Cut hose crosswise into strips and use them to fasten stems and vines to stakes and trellises. The soft, durable nylon won't damage tender plants and won't rot in wet weather, and it's a snap to cut off at season's end.

• **Save those sunflower seeds!** Just cover the entire head — it'll keep the seeds from falling off and the birds from getting to them before you do.

• **Bag those onions!** After you've cured your onions, drop one onion down a panty-hose leg and tie a knot. Repeat the process with the rest of the bunch. Hang the filled leg from a hook in a cool, dark, well-ventilated place, and whenever you need an onion, just snip one off below a knot.

• **Cover up!** Slip a "cap" over individual vegetables such as squashes, cucumbers, or eggplants, and tie the open end shut. The nylon stretches as the veggies grow, and it'll keep pests from helping themselves to your harvest.

Tools Lost and Found

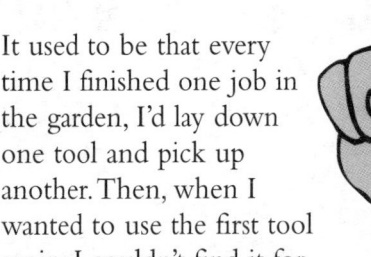

It used to be that every time I finished one job in the garden, I'd lay down one tool and pick up another. Then, when I wanted to use the first tool again, I couldn't find it for love nor money. So I came up with these two dandy ways to make sure I never lose a tool again.

Tip #1. Paint the handles of your hand tools bright yellow. That way, no matter where you put them down, you can spot them from in the garden — or from the front porch, for that matter!

Tip #2. Make temporary tool racks for long-handled hoes, rakes, and shovels. Take both ends off of some big fruit juice cans and nail them to a handy garden fence. Hang sets of them on all four sides of the garden, so no matter where you're working, when you finish with a tool, just slide it into one of the cans. That way, you'll always know where to find it!

An Inside Job

Indoors, I use a couple of old rake heads as holders for my long-handled tools. I hang them on the wall; then I slide my rakes, shovels, and hoes between the tines, and the old garage stays neat as a pin. My hand tools I keep in a bucket of clean, dry sand, handles up. It keeps them rust-free and ready for the grabbing.

Stop Commuting

Tired of running back and forth from the garden to the garage every time you need something? Then get yourself a mailbox, paint it up fancy, and fill it with all those small things you use all of the time, like hand tools, gloves, and twine. Put it in your garden so that it's always right at hand. You can even mount a whirligig on top of the box and let it do double duty as a scarecrow!

Share the Wealth

Almost every gardener needs to call on the big guns now and then — say, a shredder, sod-cutter, or heavy-duty tiller. But that kind of gear takes up a lot of space in your toolshed and a big chunk out of your wallet. Rather than buy something I use only for a couple of hours once or twice a year, I rent it. And, because most rental shops have a whole- or half-day minimum, I try to find a friend or neighbor to share the time — and the fee — with me.

Baby, It's Cold Out There

Even when you think you've got your growing season all figured out, Mother Nature can throw you a curveball or two. That's why it pays to take a tip from the Boy Scouts, and be prepared.

Give Me Shelter!

The simplest way to keep your plants from shivering their timbers, at the beginning or the end of the growing season, is to use floating row covers. Besides keeping out chilly winds, they fend off bugs and other thugs. But there are plenty of other ways to do both those things, and for much less money. Here are some of my favorite warmer-uppers:

• **Plastic milk cartons.** Cut the bottoms off. Sink them a couple of inches into the ground around each tender plant, so they don't blow away in the wind.

• **Panty hose.** Cut off a piece, knot the top, slip it over a plant, and pull the bottom closed.

• **Paper grocery bags.** Dig your planting hole, then set a bag inside so that 10 inches or so sticks up above the surface. Fill it with soil, roll the top down, and plant your seedling. At the first sign of frost, roll up the collar and fasten it with a spring-loaded clothespin or two.

SUPER Growing Secrets

READ ALL ABOUT IT!

Besides protecting your plants from the cold, there are literally hundreds of uses for newspaper in the garden. Among my favorites are:

1. **Cold frame insulation.** Line the inside of a cold frame with several sheets of newspaper on frosty nights.

2. **Compost material.** Chop, shred, or cut it up — it's one of the best of the "browns."

3. **Cutworm control.** Make little collars out of newspaper, and wrap them around the stems of tender young plants.

4. **Earwig traps.** Set out sections of dampened, rolled-up newspaper in your garden at night. The next morning, they'll be filled with earwigs. Drown 'em or crush 'em — the choice is yours!

5. **Mulch magic.** Place several sheets on the ground, and cover with grass clippings or shredded bark. It smothers the weeds, and eventually breaks down, so it can be worked into the soil.

6. **Starter pots.** Come transplanting time, plant pot and all (see page 43).

The Great Frame-Up

I never knew I needed a cold frame until I got one. Now I don't know how I ever got along without it! It's about as simple as a gadget can get: Just a box with no bottom and a top that opens up and even comes off when the weather warms up. I use it in the spring to start some of my seedlings and harden off others. Then, in fall, I plant cool-weather veggies like lettuce and spinach in it. They grow happy as clams, all winter long.

Making a cold frame is as easy as 1, 2, 3. Get a window frame (minus glass); heavy, clear plastic; and 4 boards. Then:

1. Cut the boards to the right size and nail them together to make a box that's just a tad smaller all around than the window frame.

2. Tack the plastic over the frame.

3. Set the window frame on top of the box, and you're all set to grow!

Southern Comfort

Way down South, ol' Sol can turn a cold frame into a hot frame in a hurry! To keep your young plants warm without roasting them alive, use polyester row-cover fabric on your frame instead of glass or plastic. It'll let in the right amount of light without so much heat. Make sure the covers stay put by attaching a square of Velcro® to each corner of the box and each corner of the cover.

Bedding Down

Grandma Putt used to say that a garden is like a house: If you just walk away and leave it empty, it'll head downhill like a runaway wagon. That's why I treat my garden as well after the last harvest as I do before spring planting.

BEDTIME SNACK

This Tonic is a great soil fortifier as you put your garden to bed for the winter.

25 lbs. of gypsum
10 lbs. of natural organic garden food (either 4-12-4 or 5-10-5)
5 lbs. of bonemeal

Mix these ingredients, then apply them to every 100 square feet of soil with your handheld broadcast spreader. Work them into the soil, and cover with a thick blanket of leaves and straw. Then overspray the area with my Sleepytime Tonic (see page 88).

The Bedtime Routine

Around the time I harvest my last veggies, I start pondering next year's garden. Here's how I say "Till we
meet again."

1. Clear away all the plants and add them to the
compost pile.

2. Loosen the subsoil with a garden fork. Doing
this chore in the fall, instead of waiting until spring,
gives the worms time to repair the damage it does
to their tunnels.

3. Work a helping of my Bedtime Snack
(see page 87) into the soil.

4. Spread a thick layer
of leaves over the garden
and top it off with straw.
I've found that this is the
worms' favorite mulch
combo. It keeps the little guys warm and busy all
winter long, and come spring, my planting beds
will be well fed and all set to grow.

5. Overspray the blanket of leaves and straw
with my Sleepytime Tonic.

Toodle-oo, Tools

When it's time to pack away your
garden gear for the winter, clean and
sharpen your tools, then give
them a light coat of oil. Hang
long-handled tools from racks or
hooks. Wrap hand tools in newspaper
and tuck them into a drawer.

SLEEPYTIME TONIC

Apply this Tonic to your
garden so that it'll sleep tight
over the winter.

1 can of beer
1 can of regular cola (not diet)
1 cup of baby shampoo
½ cup of ammonia
¼ cup of instant tea granules

Mix these ingredients in a bucket, pour them into your 20 gallon hose-end sprayer, and saturate the blanket of leaves and
clippings covering your garden.

In this chapter, you've learned how to make your garden fit as a fiddle. Now we'll
move on to the big challenge: protecting it from pesky pests and dastardly diseases
that can strike when you least expect them.

CHAPTER 5

Keeping Plague and Pest(ilence) at Bay

For Grandma Putt, fending off pests and diseases wasn't
a matter of waiting until the hordes attacked and then
marching out to the garden and taking aim with a spray
gun. She taught me that keeping a garden safe from bugs
and other varmints is a two-part process. First, before you
plant a single vegetable, you set up your defenses. Then
you keep an eagle eye out for trouble, so you can handle
little problems before they turn into big ones.

The Defensive Line

Grandma Putt and I had our share of encounters with pesky pests and dastardly diseases that seemed to come charging in out of nowhere. But we sent most of them scurrying off in a hurry, and our garden bounced back like a champ. That's when I learned that the surest defense against garden-variety trouble-makers is strong, healthy plants.

The Making of a Champ

Anytime you take on trouble in your garden, you'll be waging a losing battle if your plants can't join the fight. To raise plants that can put up their dukes when the need arises, you need to give them soil that's championship material. The way to do that is to call on that magic bullet we talked about in Chapter 3 — **organic matter.** Here's the simple process I use to give my plants the best possible training camp:

• Add hefty doses of organic matter to your soil, in both spring and fall.

• Use organic mulches that will break down and feed the soil.

• Apply my terrific tonics at the recommended intervals.

• Keep a batch of compost cooking and dish it up in large helpings.

• Lay out a big welcome mat for earthworms.

Staying in the Pink of Health

Besides building strong, healthy soil, there are plenty of things you can do to keep diseases from knocking your veggies down for the count. Here's my Rx for good health:

✔ **Plant disease-resistant varieties.** Just name the vegetable you want to grow, and you can find plants with built-in resistance to ailments like mildews, viruses, leaf spots, and wilts — and they're labeled that way in good seed catalogs and garden centers. Call your closest Cooperative Extension Service and ask what vegetable diseases are most common where you live. Then shop accordingly.

✔ **Look for varieties that thrive where you live.** They'll be better able to handle whatever your climate dishes up in the way of heat, cold, humidity, and wind — and the diseases that often come with them.

✔ **Give plants the conditions they like.** Or choose plants that suit the conditions you can give them. Plants grow up to be strong, healthy, and able to fend off diseases only if they get the kinds of light, moisture, and food they need.

✔ **Bide your time.** Plants that start life in the garden too early — whether as seeds or as transplants — have to struggle against cold soil, cold air, and biting winds just to survive. Like any of us under those conditions, they stress out, and a stressed plant is a weak plant: easy prey for both diseases and pests.

✔ **Rotate your crops.** Particular diseases and pests tend to favor certain vegetable families. But, as we discussed in Chapter 2, the villains don't follow their victims around. By moving the target, you nearly always get rid of the culprit.

✔ **Diversify.** Any insect or germ will zero in on a big expanse of its favorite food. But if it takes a gander at your garden and sees a crazy-quilt mix of veggies — some yummy, some so-so, and some frankly repulsive — it'll almost always turn tail and head for richer territory.

✔ **Aim your hose at the ground.** Better yet, use a drip system or soaker hose. Wet foliage — especially after dark — is an open invitation to fungus.

✔ **Steer clear of wet plants.** Fungi can travel from plant to plant on clothes, tools, or hands. After a rain shower, stay out of the garden until the foliage is good and dry.

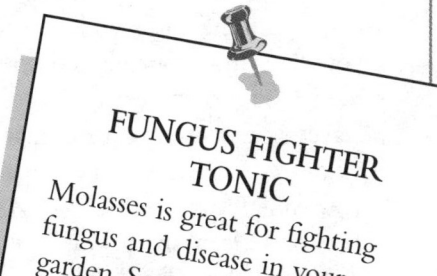

FUNGUS FIGHTER TONIC

Molasses is great for fighting fungus and disease in your garden. So, at the first sign of trouble, mix up a batch of my Fungus Fighter Tonic.

½ cup of molasses
½ cup of powdered milk
1 tsp. of baking soda
1 gal. of warm water

Mix the molasses, powdered milk, and baking soda into a paste. Place the mixture in the toe of an old nylon stocking, and let it steep in warm water for several hours. Then strain, and use the Tonic to fight fungus in your garden every 2 weeks throughout the growing season. I guarantee there'll be no more fungus among us!

More Preventive Medicine

✔ **Mulch early and often.** A blanket of fresh mulch will keep fungus in the soil from splashing up onto your plants when it rains or when you water. It also reduces disease-spreading weeds.

✔ **Go easy.** Diseases and pests hone in on broken stems, torn leaves, and damaged roots, so be careful when you cultivate. And when you plan your garden, make the paths wide enough that you can move yourself and your equipment down them without bruising leaves and stepping on soil that's been cultivated. At harvesttime, cut your veggies off with clippers or a clean, sharp knife — don't tear them from their stems.

✔ **Don't ask for problems.** When you buy transplants, inspect them carefully for any signs of pests or diseases. Look under all of the leaves and in the joints where they meet the stems. If you see traces of pesticide, like white powder or sticky-looking blotches, say "No, thanks." There could still be problems lurking that you don't want in your garden.

✔ **Go on the offensive.** Spray your plants with my All-Season Green-Up Tonic (see page 349). It'll give your plants a square meal and keep away disease germs at the same time.

✔ **Encourage allies.** Spiders, ladybugs, toads, bats, songbirds, and all kinds of beneficial insects are champing at the bit to get at your garden pests, including the ones that spread diseases. So lay out the welcome mat for them.

✔ **Search and destroy.** Inspect your garden at least every couple of days. Get rid of weeds while they're still small and harmless. Put on your reading glasses, and examine leaves and stems for any signs of pests or diseases. If you find trouble, deal with it today. Tomorrow could be too late.

Don't Break Training

Once you have your soil well on its way to health and well-being, make sure you don't accidentally set it back. In particular:

Don't walk on garden beds, and never work with wet soil. You'll make the particles stick together, drive out all the air spaces between them, and turn the soil into hostile territory for your plants' roots.

Just say no to pesticides, unless they're absolutely necessary. They'll kill off your worm allies, and they can get into the soil and cause more problems than they seem to be solving.

Go easy on chemical fertilizers. They give your plants a quick burst of energy — like the one a burger-and-shake lunch gives you — but they do nothing for your soil, and that means they do nothing for the long-term health of your garden.

Botanical Warfare

Doctors tell us, even when we're in the pink of health, that our bodies are chock-full of what we call germs. Most of the time, they just go about their business and we don't even notice them. Then one day, bingo! Something gets out of whack, and we're suddenly sick as dogs.

That's true in your garden, too — only more so. After all, your vegetable plants aren't living in a clean, tidy house. They're standing knee-deep in dirt, with millions of invisible organisms coming at them from all directions, slithering through the soil, floating through the air, and even sloshing around in rainwater. Plants have to be pretty tough customers to keep warding off attacks by this army! And you have to be Johnny-on-the-spot to help them do it.

The Lineup

Each plant disease tends to attack a different crowd of vegetables. (Don't panic: Plenty of home gardeners never see a single one of them raise its ugly head — these villains most often plague big, single-crop commercial growers. But to be forewarned is to be forearmed.) There are four categories:

- **Fungus**
- **Bacteria**
- **Viruses**
- **Nematodes**

The Lowdown

No. 1. Fungus. This is the biggest batch, and includes two of the worst, molds and mildews. They can attack any part of a plant. Victims wilt, rot, or get spots on their leaves. Fungi start life as spores, which are tiny, seedlike things that multiply like crazy, especially on warm, wet surfaces. During winter, they sleep in the soil or in plant debris until spring rains kick them into action. The good news is that fungi tend to spread slowly; if you catch them in time, you can send them packing.

No. 2. Bacteria. These are smaller than fungi, and there are billions of them in the garden and everyplace else. Nearly all are harmless, and many are beneficial. But the few real villains move fast and cause big-time problems, usually in the form of rot or wilt. There is no cure: Your only solution is to pull up the sick plants and destroy them.

The good news here — at least for folks up North — is that most of the bacteria that attack plants can't live through the winter in frozen soil. A few, though, spend the cold months in the bodies of insects, which pass on the diseases to plants the following summer.

No. 3. Viruses. These guys are even tinier than bacteria. Only a few of them are true killers, causing plants to suddenly wilt and go belly-up. If your plants' leaves become crinkly and twisted, or if the color disappears in spots, chances are there's a virus at work. These culprits spend the winter in wild plants, and they're transmitted by insects. Aphids, whiteflies, thrips, and leafhoppers all carry plant viruses.

No. 4. Nematodes (a.k.a. roundworms or eelworms). Through a strong magnifying glass, a nematode looks like a tiny snake with a needle coming out of its head. It's what they use to poke their way into stems and leaves, sucking out juices along the way. What's worse, though, is that the niches they carve out are open doors to fungi and bacteria (see pages 101–102.)

ALL-AROUND DISEASE DEFENSE TONIC

Wet, rainy weather can mean an outbreak of fungus in your garden, especially in late winter and early spring. Keep your outdoor green scene happy and healthy with this Tonic.

1 cup of chamomile tea
1 tsp. of liquid dish soap
½ tsp. of vegetable oil
½ tsp. of peppermint oil
1 gal. of warm water

Mix all of the ingredients together in a bucket, then mist-spray your plants every week or so before the really hot weather (75°F or higher) sets in.

WARNING: This is strong stuff, so be sure to test it on a few leaves before completely spraying any plant.

Dr. Jerry's Veggie Health Clinic

Here's a quick rundown of some of the most common plant diseases and what you can do to head them off at the pass. But keep in mind that once they've taken hold of a plant, your best option is to pull up the victim and destroy it.

Anthracnose (fungus)

Victims: Beans, cucumbers, eggplant, lettuce, melons, peas, peppers, potatoes, radishes, rhubarb, spinach, tomatoes, turnips.

What the Examination Shows: Small spots appear on leaves, stems, and fruit. Spots usually grow in size, and eventually the plant dies back.

How to Avoid Sick Bay: Plant resistant varieties. Rotate crops every year, and spray plants with Compost Tea (see page 351) and my All-Around Disease Defense Tonic.

Bacterial Blight

Victims: Beans, cabbage family, peas

What the Examination Shows: In the cabbage family, young plants are stunted, with one side of the plant larger than the other; mature plants lose older leaves. On beans and peas, light or dark green spots appear on leaves, then dry out and turn bronze or brown.

How to Avoid Sick Bay: Plant resistant varieties. Spray neem oil on plants with a minor infection.

Bacterial Wilt

Victims: Carrots, cucumbers, eggplant, some melons, peanuts, peppers, potatoes, pumpkins, rhubarb, squash, sweet potatoes, tomatoes.

What the Examination Shows: Soft brown lesions appear on stems and grow until the plant is girdled. Stems develop brown streaks, then dissolve into brown jelly.

How to Avoid Sick Bay: Use row covers to protect plants from cucumber beetles, which spread one form of the disease. Rotate crops on a 4- or 5-year cycle to avoid the other form, which can live in the soil for more than 5 years.

Dr. Jerry's Veggie Health Clinic

Clubroot (fungus)

Victims: All members of the cabbage family (see the clan roster in Chapter 7).

What the Examination Shows: Roots become swollen and lumpy, and wilted, yellowish leaves appear.

How to Avoid Sick Bay: Plant resistant varieties. Add compost (not manure) to the soil, and raise the pH to at least 7.2. Spray plants with my All-Around Disease Defense Tonic.

Curly Top (fungus)

Victims: Beans, beets, cabbage family, carrots, celery, cucumbers, eggplant, melons, pumpkins, spinach, squash, Swiss chard, tomatoes.

What the Examination Shows: Leaves curl upward, and grow thick and leathery-looking. On beans, the leaves curl down instead of up.

How to Avoid Sick Bay: Use row covers to protect plants from leafhoppers, which spread the disease. Spray plants with my All-Around Disease Defense Tonic. Control weeds in and around the garden.

Damping-off (fungus)

Victims: All seedlings.

What the Examination Shows: Seedlings rot, either before or after they break through the surface of the soil.

How to Avoid Sick Bay: Follow the seed-starting routine described in Chapter 3.

Downey Mildew (fungus)

Victims: Endive, lettuce, and members of the beet, cabbage, carrot, onion, and pea families.

What the Examination Shows: Leaf spots occur, then turn into fluffy, often violet-colored mold, which spreads to both sides of the leaf. Extensive rot develops as more fungi move in.

How to Avoid Sick Bay: Plant resistant varieties. Spray foliage regularly with Compost Tea (see page 351) and the Baking Soda Spray on page 99. Rotate crops every year. Remove weeds immediately, as they can harbor the disease.

Dr. Jerry's Veggie Health Clinic

Early Blight (fungus)

Victims: Carrots, onions, potatoes, tomatoes.

What the Examination Shows: Brown, circular spots surrounded by rings. This usually occurs during periods of warm, humid weather before fruits have ripened.

How to Avoid Sick Bay: Plant resistant varieties. Weed regularly. Spray plants with Compost Tea and my All-Around Disease Defense Tonic. Use row covers to keep out flea beetles, which can spread the disease.

Fusarium and Verticillium Wilts

Victims: Beans, cucumbers, melons, pumpkins, squash, sweet potatoes, tomatoes.

What the Examination Shows: Leaves turn yellow, then brown. Stems may turn brown and split.

How to Avoid Sick Bay: Plant resistant varieties. Rotate crops every year. Remove and destroy infected plants immediately. Before the next growing season starts, solarize the soil, then add plenty of organic matter.

Gray Mold, a.k.a. Botrytis (fungus)

Victims: Pretty much everything, both seedlings and mature plants.

What the Examination Shows: Airy-looking, gray mold appears above a water-soaked, brown, rotten area on leaves, stems, flowers, or fruit. It can be fatal to seedlings, but is usually just a nuisance on bigger plants.

How to Avoid Sick Bay: Clean seed-starting gear thoroughly. Give plants plenty of space and good air circulation. Remove dead leaves, flowers, and other debris as soon as you spot them. Spray plants with Compost Tea and my All-Around Disease Defense Tonic.

Late Blight (fungus)

Victims: Potatoes, tomatoes.

What the Examination Shows: Dark spots develop on leaves, often with a strong, unpleasant odor. Eventually, plants rot and collapse.

How to Avoid Sick Bay: Plant certified disease-free seeds or transplants. Rotate crops every year. Spray plants with Compost Tea and my All-Around Disease Defense Tonic.

Dr. Jerry's Veggie Health Clinic

Root Rot (many causes)

Victims: Just about everything.

What the Examination Shows: Plant wilts and lower leaves turn yellow. Roots turn black or brown and are often soft, easily broken, and foul-smelling. Root rot occurs in moist or wet soil, usually during cool weather.

How to Avoid Sick Bay: Rotate crops every year. Avoid overwatering. Water plants with Compost Tea before symptoms appear. Before the next growing season begins, solarize the soil and add plenty of organic matter.

Rust (fungus)

Victims: Asparagus, beans, beets, carrots, chard, corn, onions, peanuts, peas, spinach.

What the Examination Shows: Red, yellow, or orange dots, usually on the undersides of leaves. On onions and asparagus, foliage tips turn brownish red. Rust usually strikes late in the season during wet weather. Depending on the type, it can destroy crops or cause only cosmetic damage.

How to Avoid Sick Bay: Plant resistant varieties. Spray plants with Compost Tea and my All-Around Disease Defense Tonic before symptoms appear.

Southern Blight (fungus)

Victims: Just about everything.

What the Examination Shows: A white to pinkish growth appears at the base of the stem at the soil line. Leaves turn yellow and drop.

How to Avoid Sick Bay: Add compost or other organic matter before the growing season starts. Spray plants with Compost Tea and my All-Around Disease Defense Tonic before symptoms appear. When you remove infected plants, take 6 inches of soil all around them.

Tobacco Mosaic Virus

Victims: The tomato family primarily, but also beans, beets, cucumbers, melons, and potatoes.

What the Examination Shows: Leaves turn yellow to pale green, often mottled, deformed, and smaller than normal. Plants become stunted, with greatly reduced yield.

How to Avoid Sick Bay: Plant resistant varieties. Don't let anyone smoke in or near your garden, or even carry in an unlit pipe, cigar, or cigarette. While you're removing and destroying infected plants, avoid touching healthy ones (the virus is spread by contact). Change your clothes, and disinfect your hands and tools before you set foot in the garden again.

Garden Cure-Alls

No matter what pests or diseases are attacking your garden — or threatening to — I've got a pocket of surefire tricks to set things right in a hurry.

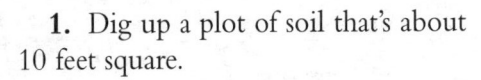

Solar Power: Seven Steps to Cleaner Soil

Big-time enemies call for big-time action. Solarizing your soil (heating it up to 150°F or so) will kill off fungi and low-life critters like nematodes and Colorado potato beetles. For this process to work, you and ol' Sol need to get cookin' during the hottest part of the year, which in most places is July and August. Here's the routine:

1. Dig up a plot of soil that's about 10 feet square.

2. Lay on a 1- to 2-inch layer of fresh manure and work it in well.

3. Rake the soil into beds or rows.

4. Water well, then let everything settle overnight.

5. Cover the plot with a sheet of clear, 3- to 6-mil plastic and pile soil around the edges to keep it in place.

Patch any holes or tears that you find. Make sure the cover has some slack in it, so it can puff up (instead of blowing away or even bursting) when the heat starts rising.

6. Wait about 6 weeks — longer if the weather's cool.

7. Take off the cover, water, and plant your crops. Don't cultivate, or you'll bring up untreated soil — nasty nematodes, fungi, and all.

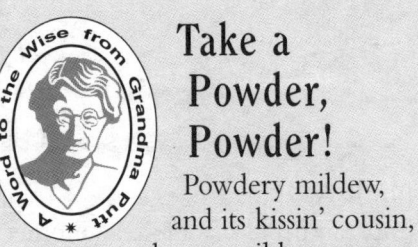

Take a Powder, Powder!

A Word to the Wise from Grandma Putt

Powdery mildew, and its kissin' cousin, downy mildew, can spell the end for plenty of veggies. Grandma Putt kept her garden growin' great guns by spraying her plants every week with her special Baking Soda Spray. I still do.

BAKING SODA SPRAY

1 tbsp. of baking soda
2 tbsp. of baby shampoo

To make this Tonic, mix ingredients in 1 gallon of warm water. Then mist-spray your plants lightly once a week, and say, "Out, out, damned spot!"

No Smoking, Please

Once tobacco mosaic virus (TMV) shows up in your garden, it's the dickens to get rid of. It often arrives courtesy of tobacco from a cigarette, but you can also carry it in on contaminated plants or even containers they've come into contact with. The nasty stuff lives in the soil for as long as 5 years, and during that time there's no telling where it could pop up. Though members of the tomato family are its most frequent victims, the virus can attack many garden plants (veggies and otherwise), including spinach, beets, cucumbers, melons, and lettuce. If TMV has attacked your garden, don't grow anything but resistant varieties for at least 3 years.

The Milk of Plant Kindness

Nobody's figured out why, but milk seems to neutralize the tobacco mosaic virus. If you know this villain is lurking somewhere in your garden, just waiting to attack, try this tactic: Whenever you're working near a likely target — especially the tomato family — keep a bowl handy that's filled with a half-and-half mixture of milk and water. Then every few minutes, dip your hands and tools into the liquid. It'll stop this dastardly disease dead in its tracks!

COMPOST TEA

Teatime is usually for people, not plants, but Compost Tea is the healthiest drink a plant could ever ask for. It delivers a well-balanced supply of all those important nutrients — major and minor — and fends off diseases at the same time. Here's the recipe I learned from Grandma Putt long ago:

1½ lbs. of fresh compost
4½ gal. of warm water

Pour the water into a 5-gallon bucket. Scoop the compost into a cotton, burlap, or panty-hose sack, tie it closed, and put it into the water. Cover the bucket and let it steep for about a week. Pour the solution into a watering can, spray mister, or even a 20 gallon hose-end sprayer, and give your plants a good spritzing with it every 2 to 3 weeks during the growing season.

Manure Tea

You can make manure tea (another wonder drink) the same way you make Compost Tea. Just substitute 1½ pounds of well-cured manure for the compost, and use the finished product the same way.

The Root of the Problem

Root-knot nematodes — those pesky, pugnacious parasites — can cause all kinds of damage in your garden. There are two branches of the family: northern and southern.

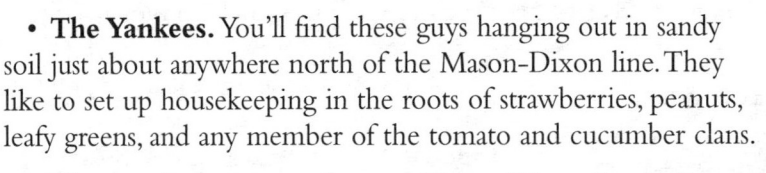

- **The Yankees.** You'll find these guys hanging out in sandy soil just about anywhere north of the Mason-Dixon line. They like to set up housekeeping in the roots of strawberries, peanuts, leafy greens, and any member of the tomato and cucumber clans.

- **The southern ungentlemen.** These slithery Sun Belt slobs also stick pretty much to sandy soil, ranging as far north as New Jersey. They can't be bothered with strawberries or peanuts, but they'll ransack plenty of other roots, including those of okra, beans, watermelon, and the whole danged tomato family.

- **The modus operandi.** Once they do their breaking and entering, root-knot nematodes inject a couple of cells with a chemical that makes them swell up like balloons. These giant cells multiply and show up on the roots as small galls that you can't break off. Often, the roots will also fork at the tips. The aboveground sign that these rascals are at work will be sickly and stunted plants — but because a lot of culprits can cause that condition, you'll have to dig up a plant or two to make sure.

If It Breaks, Don't Fix It

Healthy legume crops like peas and beans have nodules on their roots that look a lot like the galls made by nematodes. To find out whether your beans are healthy or sick, break off a root nodule. If it comes off easily, it's a beneficial bump meant for fixing nitrogen in the soil. If the thing won't budge, you know you've got trouble right there in Root City.

What's in a Name?

Not all nematodes are villains. In fact, beneficial nematodes just may be some of the best friends your garden could ask for. Like their nasty cousins, these guys are parasites. Instead of setting up camp inside your plants, however, they move into the bodies of pests like cutworms, root maggots, and Japanese beetle grubs, and polish them off.

Most garden centers and garden catalogs sell beneficial nematodes. If you buy some, read the package instructions carefully and follow them exactly. Good nematodes can't possibly harm your plants, but to get them to do their best work, you need to release them at just the right time.

Move 'em Out

If you've discovered that nematodes ride the range in your garden, you have to outwit the slimy squirts. I recommend this seven-part strategy:

1. Starve 'em out. When their favorite victims aren't around, nematodes turn from first-class delinquents into just another part of the underground scene. Grow crops they don't like. The Yankees can't stand corn; the Southerners don't care for strawberries, and none of the rascals likes rutabagas or any member of the cabbage and onion clans.

2. Bring on the enemy. Load your soil with things like eggshells, seafood meal, and shrimp hulls. They all contain chitin, which is what nematode eggs are covered with. Chitin eaters from near and far will show up and start to chow down. When they finish the free food you've given them, they'll start in on the nematode eggs with a vengeance!

3. Time your plantings. During the second half of the summer, nematode crowds are at their peak. That's when to grow the crops they don't like. In winter and early spring, there aren't many of the culprits around, so you can plant their favorite chow to your heart's content.

4. Solarize your soil in midsummer. This is a must in the Deep South before you put in fall crops of favorite nematode chow like turnips, carrots, and onions. But anywhere, it's a good idea to kill off most of the blighters just before fall planting time. See Solar Power: Seven Steps to Cleaner Soil on page 99.

5. Carry no passengers. Root-knot nematodes seldom travel more than a few feet from their hatching place — unless you give them a ride. After you've been digging in a likely nematode stomping ground, hose off all your tools, and even your gloves if you've had your hands in the soil.

6. Grow resistant varieties. Several kinds of tomatoes, hot peppers, and other veggies don't knuckle under to root-knot nematodes. New kinds of resistant crops come on the market every year, so look for them at garden centers and in catalogs.

7. Serve up big helpings of mulch and water. Some of the nematodes' favorite crops will produce in enemy territory, but they'll need more water than usual. Any mulch keeps more moisture in the soil and smothers weeds, but compost or manure will also add nematode enemies to the soil.

NO HITCH HIKERS!

Villainless Crimes

Two common ailments look and act like diseases, but they're what gardeners call "cultural problems." Here's how to head off trouble.

✔ **Blossom-end rot** hits squash, tomatoes, peppers, and watermelon. A dark, watery spot starts at the blossom end and grows until it's covered the whole thing. Small fruits usually drop off quickly. Larger ones often stay on the plant.

Causes: Too little calcium; long periods of wet weather followed by a dry spell.
Prevention: Before the growing season starts, test your soil. If it needs calcium and the pH is low, add limestone. If the pH is not low, add gypsum. Mulch to maintain even moisture. Go easy on fertilizers, and add ground-up eggshells to the can when you water.

✔ **Cracking** attacks celery, tomatoes, or rhubarb. Tomatoes crack lengthwise. In rhubarb and celery, the leaf stems split.

Causes: In tomatoes, sudden change in soil moisture, usually from dry to wet. In rhubarb and celery, it's caused by too little boron.
Prevention: In tomatoes, mulch to maintain even moisture, water during dry spells, and pick fruit as soon as it's ripe. In rhubarb and celery, test your soil before the growing season starts, and add boron if you need to.

Telling Good Guys from Bad

The way Mother Nature looks at it, there are no such things as "good guys" and "bad guys." All of those critters out there — from teeny, tiny bacteria to great big grizzly bears — are just "doin' what comes natur'lly," as Grandma Putt's favorite songwriter, Irving Berlin, put it. The problem for us gardeners is that some of those critters are doing what comes natur'lly where we don't want them to do it: in our gardens.

Heroes and Villains

Actually, we can divide garden wildlife into three kinds: heroes in big white hats, creepy villains, and a whole lot of townsfolk (townsbugs, rather) who are going about their business, not bothering anybody. To learn who the big-time felons are, and how to rally the heroes to your aid, study the **Most Unwanted List** starting on the next page.

Aphids

Likely Victims: Just name a plant, and you can almost bet there's an aphid that specializes in dining on it.

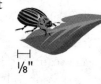

⊢⊣
⅛"

The Crime Scene: Stunted growth and deformed, often yellow leaves. Potato leaves turn brown and curl up. Tomatoes get blossom-end rot, and rolled and spotted leaves.

Be on the Lookout For: Tiny, pear-shaped guys with two little antennae coming out of their heads. At the back end, there's a pair of tubes that fire off a spray when the bugs get scared. There are dozens of kinds of aphids, and they can be almost any color in the rainbow. They like to feed on young growth, and most often cluster on buds, stems, and the undersides of leaves.

The Tonic to Reach For: Aphid Antidote. And for long term protection, call in the ladybugs.

• •

Armyworms

Likely Victims: Beans, beets, cabbage, corn, cucumbers, lettuce, peas, peanuts, peppers, spinach, and tomatoes.

⊢————————⊣
1¾"

APHID ANTIDOTE

To keep aphids and other pests out of your yard, mix up a batch of this amazing antidote.

2 medium cloves of garlic, chopped fine
1 small onion, chopped fine
1 tbsp. of liquid dish soap
2 cups of water

Put all the ingredients in a blender and blend on high. Then strain out the pulp. Pour the liquid into a handheld mist sprayer, and apply liberally at the first sign of aphid trouble.

The Crime Scene: Ragged holes in leaves and fruit.

Be on the Lookout For: Caterpillars, 1 to 2 inches long, greenish blue to brownish in color, usually with prominent stripes down their sides. They feed at night or on cloudy days, year-round in warm climates. Elsewhere, they usually show up in the fall.

The Tonic to Reach For: All-Season Clean-Up Tonic (page 349).

• •

Cabbage Loopers

Likely Victims: Beans, celery, peas, potatoes, spinach, tomatoes, and all members of the cabbage family.

The Crime Scene: Large, irregular holes in leaves. Holes in broccoli or cabbage heads where the larvae have burrowed in.

Be on the Lookout For: Green caterpillars about 1½ inches long, with white stripes down their sides. They arch their midsections as they move along. The adult version is a brown moth with a silver chevron in the center of each wing.

The Tonic to Reach For: Wild Mustard Tea (page 360).

Colorado Potato Beetles

Likely Victims: Eggplant, peppers, potatoes, and tomatoes.

The Crime Scene: Chewed leaves, with foliage stripped from plants. Distinctive black excrement on damaged leaves.

Be on the Lookout For: Beetles about the size of a fingernail, with dome-shaped shells done up in black and yellow stripes. Adult females lay clusters of orange eggs on the undersides of leaves. The larvae look like dull reddish orange blobs with black legs and heads.

The Tonic to Reach For: Beetle Juice (page 350) or Wild Mustard Tea (page 360).

Corn Earworms, a.k.a. Fruitworms

Likely Victims: Beans, corn, okra, peas, peppers, potatoes, squash, and tomatoes.

The Crime Scene: On corn: munched young shoots, chewed silk, mauled and deformed ears. Holes in tomatoes at the stem end. Pinhead-sized holes in peppers. On other crops: leaves and buds with chunks missing.

Be on the Lookout For: Caterpillars ranging in color from green to brown to yellowish tan, with dark stripes down their sides. Adults (pale tan moths) fly at night, laying single, cream-colored eggs on corn silk or leaves in spring.

The Tonic to Reach For: Garden Cure-All Tonic (page 107).

Cucumber Beetles
Likely Victims:
Cucumbers, melons, potatoes, squash, and other plants.

1/4"

The Crime Scene:
Holes chewed through leaves, flowers, and fruit. Vanished seeds (the larvae get them before they sprout).
Be on the Lookout For: Beetles about ¼ inch long, with shiny yellow wing covers with either three black stripes or 11 black spots. Larvae are thin, whitish grubs with a black or brown head. Adults winter in dead vines or garden litter and hit the chow line just as cucumber seedlings emerge. They appear most often on the undersides of leaves. Adults and larvae transmit bacterial wilt and cucumber mosaic virus.
The Tonic to Reach For:
Beetle Juice (page 350).

Cutworms
Likely Victims:

1"

Beans, the cabbage family, corn, tomatoes, and just about everything else (usually seedlings).
The Crime Scene: Sometimes chew marks on older plants, but most often seedlings gnawed off at the base. (If they looked fine when you went to bed but you find them belly-up, or even missing, in the morning, you can

bet the culprit was a cutworm: These rascals operate by night.)
Be on the Lookout For: Ugly, soft caterpillars, 1 to 2 inches long, in almost any color of the rainbow. You know you've got one if it curls up when you touch it. Adults are small, plain brown moths.
The Tonic to Reach For:
Hot Bug Brew.

HOT BUG BREW
When you've got an all-out invasion on your hands, heat up the action.

3 hot green peppers
3 medium cloves of garlic
1 small onion
1 tbsp. of liquid dish soap
3 cups of water

Purée the peppers, garlic, and onion in a blender. Pour the purée into a jar, and add the dish soap and water. Let stand for 24 hours. Then strain out the pulp, and use a handheld sprayer to apply the remaining liquid to bug-infested plants, making sure to thoroughly coat the tops and undersides of all the leaves.

Jerry's Most Unwanted List

European Corn Borers

Likely Victims: Beans, corn, and all members of the tomato family.

1"

The Crime Scene: The same mischief you get from corn earworms.

Be on the Lookout For: Caterpillars about the size of corn earworms, but lighter colored, usually tan to off-white, with brown spots.

The Tonic to Reach For: Garden Cure-All Tonic.

GARDEN CURE-ALL TONIC

At the first sign of bug activity, mix up a batch of this Tonic.

4 cloves of garlic
1 small onion
1 small jalapeño pepper
1 tsp. of Murphy's Oil Soap
1 tsp. of vegetable oil
1 qt. of warm water

Pulverize garlic, onion, and pepper in a blender, and steep in water for 2 hours. Strain mixture, and further dilute with 3 parts of warm water. Add Murphy's Oil Soap and vegetable oil. Mist-spray your plants with this elixir several times a week.

Flea Beetles

Likely Victims: Just about everything, but especially the tomato, cabbage, and beet families.

1/16–1/8"

The Crime Scene: Leaves so full of little holes that they look like screen doors.

Be on the Lookout For: Little brown to black guys about the size of a pinhead. They hop around like fleas, spreading disease as they bounce from plant to plant.

The Tonic to Reach For: Beetle Juice (page 350).

Leaf Miners

Likely Victims: Beets, lettuce, spinach, Swiss chard, and other leafy greens.

1/8"

The Crime Scene: Squiggly lines or blotches on leaves that are actually tunnels chewed by the maggots. Sometimes foliage also turns yellow.

Be on the Lookout For: Grayish white maggots. The adults are grayish yellow flies, about half the size of a common housefly.

The Tonic to Reach For: Rhubarb Bug Repellent Tonic (page 355).

Jerry's Most Unwanted List

Whiteflies
Likely Victims:
Cucumbers, potatoes, and tomatoes.

H
1/10"

The Crime Scene:
Weakened plants, often yellow and dry. Secretions like honeydew, often accompanied by fungus growths.

Be on the Lookout For:
Pinhead-sized flies with mothlike, snowy white wings. You'll usually find groups camped on the undersides of leaves or on soft, tender growth.

The Tonic to Reach For:
Whitefly Wipeout Tonic.

WHITEFLY WIPEOUT TONIC
Whiteflies will lay their eggs on just about any kind of leaf in your veggie patch — but not if you beat them to it by giving your plants a good spritz of this Tonic.

1 cup of sour milk (let it stand
   out for 2 days)
2 tbsp. of flour
1 qt. of warm water

Mix these ingredients in a bowl, pour into a mist sprayer, and lightly spray your veggie plants. Your whitefly worries will be a thing of the past!

The Specialists

Some archvillains are particular about their victims: This trio pretty much confine their lives of crime to certain plants or plant families.

Asparagus beetles. They start chowing down on asparagus as soon as the spears appear in spring. (These guys have good taste.) They lay eggs on the spear, and when the larvae hatch, everyone has a banquet. Be on the lookout for beetles about the size of ladybugs that are decked out in shells of blue, brown, black, or russet.

Cabbage worms. Unlike cabbage loopers, these creepy-crawlies restrict their diet to members of the cabbage family. They like to hang out in cabbage and broccoli heads, and they chew the dickens out of any leaf that they come across. The picture on the wanted poster shows a pale green, velvety-haired caterpillar, about an inch long, with yellow stripes down his back. The adult version is a white moth with black wing tips and black spots (males have one on each wing; females have two).

WILD MUSTARD TEA

No cabbage moth worth her spots will lay her eggs in your garden if you spray your plants with my Wild Mustard Tea. It works like a charm on loopers and potato beetles, too!

4 whole cloves
1 handful of wild mustard leaves
1 clove of garlic

Steep these ingredients in 1 cup of boiling water. Let it cool, and then spray away!

Mexican bean beetles. These bad guys are easy to mistake for one of the very best good guys: ladybugs. They start out yellow, with no spots, but mature to a shade of lady-bug-lookalike copper with black spots. Though their true calling in life is chomping on bean leaves, they sometimes moonlight by attacking cabbage, collards, kale, and mustard greens. You'll know they've been at work when you see veiny skeletons where leaves used to be.

Before you send a Mexican bean beetle to his just reward, take a good, close look. If you see little white markings on his head, this is no bad bean bozo you're looking at: It's his good cousin the ladybug.

Mite-y Good, or Mite-y Bad

These critters are so small you can hardly see them, even with a magnifying glass. But they can cause whale-sized damage. And with them, there's damage, and then there's *damage*. The bad mites (usually spider mites) gobble up just about every plant in your garden. The good mites gobble up the bad mites (and also thrips).

I never even bother trying to see the mites. It's too frustrating. Instead, I just get out my magnifying glass and hunt for webs made of stuff that looks like angel hair clinging to leaves and stems. On your plants, the bad mites' damage will show up as pale or wilted leaves or as foliage covered with yellowish specks.

SUPER SPIDER MITE MIX

Spider mites are tiny fellas, alright, but they get up to mite-y BIG mischief in your garden! When they show up, send 'em packin' with this potent brew.

4 cups of wheat flour
½ cup of buttermilk
5 gal. of water

Mix all of the ingredients together, and mist-spray your plants to the point of run-off. This magnificent mix will suffocate the little buggers without harming your veggies.

The Good Guys: Superbugs to the Rescue

Here are five of the best reasons I know to plant some flowers among your veggies, or at least along the garden fence. When these tough guys spot those blossoms and smell all of that yummy nectar, they'll zero in on your yard, and end up hanging around to polish off your pests besides.

HERO BUGS	LAY OUT THE WELCOME MAT FOR	ENTICE THEM BY PLANTING	WATCH THEM POLISH OFF
Green lacewings, a.k.a. aphid lions	Slender green insects with pale, delicate wings (the grown-ups), or fierce-looking, yellow-brown bugs with tufts of hair coming out of the sides (the youngsters)	Angelica, the carrot family, coreopsis, goldenrod, mint, Queen Anne's lace, red cosmos, tansy	Aphids by the truck-load, caterpillar eggs, leafhopper nymphs, mealybugs, scale, spider mites, thrips, whiteflies
Hover flies, a.k.a. syrphid flies	Buzzing, beelike bugs with black and yellow stripes (but no sting). The youngsters are pale green maggots.	Baby-blue-eyes, coreopsis, cosmos, dwarf morning glory, gloriosa daisies, marigolds, spearmint	Aphids, leafhoppers, mealybugs, thrips, any other small, soft-bodied insects
Ladybugs	Tiny red Volkswagens with black spots and legs. The larvae look like miniature alligators with orange spots.	Angelica, butterfly weed, goldenrod, morning glory, yarrow	Aphids, asparagus beetles, bean thrips, chinch bugs, Colorado potato beetle larvae, mites
Parasitic wasps	Wicked-looking (but nonstinging) wasps with long things that look like stingers coming out of their heads, or (in the prehatching stage) silk-like cocoons attached to bad bugs like tomato hornworms	Clover, daisies, dill, parsley, Queen Anne's lace, and almost any small, single-flowered herb or wildflower (these guys are big-time nectar hounds)	Aphids, cabbage worms, tomato hornworms, any other soft-bodied caterpillars
Robber flies	Ugly, hairy-faced, loud-buzzing gray flies that swoop and dive	Any flowering plant	Beetles, grasshoppers, leafhoppers, moths, and, now and then, a fellow beneficial (oops!)

Hired Guns

Lots of hero bugs are so good at what they do that garden centers and catalogs actually sell them — usually under the heading of "beneficial insects" or just plain "beneficials." Because these two are not so easy to bribe with flowers, I buy some when I need to round up a big posse.

Parasitic nematodes. Besides going after bad-guy nematodes, these wormy fellas polish off cutworms, grubs, onion maggots, and wireworms.

Predatory mites. These tykes are big-time enemies of spider mites and thrips. Some are hardy and will stay on in any garden year-round; others survive winters only in the South. Garden centers usually sell a mixture of types, so you're almost guaranteed protection from one year to the next.

No, Thanks, I'll Pass

Two beneficials almost every garden center sells are ladybugs and praying mantises. I never bother buying them. Here's why:

Ladybugs. The ones you usually find for sale are collected when they're hibernating. When ladybugs come out of hibernation, their standard operating procedure is to fly off to some other territory. And that's what they'll do when they wake up in your garden. Besides, all you have to do to draw ladybugs in droves is plant a few flowers they hanker for (see the chart on the opposite page) and not spray with pesticides (which will kill them right along with the bad bugs).

Praying mantises. These critters are fun for kids to watch, but as garden predators, they're practically useless. In the first place, as big as they are, they don't eat much. What's even worse, when they do decide to eat, they'll go after anything that moves. They're as likely to gobble up a honeybee, a lacewing, or even a ladybug as they are a bean beetle!

Help from the Tuffet

Whatever you might say about Little Miss Muffet, you know sure as shootin' that she was no gardener. If she had been, instead of running away from that spider, she'd have escorted him right over to her vegetable patch.

Squeamish as they make some folks feel, a few spiders are handy fellas to have around the garden. They polish off insects by the thousands, and only two kinds — the black widow and the brown recluse — are harmful to humans. If you live in a warm climate, you have a slight chance of encountering one of these, though probably not in your garden. Make sure you can identify a black widow and a brown recluse on sight; then, if that spider in your garden is any other kind, just say "Howdy" and let him (or her) get on with his work.

Giving the Good Guys a Chance

Grandma Putt used to say that if it weren't for all the critters helping her in the garden, that patch of ground wouldn't be worth a plugged nickel. She was right, too. And it wasn't just the bug-eat-bug world she was talking about. If you'll just invite them in, there's a whole army of animals that will keep the pest population down, pollinate flowers so they can turn into vegetables, and make for some pretty interesting wildlife-watching besides. Around my garden, the welcome mat's always out.

Hospitality 101

It's not hard to get aid from the animal kingdom. Here are some of the ways I attract beneficial bugs and other helpful critters to my garden:

• **Lay off pesticides.** I know that's a scary thought if you've been using them for a long time, but you can bet your bottom spray gun that a couple of weeks after you quit cold turkey, all kinds of good guys will show up and start munching on the bad guys. (Trust me. I've done it.)

• **Go with the flow.** The anything-goes cottage gardens that Grandma Putt grew are all the rage now, and that's good news for your vegetables. When you plant flowers, herbs, trees, and shrubs among your edibles, all kinds of great helpers will come calling.

• **Intercrop.** Mix up your plants so that the ones your allies like cozy up next to the ones that need their protection.

• **Let 'em bolt.** Instead of harvesting all your veggies, let a few plants take off and blossom. If you give them a chance, broccoli, Chinese cabbage, mustard, parsley, and radishes will all churn out flowers that good-guy bugs will zero in on.

• **Give them a drink.** All living things need good old H_2O. I sink old plant saucers into the ground, fill them with round pebbles, pour in water, and let some of the rocks stick up above the surface. It gives insects — and insect-eaters like toads, frogs, birds, and bats — a bar to belly up to.

• **Give them shelter.** All living things need a place to call home. I make sure I have shrub borders, flower beds, hedgerows, and even a few clumps of weeds where my allies can set up housekeeping — and where they can camp out when I'm tilling and disrupting life as they know it.

• **Don't panic.** Or, as Grandma Putt always said, "Live and let live." You won't have good guys unless they have some bad guys around to munch on. So don't reach for your spray gun (or even your baking-soda box) at the first sign of a slug or a cutworm. Instead, just think of the little creep as lunch for your heroes. And relax: Even if you lose a tomato or an ear of corn here and there, you'll still wind up with a harvest that keeps you in homegrown veggies until the next fresh-pickin' time rolls around.

Jerry Baker Says

"Even good bugs can sink their chops into you now and then. When I'm working in my garden and get stung by a bee or bitten by God knows what, I whip up a paste of baking soda and rubbing alcohol and slap it on. It takes away the pain and itch faster than you can say 'Get out, you rascal, you!'"

Help on the Wing

If you can get some songbirds to share your turf, you'll have one of the best pest-control squads around. Oh, some birds can make a nuisance of themselves, especially at planting time. But most of them will eat so many bad guys during the growing season that they're worth their weight in gold. And besides eating bugs that eat your veggies, they'll polish off the ones that munch on you. Birds that hang around for the winter will also chow down on hibernating bugs and bug eggs.

Varmint or volunteer? It's easy to tell friend from foe: If a bird has spindly legs and a short, thick, cone-shaped beak, he's a seedeater — and you want him to steer clear of your veggie patch, at least until your plants are well past the seedling stage. But if you see a bird with one of these two kinds of beaks, you've found a friend:

• **Thin and pointy.** A bird with this kind of beak eats insects, and plenty of them. Wrens, warblers, kingbirds, phoebes, and all manner of flycatchers fit this bill.

• **Short, wide, and gaping.** This kind of schnoz is made for grabbing food on the fly. Swifts, swallows, nighthawks, purple martins, and whip-poorwills all snatch pesky pests as they're streaking through the air.

What's in a Beak?

It tells you whether your fine-feathered one is friend or foe.

FRIENDS: Thin and pointy
Short, wide, and gaping

FOES: Short, thick, cone-shaped

UNDECIDED: Sturdy, midsize

Nobody's Perfect

Birds with sturdy, midsize beaks can work for you or against you. They eat so many bugs — and they're so much fun to watch and listen to — that they'll have a home in my garden forever. But, like all of us, they do have one bad habit (from a gardener's point of view, that is): When they're through polishing off bugs, they sometimes move on to seeds, fruits, or greens for dessert. Here's the policy I follow with this bunch:

• Lay out the welcome mat for ground birds like bobwhites and songbirds like robins, mockingbirds, bluebirds, cuckoos, towhees, and chickadees. (It was this crowd that one of Grandma Putt's favorite writers, Joseph Addison, was talking about way back in the 1700s when he said to "think of birdsong as a crop.")

• Discourage the more greedy rascals like crows, blackbirds, grackles, and cowbirds.

• Keep an eye on your crops and protect them when you need to, in ways that won't hurt the birds.

• Plant flowers, trees, and shrubs that have fruit the birds are crazy about, so they're less likely to munch on your seeds and veggies. Of course, you have to be willing to share the fruit harvest!

SUPER Growing Secrets

YOU'RE INVITED!

The best plants for drawing birds to your yard and then keeping them there are varieties of trees, shrubs, and flowers that are native to your neck of the woods. Your closest Cooperative Extension Service or native plant society can clue you in on what they are. To find out what kinds of birds will most likely come calling, contact the Audubon Society (www.audubon.com) or The Nature Conservancy (www.TNC.org).

A Jewel of a Pest Controller

Hummingbirds are famous as nectar drinkers, but they also eat plenty of bugs. These colorful little guys like to perch on the branches of trees and shrubs by the side of your garden, so they can swoop in for the kill. The best way to let them know that you've got a bird room for rent is to plant bright red flowers that are tubular or trumpet-shaped. Once they've set up residence, they'll go for other colors, too, but it's red that draws them initially. Some of their favorite flowers (and mine, too) are daylilies, coralbells, snapdragons, lilies, and trumpet vine.

Home, Sweet Home

I've seen plenty of birdhouses that are so fancy, I wouldn't mind shrinking down and moving into them myself. But most birds are pleased as punch with a nice, simple box to call home. I build mine out of scrap lumber and put a slanted roof on top. Then I drill a hole in front for a door and screw on a dowel for an entrance perch. The dimensions depend on what kind of birds you're trying to attract, but here are some general tips:

• Put a perch inside the house, just below the entrance hole. It'll make life easier for the baby birds when they're ready to test their wings the first couple of times.

• Make one section of the house removable so you can clean up after everybody moves out. But make it so only you can remove it — not squirrels, owls, or the neighbor's cat. I use a simple hook-and-eye fastener.

• Drill an entrance hole that's big enough for the invited birds to get through, but small enough to keep everybody else out.

• Put a piece of sheet metal on the front, with a hole cut out that's exactly the size of the entrance hole. That way, squirrels won't gnaw the hole bigger, squeeze in, boot out the birds, and set up housekeeping.

• Hang the house where cats and other bird- or egg-eaters can't get to it. It should be at least 6 feet off of the ground and well out of leaping range from fences and walls.

• Attach an anti-climbing collar to the support post or tree trunk. I like to make a cone out of aluminum sheet metal and fasten it on, wide end downward, a foot or so below the house.

Oh, Give Me a Home

Plant some of these trees, shrubs, and flowers, then stand back and watch the hungry birds beat a path to your doorstep.

FOR SEEDS	FOR FRUITS	FOR FLOWERS	FOR SHELTER	
Cosmos	Blackberries	Bee balm	Abelia	Holly
Elm	Cherries	Butterfly bush	Bayberry	Honeysuckle
Marigolds	Firethorn	Fuchsia	Birch	Mulberry
Ornamental grasses	Gooseberries	Honeysuckle	Blueberry	Oak
Sunflowers	Grapes	Impatiens	Cedar	Privet
Thistle	Peaches	Nicotiana	Elderberry	Trumpet vine
Zinnias	Plums	Penstemon	English ivy	Viburnum
	Roses	Phlox	Grapes	Virginia creeper

Don't You *Dare* Eat My Employees!

The best way to keep your garden-worker birds safe and happy on the job is to keep your cat inside. I love cats (especially my own), but they're the worst enemies a songbird could ask for, and there's no way to reason with them. If your neighbor's cats are on the prowl and gunning for the birds in your yard, secure chicken wire on the ground under the nesting areas. Ornery felines will keep their distance.

Batting 1000

Like most folks, I used to turn purple at the thought of having a bat anywhere near my house. Then I learned that, though they're not the cutest critters on the face of the earth, they are one of the most valuable. They avoid humans like the plague, but they're murder on wings to the bad-bug brigade, including the ones that spread nasty human diseases. Every night, an adult bat puts away between 150 and 600 pests an hour. And its prime targets are mosquitoes and the flying (and egg-laying) adult forms of cabbage worms, cut-worms, many kinds of beetles, and corn earworms.

In Grandma Putt's day, we didn't have to do anything to get bats into our garden. They just stopped by on their nightly rounds. At daybreak, they went back home to their caves or big, dense trees to hang out. Nowadays, where I live, there aren't nearly as many caves and big trees around as there were back then, so I hang up bat houses around my place. You can buy them at a lot of garden centers, but I build mine with plans I ordered from Bat Conservation International (www.batcon.org).

Garlic Pest Repellent

BUG BUSTERS!

Garlic is not only a great insect repellent, but it's also an amazing antibiotic for sickly plants. Mince several large cloves, and soak them overnight in mineral oil. The next day, strain the mixture, and then mix 2 teaspoons of the oil and 2 teaspoons of liquid dish soap in 1 pint of warm water. Put this in your 20 gallon hose-end sprayer, and fill the balance of the jar with warm water. Spray every 2 weeks in the evening to keep your garden in the pink!

A Prince of a Predator

Grandma Putt used to say that if a toad in her garden turned himself into a handsome prince, she'd just ask him to very kindly turn back to a toad again.

Toads are the most useful bug zappers any gardener could hope to find. The folks who study these things say that a single toad will pack away about 15,000 bad-guy bugs in a single year and — for reasons I don't understand and they probably don't, either — almost none of the good guys. Toads eat sowbugs, armyworms, gypsy moth larvae, all kinds of beetles, and even mosquitoes. But they go hog-wild over slugs and cutworms.

Easy to please. For such hotshot bigwigs, toads are pretty easygoing when it comes to living quarters. All they ask for is a place to escape the sun and hide from noisy contraptions like lawnmowers and loud radios, and from predators like snakes, skunks, big birds, and family pets.

They're not particular; any spot that's moist, cool, and shady, with some decent ventilation, suits them just fine.

I like to turn my old clay flowerpots into toad abodes. I just break a gap out of the rim to make a door, and then set the pot upside down on top of some loosened soil in a quiet part of the garden. And, of course, I make sure there's some water nearby, like a big birdbath sunk into the ground. Toads don't drink through their mouths; they absorb water through their skin, so they need a place that's deep enough to jump into. (This could be the excuse you've been waiting for to build a garden pond!)

Adopt a princeling. Grown-up toads are a lot more likely to stay around if you attract them with choice room and board rather than kidnap them from another territory. If you don't want to bide your time waiting for your prince to come, your best bet is to find a pond or ditch with tadpoles in it, scoop up a few, take them home, and give them a nice, watery place like a shallow pan or a little pool to grow up in. Before you know it, they'll make your slugs' worst nightmares come true.

Jerry Baker Says

"Don't use wood ashes anywhere when you have a toad on garden duty: They're highly toxic to the little guys."

Now What Do We Do?

Grandma Putt used to say that she didn't think of garden pests as villains: On the contrary, she thought of them and their shenanigans as a chance to give her creative brainpower a good workout. And I tell you, she had some brainpower!

A Word to the Wise from Grandma Putt

Say It with Flowers

Plenty of flowers and herbs give off chemicals that pesky pests can't stand. Here are some nice-looking and (to us humans) nice-smelling ways to keep the bad guys where they belong: elsewhere.

PLANT	TO SAY "SCRAM" TO	PLANT	TO SAY "SCRAM" TO
Basil	Flies and mosquitoes	Rue	Japanese beetles
Borage	Tomato worms	Sage	Cabbage moths, carrot flies
Daffodils & hyacinths	Mice, rats		
Dead nettle	Potato bugs	Summer savory	Bean beetles
Flax	Potato bugs	Tansy	Ants, flying insects, Japanese beetles, squash bugs, striped cucumber beetle
Garlic & onions	Groundhogs		
Hyssop	Cabbage moths		
Mint	Ants, white cabbage moths		
		Thyme	Cabbage worms
Nasturtiums	Aphids, squash bugs, striped pumpkin beetles	Wormwood	Black flea beetles, carrot flies, white cabbage butterflies
Petunias	Beetles		
Rosemary	Bean beetles, cabbage moths, carrot flies		

The Fab Five

When your garden is drawing irksome bugs of every kind, plant any of this quintet. They'll lay out the unwelcome mat in a hurry.

1. Asters
2. Calendulas
3. Chrysanthemums
4. Geraniums
5. Marigolds

Not Just Another Pretty Face

You might have a great vegetable companion growing in your yard already: yarrow (a.k.a. achillea). Grandma Putt used to plant it among her vegetables and herbs, because it repelled insects, intensified all of those good-smelling oils in her herbs, and made all the plants near it grow stronger and sturdier.

As if that talent isn't enough to give it star quality, yarrow is a beautiful, low-maintenance perennial flower.

RHUBARB BUG REPELLENT TONIC

Here's a potent plant Tonic that will say "Scram!" to just about any kind of bug.

3 medium-sized rhubarb leaves
¼ cup of liquid dish soap
1 gal. of water

Chop up the rhubarb leaves, put the pieces in the water, and bring it to a boil. Let the mixture cool, and strain it through cheesecloth to filter out the leaf bits. Then mix in the dish soap. Apply this terrific Tonic to your plants with a small hand sprayer and kiss your bug problems goodbye. This Tonic also helps reduce blight on tomatoes.

It's an Ambush!

Long before Grandma Putt's day, folks discovered that when you plant certain flowers, herbs, or veggies, certain pesky pests will flock to them — and not bother with the plants that you cotton to. Of course, while the rascals are busy polishing off their favorite chow, they're sitting ducks for you and your bucket of soapy water, your spritzer bottle full of Knock-'em-Dead Insect Spray (see page 120), or the toad who's just come to live with you.

Does it or doesn't it? Really work, that is. Some folks claim that these trap or lure crops don't live up to their billing as crop saviors. I don't recommend relying on them as your only method of pest control; but they can be useful, especially if you've just gone cold turkey on pesticides and you're waiting for the good guys to move back in. Just be sure to get the pests off the lure crop as soon as they show up. Otherwise, they'll polish off the trap and move on to whatever else they can find. In most cases, you'll want to dig up the trap plants and destroy them, too. (That's why they're also known as sacrificial plants.)

Here's a list of tried-and-true traps that have worked well in my garden:

TRAP	VICTIMS
Catnip	Whiteflies
Dill	Tomato hornworms
Mustard	Harlequin bugs
Nasturtiums	Aphids
Radishes	Cabbageworms, cucumber beetles, flea beetles, leaf miners, squash bugs
Sunflowers	Cutworms, European corn borers

Jerry Baker Says

"Whatever you do, don't plant one trap crop close to another one that attracts the same kind of pests — you'll wind up drawing creepy-crawlies from miles around!"

Serendipity

The best sacrificial crops usually turn out to be the ones you hadn't intended to sacrifice. Sometimes I'll walk into my garden and spot a plant — or a lot of plants of the same variety — smothered with pesky pests. When that happens, I throw a sheet over the whole thing, pull it up, and get it out of there fast, bugs and all. Then I scratch that veggie variety from my good-for-eating list and give it a new job luring pests into hot water. (See Chapter 7 for potential vegetable saviors.)

KNOCK-'EM-DEAD INSECT SPRAY

When the bad-guy bugs are coming in too fast for the good guys to polish 'em all off, let 'em have it with a dose of my Knock-'em-Dead Insect Spray.

6 cloves of garlic, chopped fine
1 small onion, chopped fine
1 tbsp. of cayenne pepper
1 tbsp. of liquid dish soap

Mix all of these ingredients in 1 quart of warm water and let it sit overnight. Strain out the solid matter, pour into a spray bottle, and let 'er rip!

The Vilest Villains

UNWANTED

Some veggie-gulping villains confine their lives of crime to specific kinds of plants or certain parts of the country. But for others, anyplace they hang their hat is home, and anything with roots is fair game. At least it seems that way. Here's a rundown of some of the vilest varmints around, and some tips on keeping them off of your turf.

Slimy Slugs

These ugly guys slither their way into just about every garden in the country. But don't let 'em get you down — you're bigger and smarter than they are. Try some of these remedies.

Repel them

Sometimes the easiest method is to make your garden a "bad neighborhood" for slugs. Here's how to do it:

• **Keep it clean.** Slugs like to hide in dead leaves and decaying vegetation, so keep your garden beds tidy, especially around their favorite targets. The one exception to the no-leaves policy is oak: Slugs can't stand the bitter taste.

• **Be careful what you compost.** Especially if you live in cool, damp territory, don't add anything to the pile unless you're sure that it's slug-free.

• **Grow repellent plants near slugs' favorites.** For instance, slugs hate wormwood and prostrate rosemary.

• **Surround their target plants.**
Try any of these materials, and the slug population'll head for a friendlier neighborhood:

Fennel, fresh-cut into 2- to 3-inch pieces
Ginger, powdered
Hair (human, horse, dog, whatever: slugs hate it all)
Limestone, crushed
Oak leaves, shredded
Seaweed
Window screen in 6-inch squares (with an opening in the center of each piece, of course, for the stem)
Wood ashes

Fence 'em out

It's easy to keep slugs out of beds by surrounding the areas with mini fences. Thin copper sheeting works best. It gives the rascals a jolt of electricity when they try to squirm over the top. Just make sure that you get every last slug *out* of the bed before you put up the barrier. Otherwise, they'll have a field day inside the ballpark!

Execute them

Any of these terrific tactics will send the creeps to their just reward:

• **Send out the hit squad.** Toads, turtles, and garter snakes consider slugs to be gourmet chow. So do ducks and geese, but they might trample your plants in the process of rounding up dinner.

• **Catch 'em at night.** That's when they do their dirty work. Blast 'em with a half-and-half spray of vinegar and

SUPER SLUG SPRAY

For slugs that are too small to handpick or be lured into traps, try this super spray.

1½ cups of ammonia
1 tbsp. of Murphy's Oil Soap
1½ cups of water

Mix all of the ingredients in a handheld mist-sprayer bottle, and overspray any areas where you see signs of slug activity.

water. Don't make it any stronger than that or it'll burn your plants.

• **Make traps** out of oranges or grapefruits: Cut them in half and scoop out the insides. In the evening, turn them upside down in the garden. In the morn-ing, they'll be full of slugs. Pick them up and drop them into a bag of salt.

Lure 'em in

The classic, old-time method of slug control is to sink empty cat food or tuna cans into the ground, fill 'em with beer, and wait for the varmints to belly up, fall in, and die happy. It works, but why waste good beer on your enemies? Scientists have found that it's the yeast that attracts the varmints, not the idea of a good time at the local saloon. So mix up a batch of Slugweiser and serve it to the slugs (see page 122). Save the good stuff in the fridge for a victory toast.

Plant what they don't like

Believe it or not, there are some veggies and herbs that slugs won't bother. If they had noses, they'd turn them up at:

Beans   Rhubarb
Chard   Sage
Corn   White
Parsley   winter
Pumpkins   radishes

SLUGWEISER

To drown your slug sorrows, try this Tonic.

1 lb. of brown sugar
½ pkg. (1½ tsp.) of dry yeast

Pour these ingredients into a 1-gallon plastic jug, fill it with warm water, and let it sit for 2 days, uncovered. Then pour it into slug traps, and let the good times roll!

Classic Slug Brews

Try each of these menu offerings to see which attracts the most sluggish customers to your traps.

- Beer and/or grape juice
- A 50-50 mix of sugar and cider vinegar
- A mixture of fermented fruit peelings, water, ½ package of dry yeast, and ½ can of beer (regular or lite)

Calculating Cutworms

For such a peaceable lady, Grandma Putt could get really riled up about cutworms. No way was she going to let those slimy good-for-nothings wipe out her baby seedlings! Her favorite way to get at 'em was to plow up the garden plot early in the spring, then turn her pet pig, Henrietta, loose. When Henrietta got through, there wasn't a cutworm left in the county.

If you don't know a pig to invite to lunch, you could have some birds over instead. Till your soil so the cutworms are close to the surface. Then get out your binoculars and your Audubon field guide and watch who shows up. Within a few days, robins, meadowlarks, blue jays, and blackbirds should have that plot of yours picked clean as a whistle.

Run 'em Off

To keep cutworms from moving in next year, plant onions, garlic, or tansy among their favorite targets.

Curses on You, Cutworms!

Cutworms are the worst enemy a bed of seedlings ever had. Here's how to protect your baby plants:

Collar 'em

The best way to head the varmints off at the pass is to put a collar around each seedling. I sink mine 2 inches into the ground, with about 3 inches showing above. Any of these materials will give first-rate protection:

- Aluminum foil
- Corrugated drain tile
- Linoleum
- Mailing tubes
- Paper or plastic cups with the bottoms cut out
- Rolls from wrapping paper, toilet paper, or paper towels
- Plastic wrap
- Tin cans with both ends removed

Go for the soft underbelly

Cutworms don't like to slink across stuff that prickles their skin. So once my plants have outgrown their collars, I sprinkle the soil around them with one of these rib-ticklers:

- Chicken manure
- Eggshells
- Hair
- Kitty litter
- Oak leaves
- Wood ashes

Plan an attack

Once plants are past the seedling stage, cutworms rarely cause fatal damage, but they'll still make a nuisance of themselves. They'll also turn into moths and lay next year's supply of eggs. That's why I keep up my patrols all through the growing season.

Set out traps in the evening. Come morning, scoop up traps, cutworms and all. Then squash the creeps, burn them, or dump them into hot, soapy water. The traps that work best for me are:

- Boards
- Cabbage leaves
- Grapefruit halves
- Potatoes

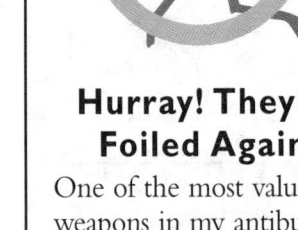

Hurray! They're Foiled Again!

One of the most valuable weapons in my antibug arsenal is good old aluminum foil. Here's a trio of terrific uses for the shiny stuff in the garden:

1. Use it as mulch around squash, cucumbers, and corn. The foil will reflect the sun's light upward and drive a lot of bugs batty, including aphids and squash bugs!

2. Loosely wrap a 4-inch square of foil around the stems of your tomato, pepper, and eggplant seedlings. Cutworms and other chewing marauders will chaw elsewhere.

3. Cut cardboard into stars, circles, triangles, and other shapes. Wrap each one in foil, and hang them in and around your garden. The flashing light will make flying felons flee — fast!

Not-So-Fine Feathered Friends

Grandma Putt used to say that birds were just about the smartest critters she'd ever come across. That's why it's so much fun to watch them when they're making nests or flitting around, getting food for their young'uns.

It's also why you can drive yourself crazy trying to keep the hungry little devils from snatching a harvest out from under your very nose.

Say "Bye-bye, Birdies"

I have to admit that it hasn't been easy, but I've come up with a few scare tactics that actually do send the wily wingers on their way (most of the time). Here's my basic, four-part strategy:

Part 1. Make it colorful. Birds see in color, just as we do. Bright colors stand out better and look scarier than earthy tones, which blend in with the scenery. Small, colorful flags are a good bet, as are pinwheels — your local garden store should have a festive array to choose from.

Part 2. Make it noisy. Birds usually steer clear of sounds they're not used to. But don't put on loud music or tapes of booming cannons that'll rile up your neighbors and set you on edge! As long as the birds can hear it when they get close, it'll make them turn around and head elsewhere. Bells, wind chimes, ice-cream sticks tied together — whatever makes a little noise when a breeze comes up — will throw them off-kilter.

Part 3. Make it look dangerous. Birds are coming to your garden to *have*

dinner, not to *be* dinner. If they look down and see the enemy, they'll hightail it out of there. Pick up a couple of realistic statues of cats, owls, foxes, and dogs, and place them in your garden.

Part 4. Keep it moving. Because they are so smart, birds catch on in a hurry. You can build a scarecrow with rubber snakes coming out of his head and put a tape player in his pocket that blares cat meows, but if he just stands in the same spot, day after day, it won't take the birds long to figure out that they can eat every seed in your corn patch, and this funny-looking guy won't lift a finger to stop them.

Jerry Baker Says

"Birds do most of their damage in the morning, so whatever scare devices you rig up, move them around in the evening. That way, when the birds show up for breakfast, they'll have a surprise in store."

The Mad Hatter

The best scarecrow Grandma Putt and I ever had was a dress-store dummy we bought for a couple of dollars at a going-out-of-business sale. We took her home, named her Mabel, and decked her out in an old, bright red dress of Grandma Putt's. We tied a long, lightweight, yellow-and-purple scarf around her neck so that it was always blowing every which way. Then we made her a hat. We found an old straw sombrero in the attic, looped shiny ribbons through the openings in the straw, and tied little bells on the ends. Every time a breeze came up, those bells would jingle and flash. The birds didn't like that one little bit.

But what really kept them out of our garden was the fact that they never knew what Mabel was going to do next. Birds generally pay a visit early in the morning, so every evening when the crops were coming up, I'd go out and move her to a new spot and bend her into a different position. Now and then, we'd put a sweater or a new scarf on her, so she'd look different. And every so often, we'd change her hat. In fact, making crazy hats for Mabel got to be one of our favorite wintertime hobbies. All year long, we'd keep our eyes out for old hats, shiny trinkets, little mirrors, odd bits of yarn and ribbon, and even toy snakes and lizards. We'd stash them in a box in the hall closet. Then, once in a while, on a cold winter night, Grandma Putt would say, "Well, Junie, how 'bout this evening we try to think like a bird?" We'd pop a big bowl of popcorn, haul that box out of the closet, and set about making the scariest topper we could come up with.

Methods to Your Madness

Here's a trio of other ways to send the fiends flying:

1. **Create an arsenal.** The only guaranteed way to protect your crops from hungry birds is to cover them with nets or floating row covers. But setting out or stringing up any of the things on this list, in or on the edge of your garden, will at least keep the damage to a manageable level. Just remember to use a combination of objects, not just one, and change them every so often, so the birds don't get to thinking of them as just another part of the greenery scenery.

Aluminum pie and cake tins	Small mirrors	Whirligigs
Gas-filled Mylar balloons	Strips of Mylar	Wind socks

2. Make a snake in the grass. Birds are as scared of snakes as a lot of people are, and for better reason: There's nothing most snakes like better than a plump, juicy bird. If you don't have a lot of real snakes in your garden (and are just as glad that you don't!), a rubber stand-in works as well as the real thing, and (for my money, at least) it's more pleasant to have around.

I make my menacing pretenders by cutting old black or green hoses into 4- or 5-foot lengths. Then I wrap strips of red or yellow tape around the hose every few inches to look like stripes. If you really want to be authentic, check out a book on snakes that are native to your area and use paint or tape to make that piece of hose look *just* like your local serpent type. Get the kids to help you, and turn it into a biology lesson.

3. Good vibrations. For up-close protection when I don't want to use row covers, I push stakes into the ground at either end of a planting bed and string old audiocassette tape between them, about 1 foot off the ground. I stretch it good and tight, so that it hums as it vibrates in the wind. Birds keep their distance.

When the Big Guys Come Around

Back when Grandma Putt and I were tending our garden, we had visits now and then from rabbits and skunks and such, but we didn't have nearly the problems with wildlife that folks have today. In those days, critters had plenty of places to call their own, and, especially during the summer growing season, they could get pretty much all of the food they needed without venturing into human territory.

Nowadays, though, in most parts of the country, there's not a lot of roaming room left, and wherever you live, it's all but guaranteed that some hungry visitors are going to show up and start munching their way through your garden.

Advance Planning

The time to keep wildlife out of your garden starts long before any footprints show up in the vegetable patch. In fact, it's way back when you do the rest of your garden planning. Here's the beginning strategy I recommend:

• **Identify the enemy.** Talk to your neighbors and find out what kinds of critters they've had trouble with, what they've done about it, and how well it's worked for them.

- **Know the enemy.** Once you've found out what animals are roaming the neighborhood, whether they're groundhogs, raccoons, possums, deer, or the dogs and cats who live down the street, do some homework. Learn all you can about their eating habits and general behavior patterns.

- **Build a fence.** The size and type will depend on what critters you need to keep out, but in almost every case, a good, solid barrier is your only guaranteed defense.

- **Plant smart.** Most animals are just like us: Some foods they'd crawl through 60 miles of burning sand to get to, some they'll munch on if there's nothing else close by, and some they won't touch unless they're all but starving to death. You probably can't avoid planting some of your enemies' favorite chow; it's undoubtedly the stuff you like, too. But you can surround their top choices with things that are farther down on their list. (See the individual plant portraits in Chapter 7 for menu listings.)

- **Plant a lure crop.** Critters that turn up their noses at some kinds of plants usually go gaga over others. Give your four-footed friends a plot of their favorite chow, well removed from the rest of the garden, and chances are they'll stay out of your prized plantings.

Turn 'em Off

Just like bugs and other creepy-crawlies, some of our four-legged friends find certain plants revolting. Here are a few big-time critter enemies from the plant kingdom:

To Chase	Plant
Cats	Rue
Gophers	Daffodils, squill
Rabbits	Mexican marigolds, dusty miller, garlic, onions

The Smaller Bunch: Gophers, Rabbits, Groundhogs, Squirrels, Rats, Mice, and Voles

I don't know any gardener anywhere who hasn't had at least a few members of this crowd charge in and belly up to the salad bar. And because these guys are small, fast, agile, and a lot smarter than they look, keeping them out can be a real challenge. Here's a Baker's half dozen general-purpose critter deterrents:

- **Call out the archenemy.** Or at least make the pests think you've done that. Get some ferret droppings from a zoo, pet shop, or ferret-owning friend and sprinkle the stuff in and around the critters' holes. It'll make 'em scurry in a hurry!

- **Sound 'em out.** Gather up six or eight empty glass pop bottles and half-bury them, top ends up, in a line near the critters' hangouts. When the wind passes over, it'll make a scary sound that will send them packing.

- **Shine light in their eyes.** Fill 1-gallon glass bottles with water and set them among your plants. Sunlight bouncing off the glass startles the animals, especially rabbits, and makes them flee.

- **Make 'em smell danger.** Round up all of the old shoes you can find, and scatter them around your garden. Set out a new supply every few days, so the human odor is, shall we say, always fresh.

- **Give 'em the hair of the dog.** And the human. And the cat. Lay circles of it around your plants, and hang bags of it from fences, trellises, and branches. I've found that hairdressers and dog groomers are always happy to supply as much as you care to carry off.

- **Make up a big batch of Grandma Putt's All-Purpose Varmint Repellent.** Use it in and around your plants, near the critters' stomping grounds, and on your fences.

- **For a change of pace,** give them a snoutful of my All-Purpose Pest Prevention Potion.

ALL-PURPOSE VARMINT REPELLENT

No matter what kinds of crafty critters are helping themselves to your harvest, this'll make them keep their paws to themselves.

2 eggs
2 cloves of garlic
2 tbsp. of hot chile pepper
2 tbsp. of ammonia
2 cups of hot water

Mix these ingredients, let the mixture sit for 3 or 4 days, then paint it on fences, trellises, and wherever else unwanted varmints are venturing.

ALL-PURPOSE PEST PREVENTION POTION

There's no doubt about it: There are a lot of crafty veggie-gulpers just waiting to sink their sharp teeth into your harvest. But gophers, moles, skunks, possums, and just about any other critter I can think of will turn tail and run when they get a whiff of my All-Purpose Pest Prevention Potion.

1 cup of ammonia
½ cup of liquid dish soap
½ cup of urine
¼ cup of castor oil

Mix all of the ingredients in a 20 gallon hose-end sprayer and thoroughly saturate the area to be protected, including all animal runs and burrows.

The Bigger Fellas: Raccoons, Skunks, Deer, Dogs, and Cats

Keeping this crowd out of your garden can really put your gray cells to the test! In fact, I could write a whole book about big-critter deterrents alone! But here's a trio of basic tips for making sure the four-legged felons don't run off with your harvest.

• **Keep garbage in closed containers,** so the scent won't draw critters. If they're already on your doorstep, keep your containers indoors until collection day.

• **Never throw meat, fish, or fats on the compost pile** — you'll have scavengers crawling out of the woodwork!

• **Keep your yard and garden well sprayed** with Grandma Putt's All-Purpose Varmint Repellent and my All-Purpose Pest Prevention Potion.

Oh, Deer

It seems the only gardeners who don't have deer problems are the ones who grow their crops on the roofs of apartment buildings. And even *they* would have trouble if Santa and his reindeer showed up during the growing season instead of in the dead of winter.

When folks ask me how I keep these brown-eyed bruisers at bay, I tell them they're like every other kind of varmint, only more so: The only surefire way to protect your veggies is to build a good, solid fence. One that's at least 8 feet tall, with no gaps anywhere, and with a strand of electric wire running along the top for good measure, should work just fine. But so does the lower and much-less-expensive version on the next page.

DOG-B-GONE TONIC

Dogs may be man's best friends, but they sure as shootin' aren't the best buddies your garden ever had! Keep the rascals out by dousing your garden with this spicy Tonic.

2 cloves of garlic
2 small onions
1 jalapeño pepper
1 tbsp. of cayenne pepper
1 tbsp. of Tabasco Sauce
1 tbsp. of chile powder
1 tbsp. of liquid dish soap
1 qt. of warm water

Chop the garlic, onions, and pepper fine, and then combine with the rest of the ingredients. Let the mixture sit and "marinate" for 24 hours, strain it through cheesecloth or old pantyhose, then sprinkle it on any areas where dogs are a problem. If you're on the howl prowl, the hole diggers will soon go elsewhere!

The "Gotcha" Fence

This fence works by luring deer to it with the smell of peanut butter. When they reach out for a bite, they get a light but unwelcome zap on the nose or tongue. Try it — it really works!

1. Pound a 4-foot metal stake into the ground at each corner of your garden and about 10 feet apart along the sides and ends.

2. Attach an insulator to the top of each stake.

3. String a line of 50-pound-tension hot wire from post to post at the top.

4. Run the wire into an electrical source: A battery-charged generating unit will work just fine.

5. Spread peanut butter all along the wire.

6. Turn on the electric current.

7. Watch the deer come running when they get a whiff of that peanut butter. And take a good, long look, because you won't see them coming back anytime soon!

Not Now, Deer

If you don't have the time or the inclination to put up an electric fence, don't despair: Your garden isn't doomed. Just hang any of these repellents from your present fence, or scatter them among your plants:

• Bars of strong-smelling deodorant soap, like Irish Spring

• Cheesecloth or panty hose pouches filled with human or dog hair

• Cotton cloths sprinkled with baby powder or athlete's foot powder

• Old shoes, dirty laundry, smelly socks, or soiled diapers

Too good to be true? Believe it or not, there are plants that will send deer scooting off to greener pastures. Castor-oil plant is a guaranteed deer-chaser. But it's also highly poisonous to humans, so you need to use it with caution. These are much safer options:

• Catnip • Spearmint
• Garlic • Thyme
• Lavender • Yarrow
• Onions

With all these tips, tricks, and tonics at your fingertips, you're sure to produce a bumper harvest. In the next chapter, we'll see how you can sock away all that bounty so that you'll enjoy some mighty fine eatin' all winter long!

CHAPTER 6

Reaping — and Keeping — the Rewards

Like all gardeners, Grandma Putt got a real kick out
of helping her garden grow and thrive. But the real thrill
was the harvest. All summer long, we picked basketfuls
of vegetables, and ate 'em fresh from the garden.
Then, when we knew ol' Jack Frost was hightailin' it our
way, we'd gather up everything and store it for the winter.
And Grandma Putt had as many good ideas for what she
called "puttin' by" as she had for making our garden grow.

Bringing In the Bounty

Grandma Putt taught me that a great harvest starts way back in the winter, when you search out the best-tasting, best-looking, most nutrient-packed varieties you can find. But to get the most from those taste-temptin' vegetables, you need to pick them when they're at the very peak of flavor, nutrition, and good looks.

It's All in the Planning

Like every other part of gardening, a great harvest doesn't just happen: It takes planning. In winter, when the seed catalogs start showing up in the mailbox, I'm already looking forward to pulling my first young radishes. Here's what I look for to make sure I get the harvest I want, when I want it:

Weather preferences. Vegetables fall into two general categories: cool-weather crops and warm-weather crops. But even within types, some varieties of veggies can handle more heat or cold than others. By choosing carefully, I can stagger my plantings to get two or even three harvests a year.

Production period. Some varieties keep producing over a longer period of time than others. I plant some that I can pick as I want them almost all summer long — and some fast growers that work well for succession planting.

Harvest period. I look for varieties with patience — that is, ones that hold their quality on the vine for a few days or even a few weeks, so I don't have to knock myself out trying to keep the plants picked clean.

Taste. I always plant some varieties that taste best when you rush them right from the garden to the kitchen, and some that might not be the very best to eat fresh but hold their flavor well through the winter.

Best storage method. There are all kinds of ways to lay away vegetables, herbs, and garden fruits: freezing, drying, canning, belowground storing. I choose storage crops based on the method I want to use. For instance, if I've just built a new root cellar, I might plant an extra bed or two of potatoes, beets, and turnips. If there's plenty of space in the deep freezer, I grow lots of corn, broccoli, peas, and other crops that taste almost as good frozen as they do fresh picked.

The Hot and Cold of It

The first secret to getting as much good food as your garden can deliver is succession planting. This simply means that whenever you harvest a crop — usually one that matures when the weather is still cool in the spring — you plant another to take its place — typically one that likes to soak up the heat. If you're lucky, when that crop has finished producing, you might have time to plant another to harvest in fall or early winter. Here's the lineup:

COOL-SEASON CROPS		WARM-SEASON CROPS	
Beets	Lettuce	Asparagus	Okra
Broccoli	Parsnips	Beans	Onions
Brussels sprouts	Peas	Carrots	Peppers
Cabbage	Radishes	Celery	Potatoes
Cauliflower	Spinach	Chard	Pumpkins
Endive	Turnips	Corn	Rhubarb
Kale		Cucumbers	Squash
		Eggplant	Sweet potatoes
		Leeks	Tomatoes
		Melons	

How to Succeed at Succession

Planting was no onetime event at Grandma Putt's place. "Junie," she'd say, "never let a good plot go to waste." When one crop was through, we'd replace it with another. Here's my four-step succession planting process:

Step 1. Choose varieties that mature quickly or that taste good when they're immature (see Chapter 7 for some suggestions).

Step 2. Harvest veggies as soon as they're big enough to eat. Besides making room for another crop, you'll have these tasty treats at their young, tender best.

Step 3. As soon as you harvest a crop, replace it with another that will be able to mature in whatever time remains in your growing season.

Step 4. Don't replace a crop with the same vegetable or with a member of its family. Plant one from a different clan instead (see Planting in Triple Time on page 134).

The Second Coming

Of vegetables, that is. Before you plant your succession crops, work in a mix of 2 pounds of dry organic vegetable food and ½ pound of Epsom salts for every 10 square feet of garden soil. Then set your soil in motion with my Seed and Soil Energizer Tonic (see page 355).

Planting in Triple Time

In most parts of the country — with a little fancy footwork — you can get three harvests a year from the same spot. Here are some of my favorite threesomes. Plant and harvest one, then go right ahead and plant the next.

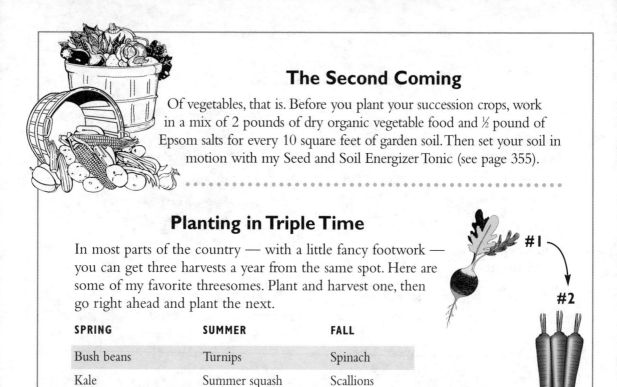

SPRING	SUMMER	FALL
Bush beans	Turnips	Spinach
Kale	Summer squash	Scallions
Mixed baby greens (a.k.a. mesclun)	Beets	Brussels sprouts
Radishes	Carrots	Leaf lettuce
Scallions	Bush beans	Beets

Time After Time

Jerry Baker Says

"Before you plant your next crop, soak your seeds in my Seed Starter Tonic (see page 355) and follow my Second Coming soil-prep routine above."

These are some of the veggies I keep planting as long as there's time left in my growing season.

VEGETABLE	WHEN I PLANT
Broccoli	Spring and late summer, 2 weeks apart
Bush beans	Summer, 2 weeks apart
Carrots	Spring and fall, 1 to 2 weeks apart
Corn	Late spring and early summer, 2 weeks apart
Peas	Spring and fall, 2 weeks apart
Radishes	Spring and fall, 1 week apart
Turnips	Spring and fall, 2 weeks apart

It's All in the Timing

Getting a good, long harvest doesn't have to mean replacing one kind of vegetable with something altogether different. When I want to give myself a big supply of a particular vegetable, I do it in one of two ways:

1. Plant varieties that mature at different times.

2. Space out planting times of the same variety.

Jerry Baker Says

"Generally, a plant yields up its biggest, best harvest during its first few weeks of production. After that, the veggies tend to be smaller and take longer to mature."

Pick Early and Often

Big commercial growers generally harvest their crops all at once and then send 'em off to market. But home gardeners can bring in the bounty all summer long. You need to keep a close eye on your plants and pick whatever is ripe, for a couple of reasons:

• **Flavor.** Most vegetables taste their best when they're young and tender.

• **Yield.** The way a plant looks at it, once it produces its offspring (in this case, seed-bearing vegetables), its job is done. If you leave overripe veggies on the vine, the plant will simply close up shop. But if you keep harvesting, the plant will keep producing.

Slowpokes and Fast Trackers

You all know the story of the tortoise and the hare. Well, veggies have the same built-in schedules. Some take more time to ripen than others. Here's what I do to make sure I catch everything at its peak.

Check these crops every day
• Broccoli
• Lettuce

Check these every other day
• Beans   • Okra
• Corn   • Strawberries
• Cucumbers • Summer squash

Check these every third day
• Beets   • Peas
• Carrots   • Peppers
• Eggplant   • Tomatoes
• Onions

Check these every so often
• Melons
• Pumpkins

One for All, and . . .

Some crops tend to peak all at once. You'll know these are ready for picking when the fruits have reached their mature size and color, the skin is so hard you can't scratch it with your fingernail, and the stems start to shrivel up. In most parts of the country, you'll catch them in time if you look in on them once a week. But if you live in a hot climate, or if the weather's hotter than normal where you live, check these guys every day.

- Gourds
- Melons
- Pumpkins
- Winter squash

It's in the Stars

In lots of ways, Grandma Putt was ahead of her time. These days, more and more scientists are telling us that the whole universe is just one giant living thing, and everything in it influences everything else, even if we can't see it at the time — which is exactly what Grandma Putt used to say. These were her guidelines for harvesting:

- **Harvest root crops intended for food** during the third or fourth quarter of the moon, and during one of the dry astrological signs (Aries, Leo, Sagittarius, Gemini, and Aquarius).

- **Harvest root crops intended for seed** (such as sweet potatoes and seed potatoes) during the full moon under any astrological sign.

- **Harvest grain** that will be stored or used for seed (like a cover crop) just after the full moon during a dry sign.

- **Harvest fruit crops** (like eggplant and tomatoes) during the waning moon in a dry sign.

SUPER Growing Secrets

FREE AND EASY

Nobody likes to be held hostage by a garden. So, if you're planning a summer vacation, pay special attention to the days-to-maturity numbers in your seed catalogs, and choose varieties that needn't be picked while you're gone. Then you won't have to worry.

Catch Me if You Can

No doubt about it: Catching everything just at its peak of flavor can be tricky. I've found that listing all my vegetables and herbs on a chart helps enormously. First, I write down the names of all of my crops and the date that I plant each one. Then I find the days-to-maturity number on the seed packet, and mark off the harvest period.

This method helps me choose varieties and time my plantings so that I'll have everything I want *when* I want it. Here's how the chart looks in the garden scrapbook I made last year:

VEGETABLE	DAYS TO MATURITY	APRIL	MAY	JUNE	JULY	AUGUST
'Bellstar' tomatoes	66–79	—	5/25	—	—	Harvest
'Gypsy' bell peppers	65–85	—	5/25	—	—	Harvest
'Costana Romanesco' zucchini	55	—	5/26	—	Harvest	Harvest
'Saffron' yellow summer squash	50	—	5/26	—	Harvest	Harvest
'Varna' leeks	85	—	5/26	—	—	Harvest

To Your Good Health

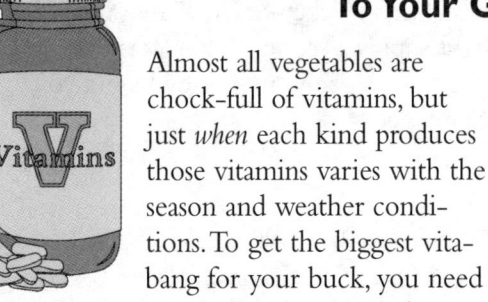

Almost all vegetables are chock-full of vitamins, but just *when* each kind produces those vitamins varies with the season and weather conditions. To get the biggest vita-bang for your buck, you need to know just when your crop is churning out its ABCs. (It's not necessarily the same time that flavor reaches its peak.) Here are some harvesttime guidelines:

• **Harvest fruit-producing veggies** like tomatoes, peppers, and eggplant as soon as they're mature.

• **Pull root crops** like carrots, parsnips, and turnips after they reach full size.

• **Gather potatoes** from large plants; they have more vitamins than those harvested from smaller plants.

• **Cut leaf crops** like lettuce and spinach when they're still growing.

• **To get maximum vitamin** production from cool-weather crops like broccoli and cauliflower, plant them in spring. They have a bigger supply of vitamins than do the same veggies started in fall.

What's the Weather?

When it's getting near harvesttime, it pays to keep a close eye on the weather, because it can cause all kinds of changes in your veggies. Here's what to watch for and why:

Moisture. Veggies like cabbages and tomatoes will swell up and burst if a heavy rainfall comes along or if you water them too much. On the other hand, root crops like beets and broccoli need plenty of water so they can grow fast and stay sweet and tender. Too little moisture can mean curtain time for them. Cukes are classic moderates: Weather that's either too dry or too wet will make them bitter.

Heat. Many vegetable plants simply stop growing when it gets too hot. They give up producing flowers and fruits, and they even cut back on photosynthesizing — a green plant's major pastime. The result is barren, bolting plants or tough, stringy, and bitter-tasting edibles.

Cold. Some veggies, like Brussels sprouts and parsnips, really come into their own after a few good frosts. Sugar — a natural antifreeze — fills up their cells, and as a result they become sweeter and more flavorful.

Cool. Lots of plants thrive in moderate temperatures, but warm-season crops like corn, tomatoes, and peppers need plenty of heat to ripen well and taste their best. (It wasn't by accident that the Midwest, with its toasty-hot summers, became known as the Corn Belt.) When temperatures stay on the moderate side, don't look for a bumper crop of these classic summertime treats.

Wind. Hard, drying winds rob moisture from leaves and make plants close up shop for a while. Unless you give them a steady supply of water and nutrients, your crops won't grow fat and tasty.

Cloudy weather or short days. Plants need plenty of sunshine to carry on the business of photosynthesis, which makes them grow. When their light supply is cut back, for whatever reason, they grow more slowly, and you can expect a delayed harvest.

A Weather Eye
Mother Nature's whims can affect your harvest for better or for worse. When you're tuned in to your local weather forecast, listen for any of these conditions:

- Moisture
- Heat
- Cold
- Cool
- Wind
- Cloudy skies

Is It Ready Yet?

When you're not sure if something is ready to pick, look for these clues:

✔ **Color.** Fleshy-fruited veggies like tomatoes, peppers, winter squash, and pumpkins turn color as they ripen. Read your seed packet or catalog description carefully, so you know what color to look for.

✔ **Gloss.** Healthy, growing veggies are shiny. If their skin is dull, you've waited too long. Watermelon is the exception to the rule: When it's ripe, its skin is dull.

✔ **Size.** Lots of crops, including peppers, potatoes, cucumbers, zucchini, and leafy greens, are ready to eat whenever they look like they are. If you're not sure you can trust your eyes, take a bite. Your taste buds don't lie.

HURRY-UP-THE-HARVEST TONIC

When I know Old Man Winter is waiting in the wings and my plants are still chock-full of unripe veggies, I give them a big drink of my Hurry-Up-the-Harvest Tonic.

1 cup of apple juice
½ cup of ammonia
½ cup of baby shampoo

Mix these ingredients in your 20 gallon hose-end sprayer jar, filling the balance of the jar with warm water. Then spray the Tonic on your garden to the point of run-off. Those veggies will ripen up pronto.

Five Steps to a Happy Harvest

When you're out there bringing in the bounty, follow these guidelines:

Step 1. Pick veggies in the morning, when their sugar content is highest.

Step 2. Never harvest (or do any other garden work) when plants are wet: You're likely to spread diseases then.

Step 3. Work carefully. Bruised or scratched vegetables spoil quickly, and damaged plants are sitting ducks for pests and diseases.

Step 4. Use your fingers to pick thin-stemmed vegetables like peas and beans, and ones that slip easily from the vine like tomatoes.

Step 5. Use a sharp knife or clippers to cut tough- or brittle-stemmed crops. Veggies like cabbage, peppers, broccoli, eggplant, and squash can be damaged badly if you try to pull or tear them from their stems.

The Spice of Life

Grandma Putt grew plenty of herbs among her vegetables, and I still do. Partly, that's because — as we talked about in Chapter 5 — they lay out a great big welcome mat for good-guy bugs and chase away lots of the villains. But I also grow them just because they taste and smell so good. For me, harvesting herbs is an ongoing process. Most mornings, I clip some chives to scramble with my breakfast eggs. Later, I pluck a handful of mint sprigs for iced tea. Then, getting on toward suppertime, I wander into the garden and gather up whatever I want to cook with.

Sometimes, though, I want larger quantities, either to store for the winter or to use fresh from the vine. Then I follow these guidelines:

• **Beat the flowers to the punch.** Most herbs reach their peak of flavor, fragrance, and quantity just before the plants bloom. If you cut them then, the plants will often grow back and give you a second harvest.

• **Clip early.** It's best to harvest herbs in the morning, after the dew has dried, but before the sun gets hot. That's when the volatile oils that give herbs their flavor and aroma reach their highest levels. The plants are also cool then, so they'll stay fresh longer. If early morning isn't possible, try to work on a cloudy day.

• **Know when to say when.** The quality of herbs goes downhill fast once they're cut, so harvest only as much as you're sure you can handle before the cuttings start to wilt. (You can always go back for more the next day.)

HAPPY HERB TONIC

Grandma Putt kept her herbs healthy and chipper with this nifty, nutritious elixir.

1 cup of tea
½ tbsp. of bourbon
½ tbsp. of ammonia
½ tbsp. of hydrogen peroxide
1 gal. of warm water

Mix all of the ingredients in a bucket. Feed your herb plants with it every 6 weeks throughout the growing season.

Look, Ma: Two Hands

The faster you can harvest your veggies and get them to the salad bowl or that pot of boiling water, the yummier they'll taste. That's why I use containers that keep both hands free for picking. For big, sturdy crops like eggplant, squash, and corn, I use a canvas apple-picking bag with a wide, comfortable shoulder strap. For more fragile fruits like strawberries and tomatoes, I clip a small bucket to my belt. It's like having a garden helper who's ready for work whenever I am!

It's Got a Hole in It

Don't haul your dirty veggies to the kitchen to clean them (and then the kitchen)! Instead, wash 'em off right in the garden. Just put them in any container that has holes in it, aim the hose, and fire away. These are some of the leaky washbasins I like to use:

• Colanders
• Dish drainers
• Plastic laundry baskets
• Plastic mesh produce bags
• Salad spinners

Come One, Come All

When most of our crops were at their peak and we had veggies coming in faster than we could keep up with them, Grandma Putt and I always threw a great big harvesting bee.

We'd invite all our friends and neighbors who didn't have gardens of their own, and we'd spend the day — kids and grown-ups alike — pickin' and shuckin' and shellin' and cookin'. Then we'd all sit down at picnic tables under the apple trees for a good, old-time country supper. At the end of the evening, we sent everyone off with baskets full of vegetables and herbs.

Jerry Baker Says

"When it comes time to harvest your crops and put 'em by for the winter, the folks at your local Cooperative Extension Service can be just as much help as they are at planting time. To find the branch closest to you, look in your phone directory under 'Local Government,' or call the nearest land-grant university."

Eating Happily Ever After

Whether you plan to eat your vegetables over the next few days or sock them away for the winter, they'll last a lot longer if you keep these terrific tips in mind:

• **Leave an inch or two** of stem on pumpkins, peppers, and squash.

• **Remove the tops** from root crops.

• **Rush anything that you pick** to the fridge or another cool place.

• **Wash only** what you plan to use right away; wash the rest later.

How to Capture Summer in Jars

When Grandma Putt was a girl, folks had to put food by if they were going to eat well through the winter. They didn't have all of the fancy frozen foods we have today. Nowadays, I see more and more folks stocking their freezers and pantries — and even building old-time root cellars.

Stocking Up

There are four major ways to store veggies. Each one has its advantages and disadvantages. Here's a quick rundown that will help you choose whatever suits you best.

Canning

Advantages: You wind up with jars of food that you just pull off the shelf and use. You don't need special storage equipment, and food won't spoil if the power goes off. Fancy pickles, preserves, and salsas (all made by the canning process) are handy to have around for guests— and they make great presents!

Disadvantages: It *is* time-consuming. If you don't do it just right, your food won't be safe to eat. Most canned veggies don't look or taste as good as frozen ones, and they don't retain as many nutrients.

Drying, a.k.a. Dehydrating

Advantages: It's easy. Dried foods take up less space than other kinds. You can dry food in small batches as crops come in. You don't need special storage equipment, and you won't lose your stash if the power goes out. Dried fruits, veggies, and herbs make great gifts.

Disadvantages: Dried foods don't look or taste anything like the fresh versions. For the best and fastest results, you need to buy a dehydrator.

Freezing

Advantages: It keeps most veggies closest to fresh in terms of looks, taste, and nutrients. It's fast and easy.

Disadvantages: The freezer in your fridge is okay for a week or so, but for long-term storage, you need one that stays at 0°F or below. Otherwise, food will spoil.

Root Cellaring, a.k.a Cold Storage

Advantages: It's fast and easy. Vegetables and fruits stay almost exactly as they were when you took them from the garden. All the storage equipment you need is either free or inexpensive.

Disadvantages: You need a storage area that will keep your crops at the right temperature and humidity.

Hold That Flavor!

If you're like me, the main reason you grow your own veggies is to get the kind of great taste you can't get from store-bought produce. To keep enjoying that great taste till the next harvesttime comes around, you need to store your crops in the way that suits them best. Here's my rundown on the most flavorful methods.

VEGETABLE	BEST STORAGE METHODS	VEGETABLE	BEST STORAGE METHODS
Beans	can, dry, freeze	Peppers	can, freeze, pickle
Beets	can, cold storage, freeze, pickle	Potatoes	cold storage
		Pumpkins	can, cold storage
Broccoli	freeze	Radishes	cold storage
Brussels sprouts	cold storage, freeze, pickle	Rutabagas	cold storage
Cabbage	cold storage, freeze, kraut, pickle	Spinach	freeze
		Squash (winter)	can, cold storage, freeze
Carrots	can, cold storage, freeze, juice, pickle	Squash (summer)	freeze, pickle
Cauliflower	freeze, pickle	Sweet potatoes	cold storage
Celery	cold storage, dry, pickle	Tomatoes	can, dry, freeze, juice, sauce
Corn	can, dry, freeze, pickle		
Cucumbers	pickle		
Eggplant	freeze, pickle		
Endive	cold storage		
Leeks	cold storage		
Okra	can, freeze, pickle		
Onions	can, cold storage, freeze, pickle		
Parsnips	cold storage		
Peas	can, dry, freeze		

Shiver Their Timbers

When I bought my new freezer, it seemed like a big investment. But now I don't know how I ever got along without it. If you're thinking about adding a freezer to the family, you need to make a few decisions:

New or used? Whichever you choose, find out how energy efficient the monster is. The cost of operating an older freezer — or a new non-self-defrosting model — will eat up a big chunk of the money you're saving by growing your own food.

Chest or upright? An upright freezer takes up less floor space than a chest type, and it's easier to see and grab exactly the veggies you want. But you have to pack them in carefully, or they'll topple out when you open the door. Cold air rushes out, too — and that adds big-time charges to your electric bill. In a chest model, the big chill stays put, and so do your veggies, no matter how you load them in. A chest freezer also costs less to buy than an upright, and it will give you extra counter space if you put it in the right spot.

How big? That all depends on how many people you expect to be feeding from your stash and what you plan on freezing. For veggies alone, my rule of thumb for a year's worth of storage space is to figure on 3 to 4 cubic feet per person.

Pack It Up

To stay in tip-top shape, frozen food must be packaged in containers that have a tight seal to keep out air, moisture, and vapor. Plenty of containers will do a fine job, provided you seal 'em up tight, but these are the ones I like best:

• **Plastic freezer boxes.** They're unbreakable, reusable, and easy to pack into whatever space you have. They have only one drawback: Plastic absorbs odors, so over time, your containers may start to smell.

• **Glass freezer containers.** You can use them over and over again, and unlike plastic, glass does not absorb odors. Glass does break, though, so you need to be more careful with it than with plastic. Make sure the glass is freezer safe. And when you thaw your food, always put the jars into cold water, never hot or even warm.

• **Boil-in bags.** They're heavy-duty plastic bags that let you blanch, cool, freeze, and then cook your vegetables all in the same container. There's almost no loss of nutrients or color from harvest to table and you save a whopping lot of time!

Six Tips for Fabulous Freezer Feasting

I like to make the most of my time, space, and money. I also like my garden veggies to taste their best and, while I'm at it, to tuck away as many of their good vitamins as possible. Here are some of my favorite save-the-harvest secrets:

Tip 1. Freeze only what freezes best. Especially if your space is limited, don't take up freezer room with veggies that you can keep in a cold basement (like potatoes and turnips) or that change texture when they're frozen (like beets and celery). And don't even think about freezing radishes, scallions, or lettuce.

Tip 2. Don't freeze any more than a year's worth. If you've stashed away as much as your family and guests will gobble up between now and the next harvest, and your garden is still offering up veggies by the wheelbarrow load, give the extras to friends, neighbors, and the local food bank. And next year, plant less!

Tip 3. Before you freeze anything for the first time, do a test batch. If you're not happy with the way it turns out, use another storage method, or give away whatever you can't eat before it goes bad.

Tip 4. Take a week's worth of veggies at a time out of your big freezer, and move them to the one in the fridge. You'll reduce frost buildup and energy costs.

Tip 5. Keep your freezer full at all times. The emptier it is, the more energy it uses. If your vegetables don't take up all of the space, fill in with ice cream, Popsicles, meat — anything but plain old air.

Tip 6. Keep an inventory checklist. That way, you'll always know how much of everything you've got. You won't discover in early February, as I once did, that all you've got left is two packages of spinach!

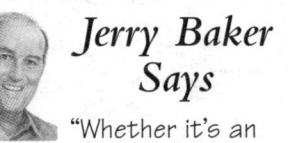

Jerry Baker Says

"Whether it's an upright or a chest model, any big freezer uses up a lot of electricity — and the emptier it gets, the more it uses. But I've found a great way to keep down the cost: Every time I take out a pack of frozen vegetables, I replace it with a zippered freezer bag full of water. That way, my freezer stays full, and all that packaged-up ice comes in handy to cool down blanched veggies come the next puttin'-by time. Or I can throw a couple in the cooler when we're going on a picnic."

I Can. Can *You?*

In this day and age, it might seem hard to believe that some people keep right on puttin' by veggies in glass jars just like Grandma Putt did. Well, I still can part of my harvest. Here's why:

1. I enjoy it. Not that I'd want to spend days on end at it. But for an afternoon or two in late August or early September, it feels good to be in an air-conditioned kitchen, doing something that reminds me of old times.

2. I like having treats on hand, like red sauerkraut and dill pickles, that I can serve to guests.

3. I like to make preserves and chutneys to give to my friends for Christmas presents.

4. Some veggies look and taste better when they're canned. Beets, for instance, get a funny texture when they're frozen. But pickled — mmm-mmm, that's good eatin'!

Canning 101

There are two major canning techniques: the boiling-water bath and the pressure method. Both accomplish the same thing: killing microorganisms that cause food to spoil, and creating a vacuum in which germs can't grow. The boiling-water bath is fine for acidic fruits, or when you're making veggie pickles, relishes, and chutneys with vinegar. But never use it for the simple canning of any vegetable — even tomatoes.

QUICK-AS-A-WINK DILL PICKLES

These pickles are a snap to make. And take it from me: You won't be able to keep them on the shelves for long!

3 QUARTS

3 cups white vinegar
3 cups water
⅓ cup pickling salt
4 pounds cucumbers, washed and cut into spears
6 heads of dill or 6 tablespoons dill seed
3 cloves of garlic, peeled
9 black peppercorns

1. Combine the liquid ingredients and pickling salt, and heat to boiling.

2. Pack cucumber spears into clean, hot 1-quart jars. To each jar add 2 heads of dill or 2 tablespoons of dill seed, 1 garlic clove, and 3 peppercorns.

3. Fill the jars with hot pickling syrup, leaving ½ inch of headroom. Adjust lids.

4. Process in a boiling-water bath for 20 minutes.

5. Stash your jars of pickles away for a few weeks, so that the flavors can blend and mellow. Then eat hearty!

How Dry I Am

Talk about old-time harvest keeping! Drying food — or, to be technically accurate, dehydrating it — goes way back to caveman days. I've dried just about every kind of fruit and vegetable you can think of, and there's almost nothing simpler: You just cut your food into small pieces, spread the pieces out in the sun or in a dehydrator until they're good and dry, pack 'em up in small containers, and stash 'em away in a cool, dark place.

They don't take up much space: Twenty-five pounds of fresh-picked veggies dries down to somewhere between 3 and 8 pounds. I keep my stash in an old wooden cupboard that belonged to Grandma Putt's mama.

What's Dry Enough?

Before you store dried veggies, you need to make sure they're good and dry. Otherwise, mold and bacteria will spoil them in a hurry. Always make sure each piece is cool when you test it — if it's still warm, it will feel more moist than it really is. Here's how I tell when my dried crops are ready for the shelf:

SUPER Storing Secrets

IT'S CONVENTIONAL

A conventional oven works just fine for drying food. It has only one disadvantage: The air can't circulate inside that box the way it does in a dehydrator or in the great outdoors, and good air movement is a *must* for even drying. But I've found a way to solve that problem: I just leave the oven door open a few inches, and I aim an electric fan at the opening. That way, moist air can't collect and put a damper on my stash!

VEGGIES	READY WHEN THEY'RE
Celery	Hard and brittle (to test, just take a bite)
Corn, dried beans, peas	Dry enough to shatter or split in half when you tap a piece with a hammer
Green beans	Dark green and leathery
Rhubarb	Crisp and brittle
Spinach and other greens	Brittle enough to crumble in your hands
Squash, pumpkins, and root veggies	Tough, leathery, and pliable, with no moisture in the center
Tomatoes	Brittle

Wild, Wild Eatin'

Back in the days of the Wild West, folks set great store by what they called leathers. I still make up lots of these — it's a great way to use up veggies and fruits that are slightly overripe. If they're just ripe, I steam them a tad first. You can make single-flavor leathers, like tomato or pepper, or combinations like strawberry-rhubarb. Here's how to make your own supply:

1. Put your veggies into the blender, and purée them until they're smooth. If you need to, add water or juice to make the purée easy to pour.

2. Line a tray with plastic wrap. If you have a dehydrator, use the special leather-making tray that comes with it.

3. Spread the purée ⅛ inch thick on the tray.

4. Set either your dehydrator or your oven at 120°F, put the tray in, and leave it there for 6 to 8 hours, or until you can pull up the leather easily from the plastic wrap. Then turn the tray upside down and pull off the plastic. Line the tray with fresh plastic and put the partially dry leather on it, bottom side up. Put the tray back in to dry some more. It should stay for another 4 to 6 hours in a dehydrator, or 6 to 8 hours in a conventional oven.

5. Roll the whole thing up in wax paper or plastic wrap, twist the ends closed, and put it into the fridge. (You can also cut it into smaller pieces and put them into glass jars or plastic bags.) Leathers will keep for months, but mine usually disappear within days!

Love Those Leathers!

Here's a handful of my favorite fruit and veggie leather combos:

- Tomato, green pepper, and onion
- Pumpkin with cinnamon, nutmeg, and walnuts
- Carrots with lemon and ginger
- Beets with orange
- Strawberry-rhubarb

Let the Sun Shine In

You can also let your leathers dry in the great outdoors, which, of course, is how the pioneers did it. Just set the tray in full sun for a day, then turn over the leather, take off the plastic wrap, and leave it for another day. (Put a cheesecloth tent over the top, so bugs can't get at your treats-in-the-making and — just to be on the safe side — take the tray indoors for the night.)

Leather Britches

Don't ask me why this drying technique is called "leather britches." I just know it's the easiest puttin'-by method I've ever heard of — and it makes for some mighty tasty veggies. I especially like to use it for green beans. Here's all there is to it:

Step 1. Pick a basketful of young, tender snap beans.

Step 2. String them on a thread, just like we used to string cranberries and popcorn for the Christmas tree.

Step 3. Hang them in the shade to dry.

Step 4. Store them in a brown paper bag.

How Much Is Enough?

There are two ways to go about socking veggies away in a root cellar. Some folks just store what hasn't been eaten fresh from the garden. Others do what Grandma Putt and I did: Plan on having enough to keep us in good eatin' all winter long. If that's your approach, too, here are some basic guidelines you can follow. For a family of four, you'll need:

- **Beets:** 1–2 bushels
- **Brussels sprouts:** 10–15 plants in the garden
- **Cabbage:** about 30 heads
- **Carrots:** 2–3 bushels
- **Kale:** 50–100-foot row
- **Kohlrabi:** ½–1 bushel
- **Leeks:** 15–40 plants
- **Onions:** 1–2 bushels
- **Parsnips:** 1–2 bushels
- **Potatoes:** 6–14 bushels
- **Sweet potatoes:** 2 bushels
- **Turnips:** about 1 bushel
- **Winter squash:** 30-40

Getting to the Root of Things

Back before there were home freezers or refrigerators, almost every house had a root cellar where folks stashed all of the food they could. Some crops, like asparagus, beets, and rhubarb, were even grown in cellars by a process called forcing.

Nowadays, not many houses have a root cellar. The good news, though, is that you don't need one. Lots of vegetables will keep fine in a toolshed or an unheated garage. Here are some other options:

- **Use a window well.** Just line it with straw, set your containers of veggies inside, and cover them with more straw.

- **Adapt a cold frame.** Surround it with bales of hay and cover the whole thing with heavy canvas.

- **Dig a pit.** Sink a big picnic cooler into it, add the veggies, and forget about it until it's time to eat.

One Size *Doesn't* Fit All

Neither does one set of storage conditions. Nowadays, for most of us, it just doesn't make sense to stash all of our crops in cold storage when there are so many other ways to keep them looking and tasting good. These are the veggies I like to keep in a root cellar and the kind of conditions they need to stay their best.

CONDITIONS	GOOD VEGGIES TO STORE
Cold and very moist (32–40°F, 90–95 percent relative humidity)	Beets Carrots Celery Horseradish Leeks Turnips Winter radishes
Cold and moist (32–40°F, 80–90 percent relative humidity)	Cabbage Endive and escarole Potatoes
Cool and moist (40–50°F, 85–90 percent relative humidity)	Cantaloupe Cucumbers Ripe tomatoes Watermelon
Cool and dry (32–50°F, 60–70 percent relative humidity)	Garlic Onions
Fairly warm and dry (50–60°F, 60–70 percent relative humidity)	Dry hot peppers Green tomatoes Pumpkins Sweet potatoes Winter squash

Okay, now you know how to take your garden from a pipe dream on graph paper to a kitchen that's chock-full of great wintertime eatin'! Now it's time to get down and dirty, and look at what each vegetable needs to make it grow big and tasty.

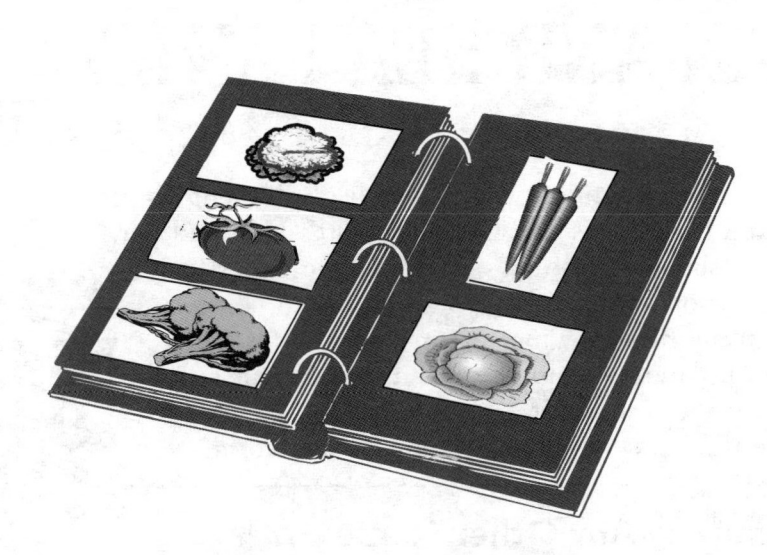

CHAPTER 7

Jerry's Favorites: A Vegetable Family Album

Grandma Putt used to say that vegetable families are just like the human kind: No matter how different they might look on the outside, and no matter how different they might act sometimes, deep down — where it really counts — they're all kith and kin. What I'm going to do in this chapter is fill you in on all of the "family secrets," so you can give each of your veggie clans the care and comfort it needs to produce *spectacular* results in your backyard.

BEAN AND PEA FAMILY

Beans • Peas

My first garden was filled with a bunch of different kinds of peas and beans. This was Grandma Putt's idea, and her theory was simple: These are just about the easiest vegetables a person can grow. She wanted me to come away from my first growing season with the taste of victory in my mouth. And it worked, too! When I counted up the bushels of crops I'd grown all by myself, I felt like the heavyweight champion of the world!

A Family by Any Other Name

The bean and pea clan also goes by the name of legume — or *Leguminosae,* in scientific lingo. Lots of things you might not think of are legumes — like peanuts. So are soybeans, including some tasty new varieties that many folks are just starting to grow in their home gardens. Besides giving an almost surefire ego boost to new gardeners and a big nutritional kick to your diet, plants in this family have another huge feather in their cap: They're good for your soil.

Cooking with Gas

All legumes take nitrogen gas from the atmosphere and turn it into the kind of nitrogen that plants need in the soil. They do it by way of good-guy bacteria that are lodged in bumpy nodules on their roots. One of the biggest favors you can do your garden is to plow under your legume crops after you harvest them, and then plant some nitrogen-loving veggies in that spot the following year — or even right away, if there's enough time left in the growing season.

Gas

On the Double

A Word to the Wise from Grandma Putt

Grandma Putt had a great maneuver that saved space and work, and increased her bounty: She grew her pole beans up her sunflower stalks. She'd sow her sunflowers as early as possible in the season to give them a good head start on the beans. Then when the time came to sow the beans, the sunflowers were already a foot or two high. By the time the beans sprouted and began to climb upward, the sunflowers were big and strong enough to support them. To use this method, sow two or three beans at the foot of each sunflower. Keep the soil damp until the beans sprout, then begin your regular feeding program.

Help Me Fix It, Please

Before beans and peas can convert nitrogen into a usable form, certain kinds of bacteria must be present in the soil. You may have heard some gardening lingo about how beans or peas "fix" nitrogen — this is what that's all about. The bacteria will be there if there's been a garden on your site before. But if you're working a brand-new plot, before you plant seeds, you'll need to coat them with a powder called an inoculant. And, no, this isn't something you inject with a syringe. You'll find inoculants and instructions for using them at garden centers and in the pea and bean sections of seed catalogs.

Legume Enemy Number One

Woodchucks (a.k.a. groundhogs) have their admirers. I have to admit it, they *are* cute as all get-out. But they can demolish a whole crop of peas and beans — and any other kind of legume — faster than you can say "Punxsutawney Phil." If these buck-toothed bandits ride the range in your territory, fence 'em out.

What You'll Need:
- Metal fence posts, 4½ feet high
- Sturdy woven or welded wire fencing, 6 feet high and long enough to go around your whole garden
- Wire for attaching the fencing to the posts

What to Do:

Step 1. Dig a very narrow trench around your garden. Make it about 2 feet deep and just wide enough so that you can insert the posts and fencing.

Step 2. Sink the metal posts into the trench about 8 feet apart, sticking up 2½ feet above the ground.

Step 3. Sink the fencing to the bottom of the trench and fasten it to the posts so it reaches up 1½ feet above the stakes.

Step 4. Bend the top of the fencing outward from your garden at about a 65-degree angle.

Step 5. Sit back and enjoy the show when the varmints try to get in. The underground part of the fence will keep them from tunneling under it. And when they try to climb over, they'll get as far as the floppy top, when their own weight will send them toppling back onto their furry little cans.

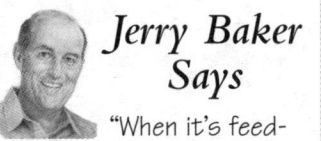

Jerry Baker Says

"When it's feeding time for peas and beans, I give them a good, well-balanced drink of fish fertilizer or Compost Tea (see page 351), and steer clear of any kind of fertilizer that's high in nitrogen. After all, that's what they've already packed for lunch."

Beans *(Phaseolus)*

Grandma Putt grew so many kinds of beans, in so many sizes and colors and shapes, that I could hardly keep track of them. I used to get a big kick out of just roaming around in her garden, looking at 'em. Today, I get an even bigger kick out of cooking and eating them in all kinds of ways throughout the winter.

A More-Than-Middlin' Muddle

Until you get the hang of it, looking through the bean section of a seed catalog can be a mighty confusing exercise — there seem to be millions of different varieties. How on earth do you ever choose? Well, it can be a challenge, but I promise it'll get easier once you understand bean lingo.

A Bean Is a Bean Is a Bean

Seed catalogs generally divide bean varieties into three main categories, depending on the stage at which folks most often pick and eat them.

Snap beans get harvested when they're young and tender. You eat them pod and all. (They got the name *snap* because that's what the crisp young pods do when you bend them.) Some folks call them green beans or string beans — even though they also come in purple and yellow, and even though many of them don't have any strings.

Shell or **shelly beans** are ready for picking when they're half mature. You eat them fresh, rather than dried, but without the pod. Catalogs also call this kind horticultural beans or flageolets.

Dry or **dried beans** stay on the vine till they're good and dry. Then you take out the seeds and store them in glass jars or gunnysacks, where they keep almost forever. (This portable, almost imperishable nourishment got the pioneers across the plains and cowboys through those long cattle drives.)

Jerry Baker Says

"You can use shell beans and dried beans interchangeably in most recipes. Just remember that shell beans stay the same size whether they're raw or cooked. Dried beans, which usually need to be soaked before you cook them, more than double in size, so you'll have to adjust the quantities you use accordingly."

A Matter of Taste

Like a great many man-made categories, bean types are generalizations, not hard-and-fast rules. Some beans make great eatin' at all three stages. And they're all technically edible at any time of their development. It's just that most varieties taste their best when you pick and eat them at one particular stage. A first-class catalog will tell you the best times to harvest each kind it offers, and the best ways to cook and store it.

One of a Kind

No matter how you plan to eat 'em, and no matter whether they grow up or bush out, all beans hanker for the same kind of home life. They like full sun, except in really hot parts of the country, where a little afternoon shade suits them just fine. Give beans well-drained soil filled up with plenty of organic matter that's low in nitrogen, and make sure the pH is on the acid side — 5.5 to 6.5.

Tall or Short?

To make matters even more complicated, all three kinds of beans come in two plant versions — tall and thin or short and stout.

Pole beans take longer to start producing (10 to 11 weeks for most types) but once they kick into gear, they'll keep churning out beans till Jack Frost knocks 'em over or until you get tired of picking, whichever comes first. You must give pole beans plenty of support, but not necessarily plain old poles. Trellises, tepees, and the garden fence will all work just as well. (See page 160 for how to make my bike wheel trellis.)

Bush types turn out a single flush of beans, usually 6 to 8 weeks after planting for the snap kind. I plant these to get an early harvest or when I want lots of beans all at once for puttin' by.

Beans by the Yard

JERRY'S FAVORITE Vegetable Varieties

'Yardlong', a.k.a. **'Asparagus Bean'**. If you're hankering to win one of your neighborhood's big-vegetable contests, the bean you need is 'Yardlong'. It really does get to be 36 inches long — sometimes longer! It needs plenty of warmth and a lot of climbing room — the vines can grow over 10 feet tall. Folks in China have been growing these sweet, tender beans for thousands of years, and using them in stir-frys (chopped up, of course). If you spend as much time in Chinese restaurants as I do, you've probably eaten yards and yards of 'Yardlong' beans without even knowing it!

Turn Up the Heat!

Lots of veggies *prefer* warm temperatures, but beans demand them! The seeds will rot in cold, wet soil, and frost will lay your seedlings out as flat as a pancake. Don't even think about sowing bean seeds before you're sure old Jack Frost has left for summer vacation and the soil temperature has reached at least 55°F.

55

Once and for All

Beans don't like moving any more than they like cold weather, so don't try to jump-start the season by sowing your seeds indoors. Plant them in the garden, right where you want them to stay. I sow my bush bean seeds in blocks, 1 inch deep and 2 to 3 inches apart. Later, I thin them to about 6 inches apart. If you live in hot, humid territory, leave 8 or even 10 inches between plants, so they'll get good air circulation. There's nothing disease germs like more than still, muggy air!

I plant my pole beans at the same depth, but the spacing depends on what kind of support I'm giving them. Whatever I use, I put it up right at planting time so I won't disturb the roots later on. When I plant seeds at the base of a fence or a flat trellis, I set them 2 to 3 inches apart, and later, I thin them to about 8 inches.

Bean TLC

I make sure my beans get about an inch of water a week, whether it's from Mother Nature or my soaker hose. I give them a little more when the pods are developing. I mulch with compost when the plants have grown their second set of leaves, and I give them a drink of Compost Tea (see page 351) or fish fertilizer every 2 weeks for the first 6 weeks, and then once every 3 to 4 weeks till the end of the growing season. That's all they need.

SUPER Growing Secrets

FREEZE 'EM

Before you store dried beans, put them in the freezer for 3 to 4 hours to kill any bugs or larvae that might be hanging around.

The Old Neighborhood

These were Grandma Putt's rules for choosing friends for her bean crops:

• **Never plant** any member of the onion family anywhere in the bean neighborhood.

• **Bush beans** like to keep company with celery, cucumbers, strawberries, and summer savory. They lend a helping hand to corn when you plant the two in alternate rows. Besides onions, they dislike fennel.

• **Pole beans and eggplant** make a terrific twosome and, like their bushy cousins, the polesters get along well with corn and summer savory. Beets don't want pole beans anywhere near their homes. Pole beans, in turn, won't put up with cabbage.

Harvesttime

How and when you harvest your beans, and what you do with them afterward, depends on which of the three kinds you've planted.

Snap beans. Depending on the variety, these are usually ready for picking in 50 to 65 days after planting. You need to keep on top of these guys, because the more you pick, the more the plants will churn out. What I can't eat right away, I freeze or put up as pickles.

Shell beans. I pick this kind when the pods are still green but I can see the seeds swelling up inside. They reach this stage 66 to 75 days after they're planted. After I shell 'em, I bake, steam, or boil 'em. They freeze well, especially in butter sauce in boil-in freezer bags, and they go great with the two other kinds in mixed-bean salads. I put by lots of jars of those for the winter.

Dry beans. These take a while. Plan on 90 to 100 days from planting time. I know they're ready when both pods and seeds are good and dry. (Just make sure you get to 'em before the pods split open, or you could lose your whole harvest.) If the weather forecast tells me a rainy spell or an early frost is headed my way before the beans are ready to harvest, I bring them in right away and let them dry out indoors. I pick the pods off of my pole beans and spread them out on screens and cake-cooling racks. But with bush beans, I pull the plants up, roots and all, and hang them up on laundry lines in a dry part of the basement.

High and Dry

When my bean pods are good and dry — whether they got that way in the basement or on the vine — I put them into a big gunnysack and pound it with a rubber mallet to break open the pods. Then I empty the sack onto sheets of weighted-down newspaper and let the wind take the pods away.

Don't Let Your Beans Be Shrinking Violets

Dried beans are some of the prettiest and most colorful veggies that ever came down the pike. They come in all shades of pink, red, black, white, yellow, green, and brown — solid or mottled like cows and Appaloosa horses. I keep them in airtight glass jars where folks can see them — and where I won't forget to use them, because they're just as good to eat as they are fun to look at.

Mix and Match

When I was a boy, I gobbled up just about any kind of food that Grandma Putt put in front of me. But there was one thing I could never get enough of: her special chile. She told me her secret way of making it so rich and flavorful: She just mixed up a whole lot of different kinds of beans — Jacob's cattle, pinto, black turtle. Whatever kind struck her fancy, she tossed into the pot. I still make my chile that way. Talk about good, stick-to-your-ribs eatin'!

On the Honor Roll

When it comes to vitamins, all beans get high marks for their ABCs. The dried kinds are also packed with calcium, iron, fiber, and protein. Just about the only things they're lacking are fat and cholesterol. Not bad, eh?

The Family Heirlooms

Grandma Putt saved her bean seeds from year to year, and she was always swapping with our neighbors and even by mail with folks far away. Some of her bean types went back hundreds of years. As a kid, I was fascinated by the names and places they conjured up. I still grow a lot of those old-time beans from the seeds Grandma Putt left me, and I swap for more with seed collectors from coast to coast. If you want to start a collection — or just want great eatin' you won't find at the grocery store — look for some of the old-timers on the next page.

Old-Time Bush Beans

JERRY'S FAVORITE
Vegetable Varieties

'Black Turtle'—an old-time southern gentlebean that's good at the snap stage but terrific, and famous, dried and cooked up into Black Turtle Soup.

'Jacob's Cattle', a.k.a. **'Anasazi'**—nobody knows where this one came from, but, just like the Native Americans who gave it one of its names, we know it goes back to ancient times. The beans taste great at either shell or dry stage. As a kid, I liked these better than any other kind of bean, because their markings — maroon splashes on white — reminded me of cows.

'Pencil Pod'—a sweet, tender snap bean that looks just like those yellow No. 2 pencils we used to tote to school. Good disease resistance, grows well anywhere, and matures in just 53 days.

'Peregion'—an old Oregon heirloom and one of the best-looking dried beans I've ever seen. Every pod has beans of a different color and pattern: solid, splotched, or marbled, in shades like bittersweet chocolate and mocha.

'Soldier'—a cool-climate classic that hails from New England. It's been showing up in Yankee baked-bean suppers since, as near as I can figure, about the time George Washington slept there. The beans are white, with a dark maroon "soldier" on the eye.

Old-Time Pole Beans

'Case Knife'—one of the oldest green beans in America, famous at least as far back as 1820. Rich-tasting beans with no strings attached.

'Cherokee Trail of Tears'—a high-yielding, good-tasting bean, best used as snap or dried, with greenish purple pods and black seeds.

'Christmas'—huge, quarter-sized lima beans that are a light cream, striped with bright holiday red. They taste great fresh, and they're my favorite of all limas for freezing.

'Kentucky Wonder', a.k.a. **'Old Homestead Brown-Seeded Pole Bean'**—a great-looking climber with big clusters of white blossoms and tender, fine-tasting, stringless pods. One of my favorites for freezing.

'Scarlet Runner'—my favorite tepee bean as a kid, because the red flowers drew hummingbirds from miles around. The pods make fine eatin' when they're young and tender, and the big, shiny, black-and-purple-mottled seeds are tasty as shell or dry beans.

Bikin' Right Along

Grandma Putt sure as shootin' knew how to get a kid out of the doldrums in a hurry. Once I had an accident on my bicycle and the front wheel got bent. I wasn't hurt, but I was definitely down in the dumps — it would take me a long time to earn enough money to buy a new one. Grandma Putt couldn't help me there, but she showed me how I could still have fun with my old wheel: We turned it into a bean trellis.

First, we found a wooden stake about 8 feet high and just wide enough to fit tightly inside the hole in the middle of the wheel. We sank the stake into the ground, slid the wheel over the top, and put some screws into the stake, just under the wheel, to make sure it stayed put. Then we ran strings from the spokes to the ground and tied each one to a short stake that we'd pounded in. I planted a couple of bean seeds beside each stake, and they grew right up the strings and over the wheel. I had a great crop of beans and a nice shady place to crawl into on a hot summer day. I still use these wheel trellises for pole beans, because they give my plants better air circulation than traditional tepees do. They make for easier pickin', too, because the spread-out vines put the pods where they're easier to see.

SUPER Growing Secrets

LIVING COLOR

It's not always easy to spot snap beans tucked away among all of those leaves. To make sure that you get 'em all — and that your plants keep crankin' out more — grow green beans of a different color; namely, yellow or purple.

Don't Be Corny!

We've all heard about how Native Americans grew their pole beans up cornstalks. Well, that works great if you're growing the kind of corn that stays on the stalk till nigh onto the first frost, and then gets popped, ground up into cornmeal, or fed to the horses. But it doesn't work with the kind of sweet corn most folks grow today and harvest long before the beans stop needing those stalks to cling to. So although it sounds great, I wouldn't recommend this method to the home gardener.

Looks Good to Me!

Folks all over North and South America were growing beans for thousands of years before all of those European explorers arrived on the scene and took some seeds back home with them. Nobody in Spain or France knew they were food crops. They just knew the plants had pretty flowers, and they grew them only for show. It took them years to figure out they could eat the pods and seeds!

What Ails 'em

Beans are prone to several diseases, but you can head off the nasties at the pass by following my guidelines for good health in Chapter 5 and by planting varieties with built-in resistance. Before you start any seed shopping, call your Cooperative Extension Service or a good local garden center, and find out which bean ailments are most common in your area. Then check catalog descriptions for these codes; if you see one beside a variety's name, you know that bean is resistant to the disease.

- Anthracnose (A)
- Bean common mosaic virus (BCMV)
- Curly-top virus (CTV)
- Bean rust (R)

Cool It

As Grandma Putt used to say, there's an exception to every rule. In the case of the beans-crave-heat rule, a big-time exception is the fava, a.k.a. English broad bean or horse bean. It actually dislikes hot weather and needs to be planted early in the spring, as soon as you can work the soil. The seeds grow up into fine and dandy bushes. The young leaves are good to eat, and good for you, to boot. I toss 'em in salads throughout spring. The beans taste great as either snap or shell types, but I like them best dried — then I either pop 'em like popcorn or roast 'em like peanuts.

Caution!

Folks who hail from the Mediterranean region, or whose ancestors did, have a gene that sometimes causes an allergic reaction to fava beans. So if you fall into this category, proceed with caution.

Peas *(Pisum sativum)*

Lots of folks tell me they don't bother to grow peas, because by the time they wade through all of the vines and pods, there's not much left. It's true, peas are not a high-volume crop. But I can't imagine my garden without them. To me, the day I chow down on my first batch of sweet early peas is the official start of summer.

Decisions, Decisions

Deciding what kind of peas to grow can be a tad tricky, because, like their beany cousins, peas come in three main types. I generally grow some of each kind, because I like them all.

Garden peas, a.k.a. **English or green peas,** are the classics that you eat without the pod. I plant two kinds. I grow the small-seeded type, called *petit pois,* for eating fresh and freezing. And I always have at least a few plants of dry, or soup, peas. I let them dry out on the vine, just like dry beans, and I cook 'em up in soups and casseroles.

Snap peas are the new kids in Vegetable Town. An Idaho plant breeder named Calvin Lamborn introduced the first one, 'Sugar Snap', in 1979, and it became an overnight superstar. Snap peas are like two peas in one: tender, sweet garden peas inside crisp — and also sweet and edible — pods.

Snow peas, a.k.a. **Chinese or sugar peas,** are the kind you get, pods and all, in Chinese restaurants.

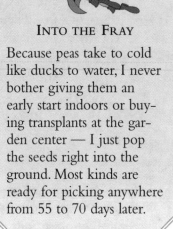

SUPER Growing Secrets

INTO THE FRAY

Because peas take to cold like ducks to water, I never bother giving them an early start indoors or buying transplants at the garden center — I just pop the seeds right into the ground. Most kinds are ready for picking anywhere from 55 to 70 days later.

In the Cool, Cool, Cool of the Springtime

Peas are cool customers. You can put the seeds into the ground as early as 5 weeks before you expect the last frost to hit your territory. If you're measuring with a soil thermometer, it can register a chilly 40°F and your seeds will still germinate — though it will take them close to 7 weeks to do so. I like to wait till the soil temperature hits 60°F. Then I know that I can expect to see tiny pea shoots about 9 days later. They take off like lightning, too, so I don't lose any good eatin' time by waiting.

Pack 'em In

Come spring plantin' time, I set my pea trellises into the ground and then plant seeds staggered in narrow bands on both sides of the supports. I sow them about 1 inch deep and 1 inch apart, and I never bother to thin the seedlings later — they're pleased as punch to grow up as close as, well, peas in a pod!

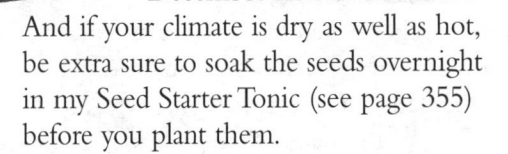

Spring in December

If you live in one of the hotter parts of the country, don't fret: Your homegrown peas will be as tasty as anyone's up North. Just plant your crop in December instead of March. And if your climate is dry as well as hot, be extra sure to soak the seeds overnight in my Seed Starter Tonic (see page 355) before you plant them.

Heat and Sun Protection

About 10 weeks before I expect the first frost, I plant a fall crop of peas. Because it's generally hot as Hades about then, I sow the seeds deep, where the soil is cooler and they're protected from the sun's heat. I dig a trench about 6 inches deep, set in my seeds 1 inch apart, and cover them with 2 inches of soil. As the plants grow, I cover them with compost until the trench is filled.

I plant fall peas where they'll get some shade from other crops. If that's impossible, I set up a trellis on the western side of the bed to block the hot afternoon sun.

Feed Me, Please, but Not Too Much

Just like beans, peas take nitrogen from the air and use it in the soil, but that doesn't mean they don't need to eat. I give my plants a light lunch of well-balanced organic fertilizer when they're 2 to 4 inches tall, and twice during the growing season I give them a drink of fish fertilizer or Compost Tea (see page 351). But I'm careful not to overfeed them: That makes for mountains of lush foliage, but not many peas. And that can be a real pain in the you-know-what come harvesting time.

Make My Bed Just Right, Please

Peas like full sun and good air circulation. They prefer their soil a shade on the acid side, with a pH of 6.0 to 6.8, and plenty of organic matter (easy on the nitrogen, because, like beans, they make their own supply). I always grow peas in raised beds; as far as they're concerned, home just isn't home unless the drainage is danged near perfect. Talk about being fussy! Peas can handle cold soil just fine, but cold *wet* soil will make the seeds rot away to nothing.

Staggering Along

Peas don't have to be just a first-crack-of-the-summer treat. Here's one way to keep a steady supply coming in pretty much all season long:

- **Plant an early crop** as soon as the soil temperature hits 60°F.
- **About 3 weeks later,** plant a different variety that's heat-resistant.
- **Eight to 10 weeks** before the first frost, plant a crop for an early-fall harvest.

Growing Up Right

All peas, even the little bushy kinds, need something steady to cling to as they're growing up. All during the fall and winter, Grandma Putt and I used to collect thin but sturdy branches that we'd pruned from our trees and shrubs or that we'd found in the woods. Come spring, when we planted our peas, we planted this "pea bush," as Grandma Putt called it, at the same time.

We'd sink the branches right into the middle of the pea beds, 6 to 8 inches into the soil, so they'd stand up good and solid. (The height we used depended on how tall each kind of pea was going to get.) Then we'd plant our peas on both sides of the bush. When the first little tendrils came out, we guided them up the branches, and the next thing we knew, they'd be twining and scrambling up like mad!

Drink Up

Young pea plants are light drinkers. They'll start out just fine on ½ inch of water a week until the flowers pop out. After that, they'll need an inch or so every week. (If your soil is very sandy, make sure the peas get an inch a week right from the get-go.)

Good Timing

Peas don't have many bad-guy bug problems, because they do a lot of their growing before most of the pesky pests appear. (For tips on getting rid of any early arrivals, see Chapter 5.) As for diseases, keep them at bay by planting resistant varieties, rotating your crops every year, and making sure your plants don't get too hot or stressed out by the weather.

The Net Result

A pea seedling's worst enemy is a hungry bird. Winged warriors like nothing better than a tender young pea sprout with a seed clinging to its bottom end. The best way I know to foil the rascals is to cover the patch with nets until the plants are past the seedling stage. Best bets: bird netting, floating row covers, or even an old tennis, volleyball, or badminton net. All work equally well.

Up, Up, and Away!

Like beans, peas come in two versions: bushy and climbing. Both will give you some mighty fine eating, but the tall, vining kinds have a couple of advantages over the smaller ones:

1. They offer up much bigger harvests.

2. When you train them on a good-looking fence or trellis, their blue-green leaves and white or lavender flowers are real showstoppers. I plant peas by my patio, where I can relax and enjoy the view.

Bless Your Little Pea-Pickin' Harvest

If you want to enjoy peas at their sweet, tender best, you need to pick them at just the right time. If they stay on the vine even a day or two past their peak, all of the sugar inside will start turning to starch — which it will also do the minute you pluck them off. Peas are like corn: The sooner you get them to the kitchen and start chowing down, the more reward you'll have for all of your hard work in the garden.

Taking Home the Blue

If you're hankerin' to walk away with top honors in an Earliest Pea Contest, first get seeds that grow up fast, like 'Dakota', which gets to pickin' stage in just 52 days. Get yourself a big container, like a half barrel, and then follow these simple steps:

Step 1. Put the container in a sheltered spot, like a deck or patio, that gets full sun. The soil inside will warm up in the blink of an eye. It'll also be nice and well drained when your garden soil is still pure mud.

Step 2. Fill the pot with good commercial potting soil and compost.

Step 3. In the middle, sink a piece of chicken wire that has been rolled into a fat tube.

Step 4. Plant the seeds around the outside of the tube.

Step 5. Keep them well watered, and feed them diluted Compost Tea (see page 351) about every 3 weeks throughout the growing season.

SUPER Growing Secrets

KEEP A WEATHER WATCH

If your pea plants just keel over and die, chances are the culprit is heatstroke — though it could possibly be cold. To stay strong and healthy, peas need temperatures that range between 55 and 75°F. Give them shelter during hot spells, and if you live in cooler climates make sure they get full sun.

Give Me Some Peanuts . . .

As some of us remember from our school days, peanuts aren't nuts at all: They're legumes, like peas and beans. Though most folks think of them as a southern crop, you can grow them as far north as southern Canada if you choose the right variety — namely, 'Early Spanish', which matures in 110 days. (Just don't expect a crop that will turn you into a peanut-butter tycoon.)

Way Down South

Down Dixie way, you can grow the larger Virginia peanuts that take a little longer to mature (usually 120 days) and, timing aside, don't perform well up North.

Catch the Show

Peanuts are good-looking plants, with big yellow flowers that look like sweet peas. But the base of the plant is where the action is. There, smaller flowers grow on runners, or "pegs," that actually burrow into the ground, where the seeds — a.k.a. peanuts — are formed. You can help the process by burying the runners, but they're so much fun to watch that I let 'em go to it all by themselves.

Roll Out the Barrel

I like to grow a couple of peanut plants in big containers on my patio so I can see the show up close. Use wooden barrels sawed in half, with holes drilled

in the bottom for drainage. Fill them with a mixture of good commercial potting soil and compost. Give the plants plenty of water until the pegs bury themselves, then ease off the hose trigger a little. And every 3 weeks give them a drink of All-Season Green-Up Tonic (see page 349).

Well Grounded

Like other legumes, peanuts resent having their roots tampered with. Plant the seeds outdoors when Jack Frost has gone for good and the soil temperature is at least 65°F.

Peanuts like light, well-drained soil with a pH of 6.0 to 7.0. Dig the soil deep, and work in plenty of organic matter. Peanuts also need a good supply of phosphorus and potassium, so add bonemeal and wood ashes to the soil about a month before planting time.

Down South, plant peanuts, shells and all, 3 to 4 inches deep and 5 inches apart. Up north, take off the shells (but not the skins) and set them in the ground 2 inches deep and 5 inches apart. Thin the Spanish type to 18 inches, Virginia to 2 feet.

Jerry Baker Says

"Take it from me, no matter where you grow your crop, buy seeds from a good seed company — the roasted kind they sell at the ballpark won't amount to a hill of . . . peanuts."

GRANDMA PUTT'S BLACK BEAN SOUP

When I was a kid, I could never get enough of this tummy-warmer. One sip and you'll know why!

6 SERVINGS

- 1 cup dried black beans
- 4 cups water
- ½ teaspoon salt
- 1 celery rib with leaves, chopped
- 1 medium onion, chopped
- 2 ham hocks
- 1 bay leaf
- ½ teaspoon dried thyme
- 2 tablespoons dry sherry
- 2 hard-cooked eggs

1. Soak the beans overnight, drain and put them into a kettle with fresh water.

2. Add remaining ingredients, except eggs and sherry. Bring to a boil, lower the heat, cover the pan, and simmer until the beans are tender and the meat is falling off the bones, about 3 hours.

3. Remove the ham hocks and set aside to cool. Scoop out about ½ cup of the beans and purée the rest. Return to the pan, add reserved beans and all the meat you can pick off the bones. Thin with hot water or stock, if necessary.

4. Bring almost to a boil, then stir in the sherry. Serve garnished with thin slices of the egg.

MIGHTY MINTY PEAS

To my way of thinking, peas and mint is a combination made in suppertime heaven. After one bite of these, if you don't agree, I'll eat my pea-pickin' hat!

4 SERVINGS

- 1½ cups shelled small fresh peas
- ⅓ cup chicken broth
- 4 tablespoons butter or margarine
- 2 teaspoons sugar
- 1 tablespoon minced fresh mint, or 1 teaspoon dried mint plus 1 tablespoon minced parsley, lettuce, or spinach

1. Combine all the ingredients in a saucepan.

2. Stir over high heat for 1 minute.

3. Turn the heat down, cover the pan, and simmer until tender — 10 minutes or so for very small peas, about a minute more for larger ones.

GREEN BEAN AND BLUE CHEESE PIE

Here's a crowd-pleaser that Grandma Putt used to whip up for Sunday breakfasts.

6 SERVINGS

1 single unbaked piecrust
½ pound whole trimmed green beans
2 tablespoons butter
1 cup diced onion
4 eggs, lightly beaten
2 cups light cream
dash nutmeg
½ teaspoon salt
¼ teaspoon pepper
1 cup (⅓ pound) crumbled blue cheese

1. Preheat oven to 350°F.

2. Steam the beans until they are tender crisp, about 3 minutes. Plunge into cold water, and drain.

3. Melt the butter in a sauté pan, and sauté the onion until limp, 3–5 minutes.

4. Beat together the eggs, cream, nutmeg, salt, and pepper. Pour the custard mixture into the piecrust. Scatter the onion evenly over the pie. Sprinkle the blue cheese over the onion. Lay the green beans on top of the pie.

5. Bake the pie for 45 minutes, or until golden brown. Remove it from the oven and allow it to sit for a least 15 minutes before serving.

LIMY LIMAS WITH DILL

When I was a boy, nothing could get me to eat lima beans — until Grandma Putt served 'em up this way.

4 SERVINGS

2 pounds fresh lima beans in the shell
2 tablespoons butter
1 tablespoon olive oil
3 tablespoons freshly squeezed lime juice
½ tablespoon minced fresh dill or ½ teaspoon dillweed
salt and freshly ground black pepper

1. Shell the beans.

2. Boil them in a large pot with an ample covering of water for about 20 minutes, or until they're as tender as you want them.

3. Drain the cooked limas and return them to the pot.

4. Reheat with the butter and oil, then stir in the lime juice, dill, and salt and pepper to taste.

BEETS AND GREENS FAMILY

Beets • Lettuce • Spinach • Swiss Chard

Grandma Putt used to say that the beets and greens clan was just about the best-looking family she knew — and I'm with her 100 percent! But these leafy guys will do more than dress up your vegetable patch: Fresh from the garden, they'll put the kind of flavor on your table that you won't find down at the local salad bar.

Four of a Kind

Technically speaking, lettuce belongs to a different scientific clan from beets, spinach, and Swiss chard. But because they have a couple of very important things in common, Grandma Putt always thought of them as one big happy family. What are their common threads?

• They all turn out their best performance in cool weather.

• Except for a tendency to bolt if the weather gets too hot for their liking, they're about as trouble-free as a crop can be.

Get to Calculatin'

I plant plenty of beets and greens in the early spring, but because they like cool weather so much, they also get a lot of space in my fall garden. I'm always very careful to figure out the right sowing date so I'm sure my crops have time to grow to good eating size before winter sets in for good.

Here's how I make my calculations. This may sound a little complicated, but it's really pretty simple once you do it a time or two — and believe me, being able to have crisp, fresh lettuce or spinach in the fall makes it worth the effort!

1. Look up each variety in a seed catalog, and note the days to maturity and the number of days it takes for the seeds to germinate. Then add those numbers together.

2. Add another 10 days, because that's about how much longer it takes crops to mature in late summer and early fall than it does in springtime. (That's because of shorter days and cooler temperatures.)

3. Tack on 14 more days to give the crops time to churn out their harvest.

4. Add up all those numbers and count backward from the first expected frost, and you've got a fall planting date!

Beets (*Beta vulgaris*)

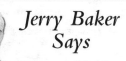

Grandma Putt always gave me beet seeds to plant in my garden because (she told me years later) once you get 'em started, they take so little care that you almost can't go wrong with 'em. I still recommend beets as a surefire winner for busy folks who don't have much time to spend in the garden — and for folks who just want a powerful lot of good eatin' for not much effort.

Keep Their Cool

Beets like cool, moist weather and loamy soil that's well drained and chock-full of organic matter. When it comes to pH, the closer it is to neutral, the better they like it; but anything from 6.5 to 7.5 will suit them just fine.

The BBC

I'm talking about the Big Beet BroadCast, not the British Broadcasting Company. Beets are just about the only root crop I know that doesn't mind being transplanted. But I never bother starting them indoors; I just sow the seeds right in my garden starting about a month before I expect the last frost.

I soak the beet seeds overnight in my Seed Starter Tonic (see page 355), then I sow them in a wide row or broadcast them in a big patch. (*Broadcasting* just means scattering seeds over the whole bed.) Then I cover them with ½ inch of soil. I make repeat sowings every 2 weeks until just after the last frost hits.

> ### Jerry Baker Says
>
> "Even small beets send their roots a long, long way into the ground. If they have to struggle through heavy soil or bump up against underground obstacles, they won't develop the way you want them to. That's why I always dig down 10 or 12 inches, and raise up my beds another 6 inches or so on top. I also make sure to clean out all of the solid objects I find as I go along (like rocks, sticks, toy soldiers, and even the flashlight I lost last fall)."

What's This About Bolting?

You've seen kids who always seem to bolt out the door when the dishes need drying or the trash needs emptying. Well, cool-weather crops like spinach and lettuce make the same fast exit whenever it gets too warm for them. They take the hot weather as their cue to go full steam ahead and grow tall, blossom, and go to seed. In the process, the leaves become bitter and tough, and are not very tasty to eat.

There's not much you can do to prevent bolting, though some varieties of these plants are more tolerant of hot weather than others — just like us folks!

A Jump Start

If you want an extra-early crop, start your seeds indoors 5 to 6 weeks before you want to move them to the garden. I always use individual pots or cell packs — it makes for an easier transition come moving day.

Spread 'em Out

Whichever way I sow my seeds, I don't pay any attention to spacing, because beets are eccentric germinators from way back when. I never know how many sprouts will come up or where, but I always know I'll have a lot of thinning to do when the seedlings get about 2 inches tall.

I leave 3 to 4 inches between small kinds, or ones that I plan to pull when they're young, and 6 inches between larger types. Don't be timid, and don't shy away from thinning a second time if the plants look crowded after they've grown for a month or so. Beet roots need all of the elbowroom they can get, if they're going to grow up (or, rather, down) the way you want them to.

Double-Dipping

Beets are a double-dip crop: The leafy green tops are as good to eat, and as good for you, as the roots. In fact, some folks grow whole patches of beets just for the greens. If you're planning to eat the tops and leave the bottoms, don't thin your crop at all. Just clip 'em off when you want to eat 'em, and forget about what's going on below the ground.

Jerry Baker Says

"When I'm thinning beet plants, I clip off the little greens at ground level with a pair of scissors. I never pull them up, because that would disturb the other roots in the patch. Then I rush right inside with those tender little greens and toss 'em up in a big salad. They're delish!"

WOODY-SEED STARTER TONIC

Seeds with woody coats, like those of beets and parsnips, get off to a faster start when you treat them to a dose of this terrific Tonic.

1 cup of vinegar
2 oz. of liquid dish soap
2 cups of warm water

Mix all of these ingredients together and soak your seeds in the mixture for 24 hours. Then plant them, and lay a strip of burlap over the row — it will create a warm environment that lets moisture in and encourages faster sprouting.

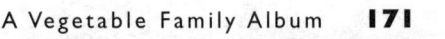

Menu Choices

If you're growing beets for the roots, feed them every 3 weeks with a liquid organic fertilizer that's low in nitrogen and high in phosphorus and potassium. But if it's only the greens you hanker for, use a fertilizer that's evenly balanced like fish fertilizer.

Keep Your Cool — Up to a Point

Though it's true that beets grow best in cool weather, they can't handle an extended cold snap after they've formed a nice, tidy bunch of leaves. If the temperature plunges below 50°F and stays there for 2 weeks or more, the leaves could bolt; if that happens, you can kiss your whole crop goodbye!

I always plan for the unexpected by keeping a few floating row covers handy. If my local weather forecaster predicts chilly days ahead, I pull the blankets up over my beets.

Another Season

Way down South, beets make a fine winter crop. Just keep your territory's temperature ranges in mind and time your plantings accordingly.

SUPER Growing Secrets

SWEET SUCCESS

Beets pack a bigger load of sugar than any other vegetable — and even so, they're low in calories. The two secrets to keeping your crop sweet and juicy are (1) raise 'em up fast in spring or fall, while the weather's cool, and (2) give 'em steady, even moisture. Hot, dry weather makes beets tough and stringy. And on-again, off-again watering can crack the roots and make ring marks form inside.

Under the Big Top

If you're a hard-core beet-green fan, grow a variety that's bred especially for great-tasting greens, and plenty of them. The two I like best are 'Early Wonder Tall Top', which gives me bunches of bright, glossy greens (and tasty young roots, to boot) in just 45 days, and — to spread out the feast — 'Big Top', which delivers its crop in about 55 days from the time you plant them.

The Nutritional Scorecard

• Beet roots have a good supply of vitamins B and C.

• Beet greens are loaded with calcium, iron, and — best of all — cancer-fighting beta carotene.

Into the Oven

I like to roast my beets just like potatoes. All of that dry heat locks in the nutrients and brings out the sweetness better than any other cooking method. It takes some time, though, so either I pop 'em into the oven when I'm baking something else, or I do up a whole passel of 'em at once, and then chill 'em to use later in salads. Here's my favorite roasting method:

1. Wrap the beets in aluminum foil and put them into a baking pan.

2. Bake them at 350 to 400°F until they're tender. (This will take 1½ to 2 hours, depending on the size of the beets.)

3. Take off the foil and let them stand until they're just cool enough for you to handle.

4. Peel them while they're still warm, and then dig in.

Can't-Beat-'em Beets

JERRY'S FAVORITE Vegetable Varieties

BEET RED? Beets aren't always ruby red. They also come in white and yellow. If you want to surprise folks at dinnertime, do what I do: Grow a variety like **'White Beet'** or **'Golden'**. Besides fine taste and good looks, beets of a different tint earn another feather for their cap: They keep their color to themselves instead of sharing it with everything else on your plate the way red beets tend to do.

CANDY LAND There's even a beet that's striped red and white like peppermint candy. In fact, some catalogs list it as 'Peppermint', but more often it's called **'Chioggia'**. It's a real head-turner when you shred it raw or slice it up thin and toss it in a salad. If you prefer cooked beets, roast 'Chioggias', because when you boil them, they lose their stripes. Either way, they taste great.

SLICE 'EM UP For nice, uniform slices for canning or pickling, grow a long, cylindrical beet like **'Forono' or 'Cylindra'** instead of one that's globe-shaped.

You Can't "Beet" 'em

Once they're out of the oven, I like to serve beets up in all kinds of ways. Here's a sampling of my favorites:

• Sliced warm with a little butter, orange juice, and freshly ground pepper

• Warm or chilled with a sauce made of yogurt with a spoonful or two of horseradish for zip

• Chilled in a salad with oranges and onions

• Warm with a sweet-and-sour dressing (4 parts cider vinegar to 1 part sugar)

A Heart of Black

Beets become discolored in the middle if the soil they call home is lacking in either boron or phosphorus. It's a condition called black heart (though the beets' innards turn brown, not black). Before you plant your seeds, have the folks at the Cooperative Extension Service or a private testing lab give your soil a thorough examination. A good soil test is especially important if you live in certain parts of the Northeast, Midwest, or Northwest, where boron is often AWOL.

Too Darn Hot

If your soil passed its test with flying colors, but your beets are still getting failing grades, you can probably blame Mother Nature: Roots that develop when temperatures are high often don't color up the way they should.

Good Buddies

Beets and kohlrabi make great companions in the veggie garden. They like the same growing conditions, and they take their nourishment from different levels of the soil: beets way down deep and kohlrabi more toward the surface. Beets also get along well with lettuce, most members of the cabbage family, and bush beans — but they don't want anything to do with pole beans!

In the Pink of Health

As long as you give 'em good air circulation and a soil pH that's close to neutral, beets don't spend much time in sick bay. But to be on the safe side, keep their home clean and rotate your crops every year: Germs that cause scab and leaf spot spend the winter in the soil and in plant debris, and they could attack your beets in spring.

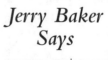

Jerry Baker Says

"The sooner you harvest your beets, the sweeter and more tender they'll taste. I try to get mine out of the ground when they're 1½ to 2½ inches in diameter."

Lettuce *(Lactuca sativa)*

Grandma Putt used to say that she felt sorry for folks who had to use store-bought lettuce in their salads. I feel the same way. Even nowadays, when you can get some pretty fancy greens in the supermarket, the only way to get lettuce that's really worth its weight in vinaigrette is to grow it yourself. Here's how to do it.

Let the Sunshine In — Maybe

If you live in cool-climate territory, plant your lettuce where it will get full sun. But in warmer parts of the country, or when you plant a summer crop, give it some relief from ol' Sol's rays. Like a delicate lady beneath her parasol, lettuce plants like to bask in the shade of tall veggies like pole beans, corn, and tomatoes. They also feel — and look — right at home tucked in among taller ornamentals in a flower bed.

Starting Out

I sow most of my lettuce crops directly in the garden as soon as I can work the soil in springtime, which is generally about a month before the last frost hits. When I want an early start, I sow my seed indoors about a month before I plan to move the plants to the garden. They're hardy youngsters — they'll take to life in the great outdoors as soon as the mercury stays above 30°F at night (after they've gone through their hardening-off week, of course; for a refresher course, see pages 39–40 in Chapter 3).

SUPER Growing Secrets

PLANT EARLY AND OFTEN

Any kind of lettuce comes and goes in the blink of an eye. To keep your salad bowl from running out, comb the seed catalogs for varieties that mature at different times, and sow a new crop every 10 days.

Seeing the Light

Lettuce seeds need lots of light to germinate. Whether I'm starting them indoors or out, I scatter them on top of the soil and then barely cover them up.

Home, Sweet Home

Lettuce prefers soil in the 6.5 to 7.0 pH range, that holds moisture but drains well. Dig in plenty of compost, and before you sow seeds, remove solid obstacles like rocks and soil clumps that could stand in their way at sprouting time.

A Healthy Meal: The Big N

During the growing season, I give my lettuce an extra nitrogen boost with soybean meal. I just sprinkle it along the row as I harvest the early leaves. Then I dig it into the first 2 inches or so of soil before I plant my follow-up crops. Alfalfa meal does the job just as well as soybean meal. You can buy both at most good garden centers.

Water from Above

For most crops, nothing beats soaker hoses or a drip irrigation system for fending off diseases and saving on water bills. But lettuce actually performs better when you water it with an overhead sprinkler. The plants stay cooler, and they're less likely to bolt or come down with heat-related diseases. As with all crops, water lettuce early in the day, so the leaves aren't wet through the night, when fungi are on the prowl.

Jerry Baker Says

"Every year, in the fall, I work manure into my lettuce beds. It ages over the winter, and come spring, it gives my plants the nitrogen boost they need to grow great gobs of tasty leaves."

Side by Side

Here's one of my favorite space-saving methods: When Brussels sprouts, cabbage, and broccoli seedlings are a few inches high, I plant quick-growing lettuce among them. By the time the other crops start needing elbowroom, all of the lettuce is long gone to the salad bowl.

A Short, Happy Life

Thanks to the fact that it doesn't hang around the garden too long before heading for the salad bowl, lettuce doesn't have as many bad guys gunning for it as most crops do. Slugs can be a problem in cool, damp territory like the Pacific Northwest, though. These slimy creeps are especially partial to 'Deertongue', an old-time, leaf-type lettuce.

Tips Burned?

If the tips of your lettuce leaves turn brown and are burned-looking, they've come down with tip burn. It's caused by a combination of an irregular water supply and heat. Make sure you water steadily and evenly, and put up a barrier between your tender plants and the brutal sun — a piece of lattice or a heat-loving crop growing on a trellis would be just the ticket! And don't worry: You can still eat your crop; just cut off the tips.

Ah, Sweet Mystery of Lettuce

When it comes time to shop for lettuce seed, I always feel like a kid in a candy store: There are hundreds of kinds to choose from, and I want one of everything. Lettuce is grouped into five major types, which are based on the plants' shapes and growing habits. I generally wind up with a few varieties from each group.

Leaf types are the easiest to grow. They don't form heads, and they mature in a flash — they're the best choice if your home turf heats up fast in spring. Leaf lettuces have a tender, sweet taste, and they're pretty plants, with frilly, curly, or lobed leaves, in all shades and combinations of red and green.

One of my favorites is 'Black-Seeded Simpson', an old-timer that Grandma Putt grew. It has juicy, crinkly, lime green leaves that are ready to eat, baby-sized, in just 26 days, and it reaches full size in 46 days.

Romaine, or **cos lettuce** comes in both red and green, with oblong leaves that form loose, upright heads. They're crisp and slightly tart. If you want lettuce that's as much fun to look at as it is good to eat, try 'Freckles'. It has bright green leaves with red spots that look just like Howdy Doody's freckles.

Butterhead, a.k.a. **Boston, bibb,** or **looseleaf,** has loose heads of wavy leaves with a creamy texture and delicate flavor. 'Ermosa' is a standout. It grows just as well in spring, fall, and even summer. It heads up in 48 days.

Summercrisp, a.k.a. **French crisp,** is midway between butterhead and crisphead. The leaves have an open form when the plants are young; as they mature, they form compact heads. At whatever stage you eat them, they're crisp and juicy. 'Sierra' has puckered, red-tipped leaves and a heavenly taste. It matures in 48 days and stands up to summer heat better than any other lettuce I've grown.

Crisphead can be tricky, so choose varieties carefully. One branch of this group, the classic iceberg type, needs a long, cool growing season and just about constant attention or the plants will bolt — and your crop will be history.

But the best crispheads, like 'Crispino', 'Cardinale', and 'Canasta', can take some heat and will give you plenty of sweet, juicy, crunchy leaves for salads and sandwiches. All crispheads form heads, though generally the warmer the climate, the looser they'll be.

SUPER Growing Secrets

SLOWIN' THE GROWIN'
To keep lettuce from going to seed, puncture the soil at the base of the plant. Go in at an angle with a sharp spade to *slightly* wound the roots.

The End Result?

When you're having trouble deciding what kind of lettuce to grow, it helps to think about how much you'll want to pick and use at any one time.

• **Keep clipping.** With all types except the solid-headed icebergs, you can take as many outer leaves as you want, starting as soon as they're big enough to eat, and keep at it until a central stem starts to form. Any leaves that grow after that will have a bitter taste.

• **Harvest the whole plant.** This works for all types. Wait until the plant reaches full size but is still young and tender, and harvest the whole thing.

• **Cut and come again.** Let leaf types get as big as you want them to, then cut off the whole plant about an inch above the soil. (Slice the stem cleanly with a sharp knife.) It will grow back, sometimes twice.

Jerry Baker Says

"In the spring, when I harvest my first green onions, I pull every other one. Then I plant lettuce in all the empty spots. The lettuce makes the onions grow better, and the onions return the favor by keeping those rascally rabbits away from the good greens."

A Word to the Wise from Grandma Putt

Not for Cabbage Only

Grandma Putt used to make some of her sauerkraut with iceberg lettuce instead of cabbage. It has a milder flavor that's a nice change of pace from regular sauerkraut, and it's easier to digest.

Wilt City

The only bone I have to pick with lettuce is that it's not a very good keeper. Leaf lettuces wilt or rot more quickly than the firmer types, but even the crunchiest crisphead goes downhill fast. For the longest after-harvest life, pull up the whole plant and put it, roots and all, into a glass full of water, just as you'd do with a cut flower. Then put a big plastic bag over the whole thing and set it in the fridge.

Munchin' on Mesclun

With the price tag they put on those fancy mesclun mixes in the supermarket, you'd think it was the most exotic stuff that ever came down the pike. But it's just baby greens, and you grow them in basically the same way you would if you planned to wait until they were all grown up before you ate them. Here's the routine:

1. Choose your greens. Although most seed companies sell mixtures, I make my own. That way, I get exactly the kinds I want. Just make sure they all mature about the same time.

2. Mix 'em up. Pour all of the seeds into a jar and really stir 'em up.

3. Plant. Sow seeds good and thick in beds that are about 3 feet square. Don't fuss with thinning — the plants get picked when they're still small, so they don't need room to spread out.

4. Plant more. Sow a new crop every week to 10 days.

5. Clip early and often. When the plants are about 4 inches tall, cut them off an inch above the ground.

6. Give them a drink. Water the bed with my All-Season Green-Up Tonic (see page 349) and wait for the plants to sprout back up. It generally takes about 3 weeks.

SUPER Growing Secrets

SAVE ME!

All lettuce plants are what scientists call open-pollinated. That means you can save seeds from the hardiest, best-tasting plants, and grow their offspring next year.

Other Strokes for Other Folks

You can get only two or three harvests from one bed of mesclun, so some folks don't bother to let it regrow. Instead, they harvest whole plants as soon as they get big enough, then sow a new crop.

Beyond Lettuce

The mesclun you find in most supermarkets is a mix of baby lettuces. It makes for some mighty fine salads, but I like to broaden the scope of things. After all, that's one reason I grow my own! Here are some of the crops that cozy up to the lettuce in my mesclun beds:

- Basil
- Beets
- Chives
- Kale
- Mustard
- Nasturtiums
- Parsley
- Spinach
- Swiss chard
- Violets

A Salad-Lover's Garden

If you like to belly up to a salad bar as much as I do, you owe yourself a salad garden. I have mine in the same place Grandma Putt kept hers: right by the kitchen door. That way, I can wander out with my salad bowl and a pair of scissors, clip off whatever I'm hankerin' for, and head back to the kitchen to toss all those fresh, crisp veggies in my favorite dressing.

Plan on It

Just as with any other garden, a salad patch needs a little advance planning if it's going to give you a harvest you'll be happy with. The basics are the same as the ones we talked about in Chapter 2, but when it comes to a specialized garden like this one, you need to make another planning decision — namely, which of the two main salad camps you fall into:

• **The purists.** If your idea of salad heaven is a big bowl of leafy greens with a great dressing on top and nothing else to complicate the scene, you're in this category. When it comes time to send off your seed order, you'll have a field day.

Every year plant breeders come out with new kinds of greens — and rediscover old-timers — that stand right up to heat and cold. And the colors and leaf shapes will knock your apron off!

• **The adventurers.** If you like a little bit of everything in your salad, make sure you leave room for your favorites, especially such classics as carrots, scallions, beets, cucumbers, radishes, and (of course) a tomato plant or two.

The Well-Rounded Salad Garden

If you fall into the adventurers category, grow small or "baby" varieties. They are generally tastier in their raw state than bigger veggies, and they take up less room, besides. Here are some of my favorites:

JERRY'S FAVORITE Vegetable Varieties

Carrots	Cucumbers	Tomatoes	Beets
'Gold Nugget'	'Bush	'Goldie'	'Gladiator'
'Lady Finger'	Champion'	'Pixie'	'Kleine Bol', a.k.a.
'Little Finger'	'Patio Pik'	'Tiny Tim'	'Little Ball'
	'Spacemaster'		

Looks Good Enough to Eat

Just as a lot of veggies look as good as they taste, plenty of flowers taste as good as they look. Here's a trio of my favorites:

Borage. Grandma Putt always swore by borage as a surefire cheerer-upper. Anytime I was feeling down in the dumps, she'd make me a big dish of potato salad made special with borage flowers. Nowadays, I also add them to tossed salads, sprinkle them on cottage cheese, or blend them with cream cheese to make a sandwich spread.

Both flowers and leaves are mild, but flavorful. Use one or the other, though: The leaves taste their best before the flowers appear. Besides being a mood lifter and a taste treat, borage packs a good supply of calcium and potassium.

Chrysanthemums. The Chinese believe that chrysanthemums give you more vitality and lengthen your life. That sounds like a pretty good deal to me, so I eat 'em every chance I get. I float the petals in soups or toss 'em in salads, and I use whole flowers as a garnish for fruit salads. They have a slightly bitter taste that sets off the sweetness of the fruit.

Nasturtiums. Somehow or other, Grandma Putt got hold of General Dwight Eisenhower's recipe for vegetable soup and found out that his "secret" ingredient was chopped-up nasturtium stems. He said he boiled 'em briefly and then tossed 'em in at the end of the cooking time.

Well, Grandma Putt figured that if it was good enough for Ike it was good enough for her. We ate plenty of nasturtiums after that, and I still do. I like the flowers coated with a dressing made from olive oil and lemon juice, or stuffed with tuna salad. (The pistils are bitter, so pull them off before you serve up the flowers.) The leaves have a tangy taste, and they're loaded with vitamins A, C, and D. I use them instead of lettuce on sandwiches.

Wait — That's Not All!

Here are some more good-lookers that can go right from the garden to the dinner table.

Bachelor's buttons	Hollyhocks	Pansies
Calendulas	Johnny jump ups	Petunias
Carnations	Marigolds	Violets
English daisies		

Spinach *(Spinacia oleracea)*

Like any other red-blooded American kid, I hated spinach. Grandma Putt had to practically stuff it down my throat — Popeye or no Popeye. And as for growing the foul stuff in my little garden — forget it!

As Grandma Putt always said, though, time changes all things. Ever since I decided I was grown up enough to make my own decisions, I've been gobbling up all of the spinach I can get my fork into, and planting every variety that will grow up happy in my territory.

If you love spinach salads and eggs Florentine, you owe it to yourself to grow a big patch of Popeye's favorite. Spinach needs cool weather to thrive, but if you choose planting times carefully and look for heat-resistant varieties, you can grow it anywhere in the country.

The Home Turf

Spinach likes full sun in cool climates, but in hotter areas, give it some afternoon shade. Test your soil's pH before you plant: Spinach rebels if its home is either too sweet or too sour. A pH of 6.5 to 7.5 is just right. Like any other leaf crop, spinach needs nitrogen to develop well, so work manure into the soil in the fall. Come springtime, dig in plenty of com-post, because spinach likes all the organic matter it can get.

Ready to Grow

Spinach doesn't like to be transplanted, so I always sow seeds right in the garden, 4 to 6 weeks before the last frost will be heading my way. I set them in the ground ½ inch deep and 2 inches apart, and when the seedlings get their second set of leaves, I give them a drink of my Seedling Strengthener Tonic (see page 356) or fish fertilizer.

When the little guys are about 4 inches tall, I thin them out so they're 6 inches apart. That bed of little dark green plants looks so pretty that it can be tempting to just let them be, but don't — plants that don't have enough elbowroom tend to bolt. Besides, just think of the salad you'll be able to make with all of that tender baby spinach!

Jerry Baker Says

"When I add manure to my spinach bed in the fall, I prepare the area just as I would if I were about to sow the seed — furrows and all. That way, I get a jump on spring planting — and avoid digging in the mud. As soon as the ground thaws, I just drop my seeds into the furrows and cover them up with potting mix."

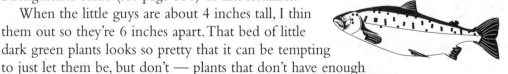

Time and Again

Spinach grows best in the 60 to 65°F range, so for show-stopping results wherever you live, time your plantings so your crop is up and growing when that kind of weather is gracing your territory. If it heats up fast in your neck of the woods, look for bolt-resistant varieties that mature early, like **'Melody'** (savoy-leaved, 40 days), **'Bloomsdale Long Standing'** (savoy-leaved, 45 days), and **'Sohshu'** (smooth-leaved, 40 days).

Sourpuss

If your spinach seeds don't germinate, or the leaves come up brown or yellow around the edges, it means their soil is too acid. To solve the problem, dig in one of the anti-acids I recommend in Chapter 4 (see page 73).

Next to Peas, Please

To save space in the garden, plant your first spinach crop right beside your early peas. By the time the peas are ready for picking, the spinach will already have found its way to the salad bowl.

By the Light of the Moon

Grandma Putt was a great believer in gardening according to the phases of the moon. She always planted her spinach crops during the first quarter of the moon, in one of the three water signs: Cancer, Scorpio, or Pisces.

Let There Be Light — But Not Too Much

Besides being finicky about heat, spinach is sensitive to the amount of light it gets. No matter how well you tend your crop or how cool the temperature stays, the plants will start to bolt when they get more than 14 to 16 hours of daylight. For my later-spring plantings, I try to slow down the process by growing bolt-resistant varieties like 'Olympia' (savoy, 45 days), 'Nordic IV' (savoy, 45 days), and 'Italian Summer' (semi-savoy, 40 days).

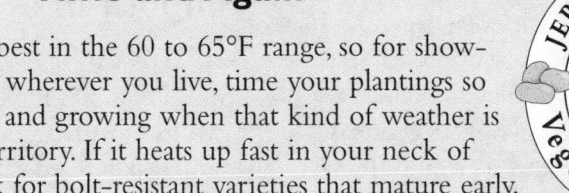

It's the Berries

Grandma Putt always planted spinach and strawberries together. She told me that spinach releases a chemical called saponin that helps the strawberries grow bigger and better.

Spinach Through the Year

I keep sowing spinach every week to 10 days until the temperature hits 75°F. Then I start again in the fall. Some years, when Old Man Winter goes easy on us, I can even grow a crop in my cold frame — that keeps me in fresh spinach right up to spring planting time.

The Relief Pitcher

In summertime, when regular spinach would knuckle under to the heat, I bring in my relief pitcher: New Zealand spinach. It's not really spinach (its scientific moniker is *Tetragonia tetragonoides*), but it looks and tastes enough like spinach that even Popeye wouldn't know the difference. I sow the seeds as soon as it's safe to set out tomatoes and peppers. Later, I clip the leaves anytime I want them, just like I do with spinach.

Spinachsicles

By the time I get the last of my spring crop into the ground, the temperature is reaching the upper limits of the spinach comfort range. In that kind of weather, the seeds germinate

Smooth or Crinkled?

Spinach comes in two leaf forms: smooth and crinkly (seed catalogs call it savoy or savoyed). The smooth-leaved varieties are sweet and tender — just right for salads. I use the savoy types for cooking, because their thicker leaves hold up better to the heat.

better when I give them the old cold-storage treatment. I freeze them for a few days, then take them out, soak them in my Seed Starter Tonic (see page 355), and then put them into the fridge for a few more days to chill out.

Sick Call

Spinach rarely calls in sick, but when it does, what ails it is usually blight, fusarium wilt, or downy mildew. If any of that trio tends to stalk your homestead, grow a disease-resistant variety like 'Melody', 'Indian Summer', or 'Winter Bloomsdale', and pay special attention to the guidelines for good health in Chapter 5 (see pages 90–91).

Jerry Baker Says

"If your plants start turning pale green during the growing season, give them a booster shot of nitrogen — 2 tablespoons of Epsom salts per gallon of water. Don't overdo it: Too much nitrogen gives spinach a sharp, metallic taste, and you don't want that."

It's Good for You, But . . .

Those dark green leaves pack a big load of vitamins and minerals, but if it's iron or calcium you're hankerin' for, you need to look elsewhere. Spinach has plenty of both, but it also contains a chemical called oxalic acid that teams up with the iron and calcium to make a combo that your body can't absorb very well. Other veggies, like turnip greens and broccoli, are much better equipped with the kinds of iron and calcium that build strong bodies.

Harvest Duo

With spinach, you've got two choices at harvesting time:

   1. Start snipping outer leaves as soon as they get big enough to eat. The rest of the plant will keep growing.

   2. When the leaves get large and meaty, cut off the whole plant an inch above soil level. If the weather is still cool enough, the plant will grow another crop of leaves.

Don't Overcook It

When I hear folks say they just don't care for spinach, I can almost bet they've had it cooked only the old-fashioned way: boiled down to a gray-green glop. To cook spinach even a finicky 5-year-old will gobble up, keep these cooking times in mind:

- **Steam:** 3 to 5 minutes
- **Blanch:** 2 to 4 minutes
- **Sauté or stir-fry:** 3 to 5 minutes

Salad Days

To my way of thinking, spinach salad is one of the greatest treats any garden could offer up. Here are some of my favorite combinations:

- Spinach, apple, fennel, and walnuts with a dressing of lemon juice and olive oil
- Spinach, cherry tomatoes, sliced red onions, and croutons topped with your favorite Caesar dressing
- Spinach, sliced celery, and sliced apples tossed in blue cheese dressing

Splish-Splash

Believe you me, spinach leaves can hold a mountain of dirt in all their crinkly crevices. But washing it off isn't nearly as tricky as some folks make it out to be. Here's my foolproof system:

   1. Fill the sink with lukewarm water (it's more comfortable on the hands than cold), and swish the spinach around.

   2. Lift it out and drop it into a colander.

   3. If you still see dirt on the leaves, fill the sink with clean water and repeat the process.

Swiss Chard *(Beta vulgaris cicla)*

The way garden writers carry on these days about Swiss chard as an "edible landscape" plant, you'd think they invented it! But Grandma Putt grew bushels of chard in both her vegetable garden and her flower beds. I still do, because as hard as I've looked, I've never seen a prettier plant — and I haven't found many that are tastier, either.

Bring On the Heat, Bring On the Cold

Unlike its relatives in the beets and greens clan, Swiss chard is no fussbudget. Its seeds will germinate in any temperature from 50 to 85°F. It'll breeze through spring frosts and keep right on churning out tender, great-tasting leaves when the rest of the family has gone belly-up in the heat. Plus, it'll keep going through the first few mild freezes in the fall. You can't beat that!

Ah — Success!

Because I can sow it anytime during the growing season, Swiss chard is one of my favorite crops for succession planting. But whether I use it to replace a cool-weather-only vegetable or give it a new bed of its own, I plant a batch every 2 weeks until freezing time closes in.

A Perennial Act

In mild climates, you can have chard plants growing and producing for several years. Just keep them well fed, and every time the leaves get about a foot high, slice off the whole plant about an inch above the ground.

A Happy Camper

Swiss chard will get along just about anyplace you want to plant it; but given its druthers, it likes full sun (a little shade in hot climates), well-drained soil that's chock-full of organic matter, and a pH between 6.0 and 7.0. Grandma Putt taught me to dig some well-cured manure into the soil before planting time, just to give those leaves a good, healthy nitrogen boost.

First of the Season

I start my first crop of chard right in the garden as soon as the soil can be worked, when the temperature belowground is at least 50°F. I sow the seeds 4 inches apart and ½ inch deep, and thin them out when the plants get about 6 inches tall. When I know I'll want to harvest whole plants, I leave 4 to 5 inches between them. But if I plan to clip individual leaves and let new ones grow in their place, I give the plants a little more elbowroom — say 8 to 10 inches.

Eat or Transplant?

I do both with the chard seedlings I pull up. Some of them go right into the kitchen. (They're terrific in salads or just lightly steamed and tossed with a little butter and garlic.) The rest I replant in the garden or in big pots by the front porch — Swiss chard is so great-looking, it's nice to let the neighbors get a look at the show.

Company's Coming

Swiss chard keeps good company with lettuce, and gets along with any member of the cabbage and bean and pea clans. But it prefers not to grow up next to beets or spinach.

SUPER Growing Secrets

I ♥ BORON

Like its brother the beet, Swiss chard needs boron in its soil. If it doesn't get enough, the stems crack. To add boron to the soil, sprinkle a little borax in and among the rows at planting time.

Ancient Roots

While we were working in our garden, Grandma Putt loved to tell me tales of how all of the vegetables we were growing came to be here. (I reckon she thought of it as a painless way to teach me some history.) She said that folks in what's now Europe have been growing Swiss chard since Aristotle's time, and that here in our part of the world, George Washington grew bumper crops of it at Mount Vernon.

Food and Drink

When my plants are about 4 weeks old, I give them a drink of Seedling Strengthener Tonic (see page 356). Throughout the growing season, I make sure they get a steady, even supply of moisture, and then I regularly feed them with my All-Season Green-Up Tonic, especially as the temperature starts rising (see page 349). Laid-back as chard is, it can still stress out and bolt if a drought hits. Then you've got problems, because even if it keeps growing, the leaves and stalks will be stringy and bitter.

A Star Stand-In

Swiss chard makes a tasty stand-in for any kind of greens, cooked or raw. I like to use it instead of spinach in vegetable lasagna, because it holds its crunch better than spinach.

Colorful Decisions

It takes a more decisive guy than I am to stick with just one variety of Swiss chard. Most kinds reach the young-eating stage in 5 weeks and grow to full size in 55 to 60 days. Here are some of my favorites — for looks, taste, and performance.

JERRY'S FAVORITE Vegetable Varieties

'Argentata'—a hardy old-timer from Italy, with silvery white ribs, deep green leaves, and flavor worthy of a Roman emperor.

'Rhubarb'—a classic from this side of the ocean, with ruby red stalks and veins and dark green leaves. (In fact, some catalogs list it as 'Ruby Red'.) I plant this one a little later than other varieties — it tends to bolt if a late-spring frost comes a-callin'. But its good looks and great taste make it worth a little extra attention.

'Bright Lights'—a star attraction if ever there was one. It has a delicate flavor and a nice, crunchy texture. But it's not the taste that draws oohs and ahs from visitors: It's the bright green leaves and stalks of red, white, pink, sunshine yellow, and bright orange — all mixed together in the row!

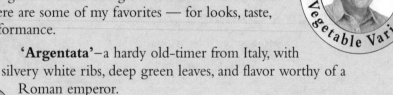

RUBY RED SAUCE

Grandma Putt always had a bumper harvest of beets, and a lot of them went into this terrific-tasting sauce. She served it up with chicken or pork — and, believe you me, nobody at the table turned down second helpings!

3 CUPS

   2 cups raw beets, grated
1½ cups apple, peeled and grated
   3 tablespoons dry red wine
   2 tablespoons honey
   2 tablespoons lemon juice
   1 teaspoon grated lemon rind
      water
3–4 tablespoons prepared horseradish
      salt and pepper

1. In a medium-size saucepan, combine the beets, apple, wine, honey, lemon juice, and lemon rind. Add just enough water to cover. Cook for 15 to 20 minutes, or until the beets are tender.

2. Place the mixture in a food processor or blender and process until smooth. Add the horseradish, season to taste with salt and pepper, and reheat.

3. Spoon the sauce over sautéed chicken breasts or pork chops.

GARLIC LOVER'S CREAMED SPINACH

If you like spinach even a little bit, you'll love this version spiced up with garlic.

4 SERVINGS

24 cups spinach
 2 tablespoons butter
 2 large garlic cloves, minced
 2 tablespoons flour
 1 cup milk
 2 tablespoons heavy cream
¼ teaspoon dried marjoram or thyme
   salt and pepper

1. Steam the spinach until limp, 3–5 minutes.

2. In a small saucepan, melt the butter and sauté the garlic. Stir in the flour to make a thick paste. Add the milk a little at a time, stirring well after each addition to prevent lumps.

3. Transfer the sauce and the spinach to a food processor or blender and process until well blended. Reheat the mixture.

4. Add the cream and marjoram or thyme, and season to taste with salt and pepper.

DANDY DANDELION SALAD

Who says nothing good ever came from a weed patch? Why, sometimes a common old weed is the best friend a salad bowl ever had!

4 TO 6 SERVINGS

8 cups dandelion greens
½ cup peeled, julienne-sliced Jerusalem artichokes
½ cup grated carrots
2 tablespoons dried currants
2 teaspoons finely minced onion
¾ teaspoon prepared horseradish
½ teaspoon Dijon mustard
4 teaspoons lemon juice
¼ cup vegetable oil
¼ cup olive oil
¼ teaspoon salt
¼ teaspoon white pepper

1. Combine the dandelion greens, Jerusalem artichokes, carrots, and currants in a salad bowl.

2. Whisk together the remaining ingredients and pour over the salad.

3. Toss to coat, and serve at once.

CREAM OF LETTUCE SOUP

Folks nowadays make a big deal out of "thinking outside the box." But to Grandma Putt, that kind of creative brainwork was just business as usual. Take lettuce, for instance. To most folks, it belongs in a salad, and that's that. But to Grandma Putt . . . well, just try this super soup of hers, and you'll know what I mean.

6 TO 8 SERVINGS

2 tablespoons butter
¼ cup chopped scallions
16 cups chopped mild-flavored lettuce or greens
3 cups chicken broth
⅛ teaspoon white pepper
salt
6 ounces cream cheese

1. In a large soup pot, melt the butter, and sauté the scallions and lettuce until the lettuce is limp, 2–4 minutes.

2. Add the chicken broth and pepper. Simmer for 5 minutes. Season to taste with salt.

3. Cool the soup slightly and purée in a food processor or blender. Return the soup to the pot and reheat.

4. Dice the cream cheese and add to the soup. Heat until melted. Serve hot, garnished with minced herbs or flowers.

CHARD WITH LEMON AND BACON

To my way of thinking, greens and bacon go together like boats and water. Just about any kind of young, tender green is great in this recipe, but Swiss chard is my favorite.

6 SERVINGS

- 2 tablespoons olive oil
- ½ cup diced Canadian bacon
- 1 large clove of garlic, minced
- 16 cups roughly chopped greens
- 2 tablespoons lemon juice

1. In a large sauté pan, heat the olive oil, and sauté the Canadian bacon and garlic for 5 minutes.

2. Add the chopped greens and toss to coat. Add the lemon juice and cover.

3. Cook, stirring occasionally, until the greens are limp, 3–7 minutes (more for collards).

4. Season to taste with salt and pepper.

PURPLE EGGS AND PICKLED BEETS

If you have trouble getting your young 'uns to eat their veggies, try this kid-pleasin' favorite. It sure made a vegetable lover out of me!

8 TO 10 SERVINGS

- 6 cups diced cooked beets
- 6–12 hard-cooked eggs, peeled
- 2 cups water
- 1½ cups white vinegar or wine vinegar
- 1½ cups sugar
- 1 cinnamon stick
- 20 whole cloves
- 5 allspice berries

1. Place the beets and eggs in a large glass or ceramic jar.

2. Combine the remaining ingredients in a saucepan and heat. Pour the mixture over the beets and eggs.

3. Refrigerate for 1 or 2 days before eating. The eggs will keep for 1 week, the beets for 2 weeks.

CABBAGE FAMILY

Broccoli • Brussels Sprouts • Cabbage
Cauliflower • Collards • Kale • Kohlrabi
Radishes • Rutabagas • Turnips

Talk about big families! When this bunch — a.k.a.
Brassica, mustard, and cole crops — get together for
reunions, they have more cousins and kissin' cousins than
you can shake a stick at. Grandma Putt grew all of them, and she
made darned sure I chowed down on them, too. She knew they were
good for me, but back then nobody knew just how good, or why.
Nowadays, scientists tell us that every single member of the family
produces a chemical called sulforaphane that helps ward off cancer.
And we all can use a little help.

The Family That Grows Together

Aside from their talent in the health-care field, the cabbage clan have a lot of other things in common:

Weather preferences. The whole Brassica crowd likes its temperatures on the cool side, so members feel right at home in climates that make a lot of other veggies pull on their long johns and go to sleep.

Eating habits. All cabbage family plants (except radishes) are big eaters, and they appreciate it when you dig plenty of compost or well-cured manure into their beds before they put down their roots.

Drinking habits. These guys like their water supply to be even and steady, and they appreciate a blanket of organic mulch to keep the right level of moisture in the ground.

Enemies. As far as certain kinds of pesky pests are concerned, one cabbage crop is as good as another — very good, in fact. (After all, how do you think cabbage moths, cabbage worms, and cabbage loopers got their names?) See Chapter 5 for some surefire ways to keep these diners out of your Brassica Bistro.

Diseases. Bacterial leaf spot, black rot, and clubroot consider themselves to be part of the family. But with a little care at planting time, you can keep them from joining the otherwise happy, healthy household.

Friends. Everybody in the cabbage clan thrives in the presence of celery, dill, sage, chamomile, peppermint, rosemary, onions, and potatoes. So make sure you plant plenty to keep the Brassicas happy.

Mint to the Rescue — but . . .

Planting mint among your Brassica crops will keep cabbage moths from flitting into your patch. But you need to contain its enthusiasm. Otherwise, you'll have more mint than you bargained for, and you'll have it in a hurry!

In the main veggie garden, I grow spearmint and peppermint in clay drainage tiles sunk right into the soil. But up on the patio, among my container plants, I pull out all the stops.

Mint comes in dozens of flavors, and I grow big pots of most of them, including chocolate, orange, pineapple, nutmeg, apple, and vanilla. Besides keeping pests at bay, they make the place smell like an old-time soda fountain!

When Clubroot Comes Calling

All the cole crops are prone to clubroot, a fungal disease that invades your garden on infected transplants. You'll know it's struck if your plants look stunted and yellowish and they wilt easily (because their roots can't take up enough water). When you pull them up, you'll see that the roots are gnarled and misshapen.

If clubroot calls on your garden — or if you've just set up gardenkeeping in a place it's visited recently — here's what to do:

• **Pull up all infected plants** as soon as you spot trouble, and burn them immediately. (This stuff spreads like wildfire.) Make sure you get out every trace of of the roots — clubroot spends its winter vacation in among the decomposing roots.

• **Don't plant any member** of the cabbage family in that part of the garden for the next 4 to 7 years.

Don't Join the Club

Because there is no cure for clubroot, here's how to head off trouble at the pass:

• **Grow your Brassica crops** in a different spot every year. (Besides keeping clubroot at bay, you'll also foil pesky cabbageworms.)

• **Keep the soil pH** at 7.2 or above — clubroot loves acidic soil.

• **Plant only disease-resistant varieties.**

• **If clubroot runs rampant** in your neck of the woods, don't buy transplants or seeds that were locally grown. Instead, use seeds from elsewhere.

Leave My Leaves Alone!

Instead of attacking the roots of cole crops, bacterial leaf spot and black rot go gunning for the leaves. Bacterial leaf spot most often attacks gardens in the Northeast and Mid-Atlantic regions. It shows up as small, purplish or brown spots on leaves, which may turn yellow and then drop off.

Black rot can strike anywhere. It starts out as V-shaped, yellow wedges running from the leaf edges to the veins. The veins turn black, and then the leaves dry out and drop off.

For both nasties, control and prevention are the same: Rotate your crops, plant disease-resistant varieties or seed that's certified disease-free, and follow the guidelines for good health in Chapter 5. And at the first sign of symptoms, get the victims out of the garden pronto, and destroy them before they spread their germs to the rest of your plants.

Two for the Show

Because the whole cabbage clan takes to chilly weather like monkeys to trees, I get two harvests every year from most of them: one early — just about the time last year's freezer stash is running low — and another one just before I put my garden to bed in the fall.

Jerry Baker Says

"One of the things I like best about a fall crop is that I almost never have problems with insects or diseases. Those pests do most of their dirty work in the late spring and early summer. By the time the weather starts cooling off, they're more interested in finding a place to bed down for the winter than in picnicking on my plants."

In the Good Old Autumntime

Here's how I time the fall plantings for my cabbage clan crops:

VEGETABLE	WEEKS BEFORE FIRST FROST
Broccoli	10–12
Brussels sprouts★	12–16
Cabbage	10–12
Cauliflower	10–12
Chinese cabbage	8–10
Kale	8–10
Radishes	4–6
Turnips	8–10

★In most parts of the country, Brussels sprouts are a fall-only crop, so plan accordingly.

Broccoli *(Brassica oleracea)*

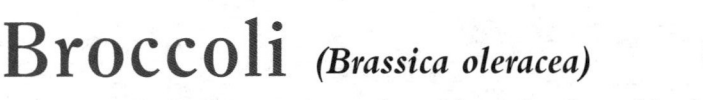

Broccoli is the Italian cousin in the cabbage family, and back in Grandma Putt's day, not many folks grew it on this side of the Atlantic. The ones who did mostly thought of it as green cauliflower, and a lot of seed catalogs even listed it that way. But, boy, how times have changed! Nowadays, broccoli is riding high on the veggie hit parade — thanks to all those medical researchers who keep saying that out of the whole cancer-fighting family, broccoli is the champ. Of course, the fact that it's one of the tastiest veggies around hasn't hurt its popularity any, either.

The Right Home

Broccoli will tolerate light shade, but it does best in full sun. It needs good drainage and air circulation, in a place where none of its relatives have grown for at least 4 years. And because broccoli grows about 3 feet tall, plant it where it won't shade other crops.

Add plenty of compost or well-rotted manure to the soil, and always test the pH before planting. Broccoli will do fine anywhere in the 6.2 to 7.2 range, but the closer you can get to neutral (7.0), the bigger your harvest will be.

Nix the Elbowroom

Some folks spread their broccoli plants out 18 to 24 inches apart. That's fine if your objective is big main heads. When you set them just 8 inches apart, however, you get smaller central heads, but the side-shoot population will explode, giving you a much bigger harvest.

SUPER Growing Secrets

BE PICKY

The secret to making a weather wimp like broccoli feel at home is planting the right variety at the right time. In spring, look for ones like **'Arcadia'** and **'Green Comet'** that grow fast and can take some heat as harvesttime approaches.

In midsummer, when you plant your fall crops, go with one that can put up with high temperatures. **'Green Jewel'** is one of the best.

Getting Started

You can start your broccoli crop in one of two ways:

1. Sow seeds directly in the garden a month or two before the last frost. (In warm climates, sow seeds in early spring, so that your crop reaches harvesting size before the weather gets hot.)

2. Get a jump on the season by starting seeds indoors 6 to 8 weeks before the last frost. Harden off the seedlings and transplant them about 2 weeks before the last frost. Plant them deeper than they were growing in the seedling tray — right up to their first true leaves.

Whichever way I've started my plants, when the central head is about an inch across, I give them a top-dressing snack of compost or well-rotted manure, and I keep their soil moist. (Broccoli likes 1 to 2 inches of water a week.)

Jerry Baker Says

"Broccoli will grow just about anyplace in the country, but it turns out that the biggest, best harvests are where nights are cool and daytime temperatures hover in the upper 60°F range."

Over the Rainbow

You might think of broccoli as a green vegetable, but it isn't always: It also comes in purple varieties like 'Violet Queen' (a sprouting type) and 'Rosalind' (a classic header). And 'White Sprouting Late' is just the color you'd expect it to be.

A Warm Crib in a Cool Room

Even though broccoli seeds can handle pretty cold ground in the spring, when I sow them indoors, I always get their seed starting mix good and warm. At 75°F, the seeds germinate in 3 to 6 days.

And I always start my fall broccoli crop in the great indoors, because I can keep the air temperature cooler than it is outside in the summer sun. Then I move the plants to the garden after the summer heat has flown the coop.

A Word to the Wise from Grandma Putt

Broccoli Bath

Lots of bugs love to hide in and among broccoli florets.

Grandma Putt had a way to make sure her broccoli was critter-free: She'd pour ¼ cup of salt and 1 tablespoon of vinegar into a sinkful of cold water. Then she'd drop in the broccoli and keep it submerged for 15 minutes or so. The bugs floated to the surface, and she had me pick 'em off. She'd rinse the veggies under cold running water and, bingo! They were ready for the pot!

Take Your Pick

Broccoli comes in two types:

• **Heading types** are the ones you see in the supermarket, and most of them are more useful for commercial growers who want a one-time-only harvest than they are for home gardeners. But some varieties, like **'Packman'** and **'Green Comet',** will send out side shoots after you cut off the central head. The more you clip, the more shoots will grow — up to a point, of course!

• **Sprouting varieties** produce a smaller central head, but a whole mini forest of side shoots. This is the kind I plant most often, because the plants give me a harvest that lasts until the weather gets so toasty that they give up the ghost. Some catalogs list the sprouting type as asparagus, Calabrese, or Italian broccoli. **'De Cicco'** and **'Calabrese'** are two of my favorites.

JERRY'S FAVORITE Vegetable Varieties

Broccoli-Raab

Broccoli's little cousin bears some family resemblance, but you'd never confuse the two if you saw them side by side. Folks grow broccoli-raab (a.k.a. rapini or rapine) as much for its leaves and shoots as for the flower heads, which are much smaller than the ones found on broccoli plants.

It likes the same growing conditions as broccoli but bolts easily, so I usually raise it as an autumn crop. Broccoli-raab has a slightly bitter taste that (at least to my way of thinking) gives a nice kick to steamed mixed vegetables.

Separate Quarters

Broccoli tastes best when it's just lightly steamed, not boiled. I like the heads and stems both, but I always cook them separately. That way, I don't risk overcooking the heads — the stems take a bit longer, even when they're peeled and cut into spears.

Harvesting Tips

When you harvest side shoots of broccoli, use a sharp knife and cut the stem at an angle. That way, moisture won't collect on the end and invite fungus disease. The broccoli heads that we eat are actually clusters of flower buds. Make sure you harvest the heads *before* they start turning yellow, because once the flowers bloom, the plants taste bitter.

Brussels Sprouts
(Brassica oleracea)

As a kid, I thought Brussels sprouts were just about the strangest-looking plants that ever came down the pike. I still do, as a matter of fact. Every time I look at my patch of them, with their tall stems full of nobby sprouts and their leaves flopping on top like palm fronds, it reminds me of some prehistoric forest. I almost expect a dinosaur to come strolling through the garden.

A Coldhearted Hero

Grandma Putt used to say that Brussels sprouts were the best friends a cold-climate gardener could ever ask for. Even in a family of cool-weather lovers, these tiny cabbages stand out. Not only do they shrug off cold spells that would turn most veggie plants to mush, but getting nipped by a few good frosts toward the end of the growing season actually improves their flavor (which bears no resemblance that I can find to that olive-drab stuff they sell at the local supermarket).

Time It Right

I like to time my planting so that my Brussels sprouts mature when the days are still warm but the nights are getting frosty. If you live in a warm climate, plant in late summer or early fall to harvest in winter or early spring. In cooler places, count backward 3 to 4 months from the date you expect your first visit from Jack Frost.

Timing can be tricky with Brussels sprouts: Though they all but stand up and cheer when frosty weather arrives, a hard freeze will lay them out flat. Experiment with your planting dates — and be patient: It may take a year or two of less-than-perfect crops before you work out the best schedule.

A Thirsty Bunch

Like all of their cabbagey cousins, Brussels sprouts like the water supply going to their roots to be steady and even. I keep a close eye on the rain gauge, and give them a drink when Mother Nature isn't sending down enough water from the sky. I also keep them well mulched to hold moisture in and keep weeds out.

SUPER Growing Secrets

WASTE NOT, WANT NOT

Two feet between plants is a lot of space in a small garden. Brussels sprouts need that much elbowroom if they're going to develop properly, but it doesn't have to go to waste. Just plant radishes and lettuces in the gaps; you'll get three harvests in the space of one!

Starting Out

Brussels sprouts like full sun and soil that's well drained and fertile, with a pH of 6.5 to 7.5. Sow seeds directly in the ground if you have a long, cool growing season (most varieties mature in anywhere from 85 to 160 days). Otherwise, start them indoors 4 to 6 weeks before you intend to plant the seedlings.

Space your plants about 2 feet apart, and put a shovelful of compost into each hole before you set in the seedlings. Then, about a month after transplanting (or about 6 weeks after germination if you've sown the seeds right in the garden), side-dress the plants with compost or spray them with fish fertilizer. Then, when the sprouts appear, pull off the leaves growing under them, along with any leaves that have turned yellow.

Stand Up, Guys

Brussels sprouts have shallow roots, so the plants may need some help staying upright. Keep your crop steady on its stems by mounding soil around the base of each plant as it grows taller, and then firming it up with the back of a hoe.

Two for the Road

Brussels sprouts come in two types, based on height:

• **Short varieties** stand 18 to 24 inches tall and tend to mature in 100 days or less. They do well in cool regions with short growing seasons, and in warmer territory where the weather heats up fast. 'Oliver' (95 days) and 'Blues' (just 75 days) are two of the best.

• **Tall types,** which grow 24 to 48 inches high, take 100 to 160 days to mature. They hanker for milder territory, like the Pacific Northwest. Whichever type you grow, you'll get about the same size and amount — the sprouts are simply packed closer together on the shorter plants.

Jerry Baker Says

"Unless you're harvesting the whole plant at once, cut your Brussels sprouts from the stem with a good, sharp knife, and leave as much of the spur as you can. Tearing or cutting into the stem can damage the plant and ruin the rest of your harvest."

JERRY'S FAVORITE Vegetable Varieties

I'd Rather Be Red

If you're planning an ornamental kitchen garden — whether in the ground or in pots — give some space to **'Rubine',** a medium-sized heirloom with deep red–purple sprouts that look like miniature red cabbages. These little guys mature in 85 days and have a rich, old-time flavor that's hard to come by in modern varieties. The ones you harvest early will turn green when you cook them, but once Jack Frost has laid a finger on them, they'll stay dark red from plant to table.

Bringing in the Harvest

You have two choices when it comes to ripening Brussels sprouts:

1. Left to their own devices, Brussels sprouts ripen slowly, from the bottom of the stem up, over a period of weeks. When I want just enough for eating fresh, I start cutting them when they're about ¾ inch in diameter, but I make sure I harvest them all before they get to be more than 1½ inches or so — they start toughening up at that size.

2. When I want most of the sprouts on a plant to ripen at the same time, I wait until the lower sprouts are about ½ inch in diameter, then I pinch off the growing tip and the top leaves. The sprouts will all mature about 2 weeks after this topping procedure.

A Portable Feast

If you want to keep right on eating fresh Brussels sprouts after Old Man Winter has settled in, dig up some of your plants and move them to a cold frame. Or do what I do when my cold frame is full of other cool-weather lovers: Grow part of your crop in containers and move them to a cool garage or basement before the first hard freeze hits.

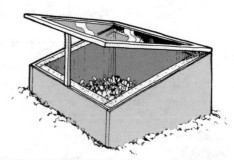

Sure Doesn't Taste Like Orange Juice

You might not think it to look at them, but Brussels sprouts actually have more vitamin C than oranges. They also pack healthful doses of potassium, iron, and fiber, and three times the vitamin A of cabbage. (All this on top of those cancer-fighting chemicals!)

The Rules

If you want to be sure that the Brussels sprouts you serve are the best, follow Grandma Putt's two rules for great-tasting sprouts:

Rule No. 1. If they're more than 1½ inches in diameter, don't even think about eating 'em — just toss 'em onto the compost pile.

Rule No. 2. Don't cook them too long. Blanch or steam them for 5 minutes, or sauté or stir-fry them for 3 to 6 minutes. (They should come out of the pan when they're still bright green and slightly crunchy.)

Rustlin' Brussels Sprouts

I can think of at least three dozen ways to eat Brussels sprouts. Here are a half dozen of my favorites:

• Steamed and sprinkled with lemon juice and freshly grated nutmeg

• Steamed and topped with a yogurt-lemon sauce with poppy seeds

• Sautéed with butter, mushrooms, and black pepper

• Sautéed in butter with a little horseradish

• Halved or quartered and then tossed into soups and casseroles

• Individual leaves floated on top of soup, like miniature lily pads

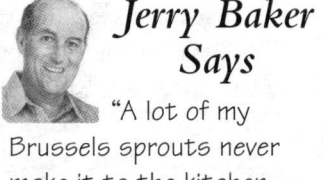

Jerry Baker Says

"A lot of my Brussels sprouts never make it to the kitchen — when they're tiny, I cut whole handfuls off the plant and eat them just like popcorn."

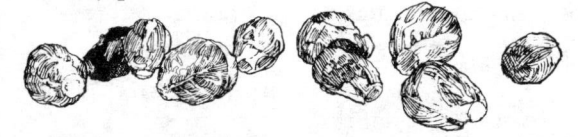

Good Keepers

When you're counting on socking away a whole winter's worth of Brussels sprouts in your root cellar, you want a variety that really holds its flavor. These are some real winners:

JERRY'S FAVORITE
Vegetable Varieties

• 'Green Pearl'   • 'Long Island Improved'   • 'Valiant'
• 'Jade Cross'   • 'Silverstar'

Cabbage *(Brassica oleracea)*

I don't know about you, but I can't imagine a very long stretch of dinnertimes without sauerkraut or coleslaw. And as I learned at Grandma Putt's knee, the kind you make from store-bought cabbage can't begin to compete with your very own homegrown stuff. Why, nobody even sells the kind of cabbages I use most often!

The Indirect Approach

I always grow cabbage from transplants. In fact, most folks do — when you see the days-to-maturity number on a cabbage seed packet, it always refers to the number of days from transplanting till harvest, not from seed sowing.

Start the seeds for spring crop 4 to 6 weeks before you expect the last frost, following the procedure described in Chapter 3 and using my Seed Starter Tonic (see page 355). Make sure to give the seeds plenty of warmth. At 80°F, they germinate in 4 to 5 days.

After the seedlings pop their little heads above the ground, move their trays to a cool, bright spot where the temperature is about 65°F during the day and a little cooler at night. Keep them well watered, and give them a drink of Seedling Starter Tonic (see page 355) once a week.

When the little guys have two or three sets of true leaves, move them to individual pots that can go right into the ground at planting time, so you don't have to disturb the roots.

SUPER Growing Secrets

BRING ON THE BORON

If cabbage isn't planted in boron-enriched soil, it will grow slowly and turn brown. To add boron to the soil, simply sprinkle borax onto the soil next to the plants.

A Booster Shot

Before you plant any cabbage seedlings, make sure the soil pH measures between 7.2 and 7.5, and has a good, balanced supply of the Big Three nutrients: nitrogen, phosphorus, and potassium, as well as boron. Then, about 3 weeks after planting day, put down a side-dressing of blood meal or well-cured manure to give your cabbages a nitrogen boost.

Moving Day

Move your hardened-off seedlings to the garden when the soil temperature measures 40°F — generally 3 to 4 weeks before the last frost. Bury them deep, so the bottom two leaves are belowground. New roots sprout from the underground part of the stem, which makes the plants grow up not only stronger but more stable.

Set plants anywhere from 10 to 20 inches apart, depending on how big they'll be when they grow up. I like to plant them so that when they're full grown, their leaves will touch. That way, they'll keep the ground below cool, shady, and weedless.

Cabbages like full sun when the weather is cool, but they take to partial shade, especially when the weather starts warming up.

Nurturing with Nutrients

If your cabbage seedlings are looking peaked or you just want them to have the best start in life, try one of these nutrient "solutions":

Pass the potassium, please. If the edges of your cabbages' leaves turn bronze, the plants need more potassium. To satisfy their craving, spray them with fish fertilizer and give them a sidedressing of wood ashes.

Into the drink. Just before Grandma Putt planted her cabbage seedlings, she dipped the roots in a mixture of well-cured cow manure and water. She made the mixture good and thick, so that some of it stuck to the roots when she pulled them out of the bucket and planted them.

The Net Result

To keep cabbage butterflies off of your veggies, use bird netting. It's reasonably inexpensive, lets light and water in, and won't blow away like row covers do. Make a frame out of wood or PVC that stands several inches above the plants, and double up the netting for safety's sake. Tack it to the ground with rocks, sticks, or earth staples. It's easy to lift up to get to your veggies, and will not take up lots of space when stored. And it beats picking those darn cabbage loopers off by hand!

How Much Is That Cabbage in the Window?

For a window-box display that will stop your neighbors in their tracks, plant cabbages. That's right — they'll grow up happy as clams, and I guarantee that your crop won't be attacked by nasty germs like clubroot. Just make sure you use a small variety like the ¾-pound 'Blue Vantage' or 'Early Jersey Wakefield', which tips the scales at a whopping ⅔ pound!

Even Steven

Cabbage likes steady, even moisture as much as the rest of the family — maybe even more so. At least it expresses its displeasure in a more obvious way: If it gets too much water all at once, especially when a heavy rain comes after a dry spell, the head will crack. Here are a couple of ways to "head" off trouble:

Do the twist. If a heavy rain comes after a drought while the heads are still forming, put both hands on each cabbage and give it a sharp quarter turn. Some of the roots will break, and they won't be able to take up enough moisture to cause damage.

Quit cold turkey. Stop watering once the round heads have formed. Then lay down a good, thick mulch of salt hay or straw, or plant a "living mulch" of low-growing plants like radishes, lettuces, nasturtiums, and

> ### CABBAGE WORM WIPE-OUT TONIC
>
> As your young cabbage plants develop heads, whip up a batch of this terrific Tonic.
>
> 1 cup of flour
> 2 tbsp. of cayenne pepper
>
> Mix the ingredients together, and sprinkle the powder on your cabbage heads. The flour swells up inside of the worms, causing them to burst, while the hot pepper keeps other critters away.

thyme among your cabbages. With either choice, you'll keep the soil's moisture level up and its temperature down — just where cabbage likes it.

Decisions, Decisions

Cabbage breeders haven't made life easy for folks who have trouble making decisions. At seed-shopping time, these are the categories you have to choose from:

Head shape. They may be round, flat, or pointed — though this matters only as far as looks are concerned. Shape has no effect on growing preferences or flavor.

Color. Cabbage comes in green, greenish white, blue-green, and red varieties. This category *does* matter if nutrition is high on your priority list: Red cabbage contains more than 30 times as much vitamin A as the greenish white kind.

Leaf type. You can choose between the more common smooth-leaved, tight-headed cabbages and the Savoy versions. The Savoys have looser, crinkled leaves and — according to serious cabbage fans — better flavor than the smooth types. And they're definitely one of the best-looking vegetables around. So if appearance matters, look no further than the Savoys.

Maturing times. Last, but not least: Actually, this is the most important category of all, because the secret to a good cabbage crop is timing it so that the heads don't develop during hot weather. Fortunately, that's not hard. Once you know your frost-free date and the time serious summertime heat usually visits your neck of the woods, all you have to do is choose varieties that mature when you need them to: in early, mid-, or late season.

Maturity date also matters for reasons besides simple growing time: Early and midseason cabbages have a milder flavor than the late ones. So I eat most of my spring crop raw, in salads or coleslaw. I use the fall planting for sauerkraut or for cooking up with pork chops or corned beef.

SUPER Growing Secrets

ONION BREATH

I always plant onions among my cabbage plants and harvest some as scallions when they're young. Others, I just leave in the ground, where they keep cabbage moths and rabbits where they belong: away from my cabbage.

A Seasonal Thing

• Early or spring cabbages mature in 50 to 60 days.

• Midseason types are also planted in early spring but take 70 to 85 days to reach full size.

• Late-season or storage varieties need anywhere from 85 to 200 days to mature — *after* you transplant them from their seedling pots.

• In the northern part of the country, cabbage is a spring and fall crop. Down South, it needs to grow up during the winter.

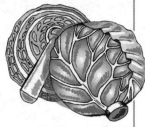

Jerry Baker Says

"To store cabbage for the winter, pull up the plants in the fall, and hang them upside down, roots and all, in a cool place like your garage or root cellar."

Cabbage Comeback

At harvesttime, instead of pulling up cabbages by the roots, I sometimes cut them off, leaving as much stalk behind as possible. Usually, a cluster of small heads will grow out of the stalk I left behind. I clip these off when they're small and so mild and tender that I can just chop 'em up and eat 'em in a tossed salad.

SUPER Storing Secrets

USE IT OR LOSE IT

Savoy cabbages types don't keep worth beans. So don't even think of socking them away in your root cellar. Instead, use them fresh from the garden. They'll give you some of the best-tasting coleslaw you've ever had!

The Root of the Matter

For an extra-early spring harvest, dig up your cabbage stalks — roots and all — at the end of the growing season. Then bury them in a trench in the garden, and cover it with a thick blanket of leaves or straw. (You can also put them into a big container of potting soil or compost, and keep them in a cold basement or garage.)

As soon as you can work the ground in the spring, plant the roots in the garden. They'll give you a crop of greens long before anything else is ready for your plate.

Sauerkraut Time — Then . . . and Now

Every year, in late fall, Grandma Putt and I made sauerkraut. I could tell it was time when Grandma started cleaning that big old 10-gallon crock. Talk about a big project! First, we put a big, clean, 100-pound flour sack inside the crock. Then we took all of the loose outer leaves off of the cabbage heads, and Grandma Putt would start shredding them into a big pan. When she'd filled the pan, she'd dump the shreds into the sack.

While she started on another round of shredding, I'd pour 2 tablespoons of salt into the sack and start kneading and bruising the cabbage until it was limp and watery. We'd keep at it until the jar was filled up, and then we'd taste the cabbage, usually add some more salt, mix it up a little more, and taste it again.

When Grandma Putt finally gave it her stamp of approval, she covered the top with grape leaves (she said they improved the flavor). Then she folded the top of the sack over the leaves and put another sack over that one. She set a plate on top of it and, finally, she laid a big rock on the plate to weight the whole thing down. We put the crock in a cool, dark place — usually the root cellar — and in 5 or 6 weeks, we had ourselves a genuine treasure!

These days, instead of filling up a big old crock, I use sterilized 1-quart glass canning jars. Here's my modern-day routine.

Step 1. Shred the cabbage in a food processor.

Step 2. Put it into a big bowl and press on it with a wooden club–style potato masher to bruise it and get the juices flowing.

Step 3. Put the shredded, bruised cabbage into sterilized 1-quart glass canning jars and pack it down firmly to within ¾ inch of the top.

Step 4. Add ¾ teaspoon of salt and a scant teaspoon of sugar to each jar. The juice from the cabbage should come to about ½ inch from the top. If it doesn't, add water to bring it to that level, then run a knife around the inside of the jar so the moisture can sink down in. Lay one or two grape leaves over the top of the cabbage.

Step 5. Cover the jars with sterilized lids and put them in a cool, dark place. As the cabbage ferments, juice will probably leak out, so line your shelves with several layers of newspaper.

Step 6. Check the jars once in a while. If any of the kraut-in-progress is starting to darken at the top, use it right away, or put it into the fridge.

Chinese Cabbage
(*Brassica rapa*)

When I want to impress the heck out of my nongardening friends, I give them one of my big-bruiser Chinese cabbages and watch their mouths drop open. Of course, once they've tasted it, they usually decide that their nongardening status has lasted long enough, and my role switches from that of a gift-giver to a full-fledged horticultural coach.

On the Orient Express

Chinese cabbage is the Asian cousin of the Brassica family but looks more like romaine lettuce. The flavor is a dead giveaway, though: It's like a mild version of domestic cabbage with a slight hint of mustard.

Family Matters

When it comes to growing conditions and weather preferences, Chinese cabbage is no different from the rest of the clan: It likes mild weather; rich, well-drained soil; lots of good food; and an even supply of water (and plenty of it). It's also prone to the family's pest and disease enemies, so follow the same good-health guidelines you'd use for any other cole crop.

Give Me Land, Lots of Land

Chinese cabbages don't like to have their roots disturbed, and they get stressed out easily in weather that's not to their liking. To avoid a plant anxiety attack — and to give them the temperature range they like best — I direct-sow mine as a fall crop, about 3 months before I expect the first frost. And because these guys can get *big* — 14 inches high and 8 inches across is nothing — I give them plenty of room to roam. Depending on the variety, I allow 1 to 2 feet between plants.

Choosing Chinese Cabbages

Napa or **barrel types** have broad, soft, light green leaves that form heads only a little taller than they are wide.

Michilili kinds grow up to be nearly three times taller than they are wide, and their leaves are darker, narrower, and coarser than the Napas'.

Lettuce types, a.k.a. **looseleaf** or **no-head,** have a white core of inner leaves surrounded by frilly green outer leaves. Most folks think they're the most decorative of the three, and they show up in a lot of ornamental gardens.

If You Taste One . . .

Having trouble deciding among the three types? Here's the good news: They all have the same great flavor! So don't worry.

Cauliflower *(Brassica oleracea)*

When I hear folks speechifyin' that the only good vegetable is an old-time vegetable, I remind them about cauliflower. Back in Grandma Putt's day, it was the most finicky food crop on the face of the planet.

For one thing, if the weather got either too cold or too hot for its liking, it went belly-up faster than you could read the numbers on a thermometer. For another, if you didn't remember to cover the heads with leaves while they were growing (what gardeners call blanching), they turned a funny color instead of that nice white shade, and they had a flavor that wasn't worth beans!

Well, cauliflower still has its share of quirks, but nowadays, plenty of new kinds don't need blanching at all, and they stand up to temperatures that would have laid their ancestors flat on their backs.

Home Turf

Cauliflower likes full sun in cool climates, but if your summers are at the warmer end of its comfort range, give it afternoon shade. It demands soil that's fertile, well drained, evenly moist, and chock-full of organic matter. The pH can range from 6.5 to 7.5, but to grow its best and fend off root diseases, cauliflower likes soil that's neutral or slightly sweet (6.8 to 7.2).

In the Beginning

For a fall harvest, sow cauliflower seeds directly in the garden, but start your spring crop indoors a month before you expect the last frost. The plants don't like to have their roots disturbed, so give each one its own pot and sow the seeds ¼ inch deep. They germinate in about 6 days when the temperature is 70°F. When the sprouts come up, thin them to one per container and move them to a spot that gets bright light and temperatures in the mid-60°F range.

Start a crop for fall harvest 10 to 12 weeks before the first frost. Sow the seeds ½ inch deep in clusters of four, and space the clusters 2 feet apart. When the first true leaves appear, thin out all but the strongest youngster in each cluster.

SUPER Growing Secrets

DON'T JUMP THE GUN

Seedlings should be no more than 5 weeks old when you plant them in the garden. Any ones older than that at transplant time are prone to shock. And if they've gotten root-bound in their pots, they may produce tiny "button" heads.

Movin' On

I move my seedlings to the garden when Jack
Frost has gone for good and the soil and air
temperatures both measure at least 50°F. I set
the plants into their holes, cover them just short
of the bottom leaves, and build a little saucer of
soil around each plant to help hold moisture.

I leave at least 2 feet between plants. Most cauliflowers are
big bruisers, and even the smallest ones have a big appetite —
they all need plenty of room to spread out and plenty of soil to
feed from. I use the space in between to grow scallions or the kinds of tangy-
smelling herbs, like tansy, that cauliflower enemies don't like.

Tolerant, but . . .

While it's true that most modern varieties of cauliflower can take the heat better
than the old-timers, not a single one of them will perform at its best in hot
weather. Wherever you live, time your planting so that the crop will mature
before the dog days of summer set in.

Blanching: A Natural Parasol

Modern self-blanching varieties don't
require this procedure, but I like to do
it anyway — pulling the leaves up over
the heads gives them some shade and
keeps them cooler and happier than
they'd be otherwise. Blanching isn't nearly
as tricky or time-consuming as some
folks make it out to be. In fact, it
couldn't be simpler. Here's all there is to it:

Jerry Baker Says

"Don't confuse
self-blanching white cauliflower (which doesn't
need blanching, but likes
it fine) with the orange,
purple, and green kinds
that don't need it and,
furthermore, don't like it."

1. Start when the flower head (also called a
curd or button) is about the size of an egg. And make sure you do it when neither it nor the foliage is wet; otherwise, the plant may rot.

2. Loop heavy twine around the leaves, gently lift them up, and tie them
loosely together.

That's all there is to it! The aim is to keep light and moisture out, but to let
air in, and also leave room for the flower to grow inside its leafy shelter.

Food and Drink

Give your cauliflower plants steady, even moisture at the rate of about an inch a week throughout their growing period. If they don't get enough water, or if the supply is erratic, they'll grow up with a strong — even foul — flavor. These guys also need a good, well-balanced diet. I give mine a dose of fish fertilizer when I first move them to the garden, and my All-Season Green-Up Tonic (see page 349) every 3 weeks after that.

Close Inspection

Once you've blanched your cauliflower, keep a close eye on it. In warm weather, it will be ready for harvesting about 4 days after you cover the head. In cool weather, it will take 10 days or so. Cut it the minute it's ready: If you wait too long, the head can rot.

Rainbow Roundup

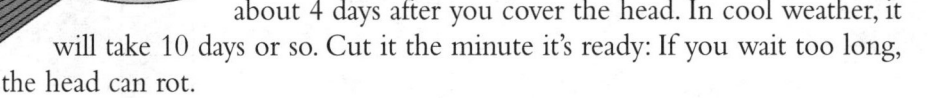

Once upon a time, bedsheets, tennis clothes, and cauliflower were all white. As Grandma Putt used to say, my, how times change! Cauliflower hasn't developed quite the color range of sheets and tennis togs, but it does come in orange, purple, and green. If you're a purist, of course, you can still get standard-issue white varieties that are a lot easier to please than Grandma Putt would ever have thought possible. Here's a rundown of the colored ones:

• Orange types like **'Orange Bouquet'** get their color from a big load of beta carotene, so they're a powerhouse of vitamin A — and pretty enough for the fanciest ornamental kitchen garden in town.

• Purple varieties like **'Violet Queen'** and **'Purple Head'** look and taste like a cross between cauliflower and broccoli.

• Green cauliflowers like **'Alverda'** and **'Chartreuse II'** are also broccoli look-alikes, with distinctive, cone-shaped heads and rich flavor.

Uptight Is Right

You'll know the time has come to harvest your cauliflower when the head is full, fairly regular, and tight. You want to reach for your harvesting knife *before* the sections start to loosen — a condition that is known as riciness. (But bear in mind that purple types always look a little irregular. They're ready when the head looks like a tight bunch of broccoli.)

Unfortunately, you get only one shot at cauliflower. No matter how you harvest it, the plant won't resprout the way broccoli and cabbage will. To extend your harvest, stagger your plantings or grow several varieties that mature at different times.

White, but . . .

You say your territory doesn't measure up to cauliflower's highest standards? Look for these easy- (or at least easier-) going campers. They can all handle more heat — and cold — than most varieties:

- 'Snow Crown'
- 'Early Dawn'
- 'Fremont'
- 'Andes'

Can't be bothered with blanching, but you still want your cauliflower dressed in classic white? So grow:

- 'White Rock'
- 'Amazing'
- 'Snowball Self-Blanching' (which also can take more heat than most)

Milky White

If your cauliflower doesn't want to keep its white color when you cook it, simply add a little milk to the boiling water.

The Sooner the Better

Cauliflower will keep for a month or so in the fridge or the root cellar, but it tastes so much better right after harvest that I don't even bother storing it fresh. What I can't use in a few days, I freeze — either plain or in a butter or cheese sauce.

Collards *(Brassica oleracea)*

Even though collards are getting around more than they did in Grandma Putt's day, when most folks think of them, they still think of greens that hail from way down South in Dixie. But collards will grow up sleek and happy anywhere in the country — and they actually taste better after a frost hits them.

The Old Plantation

Collards will perform well under almost any conditions, but they offer up their tastiest harvest in fairly sandy, fertile soil with a pH between 6.5 and 7.5. I dig manure into my patch in the fall. Like any other kind of greens, collards need plenty of nitrogen to help them grow up fast and churn out basketloads of great-tasting leaves.

Because collards are an easygoing bunch, I plant them in both spring and fall. I sow my spring crop right in the garden 3 weeks before I expect the last frost, and the fall crop goes in about 70 days before the first frost. I set the seeds in the ground ½ inch deep and 3 inches apart.

When the seedlings come up, I thin them over time, so I can use them in salads. I end up with young plants that stand 12 to 18 inches apart — if they grow up any closer together, they'll be weak and spindly.

Drink Up

Collards are a thirsty bunch. They need at least 1½ inches of water every week so their leaves will stay juicy and flavorful. And every 3 weeks, I give them a drink of my All-Season Green-Up Tonic (see page 349) so their leaves stay green and lush.

SUPER Growing Secrets

WHAT DO YOU MEAN, IT'S JUST AN OLD WIVES' TALE?

Some people claim the whole idea of companion planting is nothing but old-timey guesswork. Well, I guess they haven't talked to the folks at Cornell University's School of Agriculture lately. Scientists there have proved that when you interplant tomatoes and collards, the flea beetle population plummets dramatically. So there!

An Upstanding Crop

Collards have shallow roots, and once you've harvested the lower leaves, the plants get top-heavy. For that reason, I always give mine some help staying upright. When I've thinned my seedlings to their final spacing, I sink a metal stake into the ground beside each one.

Any kind of stake will keep a collard plant upright, but a metal one will attract electricity from the air and give those greens a good jolt of nitrogen (remember the electroculture lesson on page 81?). Tie the stems to the stakes with strips of nylon panty hose, which attracts even more static electricity.

Jerry Baker Says

"Be careful when you set stakes in the ground — and whenever you work around collard plants. Their roots are shallow, and it's very easy to damage them and you may not even know it until it's too late."

North Is North and South Is South

My cousins down in Dixie say that there's nothing they like better than collards. And they cook up their "mess of greens" the good old-time way: They boil 'em for an hour or so with a piece of salt pork. But I give mine a lighter treatment: I sauté them in a little olive oil with bacon, onion, and a splash of red wine vinegar. Talk about good down-home cookin'!

Cabbage on High

Back in Grandma Putt's day, folks called them tree cabbages, because that's what collard plants look like: loose bunches of blue-green cabbage leaves on top of stems that grow 2 to 4 feet high. They taste like cabbage, too, but richer.

Into the Kitchen

Collards take from 70 to 80 days to reach full maturity, but they taste good at any stage. Wait until six or eight leaves have appeared before you pick any — the plants need them to spur their growth. After that, you can pick single leaves as you need them or harvest whole plants.

And speaking of harvesting, here's an amazing fact: For a plant we usually think of as southern only, collards can sure take the cold! Why, they'll stand right up to temperatures as low as 10°F! So when I know the first freeze is headed my way, I lay down a heavy mulch of oak leaves or straw on top of my greens. Then my harvest keeps coming in long after the snow starts falling.

Kale *(Brassica oleracea)*

Back in Grandma Putt's day, everybody had a big patch of kale. It was just about the most popular green on the scene. And no wonder: It was (and still is) packed with vitamins, hardy enough to keep growing right through the first freeze or two, and generous enough to keep its leaves sweet and tender, so you could "store" it right in the garden all winter long. Plus, it was such a great-looking plant that folks grew it in the front yard with their showy shrubs and flowers. Nowadays, like a lot of veggies that fell by the wayside, kale is staging a comeback. As Grandma Putt would say, it's about time!

Plant It and Forget It

Well, not quite. But kale is one of the hardiest, lowest-maintenance veggies you'll ever find. It's more easy-going about its home life than any other member of the cabbage clan; but when it has its druthers, it likes soil that's rich and slightly acid (6.5 to 6.8 on the pH scale). Kale doesn't share the family's big appetite, either. In fact, too much nitrogen will make the plants churn out lush, oversize leaves that are a prime target for disease germs and bad-guy bugs. But when it grows up in a nice, moderate way, kale gets much less attention from pests and diseases than the rest of the family does — though when troublesome types do decide to pay a call, it's the same old crowd that shows up. So be prepared.

I'm Thirsty

Kale does share one family trait, though: the need for steady moisture. If the plants don't get about an inch of water every week, the leaves grow up fibrous and bad-tasting.

As far as feeding goes, kale does just fine on a balanced diet of fish fertilizer or my All-Season Green-Up Tonic (see page 349) every 3 weeks throughout the growing season.

Jerry Baker Says

"My favorite way to cook kale is to sauté it in a little olive oil with mushrooms and shallots and serve it over pasta. Talk about good eatin'!"

Shades of Light

I sow seeds for my spring crop as soon as I can work the soil. I like to give this crowd a spot that gets full sun, so they get off to a fast start. Come midsummer, though, when I start my crop for fall and winter harvesting, I plant in partial shade.

A Trio of Choices

Kale comes in three types:

• **Siberian** kinds have smooth leaves that are often frilly along the edges. A lot of folks think this kind has the best flavor.

• **Scotch** varieties have very crinkly, curly leaves that look a little like oversize parsley.

• **Ornamental** types are the pink-and-white kinds you see in flower beds, sidewalk planters, and sometimes as garnish on restaurant plates. They're edible, but if it's good eatin' you're after, forget these guys — go with either Scotch or Siberian.

Jerry Baker Says

"I like to put in my fall kale crop around the beginning of August, just after I harvest late peas and beans, and dig those plants into the soil. It gives the kale a good booster shot of nitrogen, but in a dose that's not too much for it to handle."

Green Grows the Snow

Even though it's not a member of the legume clan, kale is one of my favorite green-manure crops. I can harvest my fall planting right on through the winter: I just dig the leaves out from under the snow. Come spring, when the plants start growing again, I turn them under and they beef up the soil for my early crops.

Hey, Popeye, Ready for a Change?

When Popeye was shopping for a wonder food, he must not have known about kale. True, it does have a tad less iron than spinach, but it has three times the vitamin C, more vitamins A and B, and a bigger load of protein, calcium, and potassium.

Kohlrabi *(Brassica oleracea)*

It's too bad we didn't know about flying saucers when I was a boy. I'd have had a ball pretending that all of those spiky purple, pale green, and white balls had flown straight from Mars to Grandma Putt's garden! But back then, only a few people even dreamed about space travel. Now all I care about is that these odd-looking veggies *taste* like a dream.

Here's a little hint about the taste: If you're the kind of gardener who grows cabbage only so you can get to the tender, tasty heart, you owe it to yourself to try a monster-sized patch of kohlrabi, because that's exactly what it tastes like.

Speedy Gonzalez

Kohlrabi doesn't mind being transplanted, but it grows so fast that there's no advantage to starting seeds indoors or buying transplants. I always sow my seeds right in the garden about 4 weeks before I expect Jack Frost's last visit — once they're in the ground, they're up and growing in a week. I plant them ½ inch deep and 3 inches apart. When seedlings appear, I thin them to 6 inches to make sure they get enough light, and I mulch to keep out weeds and conserve moisture.

Kohlrabi likes a home that gets a lot of sun and has soil that drains well but retains moisture. (So dig in plenty of organic matter to ensure the right combination.) The pH of its dreams is 6.3 to 6.8.

Get 'em Launched on the Fast Track

If you don't care for the taste or texture of kohlrabi, I'll bet you dollars to doughnuts it's because you've only tasted a crop that's spent too much time growing up. The secret to great-tasting kohlrabi is rocket-fast growth — it should go from sowing to harvest in about 8 weeks.

To keep them growing at the speed of light, feed your plants with my All-Season Green-Up Tonic (see page 349) every 3 weeks, and make sure they get at least an inch of water a week.

SUPER Growing Secrets

THE LAID-BACK COUSIN

Like its cabbage-family cousins, kohlrabi prefers cool weather; but unlike those fussbudgets, it will still do its work when the mercury rises. All it asks for is plenty of water to quench its healthy thirst.

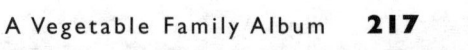

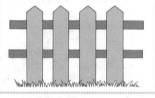

Get 'Em When They're at Par

Young kohlrabi leaves make great eatin' raw or steamed. I clip them all season long, until it's time to harvest the stems. I pick the stems when they're about the size of a golf ball. When they grow bigger than that, they get tough and bitter; all they're good for then is the compost pile.

If your bulbs are reachin' good-eatin' size faster than you can keep up with them, don't worry: Just clip them off the stems, bury them deep in the soil, and cover them with hay or straw. They'll stay crisp and fresh well into winter.

Don't You Dare Fence Me In

Kohlrabi makes a colorful addition to an ornamental kitchen garden, but, unfortunately, its long roots don't take too well to container life. So don't waste your time.

And the Winner Is . . .

I haven't come across many giant-kohlrabi contests, so maybe it's time to start one in your neighborhood. If you want to enter, get yourself some seeds of 'Superschmelz'. It's a new variety from Oregon with bulbs that regularly reach 8 to 10 inches in diameter, and (this is the best part) even at that size, they stay sweet and tender.

To grow a blue-ribbon winner, dig the soil deep, so the long roots have plenty of room to roam, and mix in a wheelbarrow load of organic matter. Plant your future monster where it has lots of elbowroom, give it an even, steady supply of water, and serve a balanced diet that is high in potassium and phosphorus.

Jerry Baker Says

"Don't let kohlrabi's offbeat, flying-saucer looks put you off — this is one of the tastiest veggies on this or any other planet! Try it sautéed in olive oil with tarragon and shallots, or slice it raw and toss it into any salad. Take my word for it: You'll be an instant kohlrabi convert!"

Radishes *(Raphanus sativus)*

When folks tell me they've just caught the gardening bug and they want to know what to grow in their first plot, I always tell 'em, "Radishes." They grow at the speed of light, so you don't have to wait long to feel the thrill of victory. And because they're the easiest crop you could ever ask for, you'll probably never know the agony of defeat.

The Dynamic Duo

Though growing radishes is so simple that a toddler could do it, deciding what kind to grow can boggle the mind. At last count, there were more than 250 radish varieties for sale. To ease the confusion a little, most folks divide them into two major types:

• **Spring radishes** are small; they reach eating size in a month or less, and they don't keep well — once you pull 'em up, the sooner you eat 'em, the better they taste.

• **Winter, a.k.a. long-season, radishes** take 2 months or more to reach full size. They get much bigger than the spring types, and they hold up better in storage. This group includes daikons and all of the other Asian types.

Two of a Kind

The growing procedures are a little different for spring and winter radishes (more on that in just a bit), but they have a few important things in common:

• They are very easy to grow.

• They like their temperatures a little on the cool side.

• They come in more colors and shapes than you can shake a trowel at.

• Their heat levels range from baby-food mild to so hot they'll send steam pouring from your ears.

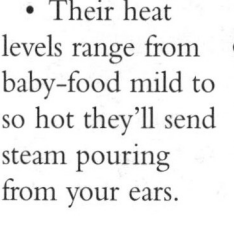
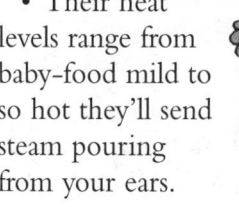

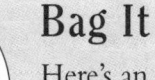

A Word to the Wise from Grandma Putt

Bag It

Here's an old-time secret that Grandma Putt showed me to get her radishes off to an even speedier start. Before planting, she would soak her seeds in water for 24 hours. Then she put them into a brown paper bag and set it in the sun. Within a day, the seeds germinated, and she put 'em right into the ground.

The Growth Plan

Spring and winter radishes need slightly different treatment at planting and harvesting time. Here's how I give my crops what they want.

Super Spring Radishes

1. Give them a spot that gets at least 6 hours of sun and has light, rich, well-drained soil with a pH of 5.8 to 6.8.

2. Till the soil to at least 6 inches, and be sure to remove rocks, sticks, or other debris that could hinder the growing roots.

3. Work in enough organic matter to get just the right soil conditions.

4. Sow seeds directly in the garden 4 to 6 weeks before the last expected frost. Set them ½ inch deep and 1 inch apart. In soil temperatures of 50°F and higher, you'll see little sprouts in a week or less.

5. Plant a new crop every 7 to 10 days until the average air temperature reaches 65°F. Then start again when the weather cools down in the fall.

6. Thin seedlings so that they're 2 inches apart, and mulch them to keep the soil moist and the weeds down.

7. As soon as the roots get big enough to eat, start pulling 'em up. Once they reach full size, they head downhill fast.

Wonderful Winter Radishes

1. Choose the same kind of site and prepare it the same way you would for spring radishes, but till the soil at least a foot deep.

2. Plant seeds in either spring or summer, depending on the variety.

3. Sow seeds 1 inch deep for small varieties, 1½ for larger ones.

4. Thin the seedlings so they're 6 inches apart, and mulch the same way you would for spring radishes.

5. Start pulling winter radishes when they're big enough to eat, but don't rush to get them all out of the ground: A frost will make them tastier.

6. Harvest all of your plants before the first hard freeze — frigid weather will knock your crop belly-up.

Radish-Raising Tips

Nix on the nitrogen. Like any other root veggies, radishes produce a pretty sorry crop when they get heavy doses of nitrogen, so go easy on the N.

Keep their cool. No matter where you live, you can grow great radishes. Just time your plantings to mature when temperatures range from 60 to 65°F. Warmer weather will make the roots tough and bitter.

It Takes All Kinds

JERRY'S FAVORITE Vegetable Varieties

Radishes come in a lot of shapes and colors you never see in the supermarket. Here are some of my favorites:

'Easter Egg'–spring; round, multicolored (red, white, pink, purple, and violet)

'French Breakfast'–spring; oblong, red and white

'Misato Rose'–winter; round, green skin and pink flesh

'Nero Tondo'–winter; round, black

'Purple Plum'–spring; globe-shaped and purple, inside and out

'Red Meat'–spring; large and round, green skin and pink flesh

'Valentine'–spring; round, green and white on the outside, red inside

Pot 'em Up

Spring radishes feel right at home in containers. Just use a pot with good drainage that's at least 12 inches deep and 10 inches wide. Fill it with potting soil that's been enriched with compost, keep the plants well watered, and give them a drink of Compost Tea (see page 351) about midway through their growing season.

The Early Bird Escapes the Worm

If cabbage-root maggots have been bugging your radishes this year, plant the seeds earlier next year. If you can get a mature crop by June 1, the tangy tubers should be all but free of the slimy culprits.

Radishes to the Rescue

BUG BUSTERS!

If you're looking for a true-blue garden hero, look no further. Radishes will draw aphids and flea beetles from peppers; protect cucumbers, squash, and melons from cucumber beetles; and rout two-spotted spider mites from tomato plants.

When you want your radishes to stand guard duty, just sow them among the plants they'll be protecting and leave them there. Then plant a separate patch for harvesting and eating.

An Old-Time Medicine Chest

Grandma Putt told me that way back in the 17th century, folks thought of the radish as medicine rather than food. From the sound of it, they seemed to think it was a miracle drug. They considered it an antidote to all kinds of poisons, and they used it to remove freckles, relieve the pain of childbirth, and cure snakebites.

They even thought it could cure baldness. For that, they ground up the radishes and mixed them with honey and dried sheep's blood to make a paste. (Don't try any of these tricks at home, kids.)

Jerry Baker Says

"Radishes rarely come down with any of the cabbage family's disease collection, but just to head off trouble, I rotate my crop every year."

Honey, We Need a Bigger Root Cellar!

Way, way back, in Greek and Roman times, folks grew giant radishes for winter storage. The monster roots often weighed in at 50 to 100 pounds or even more! Folks ate them either cooked or raw, seasoned with honey and vinegar.

Sore Throat Syrup

Radishes do have one medicinal use that I can honestly recommend. Any time I had a sore throat or a light cough, Grandma Putt would make me up a dose of radish syrup. I still take it when I feel a cold coming on. Here's her recipe:

1. Cut five or six radishes into thin slices and spread them out on a plate or in a shallow bowl.

2. Sprinkle about 2 teaspoons of sugar over the slices, cover the plate loosely with aluminum foil (to keep the flies away), and let it sit overnight.

3. In the morning, when you take off the foil, you'll find a plateful of tangy-sweet syrup. Drain it off into another container, and take a spoonful or two whenever the need strikes.

SUPER Growing Secrets

SEED TO SALAD TO SKILLET

Don't let your Good Samaritan radishes go to waste. After the tops grow up and flower, pick the seedpods while they're still green, and use them in salads and stir-frys. They're absolutely delish!

Rutabagas *(Brassica napus)*

Lots of folks think a rutabaga is nothing but a fat turnip. As Grandma Putt would say, stuff and nonsense! The rutabaga is a fine, upstanding (or, rather, downstanding) vegetable, and even though it likes the same kind of living quarters as a turnip, it's a whole other thing altogether — and better, to Grandma Putt's way of thinking.

So What's the Difference?

Well, now that you ask, plenty:

- **Taste.** Rutabagas have a sweeter, stronger flavor.
- **Color.** Rutabagas are usually yellow; turnips are usually white.
- **Shape and size.** Rutabagas are larger and rounder.
- **Growth rate.** Rutabagas take longer to mature.
- **Storage.** Once you harvest them, rutabagas keep much longer than turnips.
- **Nutrition.** Turnips contain vitamin C. Period. Rutabagas have more vitamin C than turnips, along with folicin, potassium, and beta carotene.

A Word to the Wise from Grandma Putt

Whoops!

Grandma Putt told me that long before her day, folks said the rutabaga was born from an accidental cross between a turnip and a wild cabbage.

Growing Cool

Rutabagas like to grow up in cool weather, and because they take a while to mature, they're a fall crop in most parts of the country. I sow my seeds outdoors in early summer, 3 to 4 months before I expect the first frost. (Like most root crops, rutabagas are rarely, if ever, sold as started plants.) If you live in a warm climate, plant your seeds in mid- to late summer so the tubers can develop during cooler weather.

Northern Lights

To give you an idea of just how cold-hardy the rutabaga is, it's one of the most popular veggies in all of Scandinavia. In fact, in those chilly parts, folks call 'em Swedish turnips, and they insist that the tasty tubers reach their prime after a few frosts. That's when they dig 'em up, cook and mash 'em like potatoes, and stir in a little butter and brown sugar. Talk about a real tummy-warming treat on a cold winter day!

The Home Corral

Rutabagas will take some shade, but they prefer full sun. I give my crop a soil pH of 6.8 to 7.5 and work in plenty of organic matter. I always till down to at least 14 inches, getting out all of the rocks and sticks as I go, so the roots won't bump up against anything while they're growing.

I sow my seeds ½ inch deep and 1 inch apart. When the seedlings come up, I thin them to at least 8 inches apart. (Whatever you do, don't crowd these guys, or the roots won't develop the way they should.) Then I lay down a good blanket of mulch, like oak leaves or straw, to keep the ground cool and moist, just the way rutabagas like it.

A Small Order of P and K, Please

Rutabagas are not big eaters, but they need fair amounts of potassium and phosphorus for good root development. I satisfy their appetite by giving them a dose of my All-Season Green-Up Tonic (see page 349) every 3 weeks or so throughout the growing season, and to quench their thirst, I make sure they get at least an inch of water weekly.

Harvesttime

If winters are mild in your neck of the woods, consider yourself lucky: You can just mulch your rutabagas, and keep on pulling them up right through the winter. In colder regions, leave the roots in the garden for as long as you can, but get them up before the ground freezes. To store them for winter:

🖐 Dig or pull them up and leave them in the sun for a couple of hours, until the soil dries out and falls off.

🖐 Trim the stems to within about an inch of the tuber, but don't cut off any of the roots.

🖐 Pack them in a wooden box or plastic bin full of freshly cut sawdust, and keep them in a cold (but not freezing) place.

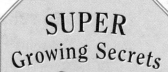

SUPER Growing Secrets

KEEP 'EM HIGH AND DRY

Don't put boxes of rutabagas — or any other fruit or root vegetable — directly onto a concrete or dirt floor. Moisture can seep in and ruin your harvest. Instead, keep your containers high and dry on shelves well above floor level.

Once Is Enough

Come spring, add the sawdust to your compost pile, or dig it right into the garden. Don't reuse it for storage — over the summer, it could pick up pests or disease germs and pass them along to your next batch of crops.

Turnips *(Brassica rapa)*

Back in Grandma Putt's day, turnips showed up at every church social, neighborhood potluck, and Saturday-night get-together that was worth a write-up in the local weekly's gossip column. Nowadays, the tasty tubers have gone into such a slump that a lot of gardening books and seed catalogs don't even mention them. Well, all I can say is that turnips have never gone out of style in my garden — or on my dinner plate — and I'll be hornswoggled if they ever will!

Old Faithfuls

Turnips will settle in and do their job under almost any conditions. But if they get their dream home, 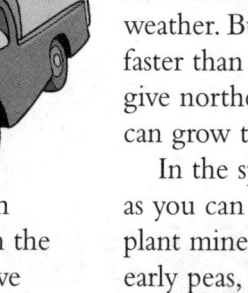 they'll return a harvest that's worth writing home about. That castle in the ground should get full sun and have well-drained, fairly rich soil with plenty of organic matter. Unless you're growing a crop for greens alone, stay away from manure and any other material that's high in nitrogen.

Turnips like a soil pH of 6.8 to 7.5, so to keep things on the sweet side, toss a few handfuls of wood ashes onto the planting bed just before you sow the seeds.

Turnip roots can really get down there, so till the soil at least 1 foot deep and remove any solid objects that the tubers could bump up against as they're growing. Keep it clean and lean, and they'll grow really mean!

Spring into Action

Like rutabagas, turnips prefer cool weather. But because they grow much faster than their yellow cousins, they give northern gardeners a bonus: We can grow them in both spring and fall.

In the spring, sow your seeds as soon as you can work the ground. I plant mine side by side with early peas, and both crops grow bigger and stronger, and turn out better harvests than they do when I grow them in separate beds.

In warmer parts of the country, plant turnips as a fall crop, timing the planting so the roots grow when the weather turns cool.

Small Appetites

Turnips grow up fat and sassy with no extra feeding during the growing season. They do like a steady supply of water, though. Give them enough to keep the soil moist but not wet, and use an organic mulch to keep moisture in the ground.

The Details

Sow your seeds ¼ inch deep and 1 inch apart. If you're hankering for a great crop of roots, thin the seedlings to stand at least 4 inches apart — those tubers need all of the elbow-room they can get! Always cut off the little sprouts with scissors instead of pulling them up, so you don't disturb the ones left behind. When you're planning to harvest only the greens, though, don't do any thinning at all.

Two Crops in One?

Maybe. Then again, maybe not. The green tops of all turnips are edible, though some are tastier than others. And varieties bred especially for their greens have roots that I wouldn't eat if you paid me a million dollars.

Seeing Green

Start clipping turnip greens as soon as they're big enough to eat, which is generally 3 weeks before the roots are ready for pulling. If you plan to come back later and dig up some roots, leave a half-dozen or more leaves on each plant. Otherwise, the tubers will stop growing, and you'll cheat yourself out of a crop.

Shopping Time

JERRY'S FAVORITE *Vegetable Varieties*

What kind of turnips I buy depends on when I want to plant them and what I intend to do with them. Here's what to look for:

WHAT I WANT	VARIETY I LOOK FOR
Great greens	'All Top'– a good, bolt-resistant hybrid that gives me a super crop of greens in 40 days
A good keeper	'Purple-Top Milan'– a flat, purple-and-white heirloom that matures in 45 days and holds up like a trouper in the root cellar
Good eatin' — pronto	'Hakurei'– an early type that gives me great-tasting greens and white roots in just 38 days
A good crop in spring or fall	'Golden Ball'– a globe-shaped heirloom that's yellow inside and out, matures in 55 days, and grows well whenever you plant it

The Root of the Matter

I pull up some turnips when they're still only an inch or 2 in diameter. At that stage, they're crisp and sweet. But they get even sweeter after a few visits from Jack Frost, so I leave most of my crop in the ground until the first hard freeze comes along. Then I dig them all up and get them ready for winter storage.

Once my crop is out of the ground, I let the tubers bask in the sun until the dirt dries out and falls off. Then I cut off the tops to within 2 inches of the roots and store them in a box of damp sawdust in a spot that stays between 32 and 40°F all through the winter.

Double Spring Greens

As your turnip and kale plants begin to go to seed, take a lawnmower and run over the rows of greens. Follow this with a thorough watering and, if your soil is not particularly rich, a good dose of compost. Soon, you'll be picking tender young greens.

Bigger Was Better

Grandma Putt told me that when *her* grandma was a girl, folks didn't bother as much with growing big tomatoes and pumpkins as we do today. Back then, the monster-veggie crowd focused its attention on turnips. It was nothing to have a 30-pounder in the garden, and — at least according to the stories — some folks grew giants that weighed as much as 100 pounds! (*The Guinness Book of Records* gives the modern heavyweight championship to a 51-pounder from Alaska.)

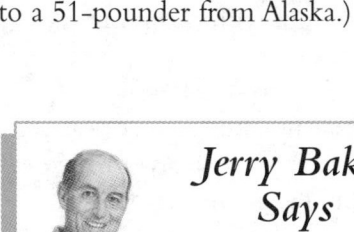

Jerry Baker Says

"I store turnips from my fall crop only — never the spring one. That's because if they (or any other root veggies) stay in storage too long, they get woody and bitter."

Bring On the Ladies

If aphids are tormenting your turnips, plant your next crop beside hairy vetch, and your troubles will be over. The reason is not a deep, dark mystery: To a ladybug, a big patch of hairy vetch is palatial living quarters, and a ladybug's idea of a four-star restaurant is a plantful of aphids. It's a simple equation: More ladybugs = fewer aphids.

Jack-o'-Turnip

Or would it be turn-o'-lantern? Whatever you want to call it, the very first jack-o'-lanterns were not pumpkins — they were turnips! The tradition started in Ireland and Scotland (long, long before Grandma Putt's day), when children would go from house to house on Halloween, carrying lanterns made out of hollowed-out turnips with candles inside.

When Irish and Scottish emigrants headed for America in the 1800s, they took the custom with them. But during the trip across the ocean, the turnip got replaced by a pumpkin.

But not at my house. Every year at Halloween, I carve up a few turnip lanterns, and hang 'em out on the porch along with my pumpkins. Here's how to do it:

1. Find a big, round turnip — the bigger and rounder, the better.

2. About a quarter of the way down, slice off the top completely.

3. Scoop out the insides with a spoon. (I like to use a spoon with a serrated tip made for eating grapefruit.)

Make the shell as thin as you can without breaking the skin. Leave a layer of flesh on the bottom. In it, hollow out a socket for the candle.

4. With a very sharp, fine knife, etch a design on the turnip. Be careful not to cut through the skin — it's a lot thinner than a pumpkin shell, and if it's broken, your lantern will collapse.

5. Push a candle into the socket.

6. With an awl or a nail, poke a hole on each side about an inch or so down from the top.

7. Thread wire or sturdy cord through the holes to make a handle. Be sure to keep it long enough so you don't burn your hand when you hold on to it.

8. Light the candle carefully, using one of those long matches that are made for lighting campfires and fireplace setups.

9. Hang it up outside, or carry it with you to your neighborhood's next Halloween party.

Winter Salad Days

You don't have to give up fresh-from-the-garden salads just because winter has camped on your doorstep. Just switch the focus from greens to the roots in your storage bin. As a for instance, grate some turnips, carrots, cabbage, and beets, add diced red onion, and toss it all with your favorite vinaigrette dressing. Mmm, mmm, good!

HITTING HIGH C BRUSSELS SPROUTS

Looking at them, it's hard to believe that Brussels sprouts have more vitamin C than oranges. For a C-packed side dish, whip up a batch of these splendid sprouts.

4 SERVINGS

1 pound small, fresh Brussels sprouts
1 tablespoon red wine vinegar
2 tablespoons minced fresh dill or
  2 teaspoons dillweed
salt and freshly ground black pepper

1. Preheat oven to 350°F.

2. Trim the sprouts and cut a little cross into the base of each one.

3. Cook the sprouts in a medium-sized saucepan in boiling water to cover for 10 minutes.

4. Drain into a colander, then quickly drench with cold water to prevent any further cooking at the moment.

5. Put the sprouts into a small, buttered baking dish. Stir in the vinegar, dill, and salt and pepper, and cover (with foil, if necessary). Bake for 10 minutes, then remove the cover and bake for another 5 minutes.

PURPLE PASSION SOUP

Purple was Grandma Putt's favorite color. And she was passionate about red cabbage. So it's no wonder she thought up this soup! It tastes equally great hot or cold.

6 SERVINGS

2 tablespoons vegetable oil
2 tablespoons butter
1½ cups diced onion
6 cups finely chopped red cabbage
2 cups apple cider
2 cups water
1 teaspoon salt
1 tablespoon lemon juice
3 tablespoons honey or brown sugar
1 cup milk
½ cup heavy cream

1. In a large soup pot, heat the oil and butter, and lightly sauté the onion; do not let it brown.

2. Add the cabbage and sauté 5 minutes, stirring constantly, then add the cider, water, salt, and lemon juice.

3. Cover the pot and then simmer for 45-60 minutes until the cabbage is very tender. Cool slightly, then add the remaining three ingredients.

4. Pour two-thirds of the soup into a blender, blend until smooth, then return to the pot with the rest of the soup.

5. Reheat and serve, or chill and serve.

SAVOY SLAW

Savoy cabbage makes terrific coleslaw. But its mild flavor and tender texture buckle under heavy slaw dressings. That's why Grandma Putt always made her Savoy slaw this way.

6 TO 8 SERVINGS

¾ cup vinegar
2 tablespoons pure maple syrup or brown sugar
1 teaspoon paprika
1 teaspoon salt
1 teaspoon ground mustard
1 teaspoon dill seeds
1 clove of garlic, minced
1 cup vegetable oil
¼ cup tomato ketchup
1 Savoy cabbage, finely chopped (8 cups)
1½ cups diced green pepper
1½ cups diced tomato
1 small red onion, cut in half and thinly sliced

1. In a small bowl, combine the vinegar, maple syrup, paprika, salt, mustard, dill seeds, and garlic.

2. Whisk the mixture as you pour in the oil in a thin stream. Add the ketchup and mix.

3. Combine the cabbage, green pepper, tomato, and red onion. Pour the dressing over the vegetables and toss.

4. Set the salad aside for at least 1 hour to let the cabbage wilt before serving.

CABBAGE KIELBASA PIE

On a cold winter night, you can't find a better supper than this hearty pie served with dark, crusty bread and dark beer.

8 SERVINGS

4 cups boiling water
4 cups finely chopped green cabbage
4 eggs, lightly beaten
½ cup milk
1 cup flour
1 teaspoon fennel seeds
1 teaspoon salt
¼ teaspoon pepper
1 tablespoon vegetable oil
2 cups thinly sliced leeks
¾ pound kielbasa, thinly sliced on the diagonal

1. Preheat oven to 375°F. Grease a 10-inch pie pan.

2. Pour boiling water over cabbage and set aside for 10 minutes. Drain, and stir in eggs, milk, flour, fennel, salt, and pepper. Pour in cabbage mixture, and press onto sides and bottom to form a crust.

3. Heat oil in a sauté pan, and sauté leeks until they are limp but not brown. Sprinkle leeks over pie. Lay kielbasa in an overlapping circle around edge of pie. Fill in center with slices of kielbasa.

4. Bake the pie for 40 minutes. Let it sit for 10 minutes before serving.

CONFETTI KOHLRABI

If kohlrabi is a new taste treat around your house, try this simple side dish. I guarantee it'll turn you and your family into the biggest kohlrabi fans in town!

6 SERVINGS

- 4 cups diced kohlrabi
- 2 tablespoons butter
- 1 cup corn kernels
- ½ cup scallions
- 1½ cups chopped tomatoes
- 1 clove of garlic, minced
- 1 tablespoon minced fresh parsley
- ½ teaspoon chili powder
- salt and pepper

1. Blanch or steam the kohlrabi until tender crisp, about 5 minutes. Drain and set aside.

2. Melt the butter in a large sauté pan, and sauté the corn, tomatoes, scallions, garlic, parsley, and chili powder for 2 minutes.

3. Stir in the reserved kohlrabi. Season to taste with salt and pepper. Serve hot.

CHEESY RUTABAGA BAKE

Rutabagas are so easy to grow that you can find yourself with a forest of 'em before you know it. So what do you do? Bake up a few of these casseroles and stash 'em away in the freezer. (Feel free to substitute turnips for the rutabagas, or use a combination of both.)

6 TO 8 SERVINGS

- 1 tablespoon butter
- 2 tablespoons vegetable oil
- ¼ cup chopped onion
- 2 cups peeled, sliced apples
- 4 cups peeled, cubed rutabagas
- ¼ cup apple cider
- 1 cup grated Swiss or Cheddar cheese

1. Preheat oven to 350°F. Grease a 2-quart baking dish.

2. In a sauté pan, heat the butter and oil, and sauté the onion until it is limp, 3–5 minutes. Add the apples and sauté 2 minutes longer.

3. Parboil the rutabagas for 5–8 minutes, or until tender crisp. Add the rutabagas and cider to the onion and apples.

4. Place the vegetables in the baking dish. Sprinkle with the cheese and bake for 30 minutes, or until the top is golden brown.

CARROT FAMILY

Carrots • Celery • Parsnips

Grandma Putt tried to teach me the scientific monikers of all the vegetable families. I never could get my tongue around the carrot clan's name: Umbelliferae. It always came out "umbrella." But Grandma Putt said that was okay; it would help me remember who belonged in the group. Every single one produces a big bunch of little flowers called an umbrel, which looks just like an umbrella.

Beyond Umbrellas

Besides their look-alike flowers, the carrot clan has some other things in common:

• **A cool nature.** Every plant in the family prefers its temperatures on the mild side.

• **Few enemies.** Not one of the veggies in this clan is much troubled by pests or diseases.

• **Opinionated roots.** All of these guys like deep, loose soil with plenty of organic matter in it.

• **Finicky seeds.** The only real family problem is poor germination. The seeds won't sprout worth a darn unless you start them in fine-grained soil (I always sift mine) and keep it moist.

The Cousins

Besides its three most famous members, the carrot family includes a lesser-known veggie (Florence fennel); several herbs, including parsley, fennel, and dill; and even a flower that most folks classify as a weed — the delicate Queen Anne's lace.

Do Yourself a Favor

If you spot some green caterpillars with black stripes munching on your carrot-family crops, don't call out the hit squad. Instead, pick them up very gently and move them to a clump of Queen Anne's lace — or even plant an extra patch of parsley or dill just for them. You'll be glad you did: In a few weeks, the crawly critters will turn into swallowtail butterflies.

Carrots *(Daucus carota)*

Grandma Putt always told me to eat my carrots: They were good for me. Well, they're even better for me now, and they taste better, to boot! That's because over the years, plant breeders have been working on reducing the size of the pale core, which has less sugar and fewer vitamins than the orange outer part.

The Family Temperament

Carrots produce their best crops when temperatures range between 60 and 75°F, so it's important to time your plantings accordingly. Start your first batch 2 to 3 weeks before you expect the last frost. Then make succession plantings every 2 weeks until the temperature reaches 80°F, but make sure the later crops get plenty of shelter from the hot summer sun.

For my spring plantings, I always put in a fast-maturing variety for eating fresh from the garden. Later, about the time I plant my tomatoes, I sow a winter-storage crop, and I always choose a variety that holds up well through the winter, like 'Bolero'.

SUPER Growing Secrets

SPEED IT UP

Carrot seeds take a long time to germinate, but soaking them overnight in my Seed Starter Tonic (see page 355) will speed up the process.

Perfectionism Pays Off

When it comes to soil, carrots are just about the biggest fussbudgets I know. If the tip comes against so much as a leaf or a piece of straw, the root can fork off in two directions or even stop growing. I always plant carrots in raised beds — even when I'm growing shorter varieties — and I dig the soil to a good 12 inches down, tossing out all of the sticks and stones I come across along the way.

Whether your soil is heavy or sandy, digging in plenty of finely sifted compost will make your carrots' dreams come true: It will lighten heavy soil, and it will help sandy soil absorb and hold water better. That's important, because carrots grow up sweeter and less fibrous in soil that stays moist.

Sitin' and Sowin' Tips

Give your carrots a site that has full sun; but if the best your garden can offer is light shade, don't worry — they'll produce a smaller harvest, but they'll still taste just fine.

Make early sowings shallow to capture warmth from the sun: Just sprinkle the seeds on the surface of the soil, tamp them lightly, and cover them with a thin layer of finely sifted compost. Later, when the soil has warmed up, plant seeds ¼ inch deep, but still cover them with compost rather than garden-variety soil. It gives them a nutritional boost and also makes it easier for them to reach up to the surface.

Aboveground

When the seedlings come up, thin them so that there's 3 to 4 inches between carrots, depending on the variety. Clip off the greens at ground level with scissors, rather than trying to pull them out and disturb their siblings. Make sure that you get at them before the tops start twining together — otherwise, it gets to be a real jungle out there!

Spray the young plants once with Compost Tea (see page 351) to get them growing on the right foot, and mulch with compost to keep moisture in the soil and weeds out.

Make Their Job Easier

Carrots can take as long as 10 days to germinate, and if a crust forms on the soil during that time, the seedlings will have to push like the dickens to get through — and a lot won't make it. Here's how to lighten their load:

• **Interplant them** with radishes. The radishes will pop up before the carrots have germinated and will loosen the soil surface in the process.

• **Water gently** every day while the seeds are germinating, so the soil stays moist and a crust doesn't form.

Procrastinator's Dream

If it's mid-July and you haven't even broken ground in your garden, don't give up. There's still plenty of time to get a crop of tasty young carrots in. Just remember to sow them deeper than you would in cooler weather, and give them some shelter from the hot summer sun.

CALENDAR

Jerry Baker Says

"Carrots like their tops to be warm and their roots to be cool. I like to plant them side by side with leafy greens like Swiss chard that will shade the soil — and keep away pesky weeds at the same time."

Rule of the Root

Carrots come in six categories, and the best kind for you depends on what kind of soil you have. My rule of thumb is that the heavier the soil, the shorter the root of the carrot should be.

For Clay Soils or Containers

If your turf tends to be on the clay side, or if you grow your veggies in containers, get one of these types:

• **Amsterdam** carrots get to be 3 to 5 inches long and about the diameter of your index finger. They grow fast and mature early, so they're also a good choice if your weather heats up quickly in the spring. 'Minicor' and 'Little Finger' are good choices.

• **Chantenay** types are stout, chunky, and anywhere from 4 to 6 inches long. 'Oxheart' grows well in heavy soil whenever you plant it. 'Tokita's Scarlet' is best for fall harvests.

• **Paris Market** varieties are little spheres about 1½ inches in diameter. They're perfect for containers, or for any garden that children have anything to do with — they can't resist the little round balls. 'Thumbelina' and 'Parmex' are both winners in my book.

For Light Soils

These longer types need good, light soil that their long roots can push through easily:

• **Nantes** varieties are the most popular home-garden carrots. They grow 5 to 7 inches long, and they're sweet and crunchy and look a little like deep orange cigars.

• **Danvers** carrots reach about the same size as Nantes types. On the minus side, they're not as sweet; on the plus side, they perform well in almost any kind of soil.

• **Imperator** types I never even bother with. They're bred for the commercial market, and they're the ones you see most often in food stores. They lack the sweetness and crunch of the other kinds (long or short), and they need deep, loose soil and just about perfect growing conditions.

End Maggot Mugging

Root maggots can polish off your carrot crop faster than you can say "Bugs Bunny." To keep the vile villains where they belong — far, far away — sprinkle coffee grounds or wood ashes over your whole carrot patch.

BUG BUSTERS!

Kaffe

Avoiding Trouble

Carrots are generally about as trouble-free as a vegetable can get, but a few problems could come your way. Here's how to head them off at the pass:

SYMPTOM	CAUSE	PREVENTION
Split roots	Too much water following a dry spell.	Keep a steady, even water supply; if a drenching rain comes along, cover plants with plastic sheets. And don't worry: Splitting doesn't affect flavor.
Green shoulders	Exposure to sunlight.	Pack soil around tops as they grow and make sure they're not shoving their way to the surface.
Forked roots	Roots have bumped into obstacles in the soil, or its nitrogen content is too high.	Make sure you get all rocks and other debris out of the soil before sowing; don't use manure or other fertilizers high in nitrogen.
Short roots	Plants are too close together; they're suffering from heatstroke.	Thin seedlings so they have plenty of elbowroom; give plants some shade during the hottest part of the day.
Hard, woody roots	Growth is too slow; they've stayed in the ground too long.	Give plants plenty of potassium and phosphorus; dig roots when they're still young and tender.
Lack of flavor	Roots pulled after their orange color peaked; they've grown at the wrong time; they've had too much nitrogen.	In summer, harvest carrots within 2 or 3 days of the time they color up. Time your planting so that carrots mature in fall, when sun is bright and nights are cool. Avoid nitrogen.

Push!

To keep the greens from breaking off when you harvest carrots, push them into the ground a little, then pull them up with a twisting motion.

Harvesttime

You know carrots are ready for harvesting when they turn deep orange (normally 60 to 80 days after planting, depending on the variety). When the weather's warm, don't waste any time — after 2 or 3 days in the ground, the flavor will go downhill fast. In cooler weather, carrots can stay in the ground for weeks without declining in either taste or appearance.

Cut 'em Off

Cut off the leaves as soon as you have the carrots out of the ground: As long as the greens are attached, they'll keep growing and drawing moisture and nourishment (and flavor) from the roots. They'll stay good for a week or so in the fridge. Just seal them up in plastic bags to lock in the moisture. For winter storage, bury them in damp sawdust and keep them in a cold place (32 to 40°F).

A Real Winter Keeper

A new variety of carrot called 'Merida' can be planted in late September or early October and will grow through the winter, to be ready for harvest May through June.

When It's Apple-Blossom Time

Grandma Putt always waited until the apple trees bloomed before she planted her carrot-family crops. She knew that by then the carrot flies had all laid their eggs and her veggies wouldn't be bothered by the pesky larvae. If you don't want to wait that long, put row covers on the beds as soon as you've sown your seeds.

Keep It Up

In parts of the country where the ground freezes, you can extend the harvest by mulching your carrots with a 2-foot layer of leaves or straw.

SUPER Storing Secrets

FASHIONABLY LATE TASTES GREAT

Carrots are one of the easiest vegetables to store, but you wouldn't know it by listening to many gardeners. They complain that stored carrots are tough and tasteless after they take them out of storage. Well, here's the answer: The carrots were tough and tasteless when they were put into storage. The biggest mistake people make with carrots meant to be stored is to sow them too early in the season. Sow your storage carrots about 4 weeks after sowing your fresh-eating carrots. Your taste buds will thank you all winter long!

Celery *(Apium graveolens)*

There are no two ways about it: Growing celery is a challenge. But it's not nearly the problem child that some folks make it out to be. As Grandma Putt used to say, it's just one of those eccentric types that have their own ideas about things. As far as I'm concerned, fresh-from-the-garden celery tastes so much better than the supermarket stuff that it's worth all of the coddling I can give it!

A Good Head Start

I start my celery seeds indoors at least 8 weeks before I expect the last frost. I use a slightly different routine from the one I use for most seeds. Here's my four-step process:

Step 1. Make a half-and-half mixture of seed-starting mix and compost; celery needs all the organic matter it can get! Use individual pots right from the get-go, so you won't have to disturb the roots at transplanting time.

Step 2. Sow the seeds on top and cover them with only a thin layer of potting mix. This is important, because celery seeds need light to germinate.

Step 3. Moisten the starting mix with my Seed and Soil Energizer Tonic (see page 355), cover the tray with clear plastic, and put it in a warm spot with indirect light. Keep the temperature between 65 and 75°F. Seedlings will start to show up in about a week. Even at this age, they've got minds of their own, so don't panic if some take longer than others to join the party.

Step 4. When the plants are up, take off the cover, move the tray to a warm,

sunny place, and keep the soil moist with my Seedling Strengthener Tonic (see page 356).

Move the seedlings to the garden when you're sure the temperature will stay above 55°F in the daytime and 40°F at night. Otherwise, they're likely to bolt, and before you know it, there's a big crop of celery seed.

Friends and Enemies

When it comes to being neighborly, celery's a pretty good crop to have around the old homestead.

A HELPING HAND
Celery and bush beans make good garden buddies — each makes the other grow better and tastier. Leeks, tomatoes, cauliflower, and cabbage are welcome in the neighborhood, too.

NOT ON SPEAKING TERMS
Celery does not get along with carrots or parsnips, so don't even think of planting them together.

Home Ground

Celery offers up its best harvest in full sun, but it will tolerate light shade, and it's happy with any soil pH from 6.0 to 7.0. What it absolutely digs in its heels about is organic matter. Work loads of compost and well-cured manure into the bed, and before you put each transplant into the ground, add compost to the planting hole. Then set the plants a little deeper than they were growing in their pots, water them with a diluted solution of fish fertilizer, and lay down an organic mulch. During the growing season, keep the soil damp, and every 4 weeks, give the plants a good healthy dose of fish fertilizer.

Round and Round

Grandma Putt always planted her celery in a circle. That way, she said, all the lacy roots would twine together and make a cozy home for the earthworms and microscopic critters that keep the soil open and fluffy, the way celery likes it.

Into the Kitchen — or the Garage

Start harvesting celery as soon as the stalks are big enough to use — they taste great at any size. Depending on how much you want, either cut off individual stems or slice off the whole plant at the soil line.

So I can have fresh celery through the winter, before the first hard freeze hits, I dig up a half-dozen plants and pot 'em in big plastic pots. I put them into the garage and water them whenever they start looking droopy. They give me crunchy, tasty snacks all winter long.

Crazy for Celery

A Word to the Wise from Grandma Putt

Back when Grandma Putt's mama was a girl, in the late 1800s, celery was all the rage. Folks went gaga over celery-flavored soda pop, celery chewing gum, and celery soup. There was even an elixir of celery that was guaranteed to cure whatever ailed you. Grandma Putt told me the fad started around 1869, when a fella who called himself Dr. Brown made up a soft drink from soda water and crushed celery seed.

Blanch It — or Not

Back in Grandma Putt's day, most folks blanched their celery to get it nice and white. What they didn't know was that left to its own green devices, celery has a little more flavor and, better still, a *lot* more nutrients.

But if you don't think it's celery unless it's white, the easiest way to blanch it is to set half-gallon, waxed paper milk cartons over the stalks as they're growing. Or plant a variety like 'Golden Self-Blanching', which will do the job all by itself.

Seeing Red

If you like to give folks a real surprise at dinnertime, serve 'em red celery. 'Solid Red' is a hale-and-hardy heirloom with a more easygoing disposition than most celery. And 'Giant Red' is a good-looking newcomer that turns even redder after the first frost.

Say Uncle

If your neck of the woods can't give celery the temperature range it needs (65 to 75°F during the day, 60 to 65°F at night), forget it. Devote the garden space to a less finicky veggie, and buy your celery from the best produce market you can find.

Celeriac *(Apium graveolens)*

Celeriac isn't as good-looking as its close relative celery, but it's just as tasty — and a lot less persnickety. It's grown for its roots (which look a lot like turnips) rather than its stalks. Most folks use celeriac as a cooked veggie, but I like it just as much in salads, shredded or sliced up thin.

You can grow celeriac the same way you do celery, and start eating the roots when they get about 2 inches in diameter. But leave most of the crop in the ground until Jack Frost has paid a few calls in the fall — it tastes much better then.

The roots are easier to dig than to pull, so loosen the soil with a garden fork and lift up the plants. Cut the tops an inch or 2 above the roots, and store them in the garage in a container full of damp sawdust.

YEAR-ROUND CELERIAC

Every fall, I plant a celeriac root in a big clay pot filled with sand, and put it in a sunny window in my kitchen. I keep the sand moist, and the next thing I know, the bulb starts sending up little stalks with frilly green tops. As long as I keep clipping them for salads, the bulb keeps churning them out, all winter long.

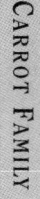

Parsnips *(Pastinaca sativa)*

Back in Grandma Putt's day, folks weren't too concerned about instant gratification. In fact, they got a kick out of planting a crop of parsnips, knowing they could just sit back and wait 6 months or a year, and then go out and dig up some of the finest-tasting veggies a body could sink a fork into.

Easy to Please

I've never figured out why more folks don't grow parsnips. As far as I'm concerned, you couldn't ask for a better vegetable — or one that's easier to please. Just about all they ask for is a spot where nobody will disturb them for a while: They take up to 150 days to mature and as long as a year to perfect their flavor.

Getting Them Started

Parsnips perform like troupers in most any kind of soil, but a pH of 6.2 to 7.2 makes the roots develop best. Dig soil to at least 18 inches for short varieties, 2 feet for longer ones, and take out any stones or other debris that could get in the way of the roots. Add plenty of compost to the soil, and, as with all root crops, say "No, thanks" to anything that's high in nitrogen.

Starting Off

Start your crop in early spring, when the soil temperature has reached 50°F. Soak seeds in water overnight in Woody-Seed Starter Tonic (see page 360) to kick-start the germination process, then sow them ½ inch deep and 1 inch apart. Keep the bed evenly moist until the seedlings pop up, 3 to 4 weeks later (I told you not to expect instant gratification from parsnips). Thin the plants to 3 to 4 inches apart, put a layer of leaf mold around them, and mulch with straw. Then just sit back and wait . . . and wait . . . and wait.

Patience Rewarded

You can dig parsnips as soon as they're big enough to use, but I never bother — there are plenty of other great-tasting veggies in the garden then. I let my crop stay in the ground until the following spring. Then, in early April, when the daffodils are about to bloom and the parsnips' sweet, nutty flavor reaches its peak — and my freezer and root cellar are close to empty — I dig up my parsnips and have a feast.

Beware of Impostors
If you see a parsnip that's growing in the wild, whatever you do, *don't dig it up and eat it* — it could be the parsnip's look-alike, the highly toxic water hemlock.

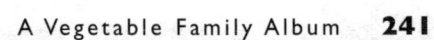

The Long and the Short of It

If your soil tends to be heavy, rocky, or shallow, plant a short parsnip like **'Fullback'** or **'Harris Early Model'.** On the other hand, if depth is not a factor in your neck of the woods and you'd like a giant parsnip for your trophy case, shop around for seeds of **'Tried and True'.** One of those guys grew to be over 12 feet long in England a few years ago!

JERRY'S FAVORITE Vegetable Varieties

Keep Your Hands from Yourself

The stems and leaves of parsnips produce a liquid that some folks are allergic to. Just to be on the safe side, wear gloves and keep your hands away from your face when you're working with parsnip tops.

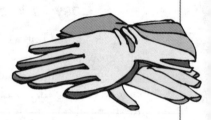

Eat Up

A Word to the Wise from Grandma Putt

Grandma Putt's favorite way to cook parsnips was to boil them until they were just tender, then toss them in a little butter and sprinkle cinnamon on top. I still like them that way, but they're just as good stir-fried, or used instead of potatoes in all kinds of recipes. Why, I even like them dredged in flour and bread crumbs and French fried.

On the Side

One of the tastiest side dishes I can think of is a parsnip purée. Fresh from the food processor, it makes a dandy addition to any plate. But what's even better for the folks who like to be prepared for last-minute company, parsnip purées are terrific keepers in the freezer.

To make one of these satisfying treats, slice up the parsnips and blanch them in boiling water for about 5 minutes, until they're barely tender. Then purée them in a blender or food processor, along with just enough liquid to give them the consistency of mashed potatoes. Season with butter, salt, and pepper to taste, and add whatever herbs you're partial to. Here's a quartet of my favorite parsnip partner combos:

- Orange juice and ginger
- Cream and thyme or rosemary
- Apple cider, brown sugar, and cinnamon
- Yogurt, garlic, and shallots

CARROT-CILANTRO SOUP

This super soup tastes equally delicious whether you serve it hot or cold. Its combined flavors of coriander and cilantro always remind me of my favorite Mexican restaurant — even though the recipe came from my cousin in Dublin!

4 SERVINGS

- 2 tablespoons butter
- 1 cup chopped onion
- 2 teaspoons ground coriander
- 1 pound carrots, peeled and thinly sliced
- 4 cups chicken broth
- ¼ cup cream (optional)
- salt and freshly ground black pepper
- ½ cup chopped cilantro

1. Melt the butter in a medium-size saucepan. Cook the onion in this over medium heat until it's nice and soft — about 10 minutes. Add the coriander and cook, stirring, for 3 or 4 minutes, then add the carrots and chicken broth.

2. Bring to a boil, turn down the heat, and simmer, covered, for ½ hour.

3. Now blend the soup in a food processor or blender until smooth. Put back into the saucepan. Add the cream, if you're using it, then season to taste with salt and pepper. Last, stir in the chopped cilantro. Reheat, if necessary. (Or chill, if you plan to serve it cold.)

PARSNIP APPLE DRESSING

For Sunday dinners in early winter, when the root cellar was brimming with tangy apples and the parsnips were reaching their peak of sweetness in the garden, Grandma Putt served up roast chicken stuffed with this heavenly concoction.

4 TO 6 SERVINGS

- 2 tablespoons butter
- 1 cup finely diced celery
- 1 cup diced onion
- ¼ teaspoon ground sage
- ¼ teaspoon dried thyme
- 4 cups grated parsnips
- 1 cup peeled, chopped apples
- 2 cups fresh bread cubes
- ⅓ cup apple cider
- salt and freshly ground black pepper

1. Preheat oven to 350°F.

2. Melt butter in a large sauté pan, and sauté the celery, onion, sage, and thyme, until the onion is limp, 3–5 minutes.

3. Add the parsnips and apples, and sauté until the parsnips are tender, about 3 minutes.

4. Mix the bread cubes and cider, and season to taste with salt and pepper.

5. Stuff the dressing into a 5- to 6-pound chicken and roast as usual, or simply serve up the dressing as a side dish. Either way, it's delish!

ONION FAMILY

Leeks • Onions • Shallots

The onion family is a large and . . . um . . . fragrant clan, and an old one, to boot. Grandma Putt told me that folks have been growing some kind of onion for at least 5,000 years. Well, all I know is that if I live to be 5,000, I'll still be growing them in my garden!

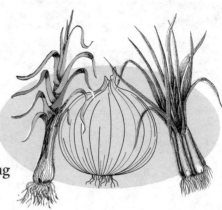

In the Pink

All members of the onion family can fall victim to pink root, a disease that stunts roots and turns them pink or red. It's usually only commercial growers who get hit with this, and it shows up in bulb onions and scallions more than it does in leeks and chives. But if the nasty stuff does head your way, here's what to do:

• Pull up and destroy the infected plants. Don't throw them onto the compost pile.

• Don't plant any onion crop in that spot for at least 6 years — that's how long the pesky fungus can survive in the soil.

Say "No, Thanks!" to Pink Root

Pink root is a lot easier to avoid than to cope with after it strikes. Follow the general guidelines for good health in Chapter 5 and also:

• Grow onions in raised beds, with lots of organic matter in the soil to ensure good drainage.

• Be extra careful when you're cultivating around onion crops — the pink root fungus often enters through wounds in the skin.

• Control onion maggots — their tunnels also let the fungus creep into the plants.

• Look for varieties with some tolerance to pink root. That won't guarantee safe passage for your onions, but it does mean that if the disease strikes, you'll stand a better chance of getting a decent harvest.

The Worst Enemies of the Worst Enemies

Maggots and cutworms are an onion crop's worst enemies. Fortunately, the worst enemies those bad critters could have are parasitic nematodes. Add them to the soil before you plant any onion family member. (See pages 122, 123, and 235 for other ways to clobber these clammy customers.)

Leeks *(Allium ampeloprasum)*

Grandma Putt grew a big patch of leeks, because she could never get enough cock-a-leekie soup. She also had a soft spot for them because the leek is the emblem of Wales, and every time she looked at one, it reminded her of her own Welsh cousins.

I grow them because they're tasty, nutritious, and a lot easier to digest than onions. They're also easy to grow and tolerant of cold weather. And why pay an arm and a leg for them in the supermarket?

Two of a Kind

Leeks come in two kinds:

• **Hardy types,** like 'Winter Giant' and 'American Flag', take 100 days or more to reach full size. They stand up to cold weather — in fact, they'll be okay in the garden all winter long. What's more, a lot of them have attractive blue-green foliage that looks great in an ornamental-edible garden.

• **Nonhardy varieties,** like 'King Richard' and 'Kilima', mature in just 70 to 90 days, so you harvest them in summer and early fall. They have a milder flavor than the hardy types, and they're great eaten fresh from the garden. On the other hand, these varieties don't store very well. They also tend to be tall and thin, with light green leaves that look just fine but when they're cooked, develop a taste that's nothing to write home about.

Start 'em Out Indoors

If your growing season is long and mild, sow leek seeds right in the garden; otherwise, buy plants for setting out about the time of the last spring frost. Start seeds indoors at least 10 weeks before the average frost-free date. I start mine in flats, and when the seedlings are about 2 inches tall, I transplant them to individual containers. While they're growing, I feed them with fish fertilizer every 2 weeks.

Move them to the garden about a week after the last frost, when they're as thick as a pencil. (Don't worry if they're a little bigger — that just means a bigger harvest.) Before you set your leeklings into their holes, trim the roots to about 2 inches.

Set them 4 to 8 inches apart, depending on the variety. If you want long, thin stems, plant them closer together; to get thicker stems, set them farther apart.

Leeks like full sun, well-drained soil with a pH of 6.2 to 7.0, and a big load of organic matter — ideally, a mix of compost and manure.

A Little Dibble'll Do Ya

There are several ways to plant leeks, all of them designed to make the stem grow straight, long, and white. But the simplest and fastest — and the one I use — is the dibble method.

A dibble is a planting tool that looks like a fat, pointed stick with a T-shaped handle. (If you don't have one, the end of a rake handle works just as well, as long as your soil is good and loose.)

Make a hole that's just deep enough to leave only the top inch of the transplant exposed. Then set the transplant into the hole, fill it loosely with soil, and water well, so that the soil settles in lightly around the plant. As the plants grow, they'll fill in the hole.

Dandy Leeks

Leeks are tastiest in the spring, when the plants are young and sweet. Grandma Putt sliced 'em up and cooked 'em with dandelion buds, then tossed 'em in butter with a little salt and pepper for some really good eating.

Growing Up

Mulch to keep moisture in the soil, and give the plants at least an inch of water a week; otherwise, the stems will get tough and strong-tasting. Once a month during the growing season, give them a nice drink of fish fertilizer or my All-Season Green-Up Tonic (see page 349) to satisfy their appetite.

Harvesttime

Leeks don't store as well as a lot of crops, so pull them only as you need them. I harvest the nonhardy kinds through the summer, starting as soon as they're big enough to use.

Hardy ones stay in the ground right through winter. Just pile a big blanket of mulch onto the bed, and then, when you get a hankering for some, loosen the soil with a spading fork and pull as many as you want.

And the Winner Is ...

Over in Wales, if you grew a giant pumpkin, probably no one would look at it twice. But grow a giant leek and you'll be a national hero! The Welsh recordholder weighed in at just over 12 pounds. If you want to try for the heavyweight title on this side of the Atlantic, start with seeds of a variety like 'Musselburgh' or 'Broad London', a.k.a. 'American Flag'.

Pow!

Grandma Putt used to say that the leek is the most versatile member of the onion family. It packs a bigger vitamin and mineral wallop than any of the others; adds just as much punch to soups, stews, and salads; and performs better as a solo vegetable. I like to cook young leeks and serve 'em up just like asparagus.

Onions *(Allium cepa)*

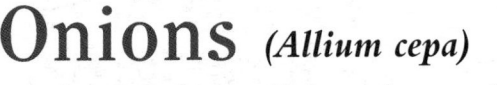

Grandma Putt always said that onions are the perfect crop for the gardener who doesn't have time to garden. All you need to do is start 'em out with what they want, and then sit back and wait.

What They Want

Onions are persnickety about their home ground. They *insist* on loose, fertile, well-drained soil — preferably a good, sandy loam — with lots and lots of compost or well-rotted manure dug into it, and a pH of 6.0 to 7.5. Give your onions a site that gets at least 6 hours of sun a day, and till the soil to a depth of about 8 inches, so the bulbs have loose quarters to develop in. Make sure you get out all traces of weeds: The grassy onion tops don't shade the ground the way the leaves of other veggies do, and once weeds come up, they'll take over the whole patch in the blink of an eye.

Three Guesses

There are three ways to give your onion crop its start in life: from transplants, from sets, and from seeds. (Sets are dormant bulbs about the size of a dime.) Each has its advantages and disadvantages, and here they are:

TYPE	ADVANTAGES	DISADVANTAGES
Transplants	They're easier to care for than seeds, at least in the beginning, and they mature sooner.	They're more expensive than seeds. You may not know exactly what kind you're getting — most garden centers buy them in bulk from growers, and the flats are often labeled simply red, white, or yellow.
Sets	They're easier to care for than seeds, at least in the beginning, and they mature sooner.	Onions that are grown from sets tend to bolt and send up seed stalks rather than develop bulbs. They often don't store as well as onions grown from seeds or transplants.
Seeds	You'll know exactly what kind of onions you're buying. You can be sure of getting a variety that will thrive in your neck of the woods.	They take a long time to mature, so you can sow them in the garden only if you have a long growing season. If you start indoors, you need to tend them for at least 2 months before you plant them in the garden.

Starting from Seed

In warm climates, you can sow onion seeds right in the garden when the soil temperature reaches 50°F. But in most parts of the country, start seeds indoors 8 to 10 weeks before the average frost-free date.

Starting from Transplants

Whether you start your own or buy them at a garden center, transplants can go into the ground 2 to 3 weeks before the last frost, when the soil temperature has reached at least 40°F.

Soak them in Compost Tea (see page 351) for 15 minutes, set them in the ground 1 to 2 inches deep, and space them 2 to 6 inches apart, depending on the size the bulb will be at maturity. If it's scallions you're after, space them 1 inch apart.

I Wouldn't Take a Dime for It

Just say no to any set that's bigger than a dime — the bigger the set, the more likely the plant will bolt. And if you want a crop of scallions, be sure the sets are white. They can go into the ground 4 weeks before the last expected frost, as long as the soil temperature is at least 40°F.

Soak the sets in Compost Tea (see page 351) for 15 minutes. Then push them into the ground, pointy end up, about ½ inch below the surface. To produce scallions, space them 1 inch apart; for mature bulbs, space them 2 to 6 inches apart.

ALL-PURPOSE ORGANIC FERTILIZER

This super stuff is the best friend your onions (or any other veggie plant) ever had.

5 parts seaweed meal
3 parts granite dust
1 part dehydrated manure
1 part bonemeal

If you want really big onions, side-dress them 2 or 3 more times during the season with the same fertilizer. And always be sure to water them after you fertilize.

SUPER Growing Secrets

TAKE YOUR TIME

Whichever way you start your onions, don't rush to get them into the ground. They like cool weather, but not prolonged cold — an extended period of temperatures in the 30s and 40s will slow their development.

A Little TLC

Even though, as Grandma Putt said, onions need a lot less attention than most crops, to get the best possible harvest, you'll still want to give them some basic care. No matter how you've started them, the routine is the same:

• **Weed often and well —** but carefully. Onions don't like weeds anywhere in their neighborhood, so keep a close eye out for trespassers and send them packing in a hurry. But because onion roots grow close to the surface, be extra careful to keep any cultivating gentle and shallow. (See My Weed Management Policy on page 78.)

• **Mulch sparingly.** A 1- to 2-inch layer of compost or chopped leaves will help keep weeds out and moisture in, but make sure you pull away the mulch from the plants once bulbs start to form.

• **Don't bury 'em.** Even though they're a root crop, onions grow best when they're on or near the surface of the soil. For the biggest onions, pull away the soil from the upper two-thirds of the bulb.

• **Feed 'em.** About a month after planting, give your onions a drink of fish fertilizer, and another one about a month after that. (Say no to anything with nitrogen in it — you'll get plenty of leaves but not much bulb.) Cut off the food supply about a month before you harvest, or as soon as the necks start feeling soft.

• **Water 'em —** up to a point. Onions don't need much water, but they like the supply to be steady. When the tops start turning yellow, stop watering completely, so that the skins can dry out. They'll hold up better in storage.

• **Bend 'em over.** When the leaves are all yellow, and about a quarter of them have toppled, bend over the rest of the tops with the back of a rake. This procedure will direct the plants' energy from the leaves to the bulbs.

Ashes, Ashes, They Won't Set Down

If you notice a lot of little flies buzzing around your onions, head for your fireplace, and add wood ashes (which contain potash) to your soil. Sprinkled around onions and cabbage, wood ashes discourage the flies whose babies are root maggots.

How Do You Like Them Onions?

Onions are one of those crops that make me glad that seed catalogs show up so early in the winter, because deciding what kind to grow can be a challenge. You can decide by color (white, red, yellow) or by shape (globe, flattened, torpedo), but most folks sort them out by how they use them.

• **Storage onions** usually have thicker skins, are a darker color, and have a more potent flavor. The best ones, like 'Copra' and 'Prince', will keep for months. Most varieties mature in 90 to 100 days from seed.

• **Slicing onions,** a.k.a. Bermuda or Spanish, are sweeter-tasting, thinner-skinned, and lighter in color than storage types. Varieties like 'Vidalia', 'Walla Walla', and 'Texas Supersweet' will perk up a sandwich or burger like nobody's business, but they don't store very well. Like storage types, they reach full size 90 to 100 days after you sow seeds.

• **Pearl or cocktail onions,** like 'Barletta', have tiny, mild-flavored bulbs that are great for pickling, tossing whole into soups or stews, or popping into Gibson cocktails. Most varieties are ready to pull in 60 to 70 days from seeds.

• **Green onions,** a.k.a. scallions, spring onions, or bunching onions, are grown for their stalks and grassy tops. Any kind of onion can be pulled early and called a scallion, but the genuine articles, like 'Evergreen White Bunching' and 'Red Welsh', are actually perennials, and they don't form bulbs at all. All of them are ready for picking 65 to 75 days from seeds.

Jerry Baker Says

"I grow plenty of onions among my other plants, because they make such good companions. But I don't depend on them for my main crop. Those I keep in separate beds — that way, I can stop watering them as harvest-time approaches without cheating my other veggies out of their weekly drinks."

Tied Up in Knots

For quick and easy storage of your onions, put one onion in an old panty hose toe and tie a knot above it. Add one after the other until you've filled the whole leg. Then hang your harvest in a cool, dry place. When you need an onion, simply cut below the bottom knot. (For more ways to use panty hose in the garden, see page 84).

Pull 'em Up

Harvest scallions, or green onions, when the tops are about 6 inches tall. As for how speedy you need to be, it depends on how pungent you like your onions: The younger they are, the milder they'll taste.

Bulbing onions are ready as soon as you think they're big enough to use, but they're fully mature when their tops turn yellow and start to topple. If you have to harvest your crop when some of the tops are still green, use them right away — they won't keep well.

How to Stash 'em

Here's how to harvest your storage crop:

1. Loosen the soil around each bulb and pull it up. Be careful, because damaged onions rot in the blink of an eye.

2. Spread the bulbs — tops attached — on a flat surface off of the ground. I use old window screens propped up on concrete blocks. Leave the bulbs there until the skins are dry and the tops have withered completely (2 to 10 days outside; roughly 2 weeks indoors, in a well-ventilated spot).

3. Cut off the tops, leaving about an inch of stem, put the bulbs into mesh bags like the ones you buy onions or potatoes in, and hang them in a place that's cool (35 to 40°F), dry, and well ventilated.

No More Tears

To stop those tears from flowing, hold onions under running water when you peel them. The H_2O will help remove a chemical called propanethial S-oxide, which turns into sulfuric acid when it comes in contact with your eyes.

Partner, Please Pass the Parsley

The next time you order a big, juicy hamburger, don't say "Hold the onions" just because you're afraid your table-mates will turn tail and run. Just order a few sprigs of parsley on the side and chew on 'em after you've finished your burger — they'll rout that onion breath faster than you can say "Medium rare."

Jerry Baker Says

"Never store onions near apples, tomatoes, or potatoes — they all give off a gas that makes onions sprout or spoil more quickly."

Seeing the Light

To mature properly, different kinds of onions need different amounts of light and darkness. Varieties are grouped by day length: short, long, and intermediate, and which kind you want to plant depends on where you live.

Up North

If you live in the northern parts of the country, plant long-day onions. They need about 14 hours of daylight and 10 hours of darkness. Some of your best choices are:

'**Borrettana**'–an old — and flavorful — Italian heirloom. It's small, flat, and yellow-brown in color and keeps well through the winter.

'**Red Burgermaster**'–great big, red and white globes with a taste that was made in hamburger heaven.

'**First Edition**'–firm, brown-skinned globes with creamy yellow flesh and a rich, pungent flavor. If you love to cook with onions — and to have a steady supply through the winter — these great keepers are the ones to plant.

Down South

If you garden in the Sun Belt states, look for short-day onions that thrive in equal amounts of daylight and darkness, like these winners:

'**Texas Supersweet**'–the best — and sweetest — onion for eating raw that you'll ever hope to find. As you'd expect from a plant that hails from the Lone Star State, these globe-shaped bulbs are BIG!

'**Granex**'–these sweet, flat bulbs come in both white and yellow, and they go by a handful of names. The white kinds are often sold as '**Miss Society**'; the yellows you'll see in both catalogs and supermarkets as '**Vidalia**', '**Maui**', or '**Noonday**'. They all have the same great taste and — unfortunately — the same short life in storage.

In the Middle

You can grow these intermediate varieties anywhere, but, just like Goldilocks, they'll be happiest where the daylight hours are that "just right" number between the long days of the North and the short days of the South.

'**Candy**'–colossal white bulbs with large, thick rings and a sweet taste that will make any lover of French-fried onion rings sit up and say "Yum!"

'**Sweet Red**'–large, flattened red globes that are perfect in salads and on burgers. Unfortunately, though, they don't store well.

Shallots *(Allium cepa)*

With the prices they charge for shallots in the supermarket, you'd think they were the most finicky crop on the face of the earth. Grandma Putt would take one look and say, "Land sakes! How can they get away with that? Don't folks know that shallots are as easy to grow as any other bulb?"

Highfalutin Alliums

Shallots have a reputation as the aristocrats of the onion family, but Grandma Putt was right: If you can grow onions, you can grow shallots. They like the same growing conditions, but shallots are much less particular about their soil. In fact, the only kind they don't like is heavy clay.

A Setup

Shallots are grown from bulbs (which are called cloves in the kitchen). I plant mine 2 to 4 weeks before the last frost. Just break up the clusters of bulbs, rub off their loose skins, and set them in the ground 6 inches apart.

Push them into the soil so the tops are about an inch below the surface, then firm the soil over them. Feed them with my All-Season Green-Up Tonic (see page 349) every 3 weeks, and make sure the plants get 1 inch or so of water every week until the tops start turning yellow. Then quit cold turkey.

If you live where the summertime temperature stays as high as 90°F for any length of time, plant shallot bulbs in the fall. Under a heavy mulch, they'll keep just fine through the winter and mature the following spring.

Harvesttime

You can start cutting shallot tops and using them the same as you would chives in salads and on eggs in as little as 30 days after planting. The bulbs mature in 90 to 120 days.

When the tops turn brown, dig up the bulbs carefully, and lay them in the sun to dry — if the weather's wet, spread them out on racks indoors. Then put them in net bags or nylon stockings and hang them in a dry place at about 60°F. They'll keep almost indefinitely.

GARLIC, SHALLOT, OR ONION VINEGAR

If you want a big bang for your gift-making buck, whip up a few batches of these simple vinegars. Grandma Putt and I used to put them in fancy bottles and give six-packs of them to friends and family at Christmas time. They're great in salad dressings, or in any recipe that calls for a flavored vinegar.

2 CUPS

⅓ cup chopped garlic, shallot, or onion
2 cups vinegar★

1. Combine the garlic, shallot, or onion with the vinegar in a screw-top jar. Store for 2 or 3 weeks.

2. Strain and bottle, inserting the appropriate thing into each bottle — a peeled clove of garlic or shallot or either a piece of onion or a tiny, peeled white onion.

★ Cider vinegar works best with the strong flavors of onions and garlic; shallots, being milder, team up better with wine vinegars.

TERRIFIC TARRAGON ONION BAKE

When you don't have time to fuss with a vegetable, this is the dish to make! The onions just sit there in the oven, getting sweeter and yummier by the minute. Any onions will do just fine, but the ones I like best are sweet varieties like Vidalia, Maui, or Walla Walla.

4 TO 6 SERVINGS

2 medium-large onions, sliced
  ¼ inch thick
2 tablespoons brown sugar
½ tablespoon fresh tarragon or
  ½ teaspoon dried
2 tablespoons butter

1. Preheat oven to 350°F.

2. Put the onion slices into a pan about 8 inches square, putting the brown sugar, tarragon, and dots of the butter between the layers.

3. Bake for 1½ hours.

4. Remove from the oven and eat up!

DILL AND SHALLOT CREAM SAUCE

This tasty sauce is one of the best reasons I can think of to grow shallots. It's got a delicate flavor that's just the ticket for dressing up vegetables, chicken, fish, or even pasta.

1 CUP

- 2 tablespoons butter
- ⅔ cup minced shallots (6–10 bulbs)
- 1½ tablespoons minced fresh dill
- 2 teaspoons all-purpose flour
- 2 tablespoons white wine
- ¾ cup heavy cream

1. Melt the butter in a sauté pan, and sauté the shallots and dill until the shallots are limp, 3-5 minutes.

2. Sprinkle the flour over the shallots, and stir in the wine and cream.

3. Simmer until the sauce is reduced by half and has thickened, about 10 minutes. Serve hot.

CREAMED CHESTNUTS AND ONIONS

There's no doubt about it: Chestnuts roasting on an open fire is a treat worth singing about. But for actually chowing down on, give me this creamy side dish every time!

6 SERVINGS

- 2 cups water
- 4 cups pearl onions
- ¾ cup peeled and quartered chestnuts
- 2 tablespoons butter
- 2 tablespoons all-purpose flour
- 1⅓ cups milk
- salt and pepper

1. In a medium-size saucepan, bring the water to a boil and add the onions. Boil for 10 minutes. Add the chestnuts and continue boiling until the onions are tender, 5–10 minutes more. Remove the onions and chestnuts from the heat, drain off the liquid, and save it. Cover the onions and chestnuts and keep them warm.

2. Melt the butter in a small saucepan, and stir in the flour to form a thick paste. Slowly add the cooking water and the milk a little at a time, stirring well after each addition to prevent lumps. Season to taste with salt and pepper.

3. Add onions and chestnuts and stir gently to coat. Serve immediately.

GRANDMA PUTT'S COCK-A-LEEKIE SOUP

*Grandma Putt always said that her Welsh ances-
try gave her a natural-born hankering for this
cockle-warming soup. To my way of thinking, it
also gave her a natural-born gift for making it!*

6 SERVINGS

2½ pounds of boneless, skinless
    chicken breasts
  3 cups water
  1 stalk celery, diced
  2 carrots, diced
 ½ cup barley
  1 cup chicken broth
  2 bay leaves
  2 teaspoons minced fresh rosemary
  1 teaspoon salt
 ½ teaspoon freshly ground pepper
 ¾ pound leeks, white and green parts
    sliced (about 1½ cups)

1. In a large saucepan, combine chicken
breasts, water, celery, carrots, barley, chick-
en broth, bay leaves, rosemary, salt, and
pepper. Heat to a boil. Reduce heat, cover,
and simmer for about 30 minutes.

2. Add the leeks, heat to a boil, reduce
the heat again, and simmer until the chick-
en is tender.

3. Remove the chicken and let cool.
When it is cool enough to handle, cut
into bit-size pieces.

4. Skim any fat from the broth and
remove the bay leaves. Put the chicken
pieces back into the broth and reheat for
about 5 minutes.

LAYERED SALAD

*Whenever we had company coming for a picnic,
Grandma Putt would make up this salad a day
ahead of time. She said she did it because it
saved her from the last-minute rush. But I know
she really did it because everybody loved it!*

8 SERVINGS

  1 large head of lettuce
3–4 stalks of celery, diced (about 2 cups)
  2 medium green peppers
  1 medium sweet onion
  2 cups peas, lightly steamed
  1 cup mayonnaise, thinned with
    2 tablespoons milk
  1 cup sour cream or plain yogurt
  2 tablespoons sugar
 ¼ pound cheddar or Monterey Jack
    cheese, grated
  1 cup minced fresh parsley or mint

1. Quarter, wash, drain, finely cut,
and dry the lettuce. Wash, scrape, and
dice the celery. Wash, core, seed, and cut
the peppers into strips. Slice the onion
into paper-thin rings.

2. Cook the peas in a little salted water;
rinse with cold water and drain.

3. Place the vegetables in layers in a glass
bowl in the order listed, saving half of the
lettuce to put on top. Mix the mayonnaise
and sour cream or yogurt together and
spread over the salad. Do not stir.

4. Sprinkle the sugar over the salad and
cover it with the grated cheese. Cover the
bowl with plastic wrap and refrigerate for
at least 8 hours and preferably 24.

SQUASH AND CUCUMBER FAMILY

Cucumbers • Melons • Watermelon Squash • Pumpkins • Gourds

This is a big family if ever there was one — in every sense of the word! It's also one of the most popular in all of gardendom. To its close friends (like Grandma Putt and me), the clan also goes by the name of cucurbits.

The Family Temperament

The cucurbits are a close-knit clan, with important things in common:

• They all like as much heat as they can get for as long as they can get it.

• They're big plants with appetites to match.

• They have the same archenemies, the worst of which are cucumber beetles, squash bugs, and squash borers.

• They're all subject to downy mildew, especially in hot, humid climates.

Jerry Baker Says

"The best way I know to get rid of bugs in the garden is to recruit a posse of young bounty hunters. Let them know what they're after, then turn 'em loose.

Put a price on the buggy heads, hang some WANTED posters around the house, and watch how fast those villains bite the dust."

Down with Downy Mildew

Here are three ways to keep both downy and powdery mildew fungus at bay:

1. Grow all your cucurbit crops on trellises so they get good air circulation.

2. Throughout the season, spray every 7 to 8 days with liquid seaweed.

3. Spray every 2 weeks with my Powdery Mildew Control Tonic.

POWDERY MILDEW CONTROL TONIC

Once you determine that the culprit is mildew, reach for this Tonic.

4 tbsp. of baking soda
2 tbsp. of Murphy's Oil Soap
1 gal. of warm water

Pour into a handheld mist sprayer, and apply liberally every week to 10 days until the white spots on your plants are gone.

Cucumbers *(Cucumis sativus)*

Every time I look at a cucumber patch, I think about all
of those jars of pickles lined up, straight as West Point cadets, on
Grandma Putt's pantry shelves. I still grow plenty of cukes for pickling — and for
eating straight from the garden. If you've only had the store-bought kind, you're
missing a real treat!

Say, Pal, Can You Turn Up the Heat?

Cucumbers hail from India, so it should come as no surprise that they
crave warmth. They need it every step of the way, in fact, from germination on. Fortunately, they mature quickly, so no matter where you
live, you can grow cukes successfully — though way up North, you'll
need to plant short-season varieties and coddle them some.

Give Them a Home

Cucumbers prefer to bask in all-day
sun, except in hot, dry regions, where
they like some afternoon shade. I give
my crop soil with a pH of 6.0 to 7.0,
dug deeply, with plenty of compost and
well-rotted manure added.

Cucumbers don't like to be transplanted. They'll grow up happiest if you
sow seeds directly in the ground at least
2 weeks after the last frost, when both
soil and air temperatures average at least
70°F — and when you're sure
Mother Nature doesn't have any
chilling surprises in store.
Expect germination in 3 to
10 days, depending on soil
temperature. (The higher the
temperature, the faster the
seeds will sprout.)

In cooler climates, buy started
plants at the garden center for

planting after all danger of frost has
passed, or start seeds indoors 3 to 4
weeks before your transplant date. Sow
them in individual, 4-inch traveling pots,
three seeds to a pot.

Keep the soil in the pots moist and
temperatures above 70°F during the day
and 60°F at night. When old Jack Frost
has gone for good and the soil temperature measures about 70°F, move your
plants outdoors.

Make sure that you have trellises or
pole supports in place *before* you
plant your seedlings, so you don't
disturb them later. Work in the
evening or on a cloudy day, so the
hot sun doesn't stress the plants, and
be very careful not to disturb the
roots. Set vining varieties 2 to 3 feet
apart, bush types 18 inches apart.

Feed Me, Please!

Cukes need all-purpose organic fertilizer (10-30-10) at the rate of 3 pounds per 100 square feet at planting, and again 3 to 4 weeks later. Then feed the plants with fish fertilizer every 2 weeks and give them a steady supply of drinking water — especially after the flowers form. Otherwise, you'll wind up with strangely shaped, poor-tasting cukes. To extend your growing season, apply additional nitrogen to the plants as soon as you start harvesting.

Up, Up, and Away

Even bush cucumbers seem born to ramble. And vining types will sprawl across the whole garden if you don't keep an eye on them. To stop cucumber takeover — and to get a healthier, tastier crop — grow them on trellises. They'll get better air circulation, thus falling prey to fewer disease and insect problems, and they'll produce more — and straighter — fruits (gravity will help straighten 'em out).

SUPER Growing Secrets

A HUT TO CALL HOME

For a fast, easy home for your cukes (or any other small-fruited vining crop), get a piece of hardware cloth or wire construction mesh, and bend it into the shape of a Quonset hut. Plant your seedlings in the middle, underneath it. They'll scramble up and over the arch — and away from low-lying pests and disease germs that are loitering on the ground.

BUG BUSTERS!

Don't Be Bitter

Cucumber beetles are drawn to cukes by a bitter compound that most varities have in their skin. So, if cucumber beetles just won't leave your crop alone, try a bitterless variety next year. The beetles tend to steer clear of kinds like 'Jazzer', 'Holland', 'Lemon', and 'Aria', which don't have that chemical attraction. But *you* won't want to steer clear of them — they turn out some of the tastiest harvests you'll find!

A Real Pickle

A good seed catalog will tell you whether the cukes you're admiring in its pages have been bred for pickling or for slicing up and using fresh. So how do you tell the difference?

• **Picklers** have thin, pale green skin. They produce their fruit about a week earlier than slicing types, and it all comes within 10 days.

• **Slicers** generally have darker skin, and, though they start later than picklers, they continue to set fruit for 4 to 6 weeks.

If you've sent off your seed order and you're having second thoughts, don't worry: A pickler will taste just fine in a salad. And you can make dandy pickles from slicers — just be sure to pick them when they're small.

Cukes Do It

Cucumbers produce separate male and female flowers on the same plant. The first blossoms you spot will be boys. About a week to 10 days later, the girls show up, each with a tiny future cucumber attached to its base. But before the fruits can mature, pollen has to pass from the male flowers to the females. Here's where the birds and bees come in: They'll do the job quick as a wink!

Don't Move!

Whether you're cultivating or picking, don't move your cuke vines any more than necessary. Why? Moving the vines:

• Destroys blossoms
• Drives away bees
• Gets the vines all kinked into a matted mess

Any one of these is just about guaranteed to land you a crop of misshapen and all-but-inedible cukes. So you have been forewarned.

SWEET SUCCESS SPRAY

Bees are the best friends your cucumber plants could have — they ensure pollination and give you more, better-tasting cukes. To attract these willing, winged workers to your veggie patch, spritz your cuke vines with this super spray.

½ cup of sugar
2 cups of water

Boil the mixture until the sugar is completely dissolved. Let the mixture cool, dilute it with 1 gallon of water, and spray out the welcome mat!

Sugar also kills nematodes in the soil, so you get two benefits for the price of one!

Say Goodbye to Excess Bag-gage!

To get rid of those bags and dark circles under your eyes, just grate a cucumber and put the pulp into a soft cloth bag. Then lie back, place the bag over your under-eye area, and relax for 15 minutes. (You can skip the bag and apply the cucumber directly to your skin, but it's a little bit messier that way.) Repeat daily until the baggage goes bye-bye.

Don't Wait

Don't dawdle about picking cucumbers. You want to get them off the vine when they're still of moderate size — between 3 and 4 inches for pickling varieties, 6 to 8 inches for slicers. Otherwise, they'll turn seedy and bitter. Cukes mature at the speed of light, so you'll need to check your plants daily.

Cukes in a Pot

For container growing, plant a small bush variety like 'Spacemaster' or 'Salad Bush'. Use potting soil enriched with compost and a pot that's at least 12 inches deep and 8 inches wide, with good drainage. And set a circle of chicken wire in the middle of the pot for support — even bush types appreciate something to lean on as they're growing up. Water often, adding crushed-up eggshells to the can, and fertilize every 3 weeks with my All-Season Green-Up Tonic (see page 349) or fish fertilizer.

Cuke in a Bottle

As an extra treat for helping rout the buggy hordes from your cucumber vines, help your kids grow their own variation of a ship in a bottle. While one of the cukes is still tiny, slip it into a small-necked glass bottle. Then shade it with newspaper, so the fruit doesn't bake in the sun.

When the cuke gets big enough to rate oohs and ahs — but not so big that it breaks the bottle — cut it from the vine, take it indoors, and put it center stage on the coffee table.

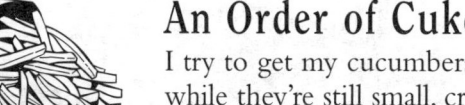

An Order of Cuke Fries, Please

I try to get my cucumbers off the vine and into the kitchen while they're still small, crisp, and tasty. But once in a while, they just get away from me and before I know it, they're past their prime for salads.

When that happens, I do what Grandma Putt did: fry 'em up. I cut them into thick slices and dip them in salted, slightly beaten eggs. Then I dredge them in flour and fry in medium-hot shortening until they turn a crispy brown. If you like fried eggplant, I guarantee you'll love these!

Melons *(Cucumis melo)*

When I was a boy growing up with Grandma Putt, summer without melons fresh from the garden would have been like the Fourth of July without fireworks or Roy Rogers without Trigger. I grow even more melons now than we did back then — and I still can't imagine a summer without them!

They All Like It Hot!

Like the rest of the cucurbit clan, melons crave heat, and most of them take their own sweet time maturing. You can get a great-tasting, juicy harvest anywhere in the country, though. Up North, just grow short-season varieties and be ready to protect your plants from chilly temperatures.

What They Like

Melons need full sun and good air circulation, but they also need protection from strong winds — they won't perform worth beans if they catch a chill.

Besides warm air, melons need soil that's at least 70°F and has a pH between 6.0 and 7.0. If it falls below 6.0, they just don't produce well. So have your soil tested before you plant, and if the pH is below 6.0, raise it pronto, using one of the methods I outline in Chapter 4 (see page 72–73).

An Inside Job

If you live in an area where it's too cold to plant seeds right in the garden, start them indoors 3 weeks before the last frost, and then move them outside when the soil temperature hits 70°F.

Once they're situated outside, cover the bed with floating row covers to protect plants from bad-guy bugs and cold winds, but take off the covers as soon as the first flowers appear. Why? Because unless bees and other insects are able to pollinate them, you'll have no crop. And all of your hard work will be for naught!

Time's Up

Where growing seasons are short, you'll need to grow melons that mature early. Some of my favorites are **'Charmel'** (78 days), **'Earli-Sweet'** (70 days), and **'Fastbreak'** (69 days).

JERRY'S FAVORITE Vegetable Varieties

The Secret to Growing Monster Melons

It's really no secret — melons need sandy soil that's high in organic matter. I always make special raised beds just for my melon crops. In those beds, I follow this three-step process:

Step 1. Dig a hole about 1 foot deep and 3 feet in diameter. In the center of it, dig a second hole that's about 1 foot wide and 2 feet deep.

Step 2. Fill the smaller, deeper hole with good, rich compost, and tamp it down firmly. It will act as a water well that will draw needed moisture up to the plants.

Step 3. Fill the larger hole with a mix of 2 parts sand, 1 part compost, 1 part professional planting mix, and 1 cup of my Mouth-Watering Melon Mix. Mound up the soil so that the center is about 6 inches above ground level. Several days before planting, soak the hill thoroughly with my Spring Soil Energizer Tonic (see page 357). When the soil is dry enough to work, plant your seeds. Thin the seedlings so that no more than three melon vines will grow from each hill, and you'll be off to the races!

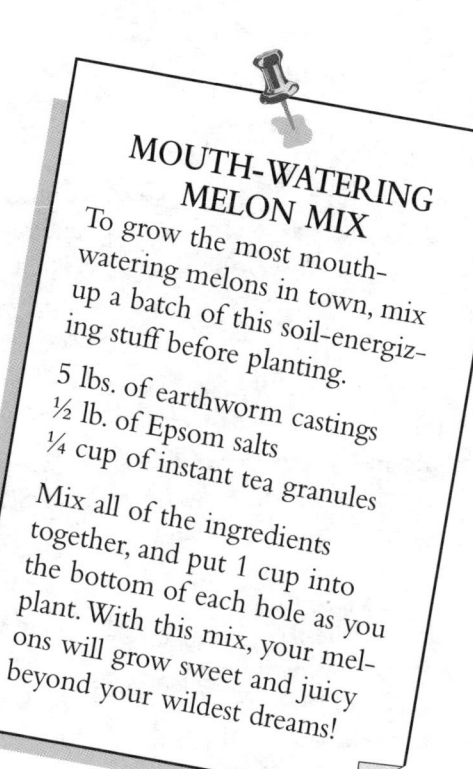

MOUTH-WATERING MELON MIX

To grow the most mouth-watering melons in town, mix up a batch of this soil-energizing stuff before planting.

5 lbs. of earthworm castings
½ lb. of Epsom salts
¼ cup of instant tea granules

Mix all of the ingredients together, and put 1 cup into the bottom of each hole as you plant. With this mix, your melons will grow sweet and juicy beyond your wildest dreams!

BUG BUSTERS!

Keep the Enemies at Bay

Melons have their fair share of pests and diseases gunning for them, but you can foil most of them by giving your plants the growing conditions they like (including soil that's rich in organic matter), encouraging insect predators, like birds, toads, and ladybugs, and growing disease-resistant varieties like 'Templar'.

SUPER Growing Secrets

GOT MILK?

Recycle your plastic milk jugs in the melon patch. Cut them in half lengthwise, and put the ripening melons inside. This will do two things: prevent the fruits from rotting and discourage mites and their cousins from nibbling on them.

Jerry Baker Says

"Most of my melons get gobbled up before they even make it to the kitchen, but if yours do get that far, they'll keep, unwashed, in the fridge for a week or so. For the best flavor, though, eat them as soon as you can — like corn and peas, they begin losing sweetness as soon as you pick them."

Keeping It Growing

As your vines start to grow, follow this procedure:

1. Keep the plants evenly moist — especially from planting time through fruit set — because melon plants will buckle under in a drought. Then, unless a prolonged dry spell strikes, stop watering when the fruits get about the size of a tennis ball — they'll develop better flavor if they don't get too much moisture in the later stages.

2. Feed the plants with fish fertilizer or my All-Season Green-Up Tonic (see page 349) every 3 weeks, starting when the fruits appear.

3. When each melon is about half grown, slide a board or milk jug under it to keep it from rotting.

I've Been Duped!

The cantaloupes you see in the grocery store — and the ones most home gardeners grow — aren't cantaloupes at all: They're muskmelons. True cantaloupes have a hard, warty rind. They're grown a lot in Europe, but almost never in North America.

Rein 'em In

Most melons need plenty of room to roam, but some of them can roam *up* instead of out. Just make sure that you select small-fruited varieties like 'Jenny Lind'. They will grow up happy as clams on trellises, so you can have fresh, sweet melons no matter how small your garden is. (Just be sure to put them where the trellises won't shade other sun lovers.)

High-Rise Melons

Even if your garden is a balcony 20 stories above the ground, you can still grow melons. Just find a big container, like a whiskey barrel sawed in half, and plant a compact variety like 'Minnesota Midget' or 'Musketeer'. Fill the pot with 2 parts sand, 1 part compost, and 1 part professional potting mix, water frequently, and feed the plants every 2 weeks with fish fertilizer.

When Is It Melon-Pickin' Time?

Make sure your melons are completely ripe before you harvest them. They won't ripen off the vine. The clue to look for depends on the type:

• **Honeydews, casabas, Crenshaws, and true cantaloupes** are ready when their skin turns either creamy gold or white, depending on the variety. Cut them from the vine using a sharp knife.

• **Muskmelons** — the melons most commonly grown in home gardens — are ripe when it takes just a little pressure to pull the fruit from its stem. If you wait just a tad longer, they'll separate, or "slip," from the vine all by themselves, but by that time, they could be overripe.

Pal o' Mine

A Word to the Wise from Grandma Putt

No matter where you plant your melons, try to give them some morning glories for company: The flowery vines make melon seeds germinate faster. Grandma Putt grew her favorite fruits next to the 'Heavenly Blue' morning glories twining around her garden fence. Melons also like the company of corn and sunflowers — but they don't want to have anything to do with potatoes.

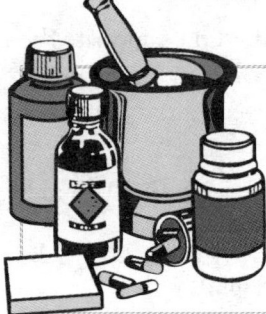

Not Just Your Garden-Variety Dessert

Most folks grow melons simply for the sweet, juicy taste, but these fruits also pack a nutritional wallop with plenty of potassium, vitamin C, and, in the orange-fleshed varieties, lots of cancer-fighting beta carotene.

Watermelon
(Citrullus lanatus

Grandma Putt's very favorite writer, Mark Twain, ranked watermelon as "chief of this world's luxuries." I'm not sure I'd go that far. But then again, maybe I would!

Finger-Tappin' Time

I grow watermelons exactly the same way I grow other melons. The difference comes at harvesttime — and it can be mighty tricky. I've tried all kinds of ways to tell when watermelons are ready for picking. My best advice is to experiment in your own garden, and then use the method that works best for you. Note the time the plants come into full bloom. Then, about 35 days later, look for one of these clues:

• The part of the melon that sits on the ground is yellow.

• The tendril closest to the melon turns brown.

• When you tap the fruit lightly, instead of a *ping,* you hear a lower-pitched *thump* or *thunk.*

Good Things Come in Small Packages

JERRY'S FAVORITE *Vegetable Varieties*

If you live in the cooler end of watermelon's comfort range, leave the Volkswagen-sized melons to folks farther south. You'll have better luck with a small variety that matures early. These are some of my favorites:

'Garden Baby'–matures in 75 days, 7 to 10 pounds
'Cole's Early'–80 days, 10 pounds
'Sugar Baby'–80 days, 8 to 10 pounds
'Fordhook Hybrid'–75 days, 14 pounds

A Watermelon by Any Other Color

Watermelon doesn't have to be red, or even pink. In fact, Grandma Putt said that when her mother was a girl, in the late 1800s, folks went bananas over *white* watermelons.

If you want to surprise folks at your summer barbecue next year, grow a watermelon of a different color, like one of these:

'Cream of Saskatchewan', creamy white flesh, 85 days, 8 to 10 pounds

'Yellow Baby', yellow flesh, 75 days, 5 to 8 pounds

'New Orchid', orange flesh, 80 days, 8 to 12 pounds

Squash (*Cucurbita*)

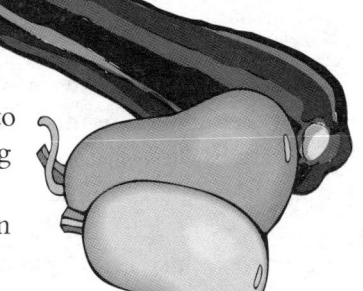

You don't have to be a gardener to know how easy it is to grow squash — or how generous the vines are in offering up their harvest. (Why do you think you get phone calls all summer long from your gardening friends — and even folks you barely know — asking, "Are you *sure* you couldn't use just a few more zucchini?")

Summer Squash

Summer squashes usually grow on bushes rather than vines, and the fruits need to be picked when they're young and tender, about 50 days from planting. They're probably the most productive vegetables on the planet, and, unfortunately, they don't store well.

So unless you need to feed a whole Scout troop — or you want to spend the summer on the phone, trying to find homes for your harvest — restrain yourself at planting time. Two or three plants will easily keep a family of four in squash all summer long.

For the sake of variety, though, I grow several different kinds and stagger the plantings, so I have a steady supply until Jack Frost arrives on the scene.

Two to Tango

Thanks to the fact that they crossbreed like crazy, there are more kinds of squashes than you can shake a rabbit at. But, fortunately for gardeners, the only thing that matters is whether the seeds they're sowing are for summer squashes or winter squashes.

Four to Grow

Summer squash is divided into four major types:

• **Cousa,** a.k.a. **Mid-East,** squashes are tapered and blocky, usually with pale green skin.

• **Pattypan, or scalloped,** types range in color from cream through gray-green to bright yellow. They're disk-shaped, with scalloped edges.

• **Yellow summer squashes** can be either straight and smooth or crooknecked and a little warty.

• **Zucchini** comes in both torpedo and globe shapes. Though most folks think of it as being only dark green, it can be yellow, almost any shade of green, or even near white.

Winter Squash

Winter squashes grow on vines — *big* vines — and they stay there until they've ripened completely, usually in 85 to 90 days. They're almost as prolific as their summer cousins, but they keep well, so you don't need to fret too much about an overpopulation problem.

And they come in such a variety of types, colors, and sizes, that it's all but impossible to keep track. Butternut, buttercup, acorn, Hubbard, and spaghetti squash are the classics. Pumpkins and gourds are also types of winter squash.

The Twain Meet

Well, in the beginning, anyway. Summer and winter squashes need the same conditions to keep them sleek and happy. The prime factor is heat: Their seeds just won't germinate in cold soil, and that's that.

I always get my planting beds ready in the fall. I dig in lots of compost or chopped leaves, and cover the beds with leaves and straw. Come spring, I take off the mulch and lay down a sheet of black plastic to warm up the soil in preparation for planting.

Take the Direct Approach

Squashes don't like to be transplanted, so it's best to wait until the soil temperature reaches 70°F, then sow your seeds directly in the garden. Plant three seeds to a hill, with the hills spaced about 18 inches apart. When the seedlings have one true leaf, thin them to one per hill. (Clip off the outcasts with scissors and don't pull them up; you may damage the survivor.)

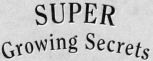

ON AND OFF

If summer gets steamy in your territory, take the sheet of black plastic off of your beds *before* you plant your seeds. Otherwise, later in the season, the soil will heat up too much. Once the plants are well on their way, spread an organic mulch around them to keep the soil cool and weeds out.

In parts of the country where the soil needs all of the warming help it can get, let the plastic stay on the ground. Just cut slits in it where you want to sow your seeds or set in your transplants. Be sure to anchor the sheet securely at planting time. If it shifts even a tad, it will cover the little seedlings and smother them in the blink of an eye.

76 Trombones

JERRY'S FAVORITE Vegetable Varieties

Seventy-six, or even hundreds! If you want a garden that's more fun than a brass band, grow **'Zucchetta Rampicante'**, a.k.a. trombone squash or climbing zucchini. It's an Italian heirloom and a real head-turner that grows in long, twisty, turning shapes. Some of them look like trombones. Others look like, well, things I've never even seen before!

This is one of the most prolific and pest-resistant summer squashes I've grown. Best of all, no matter how long it gets (and it can get really *long*), it never turns plump and seedy the way most zukes do. It stays sweet, crisp, and mmm, mmm, good.

Make the Best of It

For an early harvest, start seeds indoors 3 to 4 weeks before the last expected frost. Just be sure to use individual, 4-inch pots that can go into the ground at planting time, and be extra careful not to disturb the seedlings' roots.

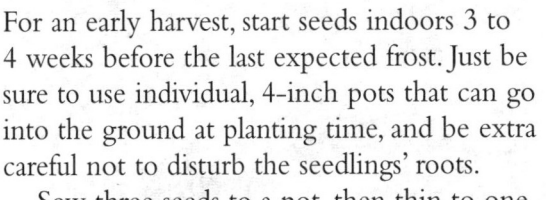

Sow three seeds to a pot, then thin to one when the first true leaf emerges. Keep the temperature at about 70°F. A week before transplanting, harden off the seedlings by cutting back on water, spraying them with salt water (see page 49), and lowering the nighttime temperature to 65°F.

Blankets at the Ready

Keep some floating row covers handy, and put them over your seedlings if the temperature dips below 65°F at night. You can leave the covers on throughout the early growth stages to keep bad-guy bugs at bay, but whisk them off the minute flowers appear on the plants. Otherwise, birds and good-guy bugs won't be able to pollinate the crop.

A Satisfied Appetite

Squashes are big eaters, but if you've packed your soil with lots of organic matter, you shouldn't need to feed them during the growing season. If the leaves are pale, or the plants just don't seem very strong, give them a dose of fish fertilizer. But go easy: Too much fertilizer, especially one that's high in nitrogen, can cut your yield.

Born to Ramble

Winter squashes are big plants, and they're born to ramble. Unless you have your strategy in place at planting time, they'll take over the garden before you know it — and then move on to conquer the whole neighborhood!

I keep my vines under control (more or less) by planting them on the edge of the garden and directing them away from the other crops. If you have an eyesore you want to cover up, like an old tree stump, point 'em toward it and let 'em go!

The Twain Diverge

The major difference in the two squash types shows up at harvesttime. To taste their best, summer squashes need to be picked as soon as they're big enough to use. The longer they stay on the vine, the bigger they grow, and the tougher, seedier, and more bitter-tasting they get.

Winter squashes are ready for picking when the stems start to dry out and shrivel up and the skin is so hard you can't scratch it with a fingernail.

Winter Wonderland

Winter squashes will keep for 6 months or more if you treat them right. Here's the process I follow:

Step 1. Get them in before the first frost. One light frost might not destroy the whole crop, but your squashes will keep much better if you don't take any chances.

Step 2. Leave at least an inch of vine on each squash, and never pick one up by its stem. If it breaks off — and it easily can — the scar will hang out a WELCOME sign for rot.

Step 3. Cure squashes in the sun for 10 to 14 days to get their skin good and hard before you store them. If old Jack Frost threatens to pay a visit, move the harvest to the garage, or cover it up well.

Step 4. Store winter squashes in a dry place (about 60 percent humidity — and not a root cellar or damp basement) where the temperature stays at 50 to 60°F. (A closed, unheated porch would work well.)

Pumpkins *(Cucurbita)*

A pumpkin is a type of winter squash, but as Grandma Putt once put it, that's like saying a Rolls-Royce is a type of car. Most any kind of squash will bake up into a tasty pie, but who'd want to ride to a ball in a Hubbard or an acorn?

A Princely Crop

Pumpkins need exactly the same planting methods and growing conditions as any other winter squashes, but if you want a harvest that'll take your fairy godmother's breath away, follow these extra steps:

• **Rotate your pumpkins** once in a while to keep them symmetrical, but move them just a little at a time, so you don't break the vines.

• **Put boards or heavy plastic** under large pumpkins to keep them from rotting.

• **Harvest orange pumpkins** at the same time you take in the rest of your winter squashes, but cut white varieties when their skin is still streaked with green. (If they're allowed to ripen outdoors, the shells turn pale yellow.)

What a Whiff!

Try sprinkling a little cinnamon and nutmeg on the lid of a jack-o'-lantern. When you light the candle, everybody who comes close will get a delicious whiff of pumpkin pie.

Small, but . . .

Miniature pumpkins are cute — kids love them — but the vines are anything but miniature: They sprawl just as far as their full-size cousins. Unlike the big bruisers, though, the tiny guys can be trained on trellises to save space, shade tender crops, add vertical interest in an ornamental-edible garden — or block your view of the compost pile. You can't beat that.

Cheek by Jowl

Squash bugs and cucumber beetles just love pumpkins. To keep those pesky pests where they belong — far away — don't plant your pumpkins anywhere near cucumbers. Instead, grow them with petunias, nasturtiums, or radishes. Beetles steer clear of all of these plants, and you'll have a much bigger and better harvest.

A Pumpkin for Every Purpose Under Heaven

JERRY'S FAVORITE Vegetable Varieties

Well, almost. If it's the world's best pie you're hankering for, plant Grandma Putt's favorite, **'New England Pie'**, a.k.a. **'Small Sugar'**.

For carvin' up at Halloween time, go with **'Ghost Rider'**, **'Howden'**, or **'Connecticut Field'**.

To have the best chance at winning your town's Tiniest Pumpkin Contest, try **'Munchkin'**, a.k.a. **'Jack Be Little'**, an orange mini that tips the scales at 3 to 4 ounces. Its white alter ego, **'Baby Boo'**, is also a good choice.

The Winner and Still Champ

As for growing the mother of all pumpkins, the process starts with choosing the right variety — namely, 'Dill's Atlantic Giant'. But it goes on from there. Here's my 12-step program:

Step 1. The fall before you plant, find a site that gets all-day sun, and where your giant vine will have room to roam — these monsters cover as much as 2,000 square feet of territory.

Step 2. Test your soil and correct the pH level if you need to: The big-time prizewinners have all grown up in nearly neutral (pH of 7.0) surroundings.

Step 3. Pile a whole boatload (and I mean boatload) of leaves, organic matter, and manure on the spot. Then sit back and wait for spring.

Step 4. Start seeds indoors in traveling pots to give them a jump on the growing season. And be sure to soak them overnight in my Seed Starter Tonic (see page 355) before you plant them.

Step 5. Come planting time, dig the rotted manure and leaves into a circle that's 30 feet in diameter. In the center of the circle, make a hill 8 to 10 feet in diameter, 12 inches high in the center, and sloping gently to ground level. If you're planting more than one giant, keep the hills 20 to 50 feet apart.

Step 6. Plant your best seedling in the center of the hill, or plant four seeds, and when the seedlings have four to six true leaves, clip off all but the biggest, sturdiest plant.

Step 7. Protect your chosen seedling from the cold, and even after the weather warms up and your plant gets bigger, shelter it from the wind. Giant pumpkin leaves can get more than 2 feet across, and if a strong breeze catches them, they can take off and rip your vines out of the ground.

Step 8. Encourage a big, strong root system by burying every leaf node that appears on the vine — the plant will grow new roots at that spot. But near the pumpkin itself, slip a sheet of plastic under the vine so no roots will form there — if the big 'un should move, it could break them.

Step 9. Until your vine is about 10 feet long and has at least 300 leaves, pinch off every flower that appears. When you decide that the time has come, zero in on the blossoms with the right stuff, and keep picking off the lesser ones. It's easy to spot potential winners: They're perfectly formed flowers that are growing on a main vine (not a secondary runner) no closer than 10 feet to the main stem, and they're growing at a 90-degree angle from the vine — otherwise, the pumpkin could push up against the vine and break it.

Step 10. At this stage, serious giant-pumpkin contestants hand-pollinate their chosen flowers, but I simply keep a few potential champs on the vine and look after them like a mother bear guarding her cubs. And when any new upstarts come along, I just pinch 'em off and send 'em to the compost pile.

Step 11. Keep the soil around the roots evenly moist. Water slowly and deeply, along the length of the whole vine. Once or twice a week will do, depending on your soil type. Avoid frequent, shallow watering, which could make your giant split. And be sure to aim the hose at the ground, not at the leaves or the pumpkin itself, where the moisture could spread diseases.

Step 12. Feed the monster. Starting when you set out the seedling, give it a gallon of diluted fish fertilizer or my All-Season Green-Up Tonic (see page 349) every week. Then, as fruit-set approaches, usually in early July, spread a 4-inch layer of well-rotted manure around the main stem.

SUPER Growing Secrets

PUMPKIN BONANZA

Here's a little secret I learned years ago: To grow the biggest pumpkins, remove all but the biggest two fruits from each vine. Give your pumpkins plenty of water — they can grow as much as 8 inches a day!

Follow-Up Hints

• **Give your pumpkin** at least 50 gallons of water a week.

• **Place all growing pumpkins** on cardboard, foam, straw, or the like, to protect them from bugs.

• **Shelter your giants** from the sun (which will cause the shells to crack) by building a sunscreen over the monsters.

• **Keep your giants on the vine** as long as you possibly can. Every few days, go out and measure them to see if they are still growing. You'll know it's time to harvest your precious pumpkins when they've reached full color and have hardened.

• **When removing your pumpkins** from the vine, use a sharp knife to cut them free. Don't damage the vine if other pumpkins are still attached and growing. Also, carry your pumpkins inside in your hands, and not by the stem. Then wash them off completely.

GRANDMA PUTT'S PUMPKIN DIP

Every year for our big Halloween open house, Grandma Putt put this special dip into a hollowed-out pumpkin and served it with gingersnaps.

3 TO 4 CUPS

2 tablespoons butter
2 cups confectioners' sugar
1 8-ounce package cream cheese
1 15-ounce can pumpkin puree
1½ teaspoons pumpkin pie spice

1. Combine the butter, sugar, and cream cheese until well blended.

2. Beat in the remaining ingredients.

3. Refrigerate until ready to use.

4. Serve in a small, hollowed-out pumpkin with gingersnaps on the side.

Safe Storage

To store your pumpkins for a long time, wash them in a mild chlorine solution (1 cup of chlorine to 1 gallon of water). This solution will kill the bacteria that causes the pumpkins to rot. Be sure to let them dry off completely before storing them away.

Pumpkins store best in cool, dry, and dark places on a board or piece of cardboard. Keep them away from anyplace that is hot and humid. They also tend to rot if they're kept on cement floors. With the proper precautions, pumpkins can be easily stored through the fall and well into the winter.

Gourds *(Lagenaria siceraria)*

I don't know many people who actually eat gourds —
though a few kinds are edible when they're young. But
I grow plenty of them, and I have since my early days at
Grandma Putt's. We made them into birdhouses, Christmas-
tree ornaments, dippers and scoops, and containers to hold odds and ends in
the workshop and garden shed. I still get a kick out of gourd projects — and judg-
ing by the miles of smiles, so do the folks who receive the results as presents.

Give 'em Time

Most gourds need a long growing season. The biggest kinds can take
up to 140 days to mature. If you live in an area where summers don't
last that long, look for varieties that mature in 95 days or so, like
'Small Spoons', 'Crown of Thorns', and 'Dinosaur Nest Egg'. Most
seed catalogs and garden centers sell mixtures of both short- and
long-season types, so you can grow several different kinds without
giving over your whole garden space to gourds.

Starting Out

If you live in a warm neck of the woods, start seeds directly in
the garden after the last frost has left and the soil has warmed
up for good.

Otherwise, you'll need to buy started plants at your local
garden center, or start seeds indoors, in individual traveling pots,
three seeds to a pot, about 3 weeks before you expect to plant
them. About a week before you set them out, thin the seedlings
so that there's only one in each pot. (Clip 'em with scissors;
don't pull 'em up.)

Whether you start
your seeds indoors or
out, they'll germinate
faster if you soak
them in water for 2
or 3 days before you
plant them.

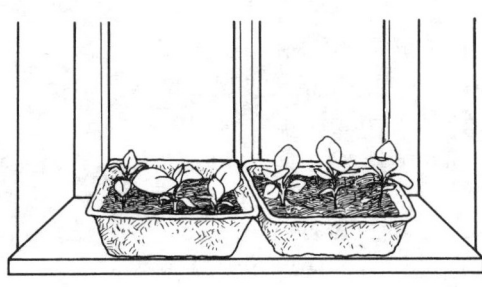

It's All Squash to Me

Gourds are a type
of winter squash,
so they like the
same kind of home
life: a spot in full
sun; rich, fertile
soil; a pH of 6.5 to
7.5; and plenty of
organic matter. I
always work com-
post or well-cured
manure into the
soil in the spring.

Movin' On

After you've hardened off the seedlings, move them to the garden and set them 2 to 5½ feet apart, depending on the variety. If you want your gourds to grow up rounded, give them a trellis to climb on. And be sure to tie them to it with something sturdy like strips of old panty hose — gourds are light as feathers when they're all dried and hollowed out, but they can get mighty heavy hanging on the vine.

If you plan to make your gourds into containers that can stand on their own, let the vines sprawl across the ground. Just make sure you lay down a good, thick straw mulch to fend off creepy-crawlies and keep the gourds cleaner. When the gourds start to form, slide a board under each one, so it gets good and flat on the side you want the finished product to rest on.

The Watering Schedule

Water your plants heavily from planting time until about a month before you expect the first frost. Then, to get the gourds ready for drying, cut back on the moisture by about a third.

SUPER Growing Secrets

BEEF IT UP

Just like other kinds of winter squash, gourds like soil that's beefed up with plenty of organic matter — especially compost. That should be all the food they need to grow up sleek and happy. In fact, you need to be careful not to overfeed them. If they get too much fertilizer, especially one that's high in nitrogen, they won't produce the big harvest you're looking for.

Gourds to the Rescue

If you have a view that's driving you nuts and you want to block it *right now,* then the answer is as near as your local garden center. Put a trellis in front of it and plant gourds at the bottom. Though the fruits mature slowly, the foliage grows so fast that it'll cover the trellis in a few weeks. Then, instead of an ugly shopping mall or a busy highway, you'll have dark green leaves and big, white, starlike flowers to gaze at all summer long.

Keep 'em on the Vine

Let gourds remain on the vine until they are completely ripe, with hard, glossy shells and dry, brown stems. Then follow these simple steps:

Step 1. Harvest all gourds before the first frost; otherwise, they'll rot.

Step 2. When the time comes, clip them off carefully, leaving at least 3 inches of stem attached. And be careful — dings and scratches will make them rot as fast as frostbite will.

Step 3. Wash them gently, one at a time, in a solution of 9 parts water to 1 part household bleach.

Step 4. Put each one into a mesh bag or the toe of a nylon stocking, and hang it up in a warm, dry place until the seeds rattle around inside. (It could take a few months for larger gourds.)

They're for the Birds

Gourds make dandy homes for your fine-feathered garden helpers — and great gifts for bird-watching friends. Here's how to make a gourd birdhouse:

1. Grow a crop of long-necked bottle gourds, like 'Birdhouse' or 'Large Bottle'.

2. Harvest and dry them as described above.

3. Put a gourd in a *padded* vise to hold it and, near the top, drill two holes, each ¼ inch in diameter.

4. In the center of the gourd's bulging stomach, cut a 1- to 2-inch-diameter entrance hole, using a keyhole saw or an expansion bit on your drill.

5. Working through the entrance hole you just made, use a serrated knife to break up the pith and seeds

inside the gourd. Carefully take them out.

6. Drill four or five ⅜-inch drainage holes in the bottom.

7. Paint the outside of the gourd with one coat of oil-based primer and three coats of white latex paint. (White will reflect the sun and keep the birdhouse cool inside.)

8. To put your new house on the bird real-estate market, insert a 1-foot piece of thick wire, like a coat hanger, through the two holes you drilled at the top in step 3. Loop one end into a circle at the top of the gourd and bend the other over a tree limb.

SQUASH PIE

Like any kid, I had a sweet tooth the size of Cleveland. And, believe me, when Grandma Putt baked this old-time pie, I was in dessert heaven!

1 9-INCH PIE

1 9-inch pie crust, unbaked
2 cups milk
4 cups cooked squash (home-canned or frozen)
3 eggs
½ teaspoon cinnamon
½ teaspoon ginger
½ teaspoon nutmeg
1 teaspoon salt
½ cup honey
½ cup whipping cream
½ cup maple syrup

1. Make your favorite pie crust, fluting the edges up high, or use a ready-made crust.

2. Put 1 cup of milk in the blender and add the squash, a little at a time. Blend until smooth.

3. Add eggs and spices, and blend. Place mixture in a large bowl and add the other cup of milk and the honey. Stir briskly until well blended.

4. Pour into unbaked pie crust and bake at 425°F. for 10 minutes, then at 325°F. for about ½ hour. Cool to room temperature. When ready to serve, beat cream until stiff, then dribble the maple syrup into the cream, folding in. Swirl onto pie.

ZUCCHINI CATERPILLARS

Talk about a funtastic vegetable! Serve these up to the kids once, and you can bet your bottom butterfly they'll ask for them again and again.

1 SERVING

1 small zucchini per serving
1 medium tomato
1 small sweet onion
minced fresh basil
butter
parmesan cheese, freshly grated
salt and pepper, to taste

1. Preheat the oven to 350° F.

2. Select one small (4- to 6-inch) zucchini for each serving. Trim off the ends.

3. Every ¼ inch, slice three-quarters of the way through the width of the squash so that the slices are still connected. Insert alternate slices of tomato and onion between the slices of squash.

4. Place each squash on a separate piece of foil and sprinkle with minced fresh basil. Dot with butter and sprinkle with cheese, salt, and pepper. Enclose the squash in foil. Bake for 20–30 minutes.

SOUTH OF THE BORDER ZUCCHINI, RICE, AND CHICKEN SALAD

If you've grown zucchini even once, you know that there's no such thing as an oversupply of zuke recipes! This one will please the palate of every salad lover you serve it to.

6 SERVINGS

3 cups diced zucchini
1½ cups cold cooked brown rice
1½ cups diced or shredded cooked chicken
½ cup chopped scallions
2 tablespoons minced fresh parsley
⅓ cup vegetable oil
3 tablespoons olive oil
¼ cup lemon juice
½ teaspoon chili powder
½ teaspoon salt
pepper
½ cup shredded cheddar cheese

1. Parboil the zucchini for 1 minute. Plunge into cold water, and pat dry.

2. In a large bowl, combine the zucchini, rice, chicken, scallions, and parsley.

3. Whisk together the oils, lemon juice, chili powder, salt, and pepper to taste. Pour over the salad and toss to coat.

4. Sprinkle the cheese on top just before serving.

FANTASTIC SQUASH

Because summer squash has a flavor that ranges from delicate to downright bland, Grandma Putt liked to spice it up with plenty of herbs. (She grew her own, of course, but if these guys don't reside in your garden, dried herbs from the super-market will work just fine.)

6 TO 8 SERVINGS

6-8 small (4- 6-inch) summer squash
½ cup all-purpose flour
¼ teaspoon salt
⅛ teaspoon pepper
2 eggs, beaten
⅔ cup bread crumbs
¼ cup grated parmesan cheese
½ teaspoon dried basil
¼ teaspoon dried thyme
¼ teaspoon dried oregano
¼ cup olive oil

1. Slice each squash lengthwise every ¼ inch, leaving all the slices connected at the "neck" of the squash. Parboil the squash for 3 minutes and drain well. Spread out each squash in a fan pattern.

2. Place the flour, salt, and pepper in one bowl; the eggs in another; and the bread crumbs, cheese, and herbs in a third. Heat the olive oil in a frying pan.

3. Dip the squash in the flour, then into the eggs, and then coat with the bread crumb-cheese-herb mixture. Brown on both sides. Serve hot.

WHOOPS! I GOOFED! SALAD

As Grandma Putt always said, nobody's perfect, especially when it comes to telling for sure when a honeydew melon is ready for picking. The next time you cut a honeydew from the vine just a tad before its time, don't toss it onto the compost pile — toss it into this sensational salad. (It's the firm texture of the underripe melon that makes this salad such a treat.)

6 SERVINGS

4 cups slightly underripe honeydew, cubed
1 cup roasted walnuts
4 tablespoons minced parsley
1 cup diced celery
1 cup finely diced sweet red pepper
4 tablespoons lime juice
2 teaspoons honey
2 tablespoons white vinegar
½ cup vegetable oil
1 teaspoon salt
⅛ teaspoon pepper

1. In a large salad bowl, toss together the honeydew, walnuts, parsley, celery, and red pepper.

2. Whisk together the remaining ingredients and pour over the salad. Toss to coat.

3. Serve at once, or chill and serve.

RED, WHITE, AND ORANGE SALAD

This summertime salad combines the sweet, cool taste of cantaloupe with the zip of radishes. Try it at your next neighborhood cookout.

4 TO 6 SERVINGS

4 cups diced cantaloupe
1 cup sliced radishes
1 tablespoon minced fresh mint
3 tablespoons lime juice
1 teaspoon grated lime rind
1 teaspoon sugar

1. Put cantaloupe and radishes in a bowl.

2. Whisk together the remaining ingredients and pour over the salad.

3. Toss to coat.

4. Serve at once.

BEYOND-THE-SALAD-BOWL CUKES

Grandma Putt used cucumbers in all kinds of salads, but she didn't stop there. She loved 'em sautéed with fresh herbs from her garden. Nothing could be simpler — or better.

4 TO 6 SERVINGS

2 tablespoons butter
1 teaspoon minced fresh basil
1½ teaspoons fresh thyme or
    ½ teaspoon dried
1 tablespoon minced fresh chives
4 cups quartered, sliced cucumbers
salt and pepper

1. Melt the butter in a large sauté pan.

2. Sauté the herbs and cucumbers until the cucumbers are tender crisp and somewhat translucent, 2–5 minutes.

3. Season to taste with salt and pepper. Serve hot.

PUMPKIN BAKED BEANS

Baked beans is a classic favorite from way back, and it seems every cook in New England has a special way of making it. Grandma Putt learned this one from her mama. It's the pumpkin that makes it special.

4 TO 6 SERVINGS

1½ cups dried navy or soldier beans
    water
½ cup diced onion
¼ cup dark molasses
1 teaspoon salt
2 cups diced pumpkin
1 teaspoon grated orange rind
juice of 1 orange (½ cup)
1 tablespoon brown sugar

1. Cover the beans with water. Bring to a boil and simmer gently for 30 minutes to tenderize.

2. Preheat oven to 350° F.

3. Combine the remaining ingredients, except the brown sugar, with the beans in a greased, covered baking dish. Add water to cover and sprinkle brown sugar over the top.

4. Bake uncovered for 4 hours, adding water if the beans become dry.

TOMATO FAMILY

Eggplant • Peppers • Potatoes • Tomatoes

Grandma Putt used to say that this family reminded her of girls at an old-time country dance: There were the belles of the ball, and then there were the wallflowers. That was her way of saying that two of the clan, tomatoes and peppers, win popularity contests hands down. From coast to coast, they get asked to dance in more gardens than any other vegetables.

Potatoes and eggplant, on the other hand, don't get invited nearly as often. They should, though — they can trip the light fantastic with the best of them!

Shades of Night

The tomato clan also goes by the names of its two black-sheep cousins: nightshade and tobacco. In scientific circles, though, the whole crowd is called Solanaceae.

A word of warning: Pile your plate high with any of this veggie quartet, but whatever you do, don't eat the leaves or stems: *They're poisonous.*

No Butts

Never ever smoke anywhere near any member of the tomato clan — and even be careful where you spray any of my tonics that contain chewing tobacco juice. Cigar, cigarette, or pipe tobacco can infect your plants with tobacco mosaic virus, and once that gets in your soil, you'll spend years getting rid of it. (See page 100 for the best ways to do battle with this nastiness.)

BEETLE JUICE

Colorado potato beetles are some of the peskiest pests known to plantkind, but this stuff will stop 'em in their tracks. Here's how to make it.

1. Collect ½ cup of beetles and whirl 'em up in an old blender with 2 cups of water.
2. Strain the liquid through cheese-cloth or panty hose.
3. Pour about ¼ cup into a 1-gallon handheld sprayer, and fill the rest of the jar with water.
4. Drench the soil around new trans-plants to keep the beetles from ever getting started.
5. If they're already on the scene, spray your plants from top to bottom, and make sure you coat both sides of the leaves.
6. If you have any extra juice, freeze it right away before bacteria can get a toehold. Just make sure you label the container in BIG letters!

The Enemy

Plenty of bad-guy bugs will ambush the tomato family if you give them half a chance. But the big guns in the hit squad are the dastardly duo of hornworms and Colorado potato beetles. I can usually head 'em off at the pass by rounding up a posse of good-guy critters and using the other varmint-control measures in Chapter 5. But here are some other methods of law enforcement.

BAD GUYS	TO KEEP 'EM OUT	TO SEND 'EM PACKING
Hornworms	Till your garden in the fall — you'll kill off the eggs before they have a chance to hatch. Plant borage, opal basil, and marigolds. Plant a trap crop of dill — hornworms love the stuff, and the slimy fiends are easy to spot clinging to dill's delicate stems.	Pick 'em off by hand. (They're big, but there usually aren't many of them.) If you have trouble spotting them among the leaves, give your plants a blast of cold water. It'll send the villains into a varmint dance that you'll be able to see from halfway across the garden.
Colorado potato beetles	Plant horseradish among your tomato family crops. These beastly beetles can't stand the stuff. They also keep their distance from catnip, coriander, dead nettle, flax, garlic, marigolds, nasturtiums, onions, snap beans, and tansy. Spray your plants with one of these: • a tea made from basil or dried cedar boughs • 2 tablespoons of Epsom salts dissolved in a gallon of water • my Beetle Juice	Feed 'em to death. Spray your plants with water. Then dust them thoroughly with wheat bran. The beetles will gobble up the stuff, then it will expand in their stomachs until the greedy varmints explode. Spray 'em with my Beetle Juice. (If the vile villains have already set up camp, this will wipe 'em out.) Pick 'em off by hand.

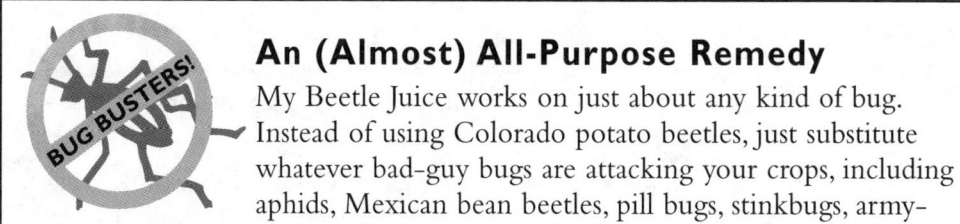

hornworm

3"

Colorado potato beetle

3/8"

An (Almost) All-Purpose Remedy

My Beetle Juice works on just about any kind of bug. Instead of using Colorado potato beetles, just substitute whatever bad-guy bugs are attacking your crops, including aphids, Mexican bean beetles, pill bugs, stinkbugs, armyworms, and even slugs. But whatever you do, don't include fleas, ticks, mosquitoes, or other insects that feed on blood and transmit diseases.

Eggplant *(Solanum melongena)*

There's no doubt about it: Growing eggplant in the North is a challenge and a half. If it won't get 5 months of hot weather where you are, you'd better be prepared to give it a lot of coddling. For me, though, it's worth all of the TLC I can give it, because I love it — baked, pickled, broiled, stuffed, fried . . . you name it!

Seven to Grow On

Here's my seven-step method for growing good eggplant in places that are not its idea of veggie heaven:

Step 1. Start with a variety that's bred to perform in your territory.

Step 2. Buy transplants at a reputable garden center rather than starting your own.

Step 3. Don't move your seedlings to the garden until the soil temperature is at least 70°F, and you're as sure as you can be that warm weather is here to stay. Eggplant needs temperatures of at least 70°F in the daytime, and 60°F at night.

Step 4. Warm up your soil with black plastic mulch before you plant (see the instructions in the winter squash section on page 268).

Step 5. Use every trick in the book to keep pesky pests at bay, and grow the crop under floating row covers — if there's a bad-guy bug anywhere in your garden, you can almost bet he'll zero right in on your eggplant.

Step 6. Grow your eggplant in raised beds, so that the soil will warm up faster and stay warm longer.

Step 7. Give it exactly the growing conditions it likes. Most crops will cut you a little slack, but not eggplant — at least not when it considers itself to be trapped in hostile territory.

A Bit of a Spoiled Brat

Regardless of where you live, eggplant insists on:

• Full sun

• Fertile, well-drained soil with a pH of 5.5 to 7.0 and plenty of organic matter

• A diet that's high in phosphorus and potassium, with only moderate amounts of nitrogen

• Plenty of water (at least 4 inches per week) throughout its growing season

Give Me Room

Standard-sized eggplants can spread 3 or 4 feet, so set them far enough apart that they won't feel cramped. I always tie my big guys to metal stakes with strips of old panty hose — it keeps the fruits off the ground, and the metal and nylon attract static electricity that gives the plants a good, healthy jolt of natural nitrogen (see page 81).

Calcium, Please

Eggplant can come down with a bad case of blossom-end rot if there's not enough calcium in the soil. Before you plant, add a good supply, in the form of lime, eggshells, or ground oyster shells. Then, when you water, make sure you add crushed-up eggshells to it for an extra boost.

Lime Away

Lime will keep flea beetles off of your eggplant. For best results, dust lightly in the early morning, when plants are still wet with dew.

Be Picky

If you live down South, almost any eggplant will grow up happy on your turf. Anywhere north of the Mason-Dixon line, though, growing a good crop (or even a crop at all) depends on starting with a variety that matures fast. **'Baby Bell'**, a.k.a. **'Bambino',** is a real speed demon — I can start harvesting 1-inch, dark purple eggplants about 45 days after I transplant the seedlings. These fighters also perform well in Yankee territory:

JERRY'S FAVORITE Vegetable Varieties

- **'Applegreen'**–small, oval, light green fruits; 62 days
- **'Little Fingers'**–Slim, deep purple fruits, 5 to 8 inches long; 65 days
- **'Orient Express'**–10-inch black, cylindrical fruits; 65 days
- **'Tango'**–7-inch, white, cylindrical fruits; 60 days

Contain Themselves

If I had to name the single best veggie for growing in a pot, it just might be eggplant. Lots of vegetables thrive in pots, but especially in colder parts of the country, growing eggplant in containers has several advantages over growing it in the ground. Here they are:

• The soil warms up much faster and stays warm longer than it does in the garden — or even in raised beds. I grow my contained crop of eggplant in big, black, plastic nursery pots because they catch and hold the sun's heat better than lighter-colored containers.

• Pesky pests can't invade your potting soil as easily as they can garden-variety dirt, and if they do, you can control them better.

• You can move your potted eggplants around to wherever the sun is brightest or the chilly winds aren't blowing. I put my containers on rolling plant dollies so I can get the show on the road any time the performers need a change of scenery.

The Kindest Cut

Don't pull eggplants from the vines. Clip them off with shears or a sharp knife, and leave about an inch of stem attached to each fruit.

Bigger Isn't Better

Don't wait until the maturity date on your seed packet to start chowing down on eggplants — start picking them as soon as they're big enough to eat, and keep at it until their skin loses its high-gloss finish. (If you slice one open and find hard or dark seeds, you've waited too long.) And don't hold back: The more you pick, the more the plant will produce!

SUPER Growing Secrets

EGGPLANTS IN A PINCH

About 3 weeks before you expect the first frost, start pinching back all of the new blossoms. That way, you'll channel the plants' energy into maturing fruits that are already on the vine, rather than churning out new ones that won't survive old Jack Frost's visit.

Hold That Shaker

Back in Grandma Putt's day, folks always salted their eggplant slices and let 'em sit awhile before they cooked 'em up — it cut the bitter taste that most eggplants had. But most varieties on the market today have had the bitterness bred out of them. They're ready for eating straight from the plant, so there's no salt needed.

Peppers
(*Capsicum annuum* and *C. chinense*)

If Peter Piper picked a peck of pickled peppers (or even fresh ones), he'd be one lucky rascal in my book. I've been growing 'em — both sweet and hot — since the early days at Grandma Putt's, and I just can't imagine a garden without 'em.

Picky, Picky

Whether they're sweet as candy or hot enough to knock your socks off, all peppers like to grow up the same way. They're a cinch once you get them started, but they take some TLC at first.

Peppers are picky about temperatures right from the get-go, so if you don't want to fuss with details, buy transplants. Otherwise, sow seeds indoors about 8 weeks before the last frost. Here are the secrets to success:

1. Sow the seeds ¼ inch deep in flats filled with professional seed-starting mix, and keep the soil temperature between 80 and 85°F. That's important, because in temperatures lower than 80°F, seeds will germinate slowly, and unless peppers get off to a fast start, they won't perform well in your garden.

2. When the first true leaves appear, move your seedlings into individual 4-inch pots and lower the soil temperature to 70°F. The air temperature should be 70°F during the day, 60°F at night.

3. At this stage, turn on grow-lights or fluorescents to make sure the plants get about 16 hours a day.

4. When the third set of true leaves appears, the plants are ready for a cold jolt: Lower the nighttime temperature to 55°F for 4 weeks. (I move my seedlings to a cold frame for an outdoor vacation.)

5. At the end of 4 weeks, you'll probably have to bring your future crop back inside — they need to grow at 70°F, day and night, until it's time to plant them in the garden.

Caution!

Hot peppers don't just *taste* hot — the juices in fruits and plants can burn your skin, and (take it from me) it hurts! So wear gloves when you're working with hot peppers, whether they're in the kitchen, the garden, or their starter pots — and keep your hands away from your face!

Out We Go

Don't rush getting transplants into the ground. If the soil temperature isn't at least 70°F, peppers kick up a mighty big fuss. Warm up the ground with black plastic mulch for a few weeks before planting. Then put floating row covers on top to keep the heat in and bugs out. Leave the covers in place until flower buds start appearing or the temperature hits 85°F.

Chow Hounds

Peppers are big eaters, and they work hard churning out a long harvest, so don't take any shortcuts as you prepare your planting site. To do their best, peppers need full sun and deep, sandy or gravelly loam. Plant them in raised beds, dig in plenty of organic matter the fall before, and make sure the pH is 5.5 to 7.0.

Come spring, before you lay down some black plastic mulch, spread about 2 inches of compost over the bed, dust the surface with a fine layer of Epsom salts, and work it all into the soil. (The Epsom salts will provide magnesium, which peppers need for good development.) Make sure your plants get about an inch of water a week. Side-dress with compost when the first flowers come out, and again 3 weeks later.

A Case of Mistaken Identity

Don't confuse garden peppers — hot or sweet — with the stuff on your spice rack. Peppercorns (whether black or any of the fancy colors you see around these days) come from a plant called Piper nigrum that hails from Ceylon and India. It's no relation at all to the bell peppers you stuff with ground beef and rice, or the chiles you chop up and toss in the salsa.

SUPER Growing Secrets

THE SALT OF THE WATER

Epsom salts help peppers develop faster and stronger. To give yours a boost, dissolve 3 tablespoons of Epsom salts in 1 gallon of warm water, and give each plant 1 pint of this mixture when they begin to bloom.

A Word to the Wise from Grandma Putt

Hold Hands, Kids

Grandma Putt used to say that pepper plants are like little kids crossing the street: They like to hold hands. By that she meant you should space them so that when the plants are mature, their leaves are just touching one another. I try to plant mine in staggered rows, 1 foot apart, 3 rows to a 36-inch bed.

Jerry Baker Says

"Peppers like slightly acid soil, so tuck a book of matches under each plant when you set it in its hole. The sulfur will make the old home ground just sour enough to suit its taste."

Good Neighbors

Grandma Putt's favorite companion plants for peppers were basil and okra. They all like the same kind of growing conditions, and the taller okra protects peppers' brittle stems from strong winds. Talk about best buds!

That's Not the Pepper I Planted!

Insects cross-pollinate peppers like crazy. So, if you plan to save seeds to plant next year, make sure you keep hot peppers and sweet peppers at least 900 feet apart. Otherwise, there's no telling what you'll end up with.

A Pepper by Any Other Color

Lots of folks think red peppers are hotter than green peppers, or that small peppers are hotter than big ones. But that just ain't so. What makes a pepper hot is certain heat-producing chemicals, the prime one being capsicin. And how much capsicin a pepper has depends on its variety and its home turf.

A jalapeño will always be hotter than an Anaheim. But a jalapeño that's grown in New Mexico, where the soil is poor and the climate dry, will always be hotter than the identical variety grown in New England, where the soil's a little richer and the weather cooler and damper — so it's no coincidence that the hottest chile peppers come from Mexico and the Southwest.

By the way, capsicin is the secret ingredient that makes all of my repellent tonics containing pepper so effective. It's an equal opportunity irritant — to man, beast, and bug!

Some Like 'em Hot

And some like 'em downright steamy. Way back in 1912, a scientist named William Scoville came up with a way to measure the amount of capsicin a pepper has — and, therefore, how hot it is. Nowadays, hot peppers are ranked according to how many Scoville Heat Units they produce. Anaheim chiles are at the bottom rung of the fieriness ladder, with fog-up-your-eyeglasses habañeros at the top.

Here's Dr. Scoville's scorecard:

PEPPER VARIETY	SCOVILLE HEAT UNITS
Anaheim chile	250–1,400
Jalapeño	4,000–6,000
Serrano chile	7,000–25,000
Cayenne	30,000–35,000
Chile Pequin	35,000–40,000
Tabasco	30,000–50,000
Habañero	200,000–350,000

I'm Confused

Most folks divide peppers into two kinds: sweet and hot. But scientists don't even think about the taste: They classify them by the shape of their pods. Seed catalogs and cookbooks list them in all kinds of ways. (Just as an example, the very same pepper is called *poblano* when it's fresh and *ancho* when it's dried.)

For me, keeping all these peppers straight is like trying to sort out people at a convention of twins. Fortunately, there's a place where you can learn everything you ever wanted to know about peppers: the Chile Pepper Institute at New Mexico State University. Check out their web site at www.chilepepperinstitute.org.

Ah, Dry Up

If you live in the Southwest, it's a snap to string your red peppers on twine, hang 'em up to dry, and wind up with a kitchen full of those great-looking pepper garlands called *ristras*. But if you try that in humid-summer territory, what you'll wind up with is a lot of moldy peppers. So if you live in the Humid Belt, instead of stringing them, dry your peppers this way:

• Put the peppers in a single layer in the bottom of a brown paper grocery bag.

• Close the bag loosely and clip it with a clothespin.

• Set it aside. In a week or 2, your peppers will be as dry — and unmoldy — as the ones in any south-of-the-border bistro.

How Dry I Can Be

If you do live where the humidity stays in the lower digits, harvest peppers for drying when they start to turn red. Just pull the plants out of the ground and hang them upside down in a cool, dry place. Or clip the peppers off the plant and string them together to make ristras. (Leave about an inch of stem on each pepper.

Anytime at All

Harvest peppers early and often — they taste great from the minute they're big enough to eat, and the more you pick, the more the plants will churn out. But their store of vitamins A and C is highest when you let them grow until they reach full size and (in the case of nongreen varieties) they've taken on about two-thirds of their destined color.

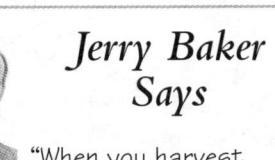

Jerry Baker Says

"When you harvest peppers, don't pull them — clip them off with sharp scissors, so you don't damage the plants."

Are You *Sure* That's a Pepper?

To wow your dinner guests, grow 'Purple Beauty' or 'Sweet Chocolate' (yes, it matures to a yummy shade of cocoa). But to get the oohs and ahs your trophies deserve, make sure you serve 'em up raw: They turn garden-variety green when you cook 'em.

More Pepper Tips

Here are a few more things to keep in mind about peppers:

• Most peppers, sweet or hot, take at least 70 days from transplanting time until you can eat the first fruits, and another 3 to 4 weeks to reach full maturity.

• In general, the hotter the pepper, the longer it takes to mature. The hottest of the hots need anywhere from 90 to 200 frost-free days.

• The days-to-maturity numbers in catalogs are based on ideal growing conditions. A pepper that takes 70 days to mature in northern New Mexico might take up to 100 days in Portland, Oregon.

• If you live in a place with wet, humid weather — hot or cool — make sure that you plant only disease-resistant varieties.

Enough Is Enough

Even peppers can get bogged down in a steamy southern summer — at least the sweet bell types can. Whatever you do, don't panic if your plants stop producing peppers in July. Just let 'em snooze until mid-August, and they'll start cranking 'em out again until Jack Frost stops by for a visit.

SUPER Growing Secrets

WATER, WATER EVERYWHERE

Here's a little secret to help you get the hottest hot peppers in town. Just before you're getting ready to harvest your peppers, produce a flood! Flooding the plants at that time stresses their roots, which sends out a signal to "turn up the heat."

On the Fast Track

If you live up North, you'll have the best chance of success with short-season varieties. I've found that these grow well in almost any part of the country:

JERRY'S FAVORITE Vegetable Varieties

Sweet

'Biscane'–7-inch tapered fruits that start out lime green, turn yellow, then red. (They're great roasted or fried. I pick mine when they're yellow-green.) 65 to 85 days.

'Sweet Chocolate'–bell peppers go from green to chocolate brown. Best of all, the plants don't mind cool nights. 65 to 90 days.

'Yankee Bell'–a great short-season, green-to-red bell, this pepper is open-pollinated, so I can save my seeds from one year to the next. 65 to 85 days.

Hot

'Early Jalapeño'–green fruits turn red (but they're best harvested green). 70 to 90 days.

'Long Slim'–vigorous plants with 6-inch, green-to-red fruits that are very hot. 75 to 90 days.

'Hungarian Yellow Wax Hot'–moderately hot fruits go from pale green, to yellow, and then to red. 70 to 95 days.

Potatoes *(Solanum tuberosum)*
Nightshade family (Solanaceae)

I've heard lots of folks say, "Why grow potatoes, when
you can find them year-round in the supermarket — and they're cheap, besides?"

I just shake my head, and tell them they don't know what they're missing.
You've never tasted anything until you've had tiny, brand-new potatoes right out
of your garden. Plus, most of the tastiest — and prettiest — spuds never even find
their way to the stores!

Give 'em What They Deserve

Potatoes like full sun and light, well-drained, acid soil with
plenty of organic matter, potassium, and phosphorus in it. Go
easy on the manure, and just say no to fertilizers with lots of
nitrogen: You'll only encourage leafy top growth at the expense
of the tubers in the ground.

Potatoes hail from the mountainy parts of South America,
so it's no surprise that they like cool climates. In fact, when the
temperature gets much above 80°F, the tubers pretty much stop
growing. Never fear, though — you don't have to live in Idaho
to grow great taters. You can compensate
for a less-than-ideal climate by juggling
your planting and harvesting times to suit
your climate and by choosing your varieties according to their maturing times:
early-, mid-, or late-season.

• **Cool regions.** In USDA Zone 6 and colder (see the Zone
map on page 362, you can plant potatoes 2 to 4 weeks before
you expect the last frost. Just be sure the soil is at least 40°F.

• **Warm regions.** If you live in Zones 7 and 8, you can get
your crop into the ground anytime from early February on
into March; just make sure you harvest it
before the hot weather sets in. Farther
south, most folks plant potatoes around
the end of September for harvesting in December and January.

No Seconds for Me, Thanks

Whatever you do,
don't overfeed your
potatoes: Too much
fertilizer can make
them develop cavities
at their centers. (It's
a cultural problem
called hollow heart).

Make Mine Sour

I like to grow my
potatoes in highly
acid soil, with a pH
below 5.5. This soil
discourages scab, a
disease that gives
potatoes pitted skin,
though it doesn't
affect their flavor.

There's No Place Like Home

Aside from choosing the right planting time, you can also help ensure yourself a good crop of spuds by selecting a variety that's been bred for your neck of the woods. Here's a sampling:

IF YOUR HOME TURF	PLANT	WHAT YOU'LL GET
Has hard, mucky clay soil	'Cherokee'	Medium-sized, late-season potato with smooth, thin, light tan skin and white flesh; good for boiling; keeps its flavor well in storage
Has a hot, dry climate	'Jemseg'	Very early-season variety with tan skin and white flesh
Has a cold, dry climate	'Denali'	Midseason variety from Alaska; good for baking or mashing
Is damp coastal territory	'Nooksack'	Late-season Russet type; good for baking, stores well
Gets very cold or very hot	'Norgold Russet'	Early-season Russet type; does not store well but matures quickly, before danger of frost in the North and high heat in the South
Is hot, with heavy soil	'Red Pontiac'	Mid- to late-season spuds with dark red skin and white flesh; good mashed or boiled

APPROVAL

Start Out Right

I always buy seed potatoes that are certified disease-free. That way, I can be sure my crop will get off to a healthy start. One pound of seed potatoes will give you anywhere from 3 to 10 pounds of spuds, depending upon the variety and your growing conditions. Most times, I buy "B-size" seed potatoes, about 2 inches in diameter, which I plant whole. When I have larger ones, I cut them into pieces, making sure each piece has two or three eyes showing.

The Eyes Don't Have It

As a youngster, I once cut up a store-bought potato and planted it in Grandma Putt's garden. I waited and waited, and nothing happened. Later, Grandma Putt told me why: Most commercially grown potatoes are treated with a chemical that keeps the eyes from sprouting. So, unfortunately, mine was doomed from the start!

A Word to the Wise from Grandma Putt

Into the Ground

Cultivate your soil well, to a depth of 12 inches or so. Potatoes aren't really too fussy about how you plant them; any of several methods works well. The crucial thing is that while your potatoes are forming on their underground stems, called stolons, you must protect them from light. Otherwise, they'll develop a bitter, toxic alkaloid called solanine — you can tell that's happened when the tubers take on a greenish tinge.

Hilling method. Dig a shallow trench and set in the seed pieces, cut side down, 12 inches apart, and cover them with about 4 inches of soil. In 2 to 3 weeks, shoots will emerge. When they've grown 6 to 8 inches tall, mound soil up around the stems to within ½ inch of the lower leaves. Keep raising and reshaping the hill throughout the growing season to encourage the stems to spread and produce more stolons.

Mulch method. This slight variation works well whenever you've got a good supply of mulching material on hand. Plant the seed pieces the way I described above; then, when the plants are 6 to 8 inches tall, put a good, thick blanket of mulch around the stems, leaving the foliage exposed to the sun. As the plants grow, keep mulching. Eventually, you'll have a layer of mulch about a foot thick chock-full of plump young spuds. I like to use leaves for mulch — it's a great way to make use of last fall's rakings. Straw works just as well, and so does hay if it's been cut before it sets seed.

Deep planting method. This is the method to use when you've got a busy summer ahead, with not much time to tend to the crop. Plant the seed pieces 7 to 8 inches deep. The stems will work their way to the surface, forming stolons along their length as they grow. A little hilling will encourage more top growth and a bigger harvest, but it's not really necessary. Deep planting has just one disadvantage over hilling and mulching: Because the tubers grow much deeper in the soil, you have to work a lot harder to dig them out come harvesttime.

Some Like It Cozy

Most folks don't think of potatoes as pot plants, but I've grown some mighty fine spuds in containers. You can, too. It's really easy, and it's the most trouble-free way to give potatoes — or any other vegetables — the kind of soil they like. Here's how I do it:

Find a container at least 18 inches deep. Anything will do as long as it's got drainage holes. I like to use old whiskey barrels sawed in half — they're sturdy, big, and most garden centers sell them at spring planting time.

Pour about 6 inches of potting mix into the bottom of the barrel. Then set the seed potatoes 6 to 8 inches apart, and cover them with 2 to 4 inches of soil. As the plants grow, keep adding more potting mix, or a combination of soil, straw, and compost. Before you know it, you've got lush green foliage spilling over the top of the barrel, and lots of future bakers or boilers growing inside.

One of my favorite varieties for container growing is 'Cherries Jubilee', a Swedish heirloom variety. It produces small round potatoes with smooth, cherry-red skin and pink flesh. And the taste — mmm, mmm, good!

Sick Bay

Late potato blight started the Irish famine, and I've contended with it once or twice on this side of the Atlantic, too — though it tends to strike commercial growers more than us home gardeners. If your potato patch does fall victim to the blight, your plants' foliage will turn black, then moldy. Burn the top growth, then wait a few weeks, and dig up the potatoes.

Raise 'em Right

If you have heavy soil and poor drainage, the secret to super spuds is to grow them in raised beds.

SUPER Growing Secrets

BUT IT DOESN'T LOOK LIKE A TULIP!

A handheld bulb planter is perfect for planting potatoes. Make holes 8 inches deep every 12 inches or so, plant the piece of potato in it, and then backfill with soil from the hole.

Let's Be Buddies

I like to plant flax (*Linum usitatissimum*) near my potato patch, because it seems to discourage the spud's worst nemesis: the Colorado potato beetle. Plus, having those sky-blue flax flowers to gaze at makes tending the taters a real treat. (For my Beetle Juice, see page 350; for other ways to control the potato beetle, see Chapter 5, The Invasion Forces.)

Not in My Neighborhood!

Potatoes and apples both rank among gardendom's best and longest keepers. But when storage time rolls around, keep them well away from each other: Apples give off ethylene gas, which tends to make spuds sprout. Furthermore — for reasons I've never figured out and Grandma Putt hadn't, either — when apples and potatoes are kept together for any length of time, they both taste "off."

Here's to Your Health

The humble spud is a powerhouse of nutrition, crammed with protein, fiber, carbohydrates, zinc, iron, copper, magnesium, iodine, and vitamins C and B. And not a smidgen of fat or cholesterol. You can't beat that!

Grow Me a Rainbow

If you still think that potatoes come only in red, tan, or russet on the outside and white on the inside, you're in for a real surprise. There are at least 5,000 varieties of potatoes in the world, in colors that will knock your socks off! So will the flavor. Here are some of my favorites:

'Alaska Sweetheart'–a real showstopper, red inside and out
'All Blue'–deep blue or purplish skin with blue flesh; rich, nutlike flavor and an added treat: blue flowers (I like to grow this one in pots on my patio.)
'Augsburg Gold'–the color its name implies — both skin and flesh — with a rich, buttery taste
'Candy Stripe'–white skin with red stripes, white flesh and terrific flavor
'Crystal'–the whitest of all, inside and out
'Donna'–red skin with yellow flesh (I like these baked.)
'German Butterball'–smooth yellow skin and flesh and a taste made in heaven
'Huckleberry'–beet-colored skin with red flesh marbled white
'Nosebag' a.k.a. **'French Fingerling'**–purple-pink outside, yellow inside
'Pinto'–yellow skin splotched with red; creamy flesh

I could go on and on — and on. But you get the idea. Order a couple of catalogs and before you know it, your potato harvest will look like a wheelbarrow full of jewels.

Tomatoes *(Lycopersicon lycopersium)*

Grandma Putt used to say that except for the fact that it's round, a store-bought tomato bears about as much resemblance to the genuine article as a goldfish does to an elephant. No wonder 90 percent of American gardeners grow their own!

Hitting High C

Flavor isn't the only feather in a homegrown tomato's cap: The ones you grow at home and pick when they're ripe and juicy are likely to have twice as much vitamin C as the ones in the supermarket. That's because tomatoes that are sold commercially are nearly always grown in greenhouses, where the vitamin content doesn't get as high as it does outdoors in the sun, or they're picked when they're still green, before the vitamin load has a chance to peak. Then they're zapped with a gas that turns them red, so they look ripe. But deep down inside, they're still green.

Home Ground

Tomatoes like full sun and fertile, light soil with a pH of 5.8 to 7.0 — and with lots and lots of organic matter in it. I get my tomato beds ready in the fall by digging in plenty of manure and chopped leaves. If I decide to add a new bed in the spring, I add lots of compost to it before I plant. And to get the soil good and warm, I put black plastic on the beds a few weeks before the big transplanting day.

Buy or Grow?

The easiest way to get your tomato crop off and running is to buy started plants — if you walk into any garden center in early spring, you'll see acres of them. But I like to start my own from seed. That way, I can control their early home life, so they grow up bigger and stronger, and give me a better harvest than most store-bought plants would. Plus, I like to grow some old-time varieties that only the seed catalogs sell.

To the Starting Gate

I start my seeds 6 or 8 weeks before I expect the last frost. And because tomatoes are especially prone to damping-off disease, I'm extra careful to follow all of the guidelines in Chapter 3. Aside from that, here are the secrets to success:

1. Sow seeds ½ inch deep and about 1 inch apart. Put them on top of the fridge or someplace else where the bottom temperature will be about 85°F. Keep the soil moist, but not wet with my Seed and Soil Energizer Tonic (see page 355).

2. When the seeds germinate, move them to a sunny window, or shine grow lights on them. Keep the bulbs an inch or 2 above the plants. Otherwise, the little guys will grow up toward the light and get thin and leggy. Feed them once a month with fish fertilizer. If the leaves start turning purple, give them a high-phosphorus liquid fertilizer.

3. Ten days after germination, move the seedlings to their own 2-inch pots. Clip off all of the leaves except the ones at the top inch of the stem, and set each seedling in its new pot up to just below the bottom leaf. New roots will grow from the buried stem. Feed with fish fertilizer, and keep the growing temperature at 60 to 70°F.

4. Two weeks later, move your crop into 4-inch pots. This time, trim off all of the leaves below the top 2 inches, then plant the same way as in step 3. Water steadily, just enough to keep the potting mix from drying out.

5. At least 2 weeks before outdoor planting day, start getting the seedlings toughened up for life in the garden. Move them to a sheltered spot outdoors for part of each day, and gradually increase the time they're outside. (See the hardening-off guidelines in Chapter 3.)

SUPER Growing Secrets

GIVE 'EM THE BRUSH-OFF

While your seedlings are growing up indoors, brush them lightly with your hand a couple of times a day, or aim a slow-turning fan in their direction so they get a nice, gentle breeze. The motion of the stems helps the plants produce a hormone called cytokinin, which makes for thicker, stronger stems.

Into the World

Move your transplants to the garden when the soil temperature is at least 55°F and when you're pretty sure the air won't get chillier than 45°F at night (and keep row covers handy, just in case). Tomatoes need a good support system, so I set them 15 inches apart down the middle of a 30-inch-wide raised bed and grow them on metal trellises. If you don't plan to use stakes or trellises, leave 2 feet between determinate types and 3 feet between indeterminate (see page 302).

Perfect Planting

There are two ways to plant tomatoes:

Holey moley method. Simply dig a hole about the size of a basketball, and in the bottom put a layer of compost or well-rotted manure mixed with a handful of bonemeal and 1 teaspoon of Epsom salts. Then set in the plant so that only about the top 4 inches sticks up above the soil. (Clip off the lower leaves with scissors first.)

Trench method. Make a 6-inch-deep trench the whole length of the planting bed. Spread a thin layer of compost along the bottom, then trim off the leaves from all but the top 4 inches of the stem. Lay each plant in the trench horizontally, with the 4-inch leafy part curved up out of the ground. Pack soil around it so it stays in place, then cover up the rest of the stem. This method works especially well in cool regions or when you're trying to get a jump on the season, because the roots grow up close to the surface, where the soil is warmer.

Wall-o'-Bottles

A great way to protect tomato seedlings from the cold is with a gadget called Wall-o'-Water. It's made of hollow, upright plastic cylinders fastened together to form a circle. You fill it with water and set it over a plant. It works great, but it gets expensive if you have a lot of tomatoes and other heat-lovers, like peppers and eggplant. I make my own warmer-uppers by taping together quart-sized pop bottles in a circle and filling them with water. They work just as well as the store-bought kind, and they're free!

Water, Please

Make sure your tomato plants get between 1 and 2 inches of water every week, whether from you or from Mother Nature. And to ensure a bumper crop, spray them with my All-Season Green-Up Tonic (see page 349) or fish fertilizer 4 times during the growing season: first, 2 weeks after transplanting, then after the first flowers appear, next when the fruits reach the size of golf balls, and, finally, when you spot the first ripe tomato.

TIMELY TOMATO TONIC

To ward off common tomato diseases, use this mix on your newly transplanted seedlings.

3 cups of compost
½ cup of powdered nonfat milk
½ cup of Epsom salts
1 tbsp. of baking soda

Sprinkle a handful of the mix into the planting hole, and then sprinkle a little of the dry milk on top of the soil after planting. Repeat every few weeks throughout the growing season.

Rushing the Season

If you want to have the very first ripe tomato on your block, plant seeds of an extra-hardy, early-maturing variety like 'Glacier' or 'Chalk's Early Jewel'. (This is an 1899 heirloom that Grandma Putt thought was the cat's meow. You can still order it through the Seed Savers Exchange in Decorah, Iowa. See www.seedsavers.org.) Then here's all you need to do:

Step 1. Start the seeds indoors 10 to 12 weeks before the last expected frost.

Step 2. When your seedlings are 4 to 5 inches tall, move them to much deeper containers. Clip off all of the leaves except ones at the top 2 inches of stem, and set them in up to the lowest leaf.

Step 3. When they reach 8 inches high, move them again, using the same procedure. But this time, put each seedling up to its neck in a half-gallon milk carton. (Either plastic or waxed paper will do fine.) This will encourage a large root system that can stand up to the cold, cruel world.

Step 4. Start hardening the plants off 4 to 5 weeks before the last frost.

Step 5. Move the little guys to the garden about 3 weeks before the last frost date. Water them well, then set them into the ground an inch or so deeper than they were growing in their cartons.

Step 6. Surround each one with my Wall-o'-Bottles. If the temperature takes a sudden dip, cover the top with plastic.

Directly into the Garden

Some folks in warm climates sow their tomatoes directly in the ground in early spring. If you want to give it a try, call your Cooperative Extension Service and ask for advice on the best varieties for your territory (not all varieties grow well from direct-sown seed, no matter what the climate is like). Then follow these simple steps:

Step 1. Sow seeds ¼ inch deep and 2 feet apart in groups of four or five, and water lightly. If frost threatens, cover the seedbed with newspaper or floating row covers.

Step 2. When the seedlings have two or three sets of true leaves (or whenever you decide they look big and strong enough), clip off all but one seedling per group.

Step 3. From then on, treat them just like your regular transplants.

Determine What to Plant

Scientists at the U.S. Department of Agriculture say there are about 25,000 varieties of tomatoes in the world. All of them fall into one of two types, based on their growing habits:

• **Determinate tomato plants** are bushes that grow to a certain size and then stop. They offer up their harvest during a certain period, which usually lasts about 6 weeks. They don't need pruning, though it helps them grow better, and they don't really need to be supported. Lots of folks just let them sprawl across the ground, but growing them in wire cages keeps the tomatoes cleaner and out of reach of at least *some* pesky pests.

• **Indeterminate tomatoes** are true vines — and to some folks, they're the only kind worth growing. That's because the bigger a tomato plant is, the tastier its fruits are. And believe me, these guys get BIG! They keep growing and churning out fruit right up to the time that Jack Frost knocks them over. It takes more time and attention to grow indeterminates: You have to train them on trellises, and you have to keep pruning them. For me, though, the results are worth the effort.

Homebodies

Tomatoes like all of the warmth they can get. If your territory can't give them as much as they'd like, plant your crop near a wall or the side of your house that faces west or south. The wall will soak up the sun's heat during the day and send it back out at night.

A Present for the Cabbages

If you already have all of the tomato plants you need, spread the pruned-off suckers on the ground among your cabbages. Freshly plucked tomato foliage gives off an odor that repels egg-laying cabbage moths — for a while, anyway.

SUPER Growing Secrets

BAG IT!

Here's one of my hotter tomato planting secrets: Bury a brown paper bag (opened and upright) approximately 6 inches deep, place your planting mix inside the bag, and set in your tomato plants. Then water well. The bag helps protect the plants from the elements and insects. And you can clip it shut with a clothespin if you're expecting frost. If the bag begins to fold over, roll it down to make a stiff collar. When the danger of frost has passed, simply cut off as much of the bag as you can.

Take That, Sucker!

Whether you're growing determinate or indeterminate tomatoes, you'll get stronger plants and bigger fruit if you keep the plants pruned. There's really nothing to it: Just pinch out all of the suckers that grow between the main stem and the branches. Then root the suckers in pots of starting mix and transplant them to the garden — you'll have a second crop for free!

Not for Monkeys Only

Tomatoes — and all potassium-loving crops —go bananas over bananas. They'll gobble up all of the overripe ones that don't make it into banana bread, but they don't need the innards; they'll be just as happy with the peels. So I place one in the bottom of each hole before I set in the plant.

And all through the growing season, every time I polish off a banana, I dig a shallow hole near the base of a plant, lay the peel in it, and cover it up. (Just be sure to dig carefully, so you don't damage shallow roots.) As thick as it is, that peel breaks down in a flash, and all the healthy minerals go right to the plant's roots.

Support the Crops

It seems to me there are almost as many ways to support tomato plants as there are gardeners who grow them. Whichever method you use, get it all rigged up before setting the plants in the ground, so you don't risk damaging their roots later. Here's a roundup of my favorite propper-uppers:

• **The good old-fashioned stake.** I always use metal ones, because they draw electrical energy from the air, and that gives my plants a good jolt of nitrogen. I use stakes that are about 7 feet tall, and drive them into the ground about 2 feet (indeterminate tomatoes are big, heavy rascals). I keep the vines pruned, so that only one or two main stems develop. As they grow, I tie them loosely every foot or so, using strips of old panty hose.

• **The classic cage.** These must be strong and anywhere from 5 to 8 feet tall to handle the big guys. They need to have openings that are large enough to let you reach in and grab a hefty tomato. Make your cages from sturdy galvanized wire mesh and bend it into 24- to 30-inch-diameter circles. (You need 3 feet of wire mesh for every foot of diameter.) Anchor each cage to a pair of 4-foot metal stakes driven about a foot into the ground.

• **The trellis.** My favorite is made from the same galvanized wire mesh that I use for cages. But instead of forming it into circles, stretch it out and attach it to metal stakes driven into the ground every 8 feet or so. As vines grow, tie them to the wire with strips of panty hose, just like you'd do with staked plants.

Jerry's Diner: Open 24 Hours

Tomatoes are heavy eaters, but you don't have to feed them: They'll chow down whenever they need to if you give them their own 24-hour diner. Here's how to build it:

1. Dig a hole that's 3 feet in diameter and 10 inches deep.

2. Put a 2-foot-high cylinder of chicken wire or hardware cloth around the hole and fill it up with compost or well-rotted manure.

3. Plant six tomatoes in a circle around the cylinder, about 1 foot away from it.

4. When you water the tomatoes, water the food supply, too. Before you know it, you'll have whopper tomatoes!

SUPER Growing Secrets

TIRE-RIFIC TOMATOES

Here's another neat way to grow great tomatoes. In good sunlight, stack up three old tires per plant. Fill the interior of the tires with rich garden soil. Insert a long metal pole or stick in the middle and plant your seedling. The tires will heat up the soil and store water for days, releasing it to the plant as needed.

The Shell Game

Tomatoes that don't get enough calcium are prime targets for blossom-end rot. To protect my crop, I add crushed eggshells to their water supply every week or 2. About six shells per quart of water does the trick. (If you don't eat that many eggs, start collecting shells from nongardening friends!)

Static Cling to the Rescue

If a storm or high wind knocks a lot of blossoms off your tomato plants, don't panic: You can still get a good crop. Just pollinate the remaining flowers yourself with an old trick Grandma Putt taught me: Rub an old nylon petticoat to build up static electricity, and lay it on the blossoms of one plant. Then take it off and shake the pollen onto another plant. You'll get 100 percent pollination every time — I guarantee it!

Gimme That Old-Time Flavor

If what you're hankering for is a tomato that tastes like the ones you grew up on, plant 'Brandywine', an indeterminate heirloom that most folks think is the best-tastin' tomato you can find, in both dark pink and yellow versions. A word of warning, though: 'Brandywine' has no built-in disease resistance, so read Chapter 5 carefully, and follow the tips to the letter!

Watch Those Bottoms

Start picking your tomatoes when their color is even and glossy, and the texture somewhere between firm and soft. Keep close watch on the bottoms — that's where ripening starts. Some varieties, primarily large heirloom types, ripen before their full color develops. Pick them when the skin still looks smooth and waxy, even if the top hasn't turned its mature color (which could be red, purple, pink, orange, or golden yellow).

Red Is So Boring!

So plant 'Green Grape', 'Pruden's Purple', 'White Beauty' (a.k.a. 'Snowball'), 'Black Krim', or yellow-and pink-striped 'Mr. Stripey'.

I Can't Decide!

With so many kinds of tomatoes in catalogs and garden centers, deciding what to grow can be downright mind-boggling. When you're starting to narrow your choices, first zero in on a variety that's bred to thrive in your neck of the woods. These are some tried-and-true winners for less-than-ideal tomato territory.

JERRY'S FAVORITE Vegetable Varieties

YOUR HOME TURF	VARIETY TO PLANT	THE RESULT
Cool	'Siberia'	Determinate plant that sets fruit at very low temperatures and performs well at high altitudes; 3-ounce red fruits
	'Caro Rich'	Determinate plant with 5-ounce orange fruits that are low in acid and high in vitamin A
Short growing season	'Gurney Girl'	Large, indeterminate plant with big, red fruits and that old-time tomato taste
Hot and humid	'Heatwave' or 'Solar Set'	Both determinate plants with tasty 8-ounce red fruits
Hot and dry	'Porter'	Indeterminate heirloom with egg-shaped pink-red fruits that weigh in at all of 1 ounce

When the End Is in Sight

About a month before you expect the first frost, start plucking all new flower clusters off of your tomato plants. That way, you'll direct the plants' energy into ripening the tomatoes that are already on the vine, rather than producing new ones that won't have time to mature. To make the remaining fruits ripen faster, spray them with my Hurry-Up-the-Harvest Tonic (see page 353).

Nutrition Bulletin

If you've gotten carried away and planted more tomatoes than you and the whole population of your town could possibly eat fresh, here's good news: When they're picked at the peak of ripeness, canned or frozen tomatoes retain their flavor and nutrients better than almost any other vegetable.

Freeze 'em

Tomatoes don't need any fancy treatment before you freeze them. Just wash them, cut out any bad spots, put them on baking sheets, and slide the sheets into the freezer. When the tomatoes have frozen, store them in plastic bags. The skins will crack during the freezing process, making the tomatoes easier to peel when they've thawed out.

Don't Let 'em See the Light

Once you've picked tomatoes (whether or not they're fully ripe), keep them out of sunlight. They'll overheat and ripen unevenly — or spoil more quickly. And never put partially ripened tomatoes in the fridge: That'll stop the ripening process then and there. Instead, store your treasures, shoulders up, in a dark place at room temperature.

But It Doesn't Look Like Butter

Even fully ripened tomatoes keep their best flavor when they're stored at room temperature, but they'll last only a day or 2. If you need to keep them longer than that (and they're small enough), put them into the butter compartment of your fridge — it's the warmest part.

Drink Your Vitamins

Don't waste all that time and effort making tomato juice the old-fashioned way: scalding, peeling, cooking, and running the fruit through a colander. Instead, just wash your tomatoes, cut out the cores and any bad spots, and run 'em through the blender, peels and all. Then can or freeze the juice. It's easier — and healthier, too, because you're keeping the vitamins you'd otherwise throw away with the peels.

Hurry Up, Guys!

To make your picked tomatoes redden up faster, put them into a paper bag with an apple or a banana. Ethylene gas given off by the fruit will speed the tomato ripening process.

Tomato Troubles? *Not!*

After weeks of pampering your tomato plants through the long, hot summer, there is nothing more frustrating than gathering fruits that look like they came from Dr. Frankenstein's laboratory. While you might want to blame insects or diseases, it may be that the variety, weather, or even your gardening habits are the actual culprit.

To help you identify what's spoiling your tomatoes, here's a list of the most common tomato problems that are not caused by insects or diseases:

Blossom-end rot. You've got this problem when the bottom of the fruit suddenly collapses and rots. The problem starts with soil. Either you don't have enough calcium or the soil alternately gets wet and dry. Add crushed eggshells to the soil, use a commercial Rot Stop spray, and keep soil moisture constant with mulch.

Blotching ripening. This condition is characterized by yellow-gray patches on the fruits, which never mature properly. It's caused by cool temperatures. Prevent it by growing varieties that produce fewer leaves and by reducing fertilizer use.

Fruit cracks. This is similar to blossom-end rot, with circular cracks developing on top of the ripening fruit. It's caused by variations in the soil-moisture level. Keeping the plants well mulched will keep the soil moisture constant. Also, if you see this condition developing, switch to a low-nitrogen fertilizer.

Sunscald. This problem causes the fruits to develop lightly colored patches that eventually rot. This is the opposite of blotchy ripening. Prevent this condition by keeping the plants leafy and the fruits shaded (use floating grow covers). Also, selectively prune out suckers and leaves.

Zippering: If you've got fruit with a thin, dark line that runs from the stem to the bottom of the fruit, then you've got zippering. Cold temperatures cause poor pollination. To avoid this, keep your young plants warm and protected early in the season with floating row cover.

SUPER
Growing Secrets

FOR TERRIFIC TOMATOES

- Don't use high-nitrogen fertilizer on your tomato plants. Lots of nitrogen encourages leaf growth at the expense of flowers and fruits.

- Avoid cultivating around your tomato plants, which can disturb the roots. Instead, use a 2-inch layer of mulch to keep out weeds.

- If you notice the leaves curling on your tomato plants, they aren't getting enough water. Be sure to soak 'em good at least once a week, especially in hot, dry weather.

Whoppers Comin' Up!

If you aim to grow the biggest danged, most terrific tomatoes in town — or simply the tastiest — treat your plants to this trio of terrific tonics.

TOMATO BOOSTER TONIC

2 tbsp. of Epsom salts
1 tsp. of baby shampoo
1 gal. of water

Mix all of the ingredients together, and liberally soak the soil around tomato plants as they flower to boost their growth to new heights.

TOMATO BLIGHT BUSTER TONIC

To ward off early blight and other common tomato diseases, use this mix when you transplant your tomato seedlings.

1 cup of compost
½ cup, plus ¼ cup of powdered nonfat milk
½ cup of Epsom salts

Mix the compost, ½ cup of the powdered milk, and the Epsom salts together. Sprinkle a handful of the mix into each planting hole. Then sprinkle the remaining ¼ cup of powdered milk on top of the soil after planting. Reapply the powdered milk every few weeks throughout the season.

TOMATO DISEASE FIGHTER TONIC

Apply this Tonic at the first sign of trouble.

1 part skim milk
9 parts water

Combine the ingredients, and mist-spray your tomato plants in early summer.

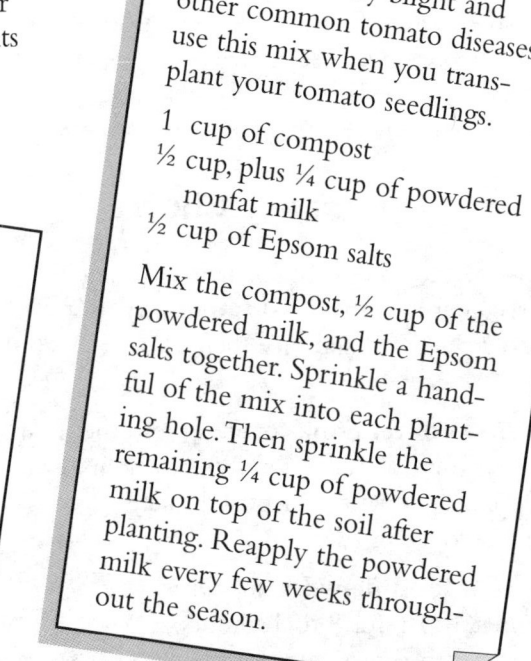

SUPER Growing Secrets

A SPOONFUL OF SUGAR

For the sweetest, juiciest tomatoes in town, take a tip from Mary Poppins and me: Add a spoonful of sugar to each hole at planting time. Your tomatoes will be so lip-smacking good, the kids will be eating them right off the vine!

Box 'em Up

At the end of the summer, rescue all of your green tomatoes before the frost zaps 'em. Wipe off any dirt, then wrap each one separately in newspaper. Pack them in a single layer in a cardboard box (so they don't squash each other), and store them in a cool, dry place.

Fancy Chow

Sun-dried tomatoes cost an arm and a leg in the supermarket, but it's a snap to dry your own. Just wash them, cut out the cores, and slice them about ⅛ inch thick. Then:

• **In a conventional oven.** Spread them out on trays and dry them at 120°F for 18 to 24 hours, or until they're crisp. Turn the slices and rotate the trays once or twice.

• **In a food dehydrator.** Dry them at 120°F for 8 to 10 hours, turn over the slices, and dry them for another 6 to 8 hours, or until they're crisp.

• **Outdoors.** Spread them out on a piece of screen in the sun, and cover them with a cheesecloth tent, so bugs and dust can't get at them. Let them dry until they're brittle (but take them in at night). They'll be dry in a day or 2.

SUPER Storing Secrets

HANG 'EM HIGH

The easiest way I know of to ripen tomatoes indoors is just to pull the vines out of the ground and hang them up in your basement or shed. Not only will the fruits ripen well, but they'll contain more vitamins than they would if you picked them off the plants. That's because the stems and leaves keep passing nutrients to the fruits. Just be sure that both vines and fruit are dry when you bring them in; otherwise, rot could set in and spoil your dinnertime fun.

Jerry Baker Says

"When I was growing up, I made plenty of pocket money by picking beetles and hornworms off of plants in every garden in the neighborhood, using nothing but my bare hands. Today, you couldn't pay me enough to touch one of those things! So when it's varmint-picking time in my garden, I reach for my trusty sidearm — a pair of long-handled barbecue tongs. You can't beat 'em!"

PATRIOTIC POTATO SALAD

Every year, when my new potatoes start coming in, I run Old Glory up the flagpole and dish up this red, white, and blue salad at a late-summer barbecue.

4 TO 6 SERVINGS

- 2 pounds small, new, blue-, red- and white-fleshed potatoes
- ½ cup dry rosé wine
- ⅔ cup extra-virgin olive oil
- 6 tablespoons fresh lemon juice or white wine vinegar
- 4 teaspoons Dijon-style mustard
- ½ cup thinly sliced green onions or shallots
- ⅔ cup minced fresh parsley
- 2 tablespoons minced fresh summer savory, rosemary, and/or chervil

salt and freshly ground black pepper to taste

1. In a saucepan, cook potatoes in boiling salted water for 20 minutes, or until tender. Do not overcook. Drain.

2. Cut the potatoes into ¼-inch-thick slices and peel them. Put the slices in a bowl and sprinkle with the wine.

3. In a small bowl, combine oil, lemon juice or vinegar, mustard, shallots, parsley, other herbs, and salt and pepper, blending well.

4. Toss the potatoes with the dressing. Serve warm or chilled.

JERRY'S SHOW-STOPPER TOMATOES WITH BASIL

This is one of my favorite ways to enjoy the tummy-boggling taste of fresh-from-the-garden tomatoes.

4 SERVINGS

- 3 large ripe tomatoes
- 2 tablespoons chopped fresh basil
- 3 tablespoons extra virgin olive oil
- 2 tablespoons lemon juice
- ½ teaspoon sugar

salt and freshly ground black pepper to taste

1. Slice the tomatoes into ½-inch slices and arrange them in a deep pie dish.

2. Sprinkle the fresh chopped basil evenly over the tomatoes.

3. In a small bowl, mix together the olive oil, lemon juice, sugar, and salt and pepper.

4. Pour this dressing over the tomatoes and basil.

5. Marinate at room temperature for 1 hour, spooning the dressing over the tomatoes occasionally. Serve at room temperature.

TOMATO FRITTATA

Frittatas look — and taste — as impressive as all get-out, but nothing could be easier to make. This one, made with fresh-from-the-garden tomatoes and basil, is one of Grandma's favorites.

1 9-INCH PIE

- 4 tablespoons extra virgin olive oil
- 2 onions, sliced
- salt
- 3 ripe tomatoes, peeled, and chopped
- 1 garlic clove, minced
- 5 eggs
- freshly ground black pepper
- 2 tablespoons chopped fresh basil
- ¼ cup chopped fresh parsley
- 2 tablespoons grated Parmesan cheese
- 1 teaspoon finely chopped pine nuts
- 2 tablespoons butter

1. In a large skillet, heat the oil and add the onions and a little salt. Cover the pan and simmer over low heat for 5 minutes. Uncover and cook until soft and golden.

2. Stir in the tomatoes and minced garlic. Simmer for 15 minutes, then drain off the oil. Set aside.

3. Preheat the oven to 350° F. In a large bowl, beat the eggs. Add the tomato and onion mixture, pepper to taste, basil, parsley, cheese, and pine nuts; mix well.

4. Melt the butter in a 10-inch pan, then pour in frittata mixture. Bake for about 15 minutes, or until the eggs are set.

5. Loosen edges, cut into wedges, and serve.

JERRY'S HEAT UP THE KITCHEN CHILE

Make the chile steamy or mild, depending on the kind of peppers you use. (To compare heat levels, check the Scoville Heat Scale on page 290.)

4 SERVINGS

- 2 pounds lean beef, ½-inch cubes
- ¼ cup extra virgin olive oil
- 2 tablespoons all-purpose flour
- 1 medium yellow onion, chopped
- 2 garlic cloves, chopped
- 3 large ripe tomatoes, chopped
- 6–8 small mild chile peppers, seeded and thinly sliced
- 3 small hot red chile peppers, seeded and thinly sliced, or 1 habañero pepper
- 4 teaspoons minced fresh oregano
- ½ teaspoon cumin seed
- 2 cups beef broth
- salt and freshly ground black pepper
- 4 cups cooked rice

1. In a large skillet, brown beef in 2 tablespoons of oil. Drain off fat; place beef in a large soup pot.

2. In the same skillet, heat oil and blend in flour, onion, and garlic. Cook until the onion is just starting to brown.

3. Add the onion mixture, tomatoes, chile peppers, oregano, cumin seed, and beef broth to the soup pot. Simmer, covered, for 2 hours, stirring occasionally.

4. Add salt and pepper to taste. Serve over rice.

SANTA'S FAVORITE CHUTNEY

Grandma Putt and I used to make up jars and jars of this chutney for Christmas presents. It's just the ticket to serve with chicken or as a topping for baked potatoes. And it's so good it would make Scrooge himself sit up and say "Ho ho ho!"

7 PINTS

- 6 pounds ripe, medium-size tomatoes (about 24)
- 6 pounds tart, green apples (about 12 medium-size)
- 2 pounds onions (about 6 medium-size)
- ½ pound red peppers (about 3)
- 1 cup minced celery
- 5 cups cider or malt vinegar
- 2½ cups sugar
- 4 tablespoons pickling salt
- 1 pound sultana-type raisins

1. Peel and chop tomatoes, apples, and onions. Chop peppers.

2. Combine with the celery, vinegar, sugar, and salt in a large kettle.

3. Boil rapidly, stirring constantly, until mixture is slightly thick. Add raisins and boil 20–30 minutes more. Keep stirring to avoid scorching.

4. When sauce is reduced to 7 pints, put into clean, hot, pint jars and seal.

5. Process in a boiling-water bath or steam canner for 15 minutes.

VERY VEGGIE PIE

This version of my favorite main-dish pie uses a passel of tomato family members.

8 SERVINGS

- 4 tablespoons butter
- 3 tablespoons diced onion
- 2 garlic cloves, minced
- 1 cup diced sweet red peppers
- 1 cup diced green peppers
- 5 cups peeled diced eggplant
- ¼ cup water
- 8 ounces cream cheese, cubed
- 5 tablespoons grated parmesan cheese
- 1 tablespoon lemon juice
- 2 tablespoons minced fresh basil
- salt and pepper
- 1 single unbaked pie crust, in pan
- 2 large tomatoes, sliced
- ½ cup wheat germ
- ¼ cup bread crumbs

1. Preheat the oven to 350° F.

2. In a large pan, melt 2 tablespoons of the butter and saute the onion, garlic, and peppers until the onion is limp. Add eggplant and water. Cover the pan and cook the eggplant for 5 minutes, stirring occasionally.

3. Add cream cheese to the eggplant. Cook until the cheese melts. Stir in 2 tablespoons of parmesan, lemon juice, and basil. Season with salt and pepper.

4. Spoon half of eggplant mixture into pie crust. Cover with the tomato slices. Add remaining eggplant.

5. Top with a mixture of wheat germ, bread crumbs, and remaining butter and parmesan. Bake 40 minutes.

QUICK LEMONY MUSTARD POTATOES

Who says fast food can't be good for you? After a long day in the garden, Grandma Putt liked to put a hearty meal on the table pronto. These tasty spuds fit the bill then, and they still do at my house.

4 TO 6 SERVINGS

      4 cups sliced or diced potatoes
      3 tablespoons butter
      2 teaspoons lemon juice
      2 teaspoons grated lemon rind
   1½ teaspoons Dijon mustard
         salt and pepper

1. Boil the potatoes until just tender, about 10 minutes. Drain.

2. In a large sauté pan, melt the butter.

3. Add lemon juice, grated lemon rind, and mustard.

4. Add the potatoes and stir to mix and heat. Season to taste with salt and pepper.

GRANDMA PUTT'S CHOCOLATE CAKE

Grandma Putt used to serve this cake to first-time guests and ask them to guess the secret ingredient. Are you ready for this? It's green tomatoes!

12 TO 15 SERVINGS

   ⅔ cup butter
   1¾ cups sugar
      4 ounces unsweetened chocolate, melted
      2 eggs
      1 teaspoon vanilla extract
   ½ cup cocoa
   2½ cups sifted all-purpose flour
      2 teaspoons baking powder
      2 teaspoons baking soda
   ¼ teaspoon salt
      1 cup beer
      1 cup puréed green tomatoes
¼–½ cup water (optional)

1. Preheat the oven to 350° F.

2. Cream together the butter and sugar. Stir in the melted chocolate, then the eggs, one at a time. Add the vanilla.

3. In another bowl, sift together the cocoa, flour, baking powder, baking soda, and salt.

4. Add flour mixture to butter mixture alternately with beer and green tomatoes. If batter is stiff, add water. Turn batter into a greased and floured 9- by 13-inch baking dish. Bake for 35 minutes. Cool, then top with your favorite frosting.

EXTENDED FAMILY

Corn • Okra • Sweet Potatoes

From a scientific standpoint, members of this trio aren't even remotely related, but Grandma Putt often thought of them as belonging together, just because they all love their weather good and hot and because, in most folks' minds, at least, they're all as American as apple pie. Actually, though, only two of them — corn and sweet potatoes — hail from this side of the Atlantic. Okra is a North African native that found its way to Europe. It never really caught on there, but it sure took root here, and ever since Colonial times, folks have thought of it as a real southern gentleplant.

Corn *(Zea mays)*

To Grandma Putt and me, summer wasn't summer until we got those first sweet, tender ears of corn off of the stalks and into the pot. More than anything else, that patch of corn still jumps up and sings out "Summertime" at my place.

My Goodness

Corn is a little picky. To grow up happy and tasty, it needs plenty of goodness — good light, good drainage, and good, rich soil. I get my planting beds ready in the fall by spreading at least an inch of well-rotted manure on top and working it into the soil with a garden fork. Then I lay down a good, thick mulch of leaves, straw, or salt hay. That keeps the ground warm enough for the worms to work all through the winter and get the soil rarin' to grow things.

Wake Up!

Come spring, I pull off the mulch and replace it with an inch or so of compost. Then I cover the beds with black plastic and start checking the ground temperature with my soil thermometer. About a week after the last frost — as long as the mercury has hit 55°F — I plant my crop. (If you're planting one of the newfangled supersweet hybrids, wait until the soil temperature is at least 65°F.)

Jerry Baker Says

"Don't water your corn seeds after you plant them — they'll rot. Instead, water their bed 3 or 4 days before you plant, and then let it dry out. The moisture level will be just right."

The Cover-Up

Once the seeds are in the ground, keep the soil evenly moist, and use floating row covers to keep the soil warm and protect the seedlings in case Jack Frost pays a late surprise visit. When the nighttime temperature is holding at 65°F, remove the covers.

Steady as She Goes

Corn is one of the heartiest eaters — and drinkers — in all of gardendom. But it has a shallow root system that can't pull water or nutrients from deep in the soil the way a lot of other plants can. This means that you need to give it a steady, even flow of both water and food.

Give plants an inch of water a week in the beginning, and a little more from flowering to harvest. Never water from overhead, though — that would wash away the pollen. And every 2 weeks throughout the growing season, give the plants a healthy dose of fish fertilizer.

Corny Friends

• Japanese beetles will leave your corn silks alone if you plant marigolds next to the corn.

• Scientists in England have proved that if you grow rows of sunflowers between corn blocks, the armyworm population plummets.

SUPER Growing Secrets

BLOCK IT OFF

Corn is pollinated by the wind, so it's important to plant your seeds in blocks, rather than in long rows. I make a grid pattern of raised beds that are 30 inches square. Then I plant my seeds 1 inch deep and 8 inches apart down the center of each bed.

The Leaning Tower of Corn

Cornstalks have a tendency to lie down on the job. This is called *lodging*. If your plants start leaning, just pull 'em to their feet and pack enough soil around the base to give 'em some support.

Planter's Choice

Depending on the weather, each crop of corn yields for 2 to 3 weeks. To keep the good times rollin' all season long, you have two choices:

1. Sow your whole crop on the same day, but plant three different varieties with maturity dates that are 10 days apart, like 65, 75, and 85 days.

2. Make succession plantings of the same variety: Every time a block of seedlings gets its fourth true leaf, sow another block.

I'll Be All in Clover

Corn is a real pain in the grass to keep weeded — the roots are so close to the soil surface that it's hard not to damage them when you're cultivating. But planting a cover crop of clover will keep weeds out of your corn patch. Wait until a month after you plant your corn. By that time, the plants are big and sturdy enough so that the clover won't be any competition for nutrients.

Then remove all of the weeds that have sprouted up, loosening the ground in the process. Scatter the seeds evenly all around the corn at a rate of about 1 ounce per 100 square feet. Then rake soil on top to cover them.

Besides keeping weeds out of the corn patch, the clover attracts bees to pollinate other crops, like squash and beans. And, as if that weren't enough, it puts nitrogen into the soil when you till it in after the corn harvest! You can use whatever kind of clover the garden center has on the shelf on shopping day. Red, yellow, and white all work just fine.

You'll Be Sor-ry!

Whatever you do, don't plant corn and tomatoes anywhere near each other. Corn earworms and tomato hornworms are almost the same critters, and they'll jump from one plant to the other faster than you can say "Jumpin' jackrabbits!"

SUPER Growing Secrets

DON'T TOUCH THE SUCKERS

Short stalks, called suckers, usually grow up from the base of a cornstalk. Back in Grandma Putt's day, folks usually clipped them off. But this is one case where the old way isn't the best: It turns out that the ears develop better when you leave the suckers in place.

Take Up a Collection

If you live in a dry climate —
or if your weather forecast
predicts drought this summer —
plant corn in a bowl. Just dig a
flat-bottomed circle about 12 inches in
diameter and 4 inches below the level of the bed. Then
plant your seeds 8 inches apart in groups of four. The
bowl will collect every drop of water that falls from the
sky or your garden hose.

In the Trenches

If your turf doesn't have a long, hot growing season, start
your plants in trenches. Here's all there is to it:

Step 1. About 2 weeks before planting time, dig a
trench 4 inches deep, and cover it with clear plastic.

Step 2. When the soil has warmed up enough, plant
your seeds in the trench, and put the plastic back on.

Step 3. When the corn grows high enough to touch
the plastic, take it off. By then, the air will be sufficiently
warm to please even a finicky corn plant.

Hostile Territory

Here are more tricks for keeping corn happy in less than
ideal surroundings:

- Start with a fast-maturing variety like 'Quickie' (65 days), 'Earlivee' (65 days), or
  'Trinity' (68 days).

  - Do what folks in *really* cold places like Russia do: Start your seeds
    indoors. Or buy transplants at the garden center, if you can find them.
    It's not the ideal way — corn resents being transplanted — but if you're
    really itchin' for that homegrown flavor, it's worth a try.

    - Plant your corn on a south-facing slope — even if you have to make
      one. Just build your raised beds the usual way (see Chapter 3), but grade
      them downhill toward the south. They'll catch the morning sun and
      warm up faster than flat beds will.

SUPER Growing Secrets

RISE TO THE OCCASION

When planting early
crops, especially those
that require high tem-
peratures to germinate,
pull loose soil from the
center of the rows to
form raised ridges about
3 inches high and
2 inches wide on top.
Plant your seeds in the
center of these ridges.
This trick is especially
good for corn, melons,
and squash, and it pre-
vents drowning out
by early rains.

When It's Dogwood Blossom Time

Like most folks, I can hardly wait to get my corn in the ground. But every year at planting time, I remember what Grandma Putt always told me: Wait until the dogwood trees are in full bloom before you plant your corn. If you do, you'll stand a better chance of foiling your crop's archenemy, the European corn borer.

Stonehenge Revisited

Here's another way to keep your corn plants warm: Build a stone circle around each one. Collect all of the rocks you can find and set them close to the stalk, but not touching it. The rocks will gather and store heat during the day, and release it toward the plant at night. They'll also do double duty as a mulch, keeping moisture in the soil and stopping weeds before they get started.

How Sweet It Is!

To a lot of folks (me included), the sweet corn section of a seed catalog can be a tad confusing. All of those terms and abbreviations have to do with scientists' breeding corn to make it sweeter and sweeter. Here's how to decipher the code:

• **Normal Sugary (su).** These are the old-time, garden-variety favorites with that good, down-home corn flavor. The sugar content varies with the variety, but in every case, the sugar starts turning to starch the minute the ears are off of the stalks. 'Golden Bantam' is a classic from Grandma Putt's day, and you still can't beat it. 'Country Gentleman' (white), 'Double Standard' (bicolor), and 'Shoepeg' (yellow) are hard to beat, too.

• **Sugary Enhanced (se and se+).** Scientists have beefed up the sugar content of these types, but they still have the flavor and tenderness of the Normal Sugary kinds. The conversion of sugar to starch is a little slower than it is with the old-timers. 'Sugar Buns' (yellow), 'Alpine' (white), and 'Peaches and Cream' (bicolor) are three good ones.

• **Supersweet (sh2).** These have loads of sugar. They've been bred to keep longer in the supermarket produce bins, but they lack the flavor and tenderness of the Normal Sugary and Sugary Enhanced types. (In fact, to a lot of folks, they taste more like candy than corn.) 'Skyline' (bicolor), 'Aspen' (white), and 'Krispy King' (yellow) are good home-garden varieties.

Tough Guys Not Allowed

If you grow any of the Supersweet hybrids, keep them separated from both Normal Sugary and Sugary Enhanced types. Otherwise, the two kinds will cross-pollinate and you'll wind up with tough, starchy kernels in both crops.

You can solve the problem in one of two ways: Either plant the two kinds at least 100 feet apart, or sow the seeds of one about 10 days before the other, so they'll bloom at different times. (You can grow Normal Sugary and Sugary Enhanced types close together with no problem.)

Personality Conflicts

Of the three types, Normal Sugary is the easiest to grow. It breezes right through the cool soil and irregular moisture that would knock the other kinds flat. Sugary Enhanced demands soil that's above 60°F at planting time and that stays neither too wet nor too dry.

Supersweet hybrids are downright fuss-budgets. They not only demand separate living quarters, far removed from the two other types, but they also insist on soil temperatures of at least 65°F. Also, they will not put up with any interruption in their steady water supply, and that's that!

Save Me!

For a bumper crop next year, do what Grandma Putt always did: Save the seeds of the plants that perform best for you this year, and then plant them next spring. Do the same every year, and before you know it, you'll have a garden full of plants that you've bred to perform like champs in whatever conditions your climate throws their way. (Remember to save seed that comes true from year to year; look for catalog descriptions that include the OP symbol we talked about in Chapter 2.)

Rainbow on a Cob

If you want some corn that will knock the socks off of the folks at your next corn roast, grow 'Rainbow Inca'. It has multicolored kernels in solid shades of red, yellow, blue, and purple — and even stripes and splotches. It reaches the good-eatin' stage in 85 days and, best of all, it has that old-time, sweet corn taste, even when it grows up where summers are cool.

It Takes All Kinds

JERRY'S FAVORITE Vegetable Varieties

When it comes to home gardens, sweet corn takes the "Most Grown" title hands down. But there are other kinds of corn that are a lot of fun to grow — and fun to use. Often, seed catalogs group them all under "Field Corn". Other times, you'll see them listed separately. And there's a lot of overlapping, because each can be used in different ways. But these are the terms you'll see most often:

• **Dent corn** gets its name because each kernel has an indentation on top. These are some of the best roastin' ears I've ever tasted. Folks also dry 'em out and grind 'em up to make flour, cornmeal, and hominy. **'Nothstine Dent', 'Blue Charge',** and **'Bloody Butcher'** are three of my favorites.

• **Flint corn** is the kind to grow if you're hankerin' to make your own cornmeal. It grinds up into coarser grains than dent types. Try **'Hispanic Pueblo Red', 'Rhode Island White',** or the multicolored **'Fiesta'**.

• **Flour corn** has soft kernels that are easy to grind into flour. It's grown mostly in the Southwest, but if your climate will cooperate, you can impress your friends with some great home-made tortillas. **'Hopi Blue', 'Hopi Pink',** and **'Mandan Bride'** are all winners — and as colorful as all get-out.

• **Indian,** a.k.a. **ornamental, corn** is the kind you see made up into bundles or wreaths around Thanksgiving — often with very high price tags attached. It's no harder to grow than an old-time sweet corn, and varieties like **'Painted Mountain'** and **'Little Jewels'** mature quick enough that you can grow them way up North.

Make Mine Mini

It's easy to have your own steady supply of those baby ears of corn that you see pickled in jars at the supermarket or cooked up in Asian restaurants. First, pick up a variety like 'Candystick', 'Delectable', or 'Bonus'. Then grow the plants as you would sweet or field corn, but space them just 2 to 4 inches apart.

As soon as the first silks appear, harvest the little ears. You'll have a much bigger harvest than with full-size plants, and in a lot less space: The stalks rarely get more than 5 feet tall, and each one produces four or five ears.

Tough Customers

Some years, our corn shucks were thicker and tougher than usual. Then Grandma Putt would look at them and say, "Well, Junie, that means there's a tough winter comin' on." And you know what? There almost always was too!

Say "Nuts" to Squirrels

And to raccoons and birds besides. Just put the toe of a nylon stocking over each ear of corn after the pollen drops. Then touch the top of the stocking with a dab of perfume. It'll keep those rampaging robbers where they belong — away from your crop.

Leave 'em Slippin' and Slidin'

There's nothing that starts a raccoon's heart to pitter-pattering like the sight of a garden full of plump, juicy corn — and there's almost nothing they won't do to get at it. To keep the rascals from eating your hard-earned harvest, fasten sheets of slippery black plastic to your garden fence. Use 36-inch-wide sheets of heavy plastic, clip them on with clothespins so they reach up about 30 inches above the ground, and let the remaining 6 inches spread out below. The coons won't be able to get a handhold on the slick stuff to climb over the fence, and they won't dig under to get in — they'd do that only if they were trapped inside and couldn't get out. Don't try to economize on the plastic — they'll shred the cheap stuff to bits. The high-quality plastic isn't cheap, but it'll last for years. (Mine has hung around the garden for close to 15 years now.)

Check the Oil, Please

Mineral oil can help protect your corn from worm damage. Simply apply a drop to the tip of each ear when the silks begin to brown. Reapply every 5 or 6 days, for a total of three applications per season. This'll keep the worms away, and when you harvest the corn, most of the silk will come off with the husk!

Don't Squash 'em

Some folks like to keep out raccoons by planting squash or pumpkins among the corn, the theory being that coons don't like to get all tangled up in the vines on their way to the corn, so they usually just give up and go away.

There's only one problem with this method: Although it works just fine if you're growing field corn, which stays on the stalks until the end of the summer, when the kernels are good and hard, it's another matter altogether with sweet corn, which you harvest earlier in the season. When *you're* trying to get to your corn, you'll get as tangled up in the vines as the coons would, and probably squash a few squashes in the process.

Don't Peek!

When you're chomping at the bit to chow down on the first corn of the year, it's hard not to pull down the husks and test an ear or two. But don't do it. Those husks are there to protect the corn from bugs and dust and gosh knows what else, and they need to stay right where they are until you have the pot of water boiling on the stove.

You can tell when corn is ready without peeking — just feel the husk to see if it's filled out and rounded. And look closely at the tassels: When the silk is supple and greenish near the top of the husk and dry and brown at the very ends, it's time to put the pot on the stove. For most varieties, that'll be about 20 days after the silks appear.

If You Have to Peek . . .

Press on the kernels starting about 20 days after the silks appear. If the juice is milky, the corn is perfect for pickin'. If it's watery, give it a few more days; and if it's pasty, you're too late, so make the best of it.

SUPER
Growing Secrets

STALKING THE STALKS

After all your corn has found its way to the pot, don't be in too much of a hurry to get the stalks out of the garden. Instead, use them to shade your late crops of peas, beets, and other fall veggies.

When the time comes to pull up the stalks, don't toss them onto the compost pile — burn them, so they don't become a winter home for corn borers and other pesky pests.

A.M. or P.M.?

Since way back before Grandma Putt's day, there's been a raging controversy in corn-loving circles: Some folks say you should pick corn in the early evening, right before dinnertime, and rush it to the pot. Other folks say it tastes sweeter if you pick it in the morning, when its sugar content is highest, then put it in the fridge — still in the husks — until dinnertime.

My advice is to experiment and see which timing suits you better. But whenever you pick your corn, shuck the ears just before you toss 'em in the pot of boiling water, and cook 'em for no more than 4 or 5 minutes after the water comes back to a boil.

Silky Smooth

To get the stubborn silk off your corn, rub a damp paper towel along the ear. The silk will cling to the paper, not to the corn.

Roastin' Ears

As far as I'm concerned, there's nothing in the world that tastes better than corn roasted on a blazing campfire — or on the barbecue grill if you're not out on the open range. And when you're the official cook at a big get-together, there's an even better reason than flavor to roast corn: The eaters do their own shuckin'!

All you have to do is soak the corn in cold water for half an hour. Then bank up the ears — husks and all — right on the coals around the base of the fire. Leave 'em there until the husks are good and charred, then take 'em off the fire and let 'em cool down a little.

How Corny Can You Get?

Sometimes, no matter how much Grandma Putt and I kept after it, a few ears of corn wound up getting over-ripe on the stalks. But Grandma didn't look at that as a loss — to her, those kernels were pure gold for the chowder pot. She had plenty of other uses for corn off-the-cob, too. These were some of her favorites:

- added to quiches and frittatas
- tossed in salads
- added to corn bread
- sautéed with tomatoes, peppers and basil
- dressed with pesto

Popcorn

If the only corn you've ever popped has come from the snack-food aisle of the supermarket, you're in for a treat! And the homegrown stuff isn't hard to come by: Popcorn has exactly the same growing needs as sweet corn. Some kinds take longer to mature, though, so find a variety that has time to grow up in your territory. ('Tom Thumb' is a good old-time New England heirloom that matures early and does well in almost any part of the country.)

A Corny Christmas

Here's an idea for a Christmas present that Santa will wish he'd thought up: Grow a few patches of popcorn, put it in nice-looking jars or bottles, and give 'em to your friends. If you really want to put on the dog, don't stick with plain old yellow. Try 'Ruby Red', 'Shaman's Blue', 'Early Pink', or even 'Calico', with kernels in a whole rainbow of red, blue, yellow, purple, and white.

Taking the Cure

The key to a successful popcorn crop is to cure it so that the kernels have just the right amount of moisture inside — otherwise, they won't pop worth beans. It's really not as hard as you might think. Here's how to cure your crop:

1. Harvest before the first hard frost, when the husks are dry and the kernels are plump, shiny, and well colored.

2. Shuck the ears and spread them out in a cool, well-ventilated place.

3. About a month later, test-pop a few kernels. If they pop up loud and fluffy (the way they should), take all of the kernels off of the cobs and store them in dark, airtight glass jars. If they

sound like they're too pooped to pop, it means they're still too moist inside; so they need more curing time.

4. Test-pop another small batch every few days — you don't want them to get too dry. And quit your complaining: The upside to this chore is that you get a tasty little snack every few days.

Time for a Drink

Popcorn won't pop any better when it's too dry than it does when it's too wet. If you leave your corn too long on the curing rack, dunk the ears in water for 30 seconds and they'll bounce right back. If the kernels are already off of the cob, just add a few drops of water to the jar they're stored in.

Okra *(Abelmoschus esculentus)*

Okra is another of those veggies that have gotten better over the years. Back in Grandma Putt's day, if you didn't live in the steamy South, you could just forget about growing okra. Nowadays, though, there are short-season varieties that can take a lot more cold than the old-timers. I grow a big crop every year.

Home Turf

Okra comes by its heat-craving tendencies naturally: It hails from northern Africa. As long as you can give it some warmth, though, it's a snap to grow. Okra needs full sun and a soil pH that's between 6.0 and 8.0. I till my soil down at least 8 inches, and work in plenty of well-rotted manure. And because the plants get anywhere from 3 to 8 feet tall, I put my crop where it won't shade other sun lovers.

Whether you live in the North or the South, okra needs a steady supply of moisture to produce well. Make sure your plants get at least an inch of water a week.

In Balmy Climates

In mild climates, you can start okra right in the garden when you're sure there are no frosts headed your way and the soil temperature has reached at least 65°F. (If the soil is any cooler than that, the seeds will rot.) Set the seeds 1 inch deep and 3 inches apart. At 65°F, they'll germinate in 7 to 10 days; at 75°F, they'll come up in 5 days.

Up North

In cooler territory, follow this routine:

1. Four weeks before the last frost, start your seeds indoors in individual pots. When the seedlings emerge, move them to bright light and feed them with diluted fish fertilizer.

2. At the same time, lay black plastic over the planting beds to get 'em warmed up.

3. When Jack Frost has been gone for 2 or 3 weeks and the soil temperature is at least 65°F, move your plants to the garden. Dig holes 12 to 16 inches apart, toss a half-shovelful of bonemeal or compost into each one, and set in your plants.

4. Cover the whole bed with floating row covers, or give each plant its own wall o' bottles (see page 300) to keep it toasty warm.

When Inhospitality Is Okay

Corn earworms are partial to okra, so I ward off trouble by keeping my crop away from the corn patch. And by  following the guidelines for good health in Chapter 5, I put out the unwelcome mat for the other problems that sometimes head okra's way: nematodes, blight, and fusarium wilt.

Harvest Early and Often

You have two good reasons to pick okra every day, or at least every other day:

1. The pods taste best when they're small and tender (I like to harvest mine when they're about 2 inches long). If you get busy and don't get to 'em until they're bigger, you just toss 'em on the compost pile. Okra pods are like summer squash: If you let them go too long, they become fibrous and bitter.

2. The more you pick, the more you'll get — the plants will keep churning out replacements until frost bowls the whole crop over.

Don't Let It Hang Around

Like corn and beans, okra tastes best the day you pick it, though it'll keep for a day or so in the fridge.

Admire Me: I'm a Flowering Plant

If the warmest spot in your garden happens to be in a flower bed, you've got the perfect home for okra — it's a close cousin to the hibiscus, and its great-looking foliage and yellow flowers with red centers give any ornamental plant a run for its money.

In Yankee Territory

Folks down South have dozens of kinds of okra to choose from. Up North, though, it pays to do some homework, and find a variety that matures early and has had a good dose of cold tolerance bred into it. Two of the best are 'Blondy' (48 days), a sturdy 3-footer that performs as well in containers as it does when it's in the ground, and 'Burgundy' (55 days), a real eye-catcher with stems, branches, leaf veins, and pods all in a deep shade of burgundy. Talk about your good-looking ornamental edibles!

Caution: Itchy Skin Ahead

Some folks break out in a rash if they rub up against okra leaves, so it's a good idea to wear long sleeves and gloves whenever you work with the plants.

Sweet Potato
(Ipomoea batatas)

Grandma Putt and I sure ate our share of sweet potatoes during the Thanksgiving and Christmas holidays, but we didn't grow our own — our climate just couldn't give them the long spell of heat they need. I grow a great crop now, though, thanks to some new varieties that can handle more of a chilling than the old-timers could.

It'll Slip By You

Sweet potatoes are grown from *slips,* which are rooted sprouts that you can buy at a garden center or from seed catalogs. Home gardeners rarely have to cope with disease problems, but to be on the safe side, make sure the slips you buy are certified to be disease-free.

Sweet and Sour

Sweet potatoes like their soil on the sour side (pH 5.5 to 6.5). They don't need very rich soil, but they do need it to be deep. They also need it to be loose, so the roots can expand easily, and well drained, so they don't rot. I dig down 10 to 12 inches and add plenty of compost. To make sure my taters' home ground stays warm and drains well, I form mounds that are about a foot high, a foot wide, and 3 feet apart. Finally, I lay black plastic mulch over the whole bed for a few weeks before planting day.

It's Not All in the Family

You'd never know it from its name or from its looks, but the sweet potato isn't even related to the regular, or Irish, spud. It's a vine, in fact, and a cousin of the morning glory.

SUPER Growing Secrets

HERE'S MUD IN YOUR EYE!

When transplanting sweet potato slips, you need to dip the roots of each one into a pan of muddy water. This process, called "puddling," covers the roots with a coating that not only prevents them from drying out while being handled, but also ensures direct contact with the soil when they are planted.

Into the Hills

About 2 weeks after the last frost, and when the soil and nighttime air temperatures are both holding steady at 60°F or above, plant your slips. Set them 4 inches deep, 12 to 18 inches apart on top of a low ridge. These ridges shouldn't be more than 6 inches high, spaced about 3 feet apart.

After that, the slips all but take care of themselves, but keep them well watered while they're settling in. Later, unless a long dry spell hits, they don't need watering — in fact, too much moisture will make the roots crack. After about 5 weeks, give them a drink of Compost Tea (see page 351) or fish fertilizer, and that'll keep them happy all season long.

Give 'em the Slip

It's a snap to grow your own slips, either from your first year's harvest or from a neighbor's crop. (Just don't use supermarket sweet taters; they've usually been treated with a chemical that prevents sprouting, and unless you live down South, you can almost bet they won't perform on your turf.) Here's what you should do:

1. Use a sweet potato that's large and firm, and start 30 to 40 days before you expect the last frost.

2. Plant the potato in a pot of sand, or stick toothpicks in its sides and suspend it above a glass that's about half full of water. Either way, about two-thirds of the tuber should stick up above the surface.

3. Put it in a sunny spot that's about 75°F. Before long, it will sprout.

4. When the sprouts are 4 to 6 inches long, gently twist them from the potato and put them in water or damp sand until roots appear — usually just a few days. Plant the slips when the roots are 2 inches long.

SUPER Growing Secrets

BAD NEWS FOR ROOTS

When your sweet potatoes go over the side of their hill, put two layers of newspaper between the plant and the ground so that roots won't form there. By confining the roots to the original planting hole, you'll have a bigger harvest. (You might have to put some rocks on the paper to hold it in place.)

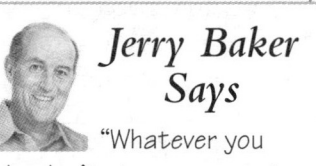

Jerry Baker Says

"Whatever you do, don't give your sweet potatoes any food that's high in nitrogen. Like any root crop, they'll pay you back with a forest full of leaves and a paltry supply of roots."

Taters for Yanks

JERRY'S FAVORITE Vegetable Varieties

When it comes to sweet potatoes, southerners have more good choices than you can shake a fried chicken leg at, but Yankees have to proceed with caution if they want a crop that'll wow the folks at Thanksgiving dinner. Two of the best are **'Georgia Jet'**, which matures in 80 to 90 days and has deep orange flesh with reddish purple skin, and **'Vardaman'**, which takes about 90 days. It has moist, orange flesh, golden skin, and — best of all for folks with small gardens — its vines don't ramble nearly as far as those of other sweet taters. And they're great-looking enough to spruce up an ornamental-edible garden.

Dig 'em, Man

You can start harvesting a few sweet potatoes as soon as they're big enough to eat, but I leave most of mine in the ground until frost kills the vines (frost sweetens the roots). Then I get them up right away. If they're left in the ground longer than a couple of days, they'll start to spoil and will soon be worthless. They'll also spoil in a flash if they're bruised or dented, so dig them very carefully with a garden fork.

Taking the Cure

Before sweet potatoes go into long-term storage, they need to be cured. Spread them out in the sun for a day so the soil dries and you can brush it off easily. Then move them to a hot (80 to 90°F), humid spot that's away from direct sun, and leave them there for a week to 10 days.

After that, wrap each one in newspaper, put them in boxes so that they're not touching each other, and sock them away in a spot that's 55 to 65°F. They'll keep for 6 months or more.

Keep the Flavor

To get the best taste from your home-grown sweet taters, follow these tips:

• Eat tiny tubers and any that are cut or bruised right away — they'll rot quickly in storage.

• Brush the soil off the potatoes before you store them, but don't wash them until just before you cook them; otherwise, they'll spoil.

• Leave your crop in storage for 2 months before you cook 'em up. Sweet potatoes behave the opposite way from corn — after the harvest, their starch begins turning to sugar, and it takes about 2 months to reach peak sweetness.

• Don't nuke 'em — bake 'em in a conventional oven. They'll have a richer flavor than they will if you cook them in the microwave.

BAKED CORN WITH THYME

*This corn casserole is so lip-smackin' good
I could make a whole meal out of it —
and sometimes I do!*

4 SERVINGS

3 cups fresh corn (cut from about
   6 ears)
¾ cup heavy cream
1 teaspoon minced fresh thyme leaves
salt and pepper to taste
4 tablespoons bread crumbs
⅔ cup minced fresh parsley

1. Preheat oven to 350°F. Mix together the corn, cream, thyme, salt, and pepper.

2. Combine the bread crumbs and parsley in a small bowl.

3. Spoon the corn mixture into a baking dish and top with the bread crumb mixture.

4. Bake for 25 minutes, then broil for another 2 minutes, until the bread crumbs are toasted.

SWEET POTATOES IN GINGER HONEY SAUCE

*Every year, this was one of the star attractions
at Grandma Putt's Thanksgiving dinner.
Just make up a batch, taste one forkful,
and you'll know why!*

6 SERVINGS

2 tablespoons minced fresh ginger root
1 teaspoon ground cardamom
2 tablespoons lemon juice
3 tablespoons honey
2 tablespoons butter
salt
1½ cups water
6 cups cubed sweet potatoes

1. In a large sauté pan, simmer the ginger, cardamom, lemon juice, honey, butter, salt, and water for 2 minutes.

2. Add the cubed sweet potatoes and simmer gently until the potatoes are just tender, 3–8 minutes.

3. Serve immediately, and politely accept the applause from your guests.

CRUNCHY OKRA ROUNDS

This crusty and delish dish was my introduction to okra way back when. It's still a great way to make the acquaintance of a taste treat that lots of folks up North shy away from. Try it — you'll like it!

4 TO 6 SERVINGS

2 tablespoons bread crumbs
3 tablespoons grated parmesan cheese
1 tablespoon cornmeal
⅛ teaspoon cayenne
¼ teaspoon salt
3 cups okra
¼ cup olive oil
2 garlic cloves, minced

1. Mix the bread crumbs, cheese, cornmeal, cayenne, and salt.

2. Add the okra and stir to coat.

3. Heat the olive oil, and sauté the okra and garlic for 5–10 minutes or until most of the roping has disappeared, and the okra is tender. Serve immediately.

HAPPY HARVEST SOUP

That was Grandma Putt's name for this soup that combines the two shining stars of American gardendom: corn and tomatoes. Celebrate your first harvest by making a big pot with fresh-from-the-garden veggies.

6 TO 8 SERVINGS

1 tablespoon vegetable oil
1 pound ground beef
3 cups corn kernels
3 cups diced tomatoes
2 cups water or beef broth
1 cup diced onion
1 garlic clove, minced
2 tablespoons minced fresh basil or 2 teaspoons dried
1½ tablespoons fresh thyme or 1½ teaspoon dried
1½ teaspoons crumbled fresh rosemary or ½ teaspoon dried
3–4 tablespoons minced fresh parsley
salt and pepper

1. In a large soup pot, heat the vegetable oil, and brown the ground beef, breaking it up with a spoon.

2. Drain off all the fat.

3. Add the remaining ingredients and simmer for 30 minutes.

4. Season to taste with salt and pepper. Serve hot.

PERENNIAL VEGETABLES

Asparagus • Rhubarb

Most of Grandma Putt's vegetables marched around her garden like a band on a football field. She took her crop rotation seriously, so every year, her plants would pop their heads up in a different place. There were some exceptions, though: her perennial crops.

Eat It Again, Sam

Most of the plants folks eat are annuals — that is, they begin and end their lives in a single growing season. But rhubarb, asparagus, and some other mighty tasty veggies will live on for years — even decades — if you take good care of them. The four most important things to remember are:

1. Give it some thought. With these guys, unlike tomatoes and beans, you probably won't want to try out a new variety every year. So shop around until you find one that's been bred to perform well in your climate. Find out what varieties your gardening friends grow and ask for a taste. Or look for a farm stand that sells its own fresh asparagus or rhubarb — ask what kind it is and where you can get some for your garden.

2. Buy the best. When a plant is going to be with you for as long as asparagus and rhubarb, you want to head off any problems *before* they start. Get your roots from a reputable catalog company, the best garden center within driving distance, or a gardening friend who has a greener thumb than anyone else you know.

3. Plan before you plant. Once they're settled in and are growing well, rhubarb and asparagus don't like to be disturbed. Give these guys a spot where you'll enjoy each other's company for the next 10 to 20 years.

4. Get it right the first time. You won't have a chance to till this bed every year and fill it up with new supplies of manure and compost. So make sure you have the soil *exactly* the way your plants like it before you put them in the ground.

Asparagus *(Asparagus officinalis)*

Grandma Putt used to say that she couldn't think of a better investment than a bed of asparagus, and I agree with her 100 percent! It takes more work at the beginning than most other veggies need and, as with most solid, long-term investments, you have to wait a while to reap your reward. But once the profits start rollin' in, they'll keep you in blue-chip eatin' for a long time to come.

Getting Ready

Because your asparagus will be on the scene for a long time, it's best to set it off from the main veggie plot. I put mine in a bed of its own, but a spot on the very edge of the garden works, too. Asparagus will put up with partial shade, but it offers up its best harvests in full sun. Just bear in mind that the plants get tall, so give them a home where they won't shade other sun lovers.

On the Double

For the main part of my vegetable garden, I don't bother with full-scale double-digging; but for new asparagus beds and rhubarb, too, I pull out all of the stops. In the fall, I get the soil good and loose to at least 16 inches deep, following the procedure on page 55. While I'm digging, I work in about a 6-inch layer of horse manure, along with big doses of Epsom salts, bonemeal, and wood ashes. And because asparagus is just about the most finicky plant I know when it comes to weeds, I remove any trace of a living plant I find as I am digging.

There's no doubt about it: Double-digging is a lot of work; but, believe me, for perennial veggies, it's worth the effort!

SUPER Growing Secrets

DO THE NUMBERS

Be sure to have your soil's pH tested before you plant your asparagus. A pH of 7.0 is its dream, but it will grow well in anything from 6.5 to 7.5. A reading below 6.0 can spell trouble!

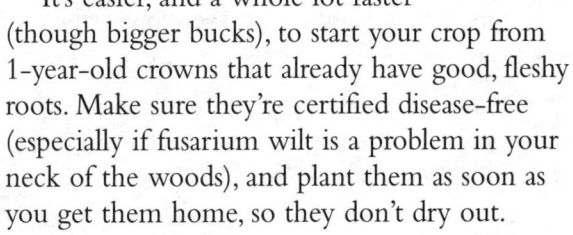

SUPER Growing Secrets

SOAK FIRST, PLANT LATER

Newly purchased asparagus roots should be disinfected by soaking them in a solution of 1 cup of regular bleach and 1 gallon of warm water before planting.

The Asparagus Crown Affair

Some folks start their asparagus from seed, but to my way of thinking, it's not worth it. For one thing, you have to sow the seeds indoors 3 months before you intend to move the plants to the garden. For another, it tacks a whole year onto the time you have to wait for your first harvest.

It's easier, and a whole lot faster (though bigger bucks), to start your crop from 1-year-old crowns that already have good, fleshy roots. Make sure they're certified disease-free (especially if fusarium wilt is a problem in your neck of the woods), and plant them as soon as you get them home, so they don't dry out.

The Good New Days

Back in Grandma Putt's time, all asparagus was open-pollinated. Nowadays, though, there are two choices:

• **Open-pollinated varieties** produce male flowers on one plant and female flowers on another, and you need both kinds. Only the females produce seeds, in the form of bright red berries, every fall. They're pretty, but they can result in crossbreeding and weak volunteer seedlings that crowd the bed and rob nourishment from the parent plants. You also need twice as many plants as you do with hybrids, because the females make seeds but no spears.

Until recently, 'Mary Washington' was the asparagus to end all asparagus. But nowadays, most folks who grow open-pollinated types opt for her off-spring, such as 'Viking', 'Waltham', and 'UC 157' (a heat-tolerant variety developed at the University of California).

• **The Jersey hybrids** are a strain of all-male plants developed by scientists at Rutgers University, in New Jersey. They produce three to four times as many spears as the old, open-pollinated kinds. And they stand right up and say "Boo" to asparagus rust, fusarium crown and root rots, and cercospora leaf spot. 'Jersey Giant' was the first of the series, and it grows especially well in colder parts of the country. 'Jersey King' and 'Jersey Knight' both perform like troupers in warmer territory.

A Daffy Cue

In most parts of the country, asparagus-planting time is when the daffodils start to bloom, or, to be more precise, in early spring, about 4 weeks before the last expected frost, when the soil temperature has reached about 50°F. (In warmer territory, though, you can plant asparagus in fall or winter.) Here's how to go about it:

1. Dig a hole that's 12 inches deep for an open-pollinated asparagus and 6 inches for one of the Jersey bunch. Put about 1 inch of compost into the hole and, for good measure, toss in a banana peel or two to give the plant a potassium boost. No matter which type you're planting, set the crowns about 18 inches apart. If you're planting in rows, keep them 4 feet apart — no asparagus likes to be crowded.

2. Soak the crowns in Compost Tea (see page 351) for 15 minutes. Then put one crown into each hole, spread the roots evenly, and cover the crown with 2 inches of soil. As the spears grow, gradually fill up the hole, but don't cover any foliage. In later years, the crowns will work their way up toward the surface.

3. Give the new plants 1 to 2 inches of water a week. After that, don't even bother thinking about H_2O unless droughtlike conditions hit your neck of the woods. Asparagus roots go down deep for moisture.

A Whale of an Appetite

Asparagus has a whale-sized appetite. Give your plants regular snacks of compost and well-rotted manure throughout the growing season. Once a year, in early spring or late fall, spread a dry organic fertilizer (10-10-10 equivalent), at a rate of 1½ cups per 10 feet of row, over the bed. Hoe out any weeds or volunteer seedlings that could compete for the food (but be careful not to damage the roots of your plants). Around midsummer, mulch with chopped leaves, salt hay, or straw to keep the soil cool and prevent weeds from moving in.

Parsley, Please

Grandma Putt used to plant parsley borders around her asparagus beds. The parsley didn't take enough nutrients from the soil to bother the asparagus, and both plants seemed to grow better together than they did separately.

Into the Drink

Asparagus beetles got their name for a good reason: They *love* those tender spears. If good-guy bugs don't home in on your patch fast enough to gobble up all the beetles, here's what to do: Go through the patch every day with a pan of almost boiling water and shake the beetles off the shoots into the drink.

Hold Your Horses!

With asparagus, there's no such thing as instant gratification. A few spears will sprout up the first year you plant your crop, but whatever you do, don't cut them: They need to grow up into ferns that will make food for the roots to grow on. Leave the foliage in place until it dies back; even when it's yellow (and adding some great-looking color to the fall landscape), it's still sending good chow to the roots.

Delayed Gratification

The second spring after you plant (or the third, if you've started your plants from seed), you can harvest a few spears, but no more than two or three per plant. Take only the ones that are 6 to 8 inches tall and at least the size of your finger — about ⅜ inch in diameter — and only for a period of 2 weeks. The third spring, you can pick as many finger-sized spears as you want for 2 to 4 weeks.

After that, let 'er rip, more or less. Keep letting the skinny spears grow up into ferns, but take all of the bigger ones you want until the plants start producing mostly small spears with loose, open tips. Then stop. That will probably happen at about the time your first pea crop comes in. Check the plants every day during harvest season, so you don't miss any.

SUPER Growing Secrets

A WEED BY ANY OTHER NAME

As far as asparagus is concerned, any plant that invades its turf — therefore, its food supply — is a weed. Period! That includes tomatoes, which lots of folks plant close to their asparagus patch because a chemical in tomatoes, solanine, repels asparagus beetles. I've found, though, that if asparagus beetles show up in enough numbers to damage my plants, their natural enemies make a beeline for the bed and polish off those pesky pests before I can say "Where's the spray gun?"

The Bedtime Story

After the ferns turn brown and brittle, cut them back and burn them, or have them hauled away. Don't throw them onto the compost pile — they could be a wintertime nest for asparagus-beetle eggs. Then test your soil's pH again to make sure nothing's gotten it out of kilter — if it has, add lime to raise the pH or sulfur to lower it (see pages 72–73). Then spread at least an inch of compost or well-rotted manure over the bed and top it off with about 6 inches of chopped leaves or straw.

SUPER Growing Secrets

ROLL OUT THE BARREL

Once a bed reaches the active harvest stage, give your crop a preseason warm-up so you can get pickin' earlier. Just put a wooden barrel over each plant and pile hot compost or fresh manure around it. Be sure the stuff touches only the barrel and not the plants — it'll give them a nasty burn. (This trick works just as well with rhubarb.)

Use Some Force

If you can never get enough fresh asparagus (and who can?), try forcing a crop to chow down on during the winter. You can buy new crowns just for this purpose. Otherwise, wait until your bed is well established and needs some thinning.

In the fall, before the ground freezes hard, dig up some roots that are at least 3 years old. Replant them in boxes or pails of potting soil mixed with compost, and put them in a shed or garage for several weeks. Then move them to a spot where the temperature is 60 to 65°F (it can be either light or dark — it doesn't matter).

Water the plants once a week, but don't let the soil get waterlogged. When spears start appearing, snap them off. You won't have enough to feed the Seventh Army, but you'll be able to keep a couple of people in asparagus heaven for a few dreary winter weeks.

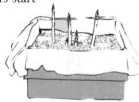

Snap or Slice?

I like to harvest asparagus spears by bending them over and snapping them off — they break naturally at just the point where the tough part ends and the tender, good-eating part begins. If you prefer to cut yours, use a sharp knife and be careful not to damage any nearby spears.

Rhubarb *(Rheum × cultorum)*

Just thinking about rhubarb — more than any other vegetable — takes me straight back to my days in Grandma Putt's garden. There's an old-timey, comforting feeling about it that even fresh-from-the-garden corn and tomatoes can't quite match. Maybe it has something to do with all those pies and cobblers Grandma used to make. Whatever it is, it's enough to make me keep a big patch of rhubarb growing in my garden today — and to cook it up just the way she did.

A No-Brainer

With most veggies, you can start your crop from either seeds or transplants. But rhubarb doesn't give you a choice, unless you just want to experiment and see what comes up: All the varieties grown today are hybrids that do not come true from seeds. (That's what the "×" signifies in rhubarb's scientific moniker.) You can sometimes find started rhubarb plants in containers, but most nurseries and catalogs offer crowns or divisions (clumps of roots, each clump with one or more "eyes," or buds).

Separate Quarters

A happy clump of rhubarb will give you its all for 20 years or more, so give it a long-term lease in a bed of its own in full sun or partial shade with fertile, well-drained soil. (Any crowns that are planted in heavy clay soil will rot faster than you can yell "Help! I'm drowning!")

When it comes to pH, rhubarb is one of the least finicky plants I know: It prefers 6.0 to 6.8, but it will produce in a pH as low as 5.3. Double-dig the beds in the fall and make them big — rhubarb has hungry roots, and they spread several feet out and several feet deep. Then work in half a bushel or so of compost and well-rotted manure for each plant.

Cool Characters

Rhubarb does its best work where winter temperatures go below 40°F and the summer ones average 75°F. When the mercury climbs above 80°F, the plants start churning out 5-foot seed stalks. They're mighty pretty to look at, with scads of little greenish white flowers, but once they arrive on the scene, you can kiss your food crop goodbye for the year.

SUPER Growing Secrets

GROWER'S CHOICE

When it comes to flavor, if you've tasted one rhubarb, you've tasted them all. The only real difference is in the color of the leaf stems: They come in pink, red, or green. Most varieties grow well in any part of the country. But if you live in a warm, dry region, you'll have the most success with **'Cherry Giant'**, which is kicked into dormancy by drought, not cold.

Get Growing

Getting your rhubarb crop off and running is a simple process. Here's how it's done:

Step 1. In the early spring (fall in mild climates), buy crowns that are about the size of your fist and have at least two buds. Keep the crowns in a cool place until you have time to plant them; otherwise, they'll sprout, and you don't want them to just yet.

Step 2. If you're planting more than one crown, dig a trench that's at least 2 feet across and just as deep. For a single one, dig a hole that's at least 2 feet in diameter and the same depth. Then refill the trench or hole partway with a 50-50 mixture of soil and compost or well-rotted manure. Space plants at least 3 feet apart.

Step 3. For each plant, make a mound of soil, then set the crown on top of it, and spread the roots over the sides. Add the rest of the soil, so that the buds are 1 to 2 inches below the surface, and firm it lightly. (Set the crowns a little deeper if your soil is sandy.)

Step 4. When the first shoots come up, mulch with compost, chopped leaves, or grass clippings, and make sure the new plants get at least an inch of water a week.

Step 5. Later in the summer, when seed stalks start popping up, clip them off right away. They'll be easy to spot: They're tall, thick, and round — very different from the edible leaf stalks. Keep on top of this job — once a plant starts producing seed stalks, it slacks off in the edible-leaf-stalk department, and you don't need slackers!

Step 6. After the plants have died back in late fall, top-dress the bed with compost or well-rotted manure. Repeat the process in spring, and then every fall and spring after that.

Step 7. Annually, in spring and fall, give your plants a dose of Grandma Putt's Robust Rhubarb Tonic (see page 355).

When Do We Eat?

Like asparagus, rhubarb is just for show in the first year of its garden life — it needs all its leaf stalks, a.k.a. "petioles", to make food for the roots. Keep on clipping off those flower stalks, though.

In early spring of the second year, you can harvest a few leaf stalks that get about as thick as your finger, but leave most of them on the plant. From the third year on, take as many finger-sized stalks as you want, and eat hearty.

Pie Time

At leaf-stalk-picking time, grab each one firmly near its base, and pull it off with a slight twisting motion. Don't cut the stalks: The stubs that stay behind will bleed, thereby inviting rot to drop in and polish off your plants.

I generally harvest rhubarb in pie-sized portions over a period of 4 to 8 weeks. But when I want enough to make pies for a family reunion or to put by for the winter, I go ahead and harvest the whole shebang. Sometimes in the fall, if it's cool and rainy, the plants send up a second round of stalks.

All Stalks on Deck

Rhubarb's good looks make it a natural on a deck or patio. Use a container that's at least 24 inches wide and deep and has good drainage. (A whiskey barrel cut in half with holes drilled in the bottom is great.) Fill it with a half-and-half mixture of high-quality potting soil and compost or well-rotted manure. Plant your crowns per my directions, water often and give the plants a drink of Compost Tea (see page 351) every 2 weeks during the growing season. That's all there is to it!

ROBUST RHUBARB TONIC

To get her rhubarb growing, Grandma Putt made up a batch of this Tonic.

1 tbsp. of Epsom salts
1 cup of tea
vegetable (nonmeat) table scraps (as much as you have on hand)
1 quart of water

Mash all of these ingredients together until it's like a slurry, and then pour the mushy mix over your plants in both spring and fall. Then watch 'em grow like the dickens!

Caution

Rhubarb's roots, leaves, and flower stalks are lethal to humans. So don't ever eat anything but the leaf stalks!

The Picture of Health

The only disease known to attack rhubarb is phytophthora crown rot, which does exactly what its name implies.

There is no cure — if your plants come down with it, dig 'em up and destroy 'em. It's a snap to keep it out of your territory, though: Just give your crop well-drained soil, apply my All-Season Clean-Up Tonic every 2 weeks (see page 349) and, to be extra safe, harvest stalks by breaking, not cutting, them.

Divide and Conquer

Once it settles in, rhubarb takes off like a freight train; after 5 years, a bed can get pretty crowded. You'll know when things are tight when the plants start sending up smaller, thinner leaf stalks.

To get them back on track, dig up the plants in late fall or early spring, when they're dormant. With a knife or a spade, cut the crown into pieces about the size of a doughnut (make sure each piece has at least one bud) and replant them, or give some to gardening friends and neighbors. If you can't plant your divisions right away (or find good homes for them), put them in the fridge. Then on plantin' day, soak them in a mixture of 1 teaspoon of Epsom salts in a pint of weak tea for 6 hours to get them plumped up and rarin' to grow.

Dr. Rhubarb Is In

Not only does rhubarb hardly ever get sick, but it can also help other plants stay healthy. To keep clubroot out of your cabbage patch, stick a few slices of rhubarb stalk into the soil near the roots of each cabbage at planting time. The oxalic acid in the rhubarb will say "Scram" to any clubroot fungus that's nervy enough to invade your cabbage's territory.

The Hit Squad

When it comes to unwelcome visitors, rhubarb is about as trouble-free as a plant can get. Mulching to keep weeds at bay will discourage two of its peskiest pests, the rhubarb curculio and the potato stem borer. Mites, which may gang up on the leaves in hot, dry climates, are usually kept under control by their natural predators: lacewings, ladybugs, and predatory thrips (all of which will show up if you don't use pesticides). If the good guys don't appear on the horizon soon enough, just send the mites packing with a spray from the garden hose.

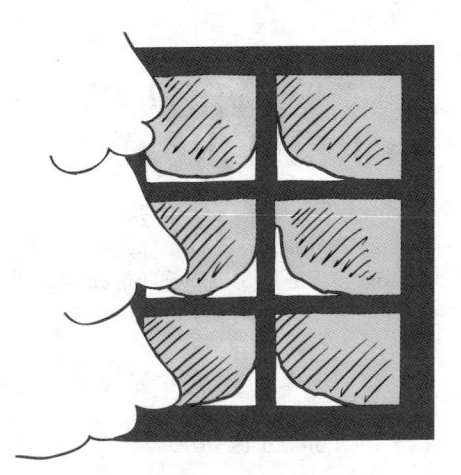

Carrying On

If that hankering for fresh rhubarb just never goes away, grow yourself a winter crop indoors. In the fall, any time after the first heavy frosts, dig up a few 2-year-old crowns with as much of the root clump as you can get. Pot each crown in a roomy container filled with a mixture of good potting soil and compost, then store it in a cold, dark place.

About a month before you want it (say, for holiday pies), move the pots to a dark spot where the temperature is about 60°F. Keep the soil moist. Just in time to start your pie baking, you'll have about 2 pounds of stalks from each crown. (Be forewarned, though: The red stalks will have small, crinkled yellow leaves on top, not the big green ones you're used to seeing outdoors.)

Come spring, move the plants back to the garden. It will take them a year to recover from their winter . . . um . . . vacation, but after that, they'll offer up as big a harvest as they did before they ever got sidetracked.

Rhubarbsicles

Want to give the kids a summertime treat you can bet they've never thought of? Make up a batch of rhubarbsicles. Here's what you'll need:

2½ pounds of rhubarb stalks
2 quarts of water
about 1 cup of sugar

ABOUT 16 SERVINGS

1. Wash and trim the rhubarb stalks, and cut them into 4-inch pieces. (Tender red stalks with few fibers work best.)

2. Put the pieces in a pan with the water and bring just to a boil.

3. Press the mixture through a jelly bag, then strain it through damp cheesecloth.

4. Measure the rhubarb juice, and add ½ cup of sugar per quart of juice.

5. Pour the juice into paper cup or Popsicle molds, and pop 'em in the freezer.

6. When the liquid is about half frozen, insert sticks.

For variations on the theme, mix the rhubarb juice with apple or strawberry juice.

GRILLED ASPARAGUS

Serve this up at your next barbecue, and I guarantee you'll be voted Outdoor Chef of the Year! Note: Asparagus cooks better on a cooler fire, so if you are grilling several things, do the asparagus last.

4 SERVINGS

    1 bunch fresh asparagus
    ½ cup olive oil
       salt and freshly ground pepper

1. In a small bowl, mix the olive oil and salt and pepper to taste, and pour into a wide, shallow dish.

2. Trim the hard butt ends off the asparagus and roll them in the oil mixture, coating them well.

3. Place the asparagus on the grill, across the grill pattern, so the stalks don't fall in.

4. Cook for about 7 minutes, rolling them slowly but continuously across the surface of the grill. Once you've rolled all of them across, pick up the first in line and place it back at the starting point.

5. Repeat the process with each stalk. This ensures that they cook evenly, and gives you an opportunity to see how well they're doing. When the stalks start to sag limply when you pick them up, they're done. The tips, the most tender parts, will singe a tad. That's okay: You want the outside to be crisp, but take care that they don't burn.

STRAWBERRY-RHUBARB PIE

The very first year I went to live with her, Grandma Putt won a blue ribbon for this pie at our county fair. Try it for yourself, and you'll know how smart those judges were!

8 SERVINGS

    2 9-inch piecrusts, unbaked
    ¾ cup brown sugar
    ½ cup granulated sugar
    2 tablespoons flour
    1 egg
       lemon zest
    2 cups fresh strawberries, sliced
    2 cups raw rhubarb, cut into ¼-inch
       pieces

1. Preheat oven to 375°F.

2. Place one piecrust in a 9-inch pie plate.

3. Combine brown sugar, granulated sugar, flour, egg, and lemon zest.

4. Toss lightly with the fruit and fill the pie shell.

5. Cover with top crust; bake 50 minutes.

CREAM OF ASPARAGUS SOUP

If you want to earn a reputation as the greatest host in town, invite the crowd over for a big pot of this super soup.

6 SERVINGS

2 tablespoons butter
2 cups sliced leeks
6 cups diced asparagus stems
1 quart chicken broth
1 cup light cream
2 tablespoons grated parmesan cheese
¼ teaspoon white pepper
salt
nutmeg

1. Melt butter in a large soup pot and sauté leeks until they're limp, 3–5 minutes.

2. Add asparagus and chicken broth, and simmer until the asparagus is tender, 10–15 minutes.

3. Cool slightly, purée in a blender, and reheat.

4. Add cream, parmesan cheese, pepper, and salt and nutmeg to taste. Serve hot.

TOMATO RHUBARB SAUCE

Some folks seem to think that rhubarb wears a sign saying "For Dessert Only." Well, if you're one of them, just make up a batch of this sauce and spoon it over chicken or fish. It'll give you a whole new slant on this versatile fruit!

6 SERVINGS

3 tablespoons butter
2 cups diced tomatoes
4 cups diced rhubarb
1 cup orange juice
4 tablespoons brown sugar
½ teaspoon ground rosemary

1. Melt the butter in a large sauté pan.

2. Add all the ingredients and simmer until rhubarb is soft, 10–15 minutes.

3. Serve with fish or chicken, or use as an omelet filling.

CHAPTER 8

Jerry's Terrific Tonics

Throughout this book, you've come across a bushel basketful of Grandma Putt's old-time mixers, fixers, and elixirs, and a boatload of my terrific tonics using common household products like beer, cola, and mouthwash. Well, here's where I let you in on the secrets behind how my tonics work, and gather them together in one handy-dandy reference place.

The Inside Scoop

- **Ammonia.** I like to call it a "thunderstorm in a bottle." It's a readily available source of nitrogen that helps encourage leafy plant growth. The ammonia you buy at the grocery store is a diluted solution of ammonium hydroxide, and it's very potent stuff. Always dilute it as specified in my tonic recipes, or you'll burn your plants. It can burn you, too, so always wear gloves when you're mixing it into tonics and be sure not to splash any into your eyes. Never, ever combine ammonia with vinegar or bleach (or products containing bleach) because the resulting chemical reaction releases fumes that can be toxic.

- **Antiseptic mouthwash.** It does the same thing in your garden that it does in your mouth — wipes out those disease germs before they have a chance to do their dastardly deeds.

- **Beer.** Whether it's cheap stuff from the convenience store, or a highfalutin microbrew from the fanciest tavern in town, beer is a miracle worker. In fact, I think of it as the "captain" of my tonic team! It acts as an enzyme activator to help release the nutrients that are locked in the soil. It also wakes up and energizes organic activity.

- **Cola.** The sugar in my favorite carbonated drink helps feed the good bacteria that condition your soil. Skip the diet brands — artificial sweeteners don't work like the real thing.

- **Epsom salts.** This terrific stuff improves the root structure of your vegetable plants — and, after all, healthy roots mean healthy, productive plants.

- **Sugar/Molasses/Corn Syrup.** These sugar sources stimulate chlorophyll formation in plants and help feed the good soil bacteria.

- **Liquid dish soap.** This occupant of your kitchen sink helps soften soil and removes dirt and pollution on your vegetable plants so that osmosis and photosynthesis can occur more easily. It also sends bugs packing — they hate the taste (especially of the lemon-scented types) and will soon be doing the "Green Apple Shuffle" to the bug bathroom.

- **Tea.** The tannic acid in tea helps plants digest their food faster. And the sooner the food gets to work, the sooner you can start raking in the harvest!

- **Tobacco.** This stuff poisons bugs when they ingest it, or when they simply come into contact with it. It does the same thing to some of the germs that cause plant diseases.

- **Urine.** Whether it comes from your dog, your baby, or a lion at the local zoo, the powerful — and frightening — smell of this stuff will keep critters like deer and gophers from helping themselves to your harvest.

ALL-AROUND DISEASE DEFENSE TONIC

Wet, rainy weather can mean an outbreak of fungus in your garden, especially in late winter and early spring. Keep your outdoor green scene happy and healthy with this elixir.

1 cup of chamomile tea
1 tsp. of liquid dish soap
½ tsp. of vegetable oil
½ tsp. of peppermint oil
1 gal. of warm water

Mix all of the ingredients together in a bucket. Mist-spray your plants every week or so before the really hot weather (75°F or higher) sets in. This elixir is strong stuff, so test it on a few leaves before completely spraying any plant. (For related text, see page 94.)

ALL-PURPOSE DANDELION CURE

Brew up this tea to cure whatever ails you — or to keep away anything that might.

2 tsp. of fresh dandelion roots and leaves
½ cup of spring water

Put the roots and leaves in the water. Bring the water to a boil, then remove the pan from the heat and let the mix steep for 15 minutes. Make a cup three times a day. (For related text, see page 80.)

ALL-PURPOSE ORGANIC FERTILIZER

This super stuff is the best friend any of your veggie plants ever had.

5 parts seaweed meal
3 parts granite dust
1 part dehydrated manure
1 part bonemeal

Work this fertilizer into the soil when you plant, then side-dress your plants with it 2 or 3 more times during the season. Be sure to always water plants *after fertilizing*. (For related text, see page 248.)

ALL-PURPOSE PEST PREVENTION POTION

Gophers, moles, skunks, possums, and just about any other critter I can think of will turn tail and run when they get a whiff of this potion.

1 cup of ammonia
½ cup of liquid dish soap
½ cup of urine
¼ cup castor oil

Mix all in a 20 gallon hose-end sprayer and thoroughly saturate animal runs and burrows. (For related text, see page 128.)

ALL-PURPOSE VARMINT REPELLENT

2 eggs
2 cloves of garlic
2 tbsp. of hot chile pepper
2 tbsp. of ammonia
2 cups of hot water

Mix these ingredients, let the mixture sit for 3 or 4 days, then paint it on fences, trellises, and wherever else unwanted varmints are venturing. (For related text, see page 128.)

ALL-SEASON CLEAN-UP TONIC

1 cup of liquid dish soap
1 cup of antiseptic mouthwash
1 cup of Tobacco Tea★

Mix these ingredients in a 20 gallon hose-end sprayer, and give your garden a good shower. Do this every 2 weeks during the growing season. (For related text, see page 82.)

★For recipe, see page 358.

ALL-SEASON GREEN-UP TONIC

1 can of beer
1 cup of ammonia
½ cup of liquid dish soap
½ cup of liquid lawn food
½ cup of molasses or clear corn syrup

Mix these ingredients in your 20 gallon hose-end sprayer. Feed the garden with this mixture 10 days after planting and then every 3 weeks during the growing season. (For related text, see page 47.)

APHID ANTIDOTE

To keep aphids and other pests out of your yard, mix up a batch of this amazing antidote:

2 medium cloves of garlic, chopped fine
1 small onion, chopped fine
1 tbsp. of liquid dish soap
2 cups of water

Put all the ingredients in a blender and blend on high. Then, strain out the pulp. Pour the liquid into a handheld mist sprayer, and apply liberally at the very first sign of aphid trouble. (For related text, see page 104.)

BAKING SODA SPRAY

1 tbsp. of baking soda
2 tbsp. of baby shampoo

Mix these ingredients in 1 gallon of warm water, and mist spray your plants lightly once a week. (For related text, see page 99.)

BEDTIME SNACK

25 lbs. of gypsum
10 lbs. of natural organic garden food (either 4–12–4 or 5–10–5)
 5 lbs. of bonemeal

Mix these ingredients together, then apply them to every 100 square feet of soil with your handheld broadcast spreader. Work them into the soil, and cover with a thick blanket of leaves and straw. Then overspray with Sleepytime Tonic. (For related text, see page 87.)

BEETLE JUICE

This stuff will stop any kind of pesky beetle in its tracks.

½ cup of beetles
2 cups of water

Collect ½ cup of beetles and whirl 'em up in the blender with 2 cups of water. Strain the liquid through cheesecloth. Pour about ¼ cup into a 1-gallon handheld sprayer and fill the rest of the jar with water. Drench the soil around new plants to keep the beetles from getting started. If they're already on the scene, spray your plants from top to bottom, and make sure you coat both sides of the leaves. If you have any extra juice, freeze it right away before bacteria can get a toehold. (Be sure to label it clearly!) (For related text, see page 282.)

CABBAGE WORM WIPE-OUT TONIC

Whip up a batch of this terrific Tonic for all your cabbage family plants.

1 cup of flour
2 tbsp. of cayenne pepper

Mix the ingredients together, and sprinkle the results on young cabbage family plants. The flour swells up inside the worms and bursts their insides, while the hot pepper keeps other critters away. (For related text, see page 204.)

. . . .

COMPOST FEEDER TONIC

Just like your plants, your compost pile needs a boost now and then. Once a month, spray it with this Tonic.

1 can of beer
1 cup of liquid dish soap
1 can of regular cola
   (not diet)

Mix these ingredients in the jar of your 20 gallon hose-end sprayer and apply generously. (For related text, see page 64.)

COMPOST TEA

Compost tea delivers a well-balanced supply of all the important nutrients and fends off diseases at the same time.

1½ gal. of fresh compost
4½ gal. of warm water

Scoop the compost into a burlap sack, tie it closed, and put it in a 5-gallon bucket with the water. Cover and let steep for 3 to 7 days. Pour the solution into a watering can or misting bottle, and spritz your plants with it every 2 to 3 weeks. *Note:* To make manure tea (another wonder drink) substitute 1½ gallons of well-cured manure for the compost. (For related text, see page 100.)

. . . .

CONTAINER GARDEN BOOSTER MIX

When it's time to plant your container veggies, add this miracle food to a half-and-half mixture of good commercial potting soil and compost. You'll get a harvest that will put many an in-ground plot to shame!

4 eggshells (dried and crushed to powder) per peck of soil
½ cup of Epsom salts
¼ cup of coffee grounds (rinsed clean)
1 tbsp. of instant tea granules

Mix the ingredients in well. Then plant away! (For related text, see page 31.)

DAMPING-OFF PREVENTION TONIC

4 tsp. of chamomile tea
1 tsp. of liquid dish soap

Mix these ingredients in 1 quart of boiling water. Let steep for at least an hour (the stronger the better), strain, then cool. Mist spray your seedlings with this Tonic as soon as their little heads appear above the soil. (For related text, see page 42.)

. . . .

DOG-B-GONE TONIC

Keep dogs out by dousing your garden with this spicy Tonic.

2 cloves of garlic
2 small onions
1 jalapeño pepper
1 tbsp. of cayenne pepper
1 tbsp. of Tabasco sauce
1 tbsp. of chile powder
1 tbsp. of liquid dish soap
1 qt. of warm water

Chop the garlic, onions, and pepper fine, and then combine with the rest of the ingredients. Let the mixture sit for 24 hours, strain it through old panty hose, then sprinkle it on any areas where dogs are a problem. (For related text, see page 129.)

FUNGUS FIGHTER TONIC

Molasses is great for fighting fungus in your garden. So at the first sign of trouble, mix up a batch of this brew.

½ cup of molasses
½ cup of powdered milk
1 tsp. of baking soda
1 gal. of warm water

Mix the molasses, powdered milk, and baking soda into a paste. Place the mixture into the toe of an old stocking, and steep it in a gallon of warm water for several hours. Then strain, and spray on your garden every 2 weeks throughout the growing season. (For related text, see page 91.)

. . . .

GARDEN CURE-ALL TONIC

4 cloves of garlic
1 small onion
1 small jalapeño pepper
1 tsp. of Murphy's Oil Soap
1 tsp. of vegetable oil
1 qt. of warm water

Pulverize the garlic, onion, and pepper in a blender, and let them steep in a quart of warm water for 2 hours. Strain the mixture, and further dilute the liquid with three parts of warm water. Add the Murphy's Oil Soap and vegetable oil. Mist-spray your plants several times a week. (For related text, see page 107.)

GARLIC PEST REPELLENT

Garlic is not only a great insect repellent, but it's also an amazing antibiotic for sickly plants.

several large cloves of garlic
mineral oil
2 tsp. of liquid dish soap
1 pint of warm water

Mince the garlic, and soak it in mineral oil overnight. The next day, strain the mixture, and then mix 2 tsp. of the oil and the liquid dish soap in the water. Put this in your 20 gallon hose-end sprayer, and fill the balance of the jar with warm water. Spray every 2 weeks in the evening. (For related text, see page 116.)

HAPPY HERB TONIC

Grandma Putt kept her herbs healthy and chipper with this nifty elixir.

1 cup of tea
½ tbsp. of bourbon
½ tbsp. of ammonia
½ tbsp. of hydrogen peroxide
1 gal. of warm water

Mix all of the ingredients together in a bucket. Feed your herb plants with it every 6 weeks throughout the growing season. (For related text, see page 140.)

HOT BUG BREW

3 hot green peppers (canned or fresh)
3 medium cloves of garlic
1 small onion
1 tbsp. of liquid dish soap
3 cups of water

Purée the peppers, garlic, and onion in a blender. Pour the purée into a jar, and add the dish soap and water. Let stand for 24 hours. Then strain out the pulp, and use a handheld sprayer to apply the remaining liquid to bug-infested plants, making sure to thoroughly coat the tops and undersides of all the leaves. (For related text, see page 106.)

HURRY-UP-THE-HARVEST TONIC

When I know Old Man Winter is waiting in the wings and my plants are still chock-full of unripe veggies, I give the garden a big drink of my Hurry-Up-the-Harvest Tonic.

1 cup of apple juice
½ cup of ammonia
½ cup of baby shampoo

Mix these ingredients in your 20 gallon hose-end sprayer jar, filling the balance of the jar with warm water. Then spray the Tonic on your garden to the point of run-off. (For related text, see page 139.)

KNOCK-'EM-DEAD INSECT SPRAY

6 cloves of garlic, chopped fine
1 small onion, chopped fine
1 tbsp. of cayenne pepper
1 tbsp. of liquid dish soap

Mix these ingredients in 1 quart of warm water and let sit overnight. Strain out the solid matter, pour into a spray bottle, and knock those buggy pests dead. (For related text, see page 120.)

MOUTH-WATERING MELON MIX

To grow the most mouth-watering melons in town, mix up a batch of this soil-energizing mix before you plant.

5 lbs. of earthworm castings
½ lb. of Epsom salts
¼ cup of instant tea granules

Mix all of the ingredients together, and put 1 cup in the bottom of each hole as you plant. (For related text, see page 263.)

MULCH MOISTURIZER TONIC

1 can of regular cola (not diet)
½ cup of ammonia
½ cup of antiseptic mouthwash
½ cup of baby shampoo

Mix these ingredients in your 20 gallon hose-end sprayer, and give your mulch security blanket a nice long, cool drink. (For related text, see page 82.)

POWDERY MILDEW CONTROL TONIC

4 tbsp. of baking soda
2 tbsp. of Murphy's Oil Soap
1 gal. of warm water

Mix all of the ingredients together. Pour into a handheld mist sprayer, and apply liberally when you see the telltale white spots of powdery mildew on your plants. (For related text, see page 257.)

RHUBARB BUG REPELLENT TONIC

Here's a potent plant Tonic that will say "Scram!" to just about any kind of bug you can think of.

3 medium-size rhubarb leaves
1 gal. of water
¼ cup of liquid dish soap

Chop up the rhubarb leaves, put the pieces in the water, and bring it to a boil. Let the mixture cool, then strain it through cheesecloth to filter out the leaf bits. Then mix in the dish soap. Apply this terrific Tonic to your plants with a small handheld sprayer and kiss your bug problems goodbye. This Tonic also helps to reduce blight on your tomatoes. (For related text, see page 119.)

ROBUST RHUBARB TONIC

To get her rhubarb growing, Grandma Putt made up a bunch of this Tonic.

1 tbsp. of Epsom salts
1 cup of tea
vegetable (non-meat) table scraps
   (as much as you can find)
1 qt. of water

Mash all of these ingredients together until you have a slurry, and then pour the mushy mix over your plants in both spring and fall. (For related text, see page 341.)

SEED AND SOIL ENERGIZER TONIC

1 tsp. of liquid dish soap
1 tsp. of ammonia
1 tsp. of whiskey

Mix these ingredients in 1 quart of weak tea, pour it into your mist-sprayer bottle, shake gently, then mist the surface of newly planted seed containers. (For related text, see page 39.)

SEED STARTER TONIC

1 tsp. of baby shampoo
1 tsp. of Epsom salts

Mix these ingredients in 1 quart of weak tea. Then bundle your seeds up in cheesecloth (one kind of seed per bundle!) and put the container in the fridge to soak for 24 hours. (For related text, see page 39.)

SEEDLING STARTER TONIC

2 tsp. of fish fertilizer
2 tsp. of liquid dish soap
1 tsp. of whiskey

Mix these ingredients in 1 quart of water. Feed the brew to your baby seedlings and they'll grow up to deliver tasty, bountiful harvests. (For related text, see page 40.)

SEEDLING STRENGTHENER TONIC

To get your seedlings off to a healthy, disease-free start, mist-spray your plants every few days with this elixir.

2 cups of manure
½ cup of instant tea granules
warm water

Put the manure and tea in an old nylon stocking, and let it steep in 5 gallons of water for several days. Dilute the "tea" with 4 parts of warm water before using. (For related text, see page 40.)

SEEDLING TRANSPLANT RECOVERY TONIC

Give your transplants a break on moving day by serving them a sip of this Tonic. It will help them recover more quickly from the shock of transplanting and make them feel right at home.

1 tbsp. of fish fertilizer
1 tbsp. of ammonia
1 tbsp. of Murphy's Oil Soap
1 tsp. of instant tea granules

Mix all of the ingredients in 1 quart of warm water. Pour into a handheld mist-sprayer bottle, and mist the seedlings several times a day until they're back on their feet. (For related text, see page 50.)

SLEEPYTIME TONIC

1 can of beer
1 can of regular cola (not diet)
1 cup of baby shampoo
½ cup of ammonia
¼ cup of instant tea granules

Mix these ingredients in a bucket, pour them into your 20 gallon hose-end sprayer, and saturate the blanket of leaves and clippings covering your garden. (For related text, see page 88.)

SLUGWEISER

1 pound of brown sugar
½ package (1½ teaspoons) of
   dry yeast

Pour these ingredients into a 1-gallon plastic jug, fill it with warm water, and let it sit for 2 days, uncovered. Pour it into slug traps. (For related text, see page 122.)

SPRING SOIL ENERGIZER TONIC

1 can of beer
1 cup of liquid dish soap
1 cup of antiseptic mouthwash
1 cup of regular cola (not diet)
¼ tsp. of instant tea granules

Mix these ingredients in a bucket or container, and fill a 20 gallon hose-end sprayer. Overspray the soil in your garden to the point of run-off. Then let the area sit for 2 weeks before you start planting. This recipe makes enough to cover 100 square feet of garden area. (For related text, see page 47.)

SUPER SLUG SPRAY

For slugs that are too small to hand-pick or be lured into traps, try this super spray.

1½ cups of ammonia
1 tbsp. of Murphy's Oil Soap
1½ cups of water

Mix all of the ingredients in a hand-held mist sprayer bottle, and over-spray any areas where you see signs of slug activity. (For related text, see page 121.)

SUPER SPIDER MITE MIX

Spider mites are tiny fellas, alright, but they get up to mite-y BIG mischief in your garden! When they show up, send 'em packin' with this potent brew.

4 cups of wheat flour
½ cup of buttermilk
5 gal. of water

Mix all of the ingredients together, and mist-spray your plants to the point of run-off. This magnificent mix will suffocate the little buggers without harming your veggies. (For related text, see page 109.)

SWEET SUCCESS SPRAY

Bees ensure pollination and give you more and better-tasting cucumbers. This sugar-packed spray will lure the buzzers to the spot. It will also kill nematodes in the soil, so with this mixture, you get two benefits for the price of one!

½ cup of sugar
2 cups of water

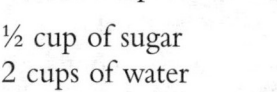

Boil the mixture until the sugar is completely dissolved. Let the mixture cool, dilute it with 1 gallon of water, and spray. (For related text, see page 260.)

TIMELY TOMATO TONIC

To ward off many common tomato diseases, use this mix on your newly transplanted tomato seedlings.

3 cups of compost
½ cup of powdered nonfat milk
½ cup of Epsom salts
1 tbsp. baking soda

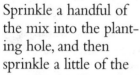

Sprinkle a handful of the mix into the planting hole, and then sprinkle a little of the powdered milk on top of the soil after planting. Repeat every few weeks throughout the growing season. (For related text, see page 301.)

TOBACCO TEA

½ handful of chewing tobacco
1 gal. of hot water

Wrap up the chewing tobacco in a piece of cheesecloth or panty hose, put it in the water, and soak it until the water turns dark brown. Fish out the cheesecloth and strain the liquid into a glass container with a good, tight lid. Then store the juice, and use it whenever a Tonic recipe calls for it. (For related text, see page 83.)

TOMATO BLIGHT BUSTER TONIC

To ward off early blight and other diseases, try using this mix on your newly transplanted tomato seedlings.

1 cup of compost
½ cup, plus ¼ cup of powdered, nonfat milk
½ cup of Epsom salts

Mix the compost, ½ cup of the powdered milk, and the Epsom salts together; sprinkle a handful of the mix into each planting hole. Then sprinkle the remaining ¼ cup of powdered milk on top of the soil after planting. Reapply the powdered milk every few weeks throughout the season. (For related text, see page 309.)

TOMATO BOOSTER TONIC

2 tbsp. of Epsom salts
1 tsp. of baby shampoo
1 gal. of water

Mix all of the ingredients together, and liberally soak the soil around tomato plants as they flower to stimulate their growth. (For related text, see page 309.)

TOMATO DISEASE FIGHTER TONIC

If your tomatoes have been bothered in the past by deadly diseases, apply this Tonic.

1 part skim milk
9 parts water

Combine the ingredients and mist-spray your tomato plants in the early part of the summer. (For related text, see page 309.)

VEGETABLE POWER POWDER

25 lbs. of organic garden food
5 lbs. of gypsum
2 lbs. of diatomaceous earth
1 lb. of sugar

Mix all of these ingredients together, and put them into a handheld broadcast spreader. Set the spreader on medium and apply the mixture over top of your garden. Follow up immediately by overspraying the area with my Spring Soil Energizer Tonic. (For related text, see page 47.)

VEGGIE TONIC #1

1 can of beer
1 cup of ammonia
4 tbsp. of instant tea granules
2 tbsp. of baby shampoo

Mix these ingredients in your 20 gallon hose-end sprayer. Then spray everything to the point of run-off. (For related text, see page 68.)

VEGGIE TONIC #2

½ cup of fish fertilizer
2 tbsp. of whiskey
2 tbsp. of Epsom salts
2 tbsp. of instant tea granules
1 tbsp. of baby shampoo

Mix these ingredients in your 20 gallon hose-end sprayer. Then spray everything to the point of run-off. (For related text, see page 68.)

WEED WIPEOUT TONIC

For those REALLY hard-to-kill weeds, try this Tonic.

1 tbsp. of gin
1 tbsp. of vinegar
1 tbsp. of liquid dish soap
1 qt. of very warm water

Mix all of the ingredients together in a bucket, then pour into a hand-held sprayer. Drench the weeds to the point of run-off, taking care not to get any on the surrounding plants. (For related text, see page 78.)

WHITEFLY
WIPEOUT TONIC

Whiteflies will lay their eggs on just
about any kind of leaf in your veggie
patch — but not if you beat them to
it by giving your plants a good spritz
of this Tonic.

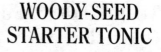

1 cup of sour milk
   (let it stand out for
   2 days)
2 tbsp. of flour
1 qt. of warm water

Mix these ingredi-
ents in a bowl and
spray the mixture over your veggie
plants. (For related text, see page
108.)

WOODY-SEED
STARTER TONIC

Seeds with woody coats, like those of
beets and parsnips, get off to a faster
start when you treat them to a dose
of this terrific Tonic.

1 cup of vinegar
2 oz. of liquid dish soap
2 cups of warm water

Mix all these ingredients together
and soak your seeds in the mixture
for 24 hours. Then plant them, and
lay a strip of burlap over the row —
it will create a warm environment
that lets moisture in and encourages
sprouting. (For related text, see
page 171.)

WILD MUSTARD TEA

No cabbage moth worth her spots
will lay eggs in your garden if you
spray your plants with this tea. It
works like a charm on loopers and
potato beetles too.

4 whole cloves
1 handful of wild mustard
   leaves
1 clove of garlic

Steep these ingredients in 1 cup of
boiling water. Let it cool, then spray
away! (For related text, see page 109.)

Well, my friends, we've come a long way from that old trunk in the attic! You've learned how you can put Grandma Putt's good old-fashioned grow-how to work in your garden — along with my new fangled tips, tricks, and tonics — to produce the tastiest tomatoes, superbest spuds, and mouth-wateringest melons you've ever tasted. I hope you've gotten as big a kick out of reading this treasure-trove of old memories and new ideas as I've had putting it together for you. So until next time, here's to great gardening!

Jerry

USDA Plant Hardiness Zone Map

Your USDA Zone number indicates the coldest temperature that hits your region in an average winter.

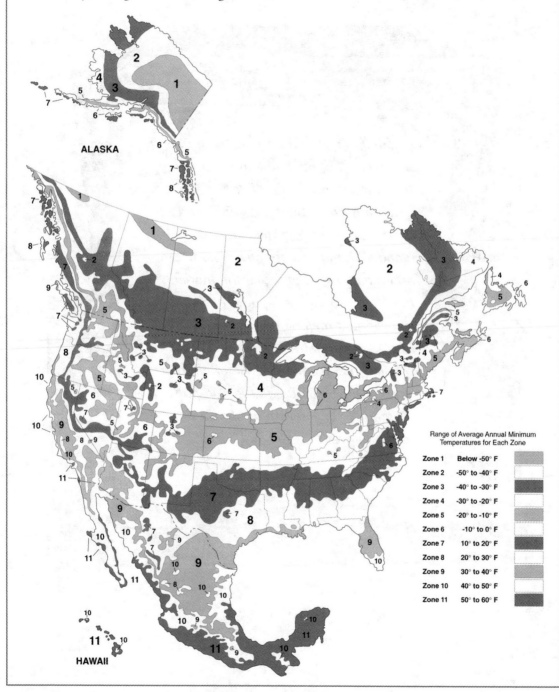

ALASKA

Range of Average Annual Minimum
Temperatures for Each Zone

Zone 1	Below -50° F
Zone 2	-50° to -40° F
Zone 3	-40° to -30° F
Zone 4	-30° to -20° F
Zone 5	-20° to -10° F
Zone 6	-10° to 0° F
Zone 7	10° to 20° F
Zone 8	20° to 30° F
Zone 9	30° to 40° F
Zone 10	40° to 50° F
Zone 11	50° to 60° F

HAWAII

American Horticultural Society
Plant Heat Zone Map

This map shows how long "real" summer lasts in your territory — that is, the number of days in a normal year when the temperature gets above 86°F. You can order a detailed, full-color version from the American Horticultural Society, 7931 East Boulevard Drive, Alexandria VA 22308. Phone: 800-777-7931; web site: www.ahs.org

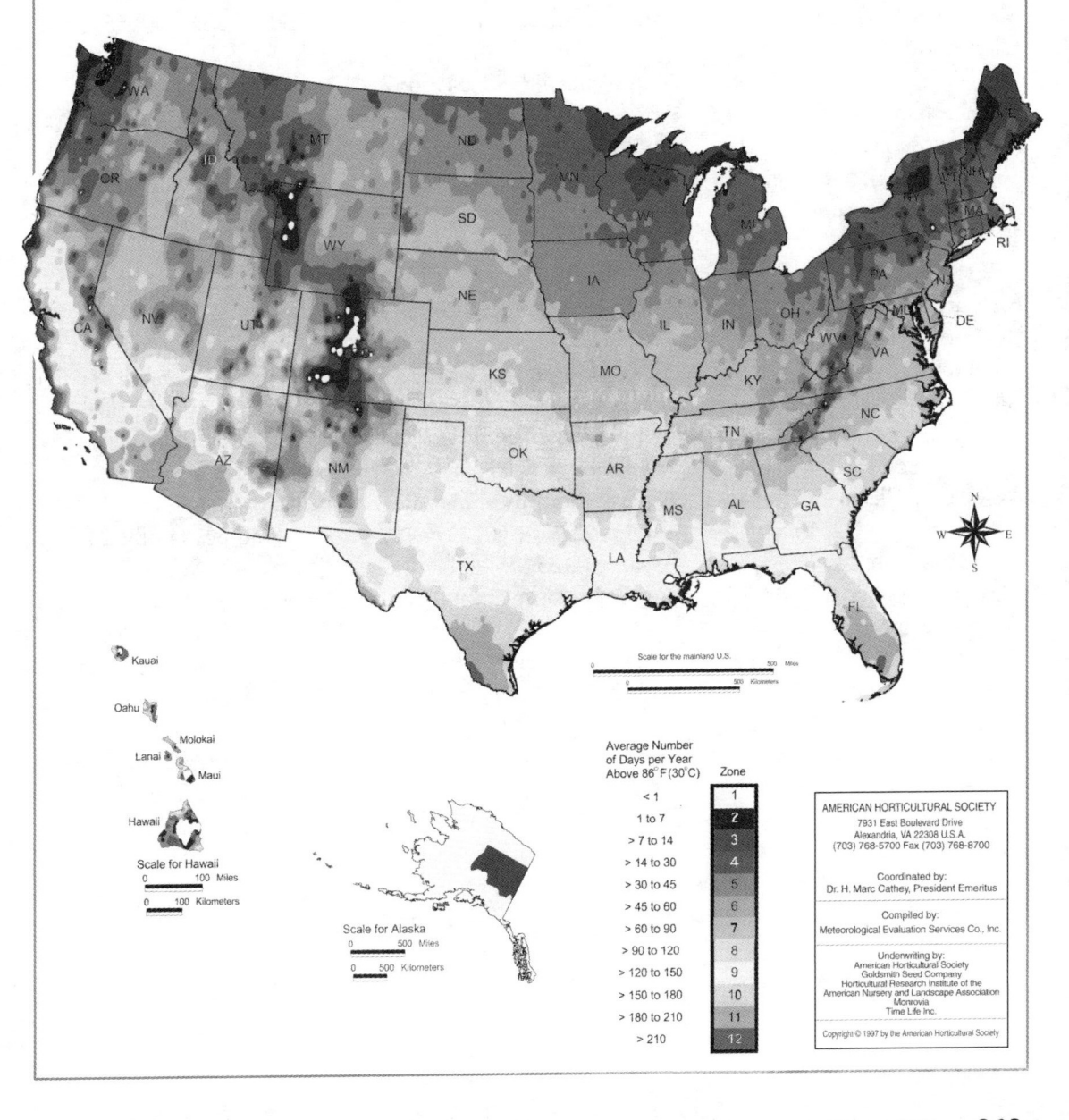

Scale for the mainland U.S.

Kauai

Oahu

Molokai

Lanai

Maui

Hawaii

Scale for Hawaii

Scale for Alaska

Average Number of Days per Year Above 86° F (30°C)	Zone
< 1	1
1 to 7	2
> 7 to 14	3
> 14 to 30	4
> 30 to 45	5
> 45 to 60	6
> 60 to 90	7
> 90 to 120	8
> 120 to 150	9
> 150 to 180	10
> 180 to 210	11
> 210	12

AMERICAN HORTICULTURAL SOCIETY
7931 East Boulevard Drive
Alexandria, VA 22308 U.S.A.
(703) 768-5700 Fax (703) 768-8700

Coordinated by:
Dr. H. Marc Cathey, President Emeritus

Compiled by:
Meteorological Evaluation Services Co., Inc.

Underwriting by:
American Horticultural Society
Goldsmith Seed Company
Horticultural Research Institute of the
American Nursery and Landscape Association
Monrovia
Time Life Inc.

Copyright © 1997 by the American Horticultural Society

Index

A

Acid (sour) soil, 14, 48, 73
Air circulation, 10
Alkaline (sweet) soil, 14, 73
All-Around Disease Defense
    Tonic, 94 (recipe), 95, 96,
    97, 98, 348 (recipe)
All-Purpose Dandelion Cure,
    80 (recipe), 348 (recipe)
All-Purpose Organic
    Fertilizer, 248 (recipe),
    348 (recipe)
All-Purpose Pest Prevention
    Potion, 128 (recipe), 349
    (recipe)
All-Purpose Varmint
    Repellent, 128 (recipe),
    349 (recipe)
All-Season Clean-Up Tonic,
    82 (recipe), 92, 104, 342,
    349 (recipe)
All-Season Green-Up Tonic,
    47 (recipe), 68, 92, 166,
    179, 188, 211, 213, 215,
    217, 224, 246, 253, 261,
    264, 273, 301, 349 (recipe)
Aluminum foil for pests, 123
American Horticultural
    Society, 7, 363
Ammonia
    secret behind, 48, 347
    in tonics, 39, 47, 50, 68,
    82, 88, 121, 128, 139,
    140, 349, 353, 354, 355,
    356, 357, 359
Animal control, 126–30
Annuals, 6
Anthracnose (fungus), 95
Antiseptic mouthwash
    secret behind, 48, 347
    in tonics, 47, 82, 349, 357
Ants, *118*
Aphid Antidote, 104 (recipe),
    350 (recipe)
Aphid lion (green
    lacewings), *110,* 342
Aphids, 104, *118, 119,* 227
Apple cider vinegar in ton-
    ics, 78
Apple juice in tonics, 139,
    353
Armyworms, 104, 117
Artichokes, *25,* 27, 190
Ashes (wood) uses, 71, 73,
    117, 249
Asparagus, *25,* 334–38
    companion planting, *28,*
    336
    double digging, 334
    flowers and, 19
    growing, 12, 27, 334–36,
    338
    harvesting, 133, 337–38
    Jersey hybrids, 335
    open-pollinated, 335
    recipes using, 344
Asparagus beetles, 108, 337

B

Baby shampoo in tonics, 39,
    68, 82, 88, 99, 139, 309,
    350, 353, 354, 355, 356,
    358, 359
Bacteria, 94
Bacterial blight/wilt, 95
Baked Beans, Pumpkin, 281
Baked Corn with Thyme,
    331
Baking soda
    bug bite relief from, 113
    in tonics, 91, 99, 350, 352,
    354, 358
Baking Soda Spray, 99
    (recipe), 350 (recipe)
Basil, 19, *25,* 289
Bats for pest control, 116
Beaks of birds, 113–14
Bean and pea family, *25,*
    152–68
Bean beetles, *118*
Beans, *25,* 154–61. *See also*
    Bush beans; Pole beans
    companion planting, 157,
    187
    cooking tips, 158
    cover crop from, 61, *62*
    dry (dried) beans, 154,
    156, 157, 158
    growing, 27, 43, 155–56,
    161
    harvesting, 133, 135, *143,
    147,* 157
    heirlooms, 158–59

nitrogen (N) and, 152–53
nutrition from, 158
recipes using, 167, 168,
  281
shell (shelly) beans, 154,
  157
snap beans, 154, 157
staking (trellises), 160
Bears, 129
Bedtime Snack, 87 (recipe),
  88, 350 (recipe)
Beer
  secret behind, 48, 347
  in tonics, 47, 64, 68, 88,
    349, 351, 356, 357, 359
Beetle Juice, 105, 106, 282
  (recipe), 283, 296, 350
  (recipe)
Beetles, 71, 105, 107, 108,
  109, 116, 117, *118*
Beetles in tonics, 350
Beets, *25,* 170–74
  boron and, 174
  companion planting, 19,
    28, 174
  cooking tips, 173
  growing, 12, 27, *45,*
    170–72
  harvesting, 133, *134,*
    135, *143, 150,* 173–74
  nutrition from, 172, 173
  recipes using, 189, 191
  roasting, 173
Beets and greens family, *25,*
  169–91
Beneficial nematodes, 101,
  111, 244
Beyond-the-Salad-Bowl
  Cukes, 281
Bibb lettuce, 177

Birdhouses from gourds, 277
Birds, 113–16, 124–26, 164,
  322
Black flea beetles, *118*
Black heart, 174
Black rot, 192, 194
Blanching, 210, 211, 240
Blight, 95, 97, 98, 296
Blossom-end rot, 103, 308
Blotching ripening, 308
Boiling-water bath canning,
  146
Bolting, 170
Bonemeal in tonics, 87, 247,
  348, 350
Borage, 181
Boron and vegetables, 174,
  187, 202
Boston lettuce, 177
Botrytis (gray mold), 97
Bourbon in tonics, 140, 353
Broadcasting seed, 170
Broccoli, *25,* 195–97
  companion planting, *28*
  growing, 27, *44, 45, 194,*
    195–96
  harvesting, 133, *134,* 135,
    143, 197
  types of, 197
Broccoli-raab, 197
Brown sugar in tonics, 356
Brussels sprouts, *25,*
  198–201
  cooking tips, 201
  growing, 27, *44, 194,*
    198–99
  harvesting, 133, *134, 143,*
    199, 200
  nutrition from, 200
  recipes using, 229

Bug bites and stings, 113
Bush beans, *25*
  companion planting, 19,
    28, 157, 174, 238
  growing, *45,* 155, 159
  harvesting, *134*
  heirlooms, 159
Butterhead lettuce, 177
Buttermilk in tonics, 357

C
Cabbage butterflies, 203
Cabbage family, *25,* 192–231
Cabbage Kielbasa Pie, 230
Cabbage loopers, 105
Cabbage moths, *118,* 192,
  303
Cabbage-root maggots, 221
Cabbages, *25,* 202–7
  boron and, 202
  Chinese cabbage, 27, *194,*
    208
  companion planting, *28,*
    174, 187, 192, 193, 205,
    342
  growing, 27, *45, 194,*
    202–6, 204
  harvesting, 133, *143, 150,*
    206
  recipes using, 229, 230
  sauerkraut tips, 207
Cabbage worms, 108, 116,
  118, 119
Cabbage Worm Wipe-Out
  Tonic, 204 (recipe), 351
  (recipe)
Calcium and vegetables, *69,*
  285, 305
Canning vegetables, 142,
  143, 146

Cantaloupes, 264, 265
Carrot-Cilantro Soup, 243
Carrot family, *25,* 232–43
Carrot flies, *118,* 237
Carrots, *25,* 233–37
  companion planting, *28*
  growing, 27, 43, 46,
    233–34, 237
  harvesting, 133, *134,* 135,
    143, 150, 237
  recipes using, 190, 243, 255
  troubleshooting, *236*
Casabas. *See* Melons
Castor oil in tonics, 128, 349
Catch (cover crops), 53,
  60–61, *62,* 317
Cats, 116, 127, 129
Cauliflower, *25,* 209–12
  blanching, 210, 211
  companion planting, *28,*
    238
  cooking tips, 212
  growing, 27, *44, 45, 194,*
    209–10, 211
  harvesting, 133, *143,* 209,
    212
Cayenne pepper in tonics,
  120, 129, 204 (recipe),
  351, 352, 353, 354
Celeriac, 240
Celery, *25,* 238–40
  blanching, 240
  companion planting, *28,*
    157, 192, 238
  growing, 12, 27, *44,* 238,
    239, 240
  harvesting, 133, *143, 147,*
    150, 239
  recipes using, 167, 243,
    255, 256, 280, 313

Chamomile tea in tonics,
  94, 348, 352
Cheesy Rutabaga Bake, 231
Chestnuts and Onions,
  Creamed, 256
Chile, Jerry's Heat-Up-the-
  Kitchen, 312
Chile pepper/powder
  recipes using, 231, 279,
    312
  in tonics, 128, 129, 349,
    352
Chinese cabbage, 27, *194,*
  208
Chinese peas, 162
Chitin eaters, 102
Chocolate Cake, Grandma
  Putt's Secret, 314
Chrysanthemums, 181
Chutney, Santa's Favorite,
  313
Clay soil, 13, 54, 60–61
Climate (weather), 6–11,
  8–9, 86–88, 132,
  138–39
Cloves in tonics, 109, 359
Clubroot (fungus), 71, 96,
  192, 193, 342
Coffee grounds
  in tonics, 351
  uses for, 31, 46
Cola (not diet)
  secret behind, 48, 347
  in tonics, 47, 64, 82, 88,
    351, 354, 356, 357
Cold composting, 64
Cold frames, 86, 87, 88
Collards, 11, *25,* 213–14
Colorado potato beetles, 99,
  105, 282, *283,* 296

Companion planting, 19,
  27, *28. See also specific*
  vegetables
Compost Activator/Acceler-
  ator, 64
Compost Feeder Tonic, 63,
  64 (recipe), 351 (recipe)
Compost in tonics, 351, 358
Composting, 63–67, *67*
Compost Tea, 100 (recipe),
  153, 156, 163, 182, 188,
  221, 247, 248, 329, 336,
  341, 351 (recipe)
Confetti Kohlrabi, 231
Container Garden Booster
  Mix, 31 (recipe), 351
  (recipe)
Container gardening, 29, 31,
  48, 221, 261, 265, 286,
  296
Containers for seed starting,
  38
Contests, gardening, 36
Cool-season crops, 7, 133
Corn, *25,* 315–25
  companion planting, *28,*
    157, 316, 323
  cooking tips, 324
  growing, 27, 43, *45,*
    315–20
  harvesting, 133, *134,* 135,
    143, 147, 323–24
  lodging of cornstalks, 316
  popcorn, 325
  recipes using, 231, 331, 332
  suckers, 317
  trench planting method,
    318
  types of, 319–21

Corn earworms (fruit-worms), 105, 116, 317, 322, 327
Corn syrup (clear) secret behind, 48, 347 in tonics, 47, 349
Cos (romaine) lettuce, 177
Cotyledons (seed leaves), 42
Cousa. *See* Squashes
Cover crops, 53, 60–61, *62,* 317
Cracking in vegetables, 103, 308
Creamed Chestnuts and Onions, 256
Cream of Lettuce Soup, 190
Crenshaws. *See* Melons
Crisphead lettuce, 177
Crop rotation, 26–27, 91
Crunchy Okra Rounds, 332
Cucumber beetles, 71, 105–6, *119,* 221, 259, 271
Cucumbers, *25,* 258–61
  companion planting, *28,* 157, 221
  cooking tips, 261
  eye bags and circles removal, 261
  growing, 27, 43, *44, 45,* 258–59, 260, 261
  harvesting, 133, 135, *143, 150,* 260–61
  recipes using, 146, 281
  staking (trellises), 259
  types of, 260
Curing manure, 60
Curly top (fungus), 96
Cutworms, 86, 106, 116, 117, *119,* 122–23, 244

D
Damping-off, 39, 40, 41, 42, 96
Damping-Off Prevention Tonic, 40, 42 (recipe), 352 (recipe)
Dandelions, 80, 190, 348
Dandy Dandelion Salad, 190
Daylight hours, 10
Deep planting method, potatoes, 295
Deer, 129–30
Dehydrating vegetables, 142, *143,* 147, *147*
Dent corn, 321
Determinate tomato plants, 302
Diapers and drought prevention, 301
Diatomaceous earth in tonics, 47, 359
Dibble planting method, leeks, 246
Digging garden sites, 55–57
Digging (spading) forks, *83*
Dill, 43, 192
Dill and Shallot Cream Sauce, 255
Dill Pickles, Quick-as-a-Wink, 146
Diseases, 95–98, 161. *See also* Pest control
Dog food (dried) for planting, 70
Dog-B-Gone Tonic, 129 (recipe), 352 (recipe)
Dogs, 129, 351
Double digging, 55–56, 334, 339
Downy mildew, 96, 99, 184, 257

Drainage of soil, 54
Drought-tolerant plants, 75
Dry (dried) beans, 154, 156, 157, 158
Drying (dehydrating) vegetables, 142, *143,* 147, *147*

E
Early blight (fungus), 97
Earthworm castings in tonics, 263, 354
Earthworms, 16, 57, 67
Earwigs, 86
Eelworms (nematodes), 94, 99, 101–2
Eggplant, *25,* 284–86
  calcium and, 285
  companion planting, 157
  flowers and, 19
  growing, 27, *44,* 284–86
  harvesting, 133, 135, *143,* 286
  recipes using, 313
Eggs/eggshells in tonics, 31, 128, 349, 351
Electroculture, 81
Enclosed beds, 58, 59
Endive, 133, *143, 150*
English peas, 162
Epsom salts
  secret behind, 48, 347
  in tonics, 31, 39, 68, 263, 309, 341, 351, 354, 355, 358, 359
Escarole, *150*
European corn borers, 106–7, *119*
Eye bags and circles removal, 261

F

F$_1$ hybrids, 33
Families of vegetables, *25.*
    See also specific vegetable
    families
Fantastic Squash, 279
Fava bean caution, 161
Fertilizing. *See also specific*
    vegetables
    composting, 63–67, *67*
    manure for, 59–60, 176,
        183
    nitrogen (N), 14, *69,* 70,
        70, 176, 288
    nutrients (secondary), *69*
    organic materials for, 68
    phosphorus (P), 14, *69, 70*
    planting and, 47, 70
    potassium (K), 14, *69, 70*
    troubleshooting, *70,* 71
    watering, 12, 73–76
Fish fertilizer
    in tonics, 40, 50, 68, 355,
        356, 359
    uses for, 153, 156, 163,
        182, 211, 239, 245, 246,
        261, 264, 269, 273, 299,
        316, 326, 329
Flea beetles, 107, *119,* 213,
    285
Flies, *118*
Flint corn, 321
Flour corn, 321
Flour in tonics, 351, 360
Flowers
    edible, 181
    pest control from, *118*
    vegetables and, 19
Forking soil, 56
Freestanding beds, 58

Freezing vegetables, 142,
    143, 144
French crisp lettuce, 177
Frittata, Tomato Pesto, 312
Fruitworms (corn ear-
    worms), 105, 116, 317,
    322, 327
Fungus, 93–94, 99
Fungus Fighter Tonic, 91
    (recipe), 352 (recipe)
Fusarium wilt, 97, 184

G

Garden Cure-All Tonic, 105,
    107 (recipe), 352 (recipe)
Garden forks, *83*
Garden peas, 162
Garden Pest Repellent, 116
    (recipe), 353 (recipe)
Garden planning, 20–36
    companion planting, 19,
        27, *28*
    container gardening, 29,
        31, 48, 221, 261, 265,
        286, 296
    crop rotation, 26–27, 91
    drawing, 22, 31
    heirlooms, 3, 32
    plant buying, 34, 35, 36
    plot selection, 17–19
    scrapbook for, 23
    seed buying, 32–34, 35
    shopping tips, 30–36
    size of garden, 17, 21, *22*
    small plots, 29
    tall plants, 24
    vegetable families, *25*
Garlands (ristras), 290
Garlic, *25*
    harvesting, *150*

recipes using, 189, 254
    in tonics, 106, 107, 109,
        116, 120, 128, 129, 349,
        352, 353, 354, 360
Garlic, Shallot, or Onion
    Vinegar, 254
Garlic Lover's Creamed
    Spinach, 189
Garlic Pest Repellent, 116
    (recipe), 353 (recipe)
Gin in tonics, 78, 359
Gophers, 127–28
Gourds, *25,* 275–77
    birdhouses from, 277
    growing, 275–76
    harvesting, 136, 277
    staking (trellises), 276
Grandma Putt's
    Black Bean Soup, 167
    Cock-a-Leekie Soup, 255
    Pumpkin Dip, 274
    Secret Chocolate Cake,
        314
Granite dust in tonics, 247,
    348
Grass family, *25*
Grass reduction, 52
Gray mold (botrytis), 97
Green Beans and Blue
    Cheese Pie, 168
Green lacewings (aphid
    lion), *110,* 342
Green manure (cover crops),
    53, 60–61, *62,* 317
Green peas, 162
Green peppers. *See* Peppers
Grilled Asparagus, 344
Groundhogs, *118,* 127–28
Groundhogs (woodchucks),
    153

Growing seasons, 6–7, *8–9*
Gypsum
  for ice protection, 71
  in tonics, 47, 87, 350, 359
Gypsy moths, 117

H
Hand trowels, *83*
Happy Harvest Soup, 332
Happy Herb Tonic, 140
  (recipe), 353 (recipe)
Hardening off, 49–50
Hardiness Zone Map,
  USDA, 7, 360
Harlequin bugs, *119*
Harvesting, 131–50. *See also
  specific vegetables*
  canning, 142, *143,* 146
  clues for, 138–39
  drying (dehydrating),
    142, *143,* 147, *147*
  freezing, 142, *143,* 144
  herbs, 140
  leathers, 3, 148–49
  planting in triple time,
    134, *134*
  production period and,
    132
  root cellaring, 142–45,
    143, 149–50, *150*
  steps for, 139
  storage tips, 142–50, *143,
    147*
  succession planting,
    133–34, *134*
  timing tips, 135–37, *137*
  vitamins and, 137
  weather impact on,
    138–39

Health of plants and pests,
  90–93, 102
Heat Zone Map, American
  Horticultural Society's,
  7, 361
Heirlooms, 3, 32
Herbs, 140
Hilling planting method,
  potatoes, 295
Hitting High C Brussels
  Sprouts, 229
Hole planting method,
  tomatoes, 300, 301
Honeydews. *See* Melons
Hornworms, *283*
Horseradish, *25, 150*
Hot Bug Brew, 106 (recipe),
  353 (recipe)
Household ingredients in
  tonics, 48, 347
Hover flies (syrphid flies),
  110
Humidity, 10
Hummingbirds, 114
Hurry-Up-the-Harvest
  Tonic, 139 (recipe), 306,
  353 (recipe)
Hydrogen peroxide in
  tonics, 140, 353

I
Indeterminate tomato
  plants, 302
Indian (ornamental) corn,
  321
Indicator plants, *53*
Ingredients (household) in
  tonics, 48, 347

Inoculants, 153
Insects, 104–9. *See also* Pest
  control

J
Jack-o'-Turnip lanterns, 228
Jalapeño peppers in tonics,
  107, 129, 352
Japanese beetles, *118,* 316
Jefferson, Thomas, 3, 36
Jell-O for seed starting, 38
Jerry's Heat-Up-the-
  Kitchen Chile, 312
  Show-Stopper Tomatoes
    with Basil, 311

K
Kale, *25,* 215–16
  cooking tips, 215
  growing, 27, *194,* 215–16
  harvesting, 133, *134,*
    216
  nutrition from, 216
  shade and, 11
Kielbasa Cabbage Pie, 230
Knock-'em-Dead Insect
  Spray, 119, 120 (recipe),
  354 (recipe)
Kohlrabi, *25,* 217–18
  companion planting, 174
  cooking tips, 218
  growing, 27, 217
  recipes using, 231
K (potassium), 14, *69, 70*

L
Ladybugs, *110,* 111, 227,
342
Lamborn, Calvin, 162

Late blight (fungus), 97, 296
Lawn food in tonics, 47, 87, 349, 358
Lawn reduction, 52
Layered Salad, 256
Leaf lettuce, 177
Leaf miners, 107, *119*
Leaf spot, 174, 192, 194
Leathers, 3, 148–49
Leeks, *25,* 245–46
   companion planting, 238
   cooking tips, 246
   dibble planting method, 246
   growing, 27, 245–46
   harvesting, 133, *143, 150,* 246
   recipes using, 230, 255
Legume (pea) family, *25*
Lettuce, *25,* 175–81
   companion planting, *28,* 174, 176, 187
   growing, 27, *44,* 46, 175, 176, 178
   harvesting, 133, *134,* 135, 178
   mesclun mixes, 179
   nitrogen (N) and, 176
   recipes using, 190, 256
   shade and, 11
   tip burn, 176
   types of, 177
Lime for flea beetles, 285
Limestone for ph adjustments, *72, 73*
Limy Limas with Dill, 168
Liquid dish soap
   secret behind, 48, 347

   in tonics, 39, 40, 47, 64, 78, 82, 94, 106, 116, 120, 128, 129, 171, 348, 349, 350, 351, 352, 353, 354, 355, 357, 359, 360
Liquid lawn food in tonics, 349
Loamy soil, 13
Looseleaf lettuce, 177
Loss prevention for tools, 85

M
Maggots, 71, 244
Magnesium, *69*
Mallow family, *25*
Manure. *See also* Compost Tea
   dehydrated, in tonics, 348
   fertilizing with, 59–60, 176, 183
   in tonics, 40, 247, 356
Maps
   American Horticultural Society's Plant Heat Zone, 7, 361
   USDA Hardiness Zone, 7, 360
Matches for sulfur, 289
Medicinal uses for radishes, 222
Melons, *25,* 262–65
   companion planting, 221
   growing, 27, 43, *44,* 262–65, 265
   harvesting, 133, 136, *150,* 264, 265
   nutrition from, 265
   recipes using, 280
Mesclun mixes, 179
Mexican bean beetles, 109

Mice, *118,* 127–28
Micronutrients, *69*
Mighty Minty Peas, 167
Milk
   for tobacco mosaic virus (TMV), 100
   in tonics, 91, 309, 359, 360
Mineral oil as worm repellent, 322
Mineral oil in tonics, 353
Mint, *25,* 193
Mites, 109, 221, 342
Molasses
   secret behind, 48, 347
   in tonics, 47, 91, 349, 351, 352
Moon and planting, 45, 183
Morning glory or bindweed family, *25*
Mosquitoes, 116, 117, *118*
Mouth-Watering Melon Mix, 263 (recipe), 354 (recipe)
Mulches, 75, 76, 77, 86, 92
Mulch Moisturizer Tonic, 82 (recipe), 354 (recipe)
Mulch planting method, potatoes, 295
Murphy's Oil Soap in tonics, 50, 107, 121, 352, 354, 356, 357
Muskmelons, 264, 265

N
N. *See* Nitrogen
Nasturtiums, 181
Neighbors and gardens, 18
Nematodes
   beneficial, 101, 111, 244

roundworms, eelworms, 94, 99, 101–2
Newspaper uses, 43, 52, 77, 86, 329
New Zealand spinach, 184
Nitrogen (N)
  beans and peas and, 152–53, 163
  composting and, 54, 65
  fertilizing, 14, *69,* 70, *70,* 176, 288
Normal sugary (su) corn, 319, 320
Nutrition
  from beans, 158
  from beets, 172, 173
  from Brussels sprouts, 200
  from kale, 216
  from melons, 265
  from potatoes, 297
  from rutabagas, 223
  from spinach, 185
  from tomatoes, 298, 306, 307
Nylon stocking uses, 84, 86, 322

O

Okra, *25,* 326–27
  companion planting, 289
  growing, 27, 43, 326, 327
  harvesting, 133, 135, *143,* 327
  recipes using, 332
Onion family, *25,* 244–56
Onions (scallions), *25,* 247–52
  breath relief from parsley, 251

companion planting, *28,* 192, 205, 250
growing, 27, *45,* 247–49, 252
harvesting, 133, *134,* 135, *143, 150,* 250, 251
recipes using, 167, 229, 230, 231, 243, 254, 256, 278, 279, 281, 311, 312, 313, 332
tears from, 251
in tonics, 106, 107, 120, 129, 350, 352, 353, 354
OP (open-pollinated), 33, 179, 320
Oxalic acid caution, 185

P

Panty hose uses, 84, 86, 322
Parasitic nematodes, 101, 111, 244
Parasitic wasps, *110*
Parsley, *25*
  companion planting, 19, 336
  growing, 43
  onion breath relief, 251
  recipes using, 231, 256, 279, 280, 311, 312, 331, 332
  shade and, 11
Parsnip Apple Dressing, 243
Parsnips, *25,* 241–42
  cooking tips, 242
  growing, 27, 43, 241, 242
  harvesting, 133, *143,* 241
  recipes using, 243
Patriotic Potato Salad, 311
Pattypan. *See* Squashes
Peanuts, *25,* 27, 166

Peas, *25,* 162–65
  companion planting, 19, *28,* 183, 187
  cover crop from, 61, *62*
  growing, 27, 43, *45,* 162–64, 164
  harvesting, 133, *134,* 135, *143, 147,* 165
  recipes using, 167, 256
  shade and, 11
  types of, 162
Peppercorns, 288
Peppermint, 94, 192
Peppermint oil in tonics, 348
Peppers (green/red), *25,* 287–92
  companion planting, 221, 289
  growing, 12, 27, *44,* 48, 287–90, 292
  harvesting, 133, 135, *143, 150,* 291–92
  recipes using, 230, 256, 280, 312, 313
  ristras (garlands), 290
  in tonics, 106, 353
Perennials, 27, 55, 333–44
Pest control, 89–130
  animals, 126–30
  bacteria, 94
  bats for, 116
  crop rotation for, 26, 91
  diseases, 95–98, 161
  flowers for, *118*
  fungus, 93–94, 99
  good bugs, 101, *110,* 110–13
  health of plants and, 90–93, 102
  insects, 104–9

Pest control *(continued)*
    nematodes, 94, 99, 101–2
    solarizing soil, 99, 102
    toads for, 117
    trap crops for, *119,*
        119–20
    viruses, 94
Phosphorus (P), 14, *69, 70*
pH (potential of hydrogen),
    14, 48, 71, *72,* 72–73
Phytophthora crown rot,
    342
Pickled Beets and Purple
    Eggs, 191
Picklers, cucumbers, 260
Pink root, 244
Planting, 37–50. *See also*
    Fertilizing; Garden
    planning; Harvesting;
    Pest control; Soil basics;
    specific vegetables; Tonics
    broadcasting seed, 170
    damping-off, 39, 40, 41,
        42, 96
    depth for, 46
    eggshells for, 44, 48
    fertilizing for, 47, 70
    hardening off, 49–50
    moon and, 45, 183
    pots for, 43, 48, 86
    seed starting, 38–44, *44,*
        48
    sowing seeds, *45,* 45–46
    stem handling, 42, 44
    transplanting, 42, 44, *44,*
        49–50
    triple time, 134, *134*
    vertical gardening, 80–81
    watering, 12, 73–76

Plastic sheets as weed-killer,
    53
Plot selection, 17–19
Pole beans, *25*
    companion planting, *28,*
        157
    growing, *45,* 152, 155,
        159
    heirlooms, 159
Popcorn, 325
Potassium (K), 14, *69, 70*
Potato bugs, *118*
Potatoes, *25,* 293–97
    companion planting, *28,*
        192, 296
    deep planting method,
        295
    growing, 27, *45, 293, 294,*
        295–96, 296
    harvesting, 133, *143, 150,*
        297
    hilling planting method,
        295
    mulch planting method,
        295
    nutrition from, 297
    recipes using, 311, 314
    tomatoes and, 25, *25*
Potato stem borers, 342
Potential of hydrogen (pH),
    14, 48, 71, *72,* 72–73
Pots for planting, 43, 48, 86
Powdered milk in tonics,
    352, 358
Powdery mildew, 99
Powdery Mildew Control
    Tonic, 257 (recipe), 354
    (recipe)
P (phosphorus), 14, *69, 70*

Praying mantises, 111
Predatory mites, 111
Pressure canning, 146
Pressure-treated lumber
    caution, 59
Production period and har-
    vesting, 132
Puddling sweet potatoes,
    328
Pumpkin Baked Beans, 281
Pumpkins, *25,* 271–74
    companion planting, *28,*
        271, 323
    growing, *44,* 271–74
    harvesting, 133, 136, *143,*
        147, 150, 274
    recipes using, 274, 281
Purple Eggs and Pickled
    Beets, 191
Purple Passion Soup, 229

Q
Quick-as-a-Wink Dill
    Pickles, 146
Quick Lemony Mustard
    Potatoes, 314

R
Rabbits, 71, 127–28
Raccoons, 129, 322, 323
Radishes, *25,* 219–22
    companion planting, *28,*
        221, 271
    growing, 27, 43, *194,*
        219–20, 221
    harvesting, 133, *134, 143,*
        150, 222
    medicinal uses for, 222
    recipes using, 280

Rainbow cob, 320
Raised beds, 57–59, 262–63
Rats, *118,* 127–28
Recipes
    Baked Corn with Thyme,
        331
    Beyond-the-Salad-Bowl
        Cukes, 281
    Cabbage Kielbasa Pie,
        230
    Carrot-Cilantro Soup,
        243
    Cheesy Rutabaga Bake,
        231
    Confetti Kohlrabi, 231
    Creamed Chestnuts and
        Onions, 256
    Cream of Lettuce Soup,
        190
    Crunchy Okra Rounds,
        332
    Dandy Dandelion Salad,
        190
    Dill and Shallot Cream
        Sauce, 255
    *Fan*tastic Squash, 279
    Garlic, Shallot, or Onion
        Vinegar, 254
    Garlic Lover's Creamed
        Spinach, 189
    Grandma Putt's Black
        Bean Soup, 167
    Grandma Putt's Cock-a-
        Leekie Soup, 255
    Grandma Putt's Pumpkin
        Dip, 274
    Grandma Putt's Secret
        Chocolate Cake, 314
    Green Beans and Blue
        Cheese Pie, 168
    Grilled Asparagus, 344
    Happy Harvest Soup, 332
    Hitting High C Brussels
        Sprouts, 229
    Jerry's Heat-Up-the-
        Kitchen Chile, 312
    Jerry's Show-Stopper
        Tomatoes with Basil,
        311
    Layered Salad, 256
    Limy Limas with Dill,
        168
    Mighty Minty Peas, 167
    Parsnip Apple Dressing,
        243
    Patriotic Potato Salad,
        311
    Pumpkin Baked Beans,
        281
    Purple Eggs and Pickled
        Beets, 191
    Purple Passion Soup, 229
    Quick-as-a-Wink Dill
        Pickles, 146
    Quick Lemony Mustard
        Potatoes, 314
    Red, White, and Orange
        Salad, 280
    Rhubarbsicles, 343
    Ruby Red Sauce, 189
    Santa's Favorite Chutney,
        313
    Savoy Slaw, 230
    South of the Border
        Zucchini, Rice, and
        Chicken Salad, 279
    Squash Pie, 278
    Strawberry-Rhubarb Pie,
        326
    Sweet Potatoes in Ginger
        Honey Sauce, 331
    Swiss Chard with Lemon
        and Bacon, 191
    Terrific Tarragon Bake,
        254
    Tomato Pesto Frittata,
        312
    Very Veggie Pie, 313
    Whoops! I Goofed! Salad,
        280
    Zucchini Caterpillars, 278
Red, White, and Orange
    Salad, 280
Red peppers. *See* Peppers
Rhubarb, *25,* 339–43
    companion planting, 342
    dividing, 342
    double digging, 339
    flowers and, 19
    growing, 27, 71, 339–40,
        343
    harvesting, 133, *147,* 341
    recipes using, 343, 344
    in tonics, 355
Rhubarb Bug Repellent
    Tonic, 103 (recipe), 107,
    119 (recipe), 355
    (recipe)
Rhubarb curculios, 342
Rhubarbsicles, 343
Ripening tomatoes, 307,
    310
Ristras (garlands), 290
Robber flies, *110*
Robust Rhubarb Tonic, 341
    (recipe), 355 (recipe)
Romaine (cos) lettuce, 177

Root cellaring vegetables, 142–45, *143,* 149–50, *150*
Root maggots, 234, 247
Root rot, 98
Rosemary, *25,* 192
Roundworms (nematodes), 94, 99, 101–2
Ruby Red Sauce, 189
Rust (fungus), 98
Rutabagas, *25,* 223–24
 companion planting, *28*
 growing, 27, 43, 223–24
 harvesting, *143,* 224
 nutrition from, 223
 recipes using, 231

S

Sage, *25,* 192
Salad gardens, 180
Sandy soil, 13, 60–61
Santa's Favorite Chutney, 313
Sauerkraut tips, 178, 207
Savoy Slaw, 230
Scab, 174
Scallions. *See* Onions
Scoville, William, 290
Scrapbook for garden planning, 23
Scuffle hoes, 84
Seaweed meal in tonics, 247, 348
Seed and Soil Energizer Tonic, 39 (recipe), 40, 42, 134, 299, 355 (recipe)
Seed buying, 32–34, 35
Seed leaves (cotyledons), 42

Seedling Starter Tonic, 40 (recipe), 202, 355 (recipe)
Seedling Strengthener Tonic, 40 (recipe), 238, 356 (recipe)
Seedling Transplant Recovery Tonic, 50 (recipe), 356 (recipe)
Seed sowing, *45,* 45–46
Seed Starter Tonic, 39 (recipe), 47, 163, 170, 184, 202, 233, 272, 355 (recipe)
Seed starting, 38–44, *44,* 48
Seed storage, 34
Seed tapes, 46
se/se+ (sugary enhanced) corn, 319, 320
sh2 (supersweet) corn, 319, 320
Shallots, *25,* 253, 254, 255
Shell (shelly) beans, 154, 157
Shopping tips for vegetables, 30–36
Shovels, *83*
Silt soil, 13
Size of garden, 17, 21, *22*
Skunks, 129
Slaw, Savory, 230
Sleepytime Tonic, 88 (recipe), 356 (recipe)
Slips of sweet potatoes, 329
Slopes for gardens, 12
Slugs (snails), 71, 117, 120–21, 176, 356
Slugweiser, 121, 122 (recipe), 356 (recipe)
Snails (slugs), 71, 117, 120–21, 176, 356
Snap beans, 154, 157

Snap peas, 162
Snow peas, 162
Soaker hoses, 74
Sod-buster pots, 43
Soil basics, 13–16. *See also* Fertilizing; Garden planning
 acid (sour) soil, 14, 48, 73
 alkaline (sweet) soil, 14, 73
 clay soil, 13, 54, 60–61
 composting, 63–67, *67*
 cover crops, 53, 60–61, *62,* 317
 digging garden sites, 55–57
 double digging, 55–56, 334, 339
 drainage, 54
 earthworms, 16, 57, 67
 forking, 56
 indicator plants, *53*
 loamy soil, 13
 mulches, 75, 76, 77, 86, 92
 nitrogen (N), 14, *69,* 70, *70,* 176, 288
 phosphorus (P), 14, *69,* 70
 pH (potential of hydrogen), 14, 48, 71, *72,* 72–73
 potassium (K), 14, *69, 70*
 raised beds, 57–59, 262–63
 sandy soil, 13, 60–61
 solarizing soil, 99, 102
 testing, 14–15, 75
 topsoil, 57
 watering, 12, 73–76
Solarizing soil, 99, 102

Sore throat syrup, 222
Sour (acid) soil, 14, 48, 73
Southern blight (fungus), 98
South of the Border
    Zucchini, Rice, and
    Chicken Salad, 279
Sowbugs, 117
Sowing seeds, 45, 45–46
Spades, 83
Sphagnum moss for
    damping-off, 39
Spider mites, 109, 221, 356
Spiders, 111
Spinach, 25, 182–85
    boron and, 187
    companion planting, 28,
        183
    cooking tips, 185
    growing, 27, 45, 182–84
    harvesting, 133, 134, 143,
        147, 185
    nutrition from, 185
    recipes using, 189
    shade and, 11
Spring, 45, 56
Spring Soil Energizer Tonic,
    47 (recipe), 55, 357
    (recipe)
Spring water in tonics, 348
Squash and cucumber
    family, 25, 257–81
Squash bugs, 118, 119, 271
Squashes, 25, 267–70
    companion planting, 28,
        221, 323
    growing, 27, 43, 44,
        267–70
    harvesting, 133, 134, 135,
        136, 143, 147, 150, 270
    recipes using, 278, 279

Squash Pie, 278
Squirrels, 127–28, 322
Staking, 160, 259, 276, 304
Stem handling, 42, 44
Storage tips, 142–50, 143,
    147
Straw as weed-killer, 53
Strawberries, 135, 157, 183,
    344
Strawberry-Rhubarb Pie,
    326
Striped pumpkin beetles,
    118
Succession planting, 133–34,
    134
Suckers of corn, 317
Sugar
    secret behind, 48, 347
    in tonics, 47, 122, 260,
        357, 359
Sugar peas, 162
Sugary enhanced (se and
    se+) corn, 319, 320
Sulfur, 69, 72, 73, 289
Summercrisp lettuce, 177
Summer squash. See Squashes
Sun-dried tomatoes, 310
Sunflowers, 25, 316
Sunlight, 11
su (normal sugary) corn,
    319, 320
Sunscald, 308
Super Slug Spray, 121
    (recipe), 357 (recipe)
Super Spider Mite Mix, 357
    (recipe)
Supersweet (sh2) corn, 319,
    320
Sweet (alkaline) soil, 14, 73
Sweet corn, 319

Sweetening tomatoes, 309
Sweet potatoes, 25, 328–30
    companion planting, 27
    growing, 328–29
    harvesting, 133, 143, 150,
        330
    puddling, 328
    recipes using, 331
    slips, 329
Sweet Potatoes in Ginger
    Honey Sauce, 331
Sweet Success Spray, 260
    (recipe), 357 (recipe)
Swiss chard, 25, 186–88
    companion planting, 187
    growing, 27, 45, 186–87
    harvesting, 133
    recipes using, 188, 191
    shade and, 11
Swiss Chard with Lemon
    and Bacon, 191
Syrphid flies (hover flies),
    110

T
Tabasco sauce in tonics, 129,
    352
Tea. See also Tobacco Tea
    chamomile tea in tonics,
        94, 348, 352
    instant in tonics, 31, 40,
        47, 50, 68, 88, 263, 351,
        356, 357, 359
    secret behind, 48, 347
    in tonics, 140, 341, 355
Tears from onions (scal-
    lions), 251
Terrific Tarragon Onion
    Bake, 254

Testing soil, 14–15, 75
Thatch Buster, 64
Thrips, 109, 342
Timely Tomato Tonic, 301
    (recipe), 358 (recipe)
Tip burn, lettuce, 176
Toads for pest control, 117
Tobacco in tonics, 358
Tobacco mosaic virus
    (TMV), 98, 100, 282
Tobacco Tea
    secret behind, 48, 347
    in tonics, 82, 83 (recipe),
        349, 358 (recipe)
Tomato Blight Buster Tonic,
    309 (recipe), 358
    (recipe)
Tomato Booster Tonic, 309
    (recipe), 358 (recipe)
Tomato Disease Fighter
    Tonic, 309 (recipe), 359
    (recipe)
Tomatoes, 25, 298–310
    cages for, 304
    calcium and, 305
    collards, 213
    companion planting, 19,
        28, 238
    freezing, 307
    growing, 27, 44, 48,
        298–303, 301, 308
    harvesting, 133, 135, 143,
        147, 150, 305, 306–7,
        310
    hole planting method,
        300, 301
    nutrition from, 298, 306,
        307
    potatoes and, 25, 25

pruning, 303
recipes using, 230, 231, 278,
    311, 312, 313, 314, 332
ripening, 307, 310
staking, 304
sun-dried tomatoes, 310
sweetening, 309
trench planting method,
    300, 301
troubleshooting, 308
types of, 302
Tomato family, 25, 292–314
Tomato hornworms, 118,
    119, 317
Tomato Pesto Frittata, 312
Tonics, 346–59
    All-Around Disease
        Defense Tonic, 94 (recipe),
        95, 96, 97, 98, 348 (recipe)
    All-Purpose Dandelion
        Cure, 80 (recipe), 348
        (recipe)
    All-Purpose Organic
        Fertilizer, 247 (recipe),
        348 (recipe)
    All-Purpose Pest
        Prevention Potion, 128
        (recipe), 349 (recipe)
    All-Purpose Varmint
        Repellent, 128 (recipe),
        349 (recipe)
    All-Season Clean-Up
        Tonic, 82 (recipe), 92,
        104, 342, 349 (recipe)
    All-Season Green-Up
        Tonic, 47, 47 (recipe), 68,
        92, 166, 179, 188, 211,
        213, 215, 217, 224, 246,
        253, 261, 264, 273, 349
        (recipe)

Aphid Antidote, 104, 350
    (recipe)
Baking Soda Spray, 99
    (recipe), 350 (recipe)
Bedtime Snack, 87
    (recipe), 88, 350 (recipe)
Beetle Juice, 105, 106,
    282 (recipe), 283, 296,
    350 (recipe)
Cabbage Worm Wipe-
    Out, 204 (recipe), 351
    (recipe)
Compost Feeder Tonic,
    63, 64 (recipe), 351
    (recipe)
Compost Tea, 100
    (recipe), 153, 156, 163,
    182, 188, 221, 247, 248,
    329, 336, 341, 351
    (recipe)
Container Garden
    Booster Mix, 31
    (recipe), 351 (recipe)
Damping-Off Prevention
    Tonic, 40, 42 (recipe),
    352 (recipe)
Dog-B-Gone Tonic, 129
    (recipe), 352 (recipe)
Fungus Fighter Tonic, 91
    (recipe), 352 (recipe)
Garden Cure-All Tonic,
    105, 107 (recipe), 352
    (recipe)
Garlic Pest Repellent, 116
    (recipe), 353 (recipe)
Happy Herb Tonic, 140
    (recipe), 353 (recipe)
Hot Bug Brew, 106
    (recipe), 353 (recipe)

Hurry-Up-the-Harvest Tonic, 139 (recipe), 353 (recipe)
ingredients (household) in, 48, 347
Knock-'em-Dead Insect Spray, 119, 120 (recipe), 354 (recipe)
Mouth-Watering Melon Mix, 263 (recipe), 354 (recipe)
Mulch Moisturizer Tonic, 82 (recipe), 354 (recipe)
Powdery Mildew Control Tonic, 257 (recipe), 354 (recipe)
Rhubarb Bug Repellent Tonic, 103 (recipe), 107, 119 (recipe), 355 (recipe)
Robust Rhubarb Tonic, 341 (recipe), 355 (recipe)
Seed and Soil Energizer Tonic, 39 (recipe), 40, 42, 134, 299, 355 (recipe)
Seedling Starter Tonic, 40 (recipe), 202, 355 (recipe)
Seedling Strengthener Tonic, 40 (recipe), 238, 355 (recipe)
Seedling Transplant Recovery Tonic, 50 (recipe), 356 (recipe)
Seed Starter Tonic, 39 (recipe), 47, 163, 170, 184, 202, 233, 272, 355 (recipe)

Sleepytime Tonic, 88 (recipe), 356 (recipe)
Slugweiser, 121, 122 (recipe), 356 (recipe)
Spring Soil Energizer Tonic, 47 (recipe), 55, 357 (recipe)
Super Slug Spray, 121 (recipe), 357 (recipe)
Super Spider Mite Mix, 357 (recipe)
Sweet Success Spray, 260 (recipe), 357 (recipe)
Timely Tomato Tonic, 301 (recipe), 358 (recipe)
Tobacco Tea, 83 (recipe), 358 (recipe)
Tomato Blight Buster, 309 (recipe), 358 (recipe)
Tomato Booster Tonic, 309 (recipe), 358 (recipe)
Tomato Disease Fighter Tonic, 309 (recipe), 358 (recipe)
Vegetable Power Powder, 47 (recipe), 359 (recipe)
Veggie Tonic #1, 68 (recipe), 359 (recipe)
Veggie Tonic #2, 68 (recipe), 359 (recipe)
Weed Wipeout Tonic, 78 (recipe), 359 (recipe)
Whitefly Wipeout Tonic, 108 (recipe), 360 (recipe)
Wild Mustard Tea, 105, 109 (recipe), 360 (recipe)

Woody-Seed Starter Tonic, 171 (recipe), 360 (recipe)
Tools, 83, 83–85, 88
Topsoil, 57
Transplanting, 42, 44, 44, 49–50
Trap crops, pest control, 119, 119–20
Trellises, 160, 259, 276, 304
Trench planting method for corn, 318
for tomatoes, 300, 301
Triple time planting, 134, 134
Turnips, 25, 225–28
companion planting, 19
growing, 27, 194, 225–26
harvesting, 133, 134, 150, 226–27
Jack-o'-Turnip lanterns, 228
recipes using, 231

U
Urine
secret behind, 347
in tonics, 128, 349
USDA Plant Hardiness Zone Map, 7, 361

V
Vegetable oil in tonics, 94, 107, 348, 352
Vegetable Power Powder, 47 (recipe), 359 (recipe)

Vegetables, 1–19. *See also* Fertilizing; Garden planning; Harvesting; Pest control; Planting; Recipes; Soil basics; *specific vegetables;* Tonics
bean and pea family, *25,* 152–66
beets and greens family, *25,* 169–91
benefits of growing, 1–4
cabbage family, *25,* 192–231
carrot family, *25,* 232–43
climate (weather), 6–11, *8–9,* 86–88, 132, 138–39
extended family, 315–32
growing season, 6–7, *8–9*
onion family, *25,* 244–56
perennials, 27, 55, 333–44
squash and cucumber family, *25,* 257–81
table scraps in tonics, 355
tomato family, *25,* 292–314
tools, *83,* 83–85, 88
watering, 12, 73–76
weeding, 52–53, 78–80

Veggie scrap soup, 16
Veggie Tonic #1 & #2, 68 (recipes), 359 (recipes)
Vernal Equinox, 45, 56
Vertical gardening, 80–81
Verticillium wilts, 97
Very Veggie Pie, 313
Vinegar, Garlic, Shallot, or Onion, 254
Vinegar in tonics, 171, 359, 360
Viruses, 94
Vitamins and harvesting, 137
Voles, 127–28

W

Wall-o'-Water, 300, 326
Walnut trees caution, 11
Warm-season crops, 133
Water hemlock caution, 241
Watering, 12, 73–76
Watermelons, 266
Weather (climate), 6–11, *8–9,* 86–88, 132, 138–39
Weeding, 52–53, 78–80, *83*
Weed Wipeout Tonic, 78 (recipe), 359 (recipe)
Wheat flour in tonics, 357
Whiskey in tonics, 39, 40, 68, 355, 359

White cabbage moths, *118*
Whiteflies, 107–8, *119*
Whitefly Wipeout Tonic, 108 (recipe), 360 (recipe)
Whoops! I Goofed! Salad, 280
Wild mustard leaves in tonics, 360
Wild Mustard Tea, 105, 109 (recipe), 360 (recipe)
Wind and vegetables, 12
Wind-sock wisdom, 10
Winter squash. *See* Gourds; Squashes
Woodchucks (groundhogs), 153
Woody-Seed Starter Tonic, 171 (recipe), 360 (recipe)

Y

Yeast in tonics, 122, 356

Z

Zippering, 308
Zucchini Caterpillars, 278
Zucchini in recipes, 278, 279. *See also* Squashes